TRY NOT TO THINK BAD THOUGHTS

The art of Matthew Revert

The art of Matthew Revert

CL4SH

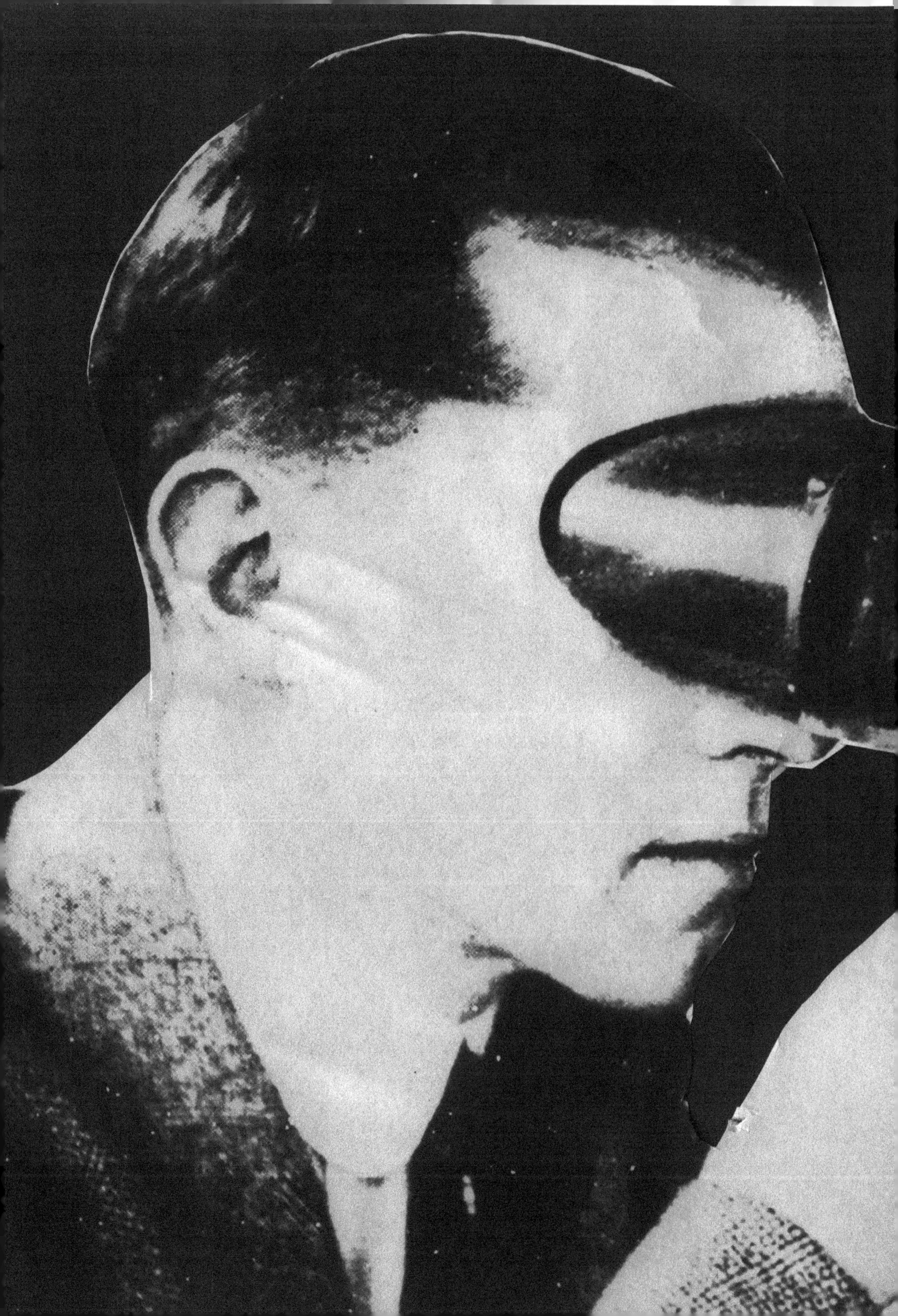

TRY NOT
TO THINK
BAD
THOUGHTS
THE ART OF
MATTHEW
REVERT
CLASH

CL◢SH

A conversation between Matthew Revert & Jon Dale

JON DALE: I was looking at the PDF of your book on the train, and I had this beautiful moment, I think it was the dicks, I was like, 'Oh my God, is anyone seeing me look at this,' but I was also, 'fuck, I hope someone sees me looking at this.'

MATTHEW REVERT: (laughs) Was it the one with the little mountaineers ascending the big dick?

JD: I think it could be. As you know, once I see dick, I'm gone.

MR: I tried to tempt you towards saying yes to the interview. (laughs)

JD: It worked!

MR: Normally, when I'm doing them, I don't think so strongly about what I want to do first. But for that one, I thought to myself, 'I'm having mountaineers going up a dick.'

JD: Why?

MR: I had a conversation with Graham [Lambkin], actually. I did a whole bunch [of artworks], and they were kind of amusing. They're not designed to be amusing, but they're silly. He made a comment about it, so I wanted to make a deliberately really silly one, so I could say, 'I made this one on purpose.'

JD: Just for him.

MR: It was kind of just for him.

JD: That's sweet. It's not even three minutes in and you're already dropping names.

MR: (laughs) That's the only name I've got.

JD: Nothing wrong with that. [In the book] you have these little sections of reflective text, and there's one where you talk about the double moment of, 'Oh God', 'oh great!'… I'm interested in that idea of dualities when it comes to what you're doing.

MR: I think it's integral. How can anything exist without its opposite also not being there? At least to bounce off. Are you talking about the story regarding childhood nudity, and the whole idea of being ashamed of your body, but loving that shame? There's everything [now] about how you've got to love yourself, but there seem to be rules about how you've got to love yourself. So, you've got to love yourself for your body, you can't love yourself for being ashamed of your body. And I find it very dogmatic, the way that we're told we're supposed to relate to ourselves.

JD: Well, it's interesting that you say, doesn't everything contain a duality

– okay, that's a dialectical thing, blah blah blah. But most things actually – they may have gestured towards that duality, but they don't actually raise it as a perspective or an important part of the thing itself. The dual movement is erased, somehow.

MR: Quite often for me, the duality itself is the subject. I find that fascinating. Also, in the anecdote where I was given the ribbon for coming second in the girls' relay. The slant of the whole piece is, why do we now reward people for not doing anything, and then juxtaposing that directly with how I felt when I was rewarded for doing nothing, and then having that reward taken away. I like the way things butt up against each other.

JD: I'm interested in the fact that you think that now we reward people for doing nothing. I think there's a great history of rewarding people for doing nothing. You're saying it's intensified?

MR: I have no doubt that when I was at school, there was a lot of that going on, and as each generation moves forward, maybe that gets a bit more pronounced. My sister has her children, my little nephews, so I see it in a way I've never seen it before. I'm really blown away by the things they celebrate. There was a legitimate graduation ceremony with robes and everything for my youngest nephew graduating kindergarten. Wow!

JD: What is it about that, that you find so…

MR: Okay, obviously it's good to instil a child with a sense of confidence, a sense of self, and to make them feel positive. But I do think that we're focusing on the wrong things. You want to reward someone for achieving a goal, rather than just trying a goal. Does that distinction make sense?

JD: It does. When you mention the thing about your nephew, and the graduation with robes, to me that isn't achievement… The question I would ask about that would be, what school does your nephew go to, and where is that school positioned in terms of society and in terms of class?

MR: It's public schooling. Beyond that, I couldn't tell you.

JD: Because of course the graduation with the robes and stuff is all about, we're preparing you to move into the space of academia, where that's the real thing, you finish your degree and you're the graduate. So, it's a performative.

MR: It is performative after having achieved something quite substantive. If you've chosen a field that you want to focus on, and whether you do that well or not, you still make it to the end of that process… Whereas this is kind of like rewarding somebody for starting the process. I know it's a balance. I just remember being told I was bad at things, a lot. I can't imagine that was all negative. (laughs)

JD: The interesting thing here is the question of achievement. What it means to achieve. A lot of the things both of us might have been rewarded for, in terms of achievement or reaching a particular goal, totally weren't achievements anyway. They're nothing, it's pointless.

MR: Achievement is a pretty abstract concept. It depends on the context within which that achievement occurs. Especially in that story, I'm trying to make it a very black and white thing, I know that. I want more people to accept the fact that they're not good at something. Maybe that's a sick desire that I have.

JD: I love it!

MR: I feel that everything is now set

up… Whether you're good at something or not, there is a platform in which you can be made to feel good about it. I do also worry that if someone is pursuing something that they have no aptitude in, and that aptitude doesn't even begin to develop with time, wouldn't they be better served focusing on something else? That's not to say that you can't do anything you're bad at, but I don't know, some people wrap up their whole identities in something that they don't necessarily have that ability in, and it can lead to some real crises down the road.

JD: This is that cruel optimism thing.

MR: Mmm. Absolutely. My main looking-glass when it comes to children today is my sister, but the impression I get is one that is not necessarily of coddling, but of side-stepping anything that might allow a child to think they haven't succeeded, or they haven't done as well as they could have. That worries me.

JD: That's the lie of happiness.

MR: Yeah. It seems so wasteful to give that lie to children. A child is probably best suited to deal with what it's like to be unhappy, before they mature to the point where it destroys them.

I almost didn't write that anecdote. There was another anecdote that I was going to write, in the 1990s, when rollerblading, in-line skating took off, because of the *Mighty Ducks* films, which I loved – I was in the right age bracket – I rollerbladed. I wasn't good at it, but if you saw me for five minutes not falling over, you might think that I had the capability to rollerblade.

There was an in-line hockey competition in Bendigo, a day-long thing, and some of the kids from school knew that I could stand up on rollerblades and asked if I wanted to be in it. I said yes, and somehow, due to some really gross miscommunication with the officials, we ended up in an age league that was younger than us. We were fourteen-year-olds playing in teams against ten-year-olds. We actually won quite soundly, but I was terrible. Even in that context, I scored, like, twice, and I was nearly falling over. It was really embarrassing, and somebody should have taken me aside and said, 'This isn't for you.'

It also coincided with my grandmother, my auntie and one of my cousins coming to Australia. The first time I'd ever met them. That was the day they were going back to the airport, and I missed that, so I could pretend I was good at hockey for a day. Seriously. (laughs) I almost wrote that one.

JD: Why didn't you?

MR: I think that I lived with the other one I ended up writing for longer.

JD: I'm interested as to why you decided to frame this work with those stories.

MR: Originally, I didn't want to include any writing, I wanted it to be just the art. CLASH Books said, 'We'd like to have some context about the pieces.' Originally it was on each page, maybe the title and a paragraph, and I didn't want that, because that's not how I like to experience any form of art. They made a good point, that while that might be true [for me], for some people, [context is] actually what they really, really like, and am I writing it purely for myself, or for an audience? So, I tried to find a middle ground.

I thought, rather than necessarily giving context into how the pieces were created, it might be interesting to give context into how who I am now was created. That might feed into the art without dictating exactly what the art should be. I wanted these two facets of me to co-exist. I thought, I will include writing, but I didn't want it to be too explanatory. Then I also thought, well, if there is an interview beforehand, that can touch upon why I did what I did, why things were created and what they mean, without having to necessarily interject that into the body of the book itself. Which is just my own personal preference…

JD: Even though it was about looking at the formative experiences that create the person who has made this art, I'm interested in [you] halting those observations at a particular point in your growth. You only really seem, from memory of reading, to be talking about these formative childhood experiences, whereas the entire set of life experiences [actually] feed into the work that's done… How does that work for you, and why are those choices made?

MR: With the art itself, what I was loving about creating it was this idea, with collage especially, with the images I was choosing, they were often very documentarian images or diagrams, something aimed to convey a fact. I love the idea that you can juxtapose bits and pieces and invent absolute false realities, and you can do that so easily. You can just take two people from two different environments, place them together, not necessarily have them doing anything, and all of a sudden, you have insinuated this whole new narrative that never existed before. I love that. Basically, all of the art is a lie. So, I thought it might be good, once again using that duality, to juxtapose that with the truth of who I actually am.

Initially my writing was really meta in a way that was making me feel sick with myself. I was questioning why anybody reading would want to know what the art means. I was focusing on that. It became a bit smug and jaded and meta, and it didn't feel right, it didn't feel honest. Because people are entitled to whatever they want from what they look at. All I could do was position it against something I felt comfortable with.

JD: What makes you think that the way you write and report your experiences is the truth of the matter?

MR: It's absolutely not. Memory is always going to be inaccurate.

JD: Which is what I mean. What's the place of memory in all of this, and what's the place of memory in informing the art you've created?

MR: Memory is so imperfect that in a way it is still creating absolute illusions. But they're illusions based on this really weird understanding of reality. I was thinking after I wrote the story where all the kids are digging up a playground, in my mind that playground is torn apart, with piles of dirt bigger than the playground. If I were shown a photo of that day I'm sure it would look nothing like that.

That stuff genuinely fascinates me. I was recently asked to write something like a memoir of my childhood, but for the framework to be my experience with video games. I was thinking about memoirs a lot after I was asked that, and how inaccurate they'd have to be, by virtue of the process of recollection.

JD: You haven't talked quite so much about the relationship between that and the artwork.

MR: Only in hindsight, not when I was doing the art.

JD: I know, but I want you to do the work of thinking about that.

MR: You bastard!

JD: Well, it's my fucking job.

MR: This also ties in with the idea of nostalgia. I think about nostalgia a lot, and how much of a distortion nostalgia is. I know that when I was selecting images to use, I would quite often get these really pleasant nostalgic pangs for eras that I wasn't even alive in, but they associate with various ideas that I have. In many of the instances, when I was creating images, I was trying to provoke my own sense of nostalgia for things I hadn't experienced. Even at the time, I'm not even thinking that I've not experienced these things, but I'm having that nice, warm, nostalgic feeling anyway.

JD: Can you think of specific moments where that happened, or specific works where that played out?

MR: In a lot of instances it's where the art has text in it as well. When I make them, I'm immediately taken to the idea of the PSA poster or the medical poster, the educational poster, and aesthetically, I love them. They always just take me back to a period of life that I wasn't even alive in, but I project myself into this idealised version of it.

I remember showing the art book to Graham – this is before there was any writing or any context, and [these nostalgic artworks] were just randomly scattered throughout other pieces. He said the artwork was so dizzying and disorienting, that by the time he got to those pieces, they almost felt like advertisements. I was like, yeah, they are, they're like advertisements! It's false, but it provokes really genuine nostalgia.

JD: With those pieces, you would have been brought up, and grown up, in the tail end of a particular period of time where there's a thing of care for community, care for society, so there's this idea that's [now] disappearing, of institutions caring…

MR: Community spirit, civic responsibility.

JD: The PSA posters, the medical posters. I always think about the in- formative public broadcasting videos – 'Kids, don't play near wells.' We both grew up in the tail end of that, and I remember seeing some of those as a kid. So, when I saw those [artworks] I was like, this is interesting, because it reminds me a little bit of [PSA posters], but it's been completely torn asunder, in some ways. But there's still that trace.

MR: It's the semiotics of the language behind it. You can convey anything if it's couched in this context which you associate with danger or education or information. You can really mess with things. You know *The Medium Is The Message*, or *The Medium Is The Massage*? I love that book, and McLuhan is so right. The older I get, the more right I think Marshall McLuhan was. It is so much of the way something is delivered that determines the message. Those pieces in particular, they strongly felt like that for me. Aesthetically, that's also inspired by Marshall McLuhan and his aesthetic.

JD: Looking at them, I thought there's a touch of the *Scarfolk Council*…

MR: I love *Scarfolk*, but I love it because I was already deeply interested in that aesthetic, rather than him introducing it to me. I actually contacted him at one point just to say, just to let you know, I love what you do, and I think we're very similar in the way we approach design. He is also provoking that exact same sense that in some ways I'm going for. He's more overtly satirical, but it's in the same realm.

JD: I'm interested in how you actually do this work. From talking about it, there was something quite fast, improvised and instantaneous about it.

MR: There was an element of that, but also beyond that, it was an absolute obsession with the cheapest possible materials. In the music world, how boring is it to hear musicians wank on about their gear? I wanted the opposite of that. I used to want to pursue visual art in my teenage years, and I always thought, I'm going to need to get this sort of paint, these sorts of canvases, these brushes, and I was inadvertently putting it further and further out of my reach, because I was building it up into this exclusivity that I couldn't afford.

Then I had this idea, that I can use literally whatever I want, and whether people like it or not, it's still art. So, the inkjet printer, public domain photos, Crayola watercolours, sometimes some markers, that's literally it. And when I started to make those [artworks], some were very quick, some took a lot longer. But no matter how long something took, I always felt a great sense of energy when I was doing it. That's similar to when I started making music again. A very similar spirit to [my first album] Not You was in these paintings.

JD: Can you tell me a little bit about how you see those things interrelating – your art, your music, the other things you do creatively, or even work-wise. In a sense, I think work-wise tells us more than the creative.

MR: Regarding the design, you mean? A lot of my graphic design obviously does call back to these eras that we were just talking about. The reality is, although aesthetically I love it, that started off as a purely pragmatic thing. I was a very new graphic designer working for small presses who didn't have much budget. The amount of money that they paid me could not encompass things like stock photographs, photoshoots or original illustrations. I had to lean on public domain, and by virtue, that means, aesthetically, they look older. I began to play into that, and that's how that really developed. It just so happened that, because I was already enthusiastic about that aesthetic, I enjoyed it.

Now I do have access to stock images, and people who can illustrate for me, but it's not even necessarily that I lean towards that aesthetic – I'm known for it, so people ask for that aesthetic. It's almost expected of me, half the time. So aesthetically, yeah, the design work probably is the closest calling card toward what I'm doing at the moment, not just because it's a visual medium. But I would say the spirit of it is closer to my music.

JD: Tell me about that.

MR: Any notoriety I ever got was from writing, before anything else. I'd written a few books and I was at a complete loss for what to do next, and I started to get really down on writing. I thought to myself, I'm just going to start thinking about something else for a while. I used to make music, in my teens and early twenties. It went nowhere, it didn't really deserve to go anywhere.

JD: Although Clinton Green did put out something of yours, didn't he?

MR: He did, he was one of the very first people to release anything by me. That was my noise project, *The Feeder*. He had *Terra Australis Incognito*, these web only releases. That was pretty cool. That was my first experience of having anything released, in any way, shape or form. I still don't think the music itself was very good, but it was cool to have that.

JD: It's a good moment, isn't it?

MR: It is. I always flirted with music, but never again with the intention of it being released. That was just because I enjoyed doing it. Then the writing thing, it did happen, quite by accident. I remember I was getting really annoyed with the whole musical thing, so I just wanted to write some funny stories that I would send to a few friends, to make them laugh. One of those friends said he'd been thinking of starting a small press, and would you be interested in a collection of your stories. That's when the whole writing thing started.

I followed that for five, six, seven years before I started doing music again. It was only because I was getting really frustrated about what to write next. I just wanted to create something really super-immediate. I had a Tascam four-track that I got from my sister for Christmas when I was sixteen, and I set that up in the same room that I do my writing. I had a five-minute cassette tape, so that would impose a limitation upon what I did, so I wouldn't meander. I limited what I could use to whatever I could reach from where I was sitting, and I recorded this shambolic bricolage shit, and that became [my first record] *Not You*. That exact same spirit, of random bricolage shit, informs the visual art.

When I'm designing, that's great, that's what earns me the most money, but it's very specific; I'm working to what a client wants. Obviously, that makes sense, it's a job. So, it was really nice to not have to think about that, and just throw it down however, which is something I wasn't having an opportunity to do.

JD: How, then, do you think the interest from a publisher for this work has affected both the way you've assembled the book, and what you'll do next?

MR: That's what I'm worried about. When I assembled the book, there was definitely a real mind toward what is the end user going to experience, which I didn't have at all when I was making the art, but which I like. Half of the work was made before I knew there was going to be a book, so there was definitely, unequivocally no considering the end user. But then, when I knew there was going to be a book, I hope it didn't change the energy of the work, but I honestly couldn't tell you. When you look at it, do you feel there's a difference in energy?

JD: I don't think so, really. I think it sits together.

MR: That pleases me a lot, because I did worry about that, because all of a sudden it became more of a job, I have a deadline to meet, I've got to produce this many pieces. I am happy with it, but the minute that you then have to consider the end user, it does change the character.

JD: One thing that interests me about the work is the colour palette.

MR: In terms of the basic yellow, blue, pink — I feel a real sense of harmony when I work with those colours. There's not any great symbolism behind the colour scheme other than that I feel great when I look at them. But the idea of only using that colour scheme, I realised I was literally making everything using those three colours, without even thinking about it. And I love the uniformity that gave it. Uniformity became very important for this book. It's almost an obsessive need to use those colours over and over and over again. That almost tells its own story. I couldn't tell you what that story is, but it's so single-minded, and that excites me.

JD: Why?

MR: Do you often wonder when somebody is just doing something obsessively, why they're doing it? I guess you're asking the question right now! (laughter)

JD: Yeah, I am.

MR: It's that interest that you have in asking me the question, that makes me interested in why I'm doing it. I love the way it looks. It almost became a game to keep using them. There were some where it would have been so good just to use a splash of red or some green, but by forcing myself to use these colours again and again and again, I had to re-imagine the composition of the images… It was something that greatly intensified my pleasure in making it. End result, symbolically, I don't think it means much, but I like the idea that some people think it will.

JD: To me it sounds like a variation on only using what you can reach while recording *Not You*.

MR: Yes, at the start, maybe. But then because I became so hellbent on this colour scheme, it became something else, it became quite difficult. I contacted Crayola, because I had to buy these sets of thirty-six colours, because that's the only one that had pink. I wanted to know whether they made separate palettes, and they didn't. Because of the shipping, it cost thirty dollars to get this palette just so I could use three colours. Then I had them shipped from the US with just those three colours cut out, because it was cheaper. It became more than just what I can reach. I had to very methodically get those. It ended very differently.

JD: Which is often the way when you work within limitations. It starts as an improvisation and ends as a dogged pursuit.

MR: Yeah, and that was something which sets *Not You* apart. That whole thing was recorded before anybody heard it, and at no point did it become a dogged pursuit. It was just me literally fucking around. When Graham said he was interested, the dogged pursuit came in ordering [the songs]. But before that, the creation of them, that was just pure, well, this is what I'm doing!

JD: I thought the dogged pursuit was listening to the fucking thing, quite honestly.

MR: I would not have listened to it. (laughter) I still find it hilarious that he put out my music.

JD: I find it hilarious, too.

MR: Well, you've been responsible for some of it.

JD: Yes, I've done it, too. It's been my fault. I love blame.

MR: The other question you asked, that is an interesting one – what's going to come next? And that slightly worries me, actually. Because now that this is happening, there becomes a foundation I wasn't expecting, and that…

JD: You'd better be careful – you might become an 'artist.'

MR: It's okay, I'll never become an artist. (laughter)

JD: You say that, but some of the best people…

MR: I also find that, when I start making something, I'm not very conscious of any concern regarding the audience at all. But that turns into some pretty brutal mind-fucking pretty quickly. There's another duality. There's this fear that some real artist is going to see it and reveal that I'm a fake, but then there's also this absolute joy at the notion that that might happen.

JD: The joy of fakery?

MR: The joy of fakery and being called out for it. Is that just a defence mechanism to stop yourself from being…

JD: Well, we all know you love punishing yourself, so it's another part of that. It's another self-inflicted wound. But you're getting in there before others can, right?

MR: Yeah, that's just the way it works. Nobody can hurt you as much as you can hurt yourself, that's the idea. (looks at JD's interview notes) Have you referred to these yet?

JD: No, most of it I've memorised. Do you want to have a look?

MR: It's hard to read. School, sports, and peer pressure. Erasure and disappearance. Power through disability and the body. That's a good one.

JD: That says, 'dissembling the body.' And then of course, there's, 'Does Matthew Revert have a God complex'?

MR: (laughs) I actually missed that. Do I have a God complex? I think we all do, don't we?

JD: I don't know… Do we?

MR: I see what you're doing. You know, I probably do. Not that I've ever thought about it, honestly, until now. I have this real urge for the world around me to be exactly as I feel it should be, and when that obviously fails, I just try to create the world around me by what I do. That's the God complex, right there, isn't it?

JD: Is it the God complex, or is it mental health?

MR: The two go hand-in-hand. Because I've obviously had my mental health issues, I still do.

JD: If you look at the list carefully…

MR: Mmmm.

JD: 'The joys of depression.'

MR: Yes, the joys of depression. And you certainly know that I have my history with it.

JD: Well, we both do.

MR: Depression's a weird one for me. When you're in a depressive episode, do you have one specific way that you will act during that, or do you find that there are different ways?

JD: I think it changes, because so much of it changes according to the circumstances within which you find yourself depressed. There's a constant deadening of the self, but things can't help but penetrate that, and how you deal with that is the manifestation of the depression.

MR: Sometimes, when I'm in a depressive episode, I begin to create obsessively, non-stop. I'm not even necessarily creating things that are 'depressed.' It's just the momentum of it is, not even an escape, but… That sense of momentum gives me some sort of mental momentum. Things are moving, and I'm pushing through. And then sometimes I'll be so utterly disabled by it, the thought of making anything makes me feel sick to my stomach. In the past I've had depressive episodes where I've destroyed everything that I've made in my life up to that point. All this music I made in my twenties, that's all been destroyed. The only way I would get any access to that is if some poor bastard out there literally had CD-Rs of it.

JD: My way of thinking of doing that, because I've done similar things, is that you've managed to wrangle a 'sensible' outcome out of depression. Because I feel like it's quite a sensible outcome for me to destroy a whole bunch of stuff that I've done in my twenties, because it's like – It's shit! It doesn't need to be around!

MR: It's interesting to think about depression in relation to outcomes. Because I guess even if your way of thinking is distorted in that moment, you do become very outcome-oriented, don't you?

JD: Sometimes, yes. Even if the outcome is just getting the hell out of it.

MR: That's still an outcome. We're both people with rather large music collections – you rather more so than me…

JD: Don't shame me in front of the reading population.

MR: Many years ago, I did a big cull — well, not even that big a cull, probably just a few hundred CDs – I wasn't culling for the right reasons, I was culling because I was in a depressive episode and I was sickening myself with everything that was around me. I thought it would be good to set up microphones around the room and record myself destroying the music. Snapping the CDs, hitting the cases with hammers. And I did that, I recorded ninety minutes of this really primal – it's like what the acting troupe in [Jacques Rivette's film] *Out 1* would have done in one of their exercises! (laughter) Just smashing it, and then afterwards I had this grand idea, I'll make some music out of me destroying my music, which is just so, so lame.

JD: It is pretty pretensh.

MR: I never ended up making anything with it.

JD: Well, that's good.

MR: That was my outcome! If I literally destroy it, then I'm gonna feel good. And I just felt kind of embarrassed. (laughter)

JD: And now that embarrassment is out there for everyone to see. (laughter)

MR: I'm okay with that. The fact that I put any of my work out there means I'm okay with embarrassment. (laughs)

JD: Same here. Maybe I'm not okay with it; maybe I'm resigned to it.

MR: I force myself to believe the former is the latter. (laughter) Just so I can feel okay.

JD: So, going back to something we mentioned earlier, and this thing about the body, and the way you ad- dress the body through the work. What's going on there?

MR: I have a long, storied relationship with the ways the body can completely break down. I was an incredibly ill baby. I couldn't tell you exactly what was wrong with me, but I have been told I was clinically dead several times. One of the times I nearly died, I mention in one of the stories – my mother's breast milk nearly killed me. I can't imagine what a mind-fuck that would have been for my mum. So, I was really, really ill. Then, when I was three, my mum gets multiple sclerosis. So, from the age of three, until she dies, when I'm fourteen, her body is just in decline. And then, of course, I have Crohn's disease. That's a shit time.

I've been very intimately familiar with the ways bodies can break down from my earliest memory. In fact, my relationship to bodies makes more sense in terms of how they can break, regarding health, because that's just been my childhood experience. When I'm making all this stuff, which includes distorted bodies, bodies that are coming together to create new things, that is the most natural thing in the world for me, to the point where I don't really even think about doing it. It just makes perfect sense.

The thing is, to me it's no longer even a negative thing. I think it's kind of magical, just how destroyed the body can become. It's like, at any minute, anything can happen. It doesn't require any interjection from outside, your body could just decide, I'm going to destroy you now. That's amazing that we live in such a destructive shell.

JD: It's perpetual vulnerability.

MR: There's something powerful about embracing that vulnerability. I've been fairly lucky – Crohn's sucks, but I've never been completely debilitated. If I had multiple sclerosis like mum, if I could not walk, I might not have such a philosophical stance about how wonderful the body breaking is. I also feel that because of the inevitability of our decline, if you can embrace that as early as possible, you are probably going to be protecting your fragile mental state…

JD: Psychological armour, right?

MR: Yeah. The films that used to scare me when I was obsessed with horror, they weren't the gore films or the slasher films, it was always the body horror films. It's not even that they scared me as much as they utterly fascinated me. They were the ones that resonated the most. Because the horror that just exists in you is incredible. I mean you specifically. (laughs)

JD: I was hearing that, and I was fine with it.

MR: So, it's always a preoccupation of mine. My second book, *The Tumours Made Me Interestin*g, that is really also obsessed with the body, to the point where the mother in that story is an arm with a head. I did a portrait of her in the art book, called Bruce's Mother. The one thing I'm also careful to — I can't control whether people who view the pieces feel this way, but at least when I'm making it, I don't necessarily just want to invoke this whole idea of the freak show.

JD: I don't think that's what it's doing.

MR: I'm glad to hear that, because I know that can be so easy to do.

JD: I can see how people might come at it that way, but I think if you're taking in the work carefully, it's so obviously not what's happening.

MR: I'm hoping that the culmination of the pieces means more than the individual things. There's a guy in there that has fish for arms, that's a bit of a freak show, but hopefully he feeds on the other body-related pieces.

JD: You've already mentioned this in terms of the vulnerability of the body being something that has been present for you from a very early age, how then does that stuff around the body that you're dealing with map on to your obsession, not so much with being a baby, as with childhood experiences?

MR: With childhood experiences, when I was writing those, it wasn't necessarily an obsession with childhood experiences as much as wanting to chart situations before I had too much of my own agency to dictate the world around me. I wanted all of the anecdotes to exist in a world where everybody else was in control of my actions. It's not hopelessness, that's the wrong word, but being divorced from personal responsibility, and then how I reflect upon it later. I started to think about other anecdotes relating to later on in life, and they didn't have that same internal resonance.

It might be because of what I just discussed, I don't know, but I kept coming back to this idea of me as a child, and this idea that I'm remembering it so imperfectly, and over the years, the way that expands. I think the distance between who I am now and the time those memories occurred was very appealing to me, because of the way they almost become mythology. That's also why I was really interested in trying to write a very first memory. Really going back to the absolute genesis, and then questioning the idea over whether that memory even happened, because that is really interesting to me. How much of who I am do I actually remember accurately?

JD: I'm interested in you mentioning agency, and thinking about when do you achieve agency? When do you achieve bodily autonomy?

MR: When do we achieve bodily autonomy… The first time we cum and don't feel ashamed of it.

JD: So, you're waiting.

MR: (laughs) That's hard. I don't even know if I do experience bodily autonomy yet.

JD: Well, I was going to say, you don't. Because of Crohn's disease, your body is always already medicalised, or it's always connected to that institution somehow. There's no space away from it. But that's the same for pretty much every human being. People talk about the natural body, and your body isn't 'natural' before you're born.

MR: The whole idea of autonomy, it really is illusory, isn't it? For me, it's very stark. No, I don't have that autonomy. Also, [there are] the structures I have to rely on in order to feel okay. Having to take gasbuster pills just so I can swallow without feeling like I'm going to die. One thing I think about sometimes is that whole desert island scenario. You're on *Lost* or something, where you're just forced to survive, and all of a sudden, I don't have my anti-depressants, I don't have my antacid tablets, I don't have my gas tablets, I don't have any of the things I need to have. What the hell would become of me?

JD: How much of what you're dealing with in terms of needing those things to help you survive is to do with societal pressure and anxieties?

MR: A societal pressure to medicate my body in a certain way?

JD: No, just the fact that your body is probably at least partly responding to societal pressure, cultural pressure, just the pressure and anxiety of being in the world. Well, being in the world as presented to you living in Melbourne at this point in time. In a different space, perhaps the body responds differently, perhaps it doesn't.

MR: I can tell you for a fact, my Crohn's disease, the first time it manifested in a way where I noticed it, and it required medical intervention, was a direct result of stress. I think the environment is very intricately linked.

JD: So, in the desert island scenario, you're in a completely different environment. It doesn't mean you don't need any of that other shit to survive, but it's something to consider.

MR: I have to take Peroxetine every day. If I don't take it, it's not just a case of anxiety or depressive symptoms being worse than normal. I also get these really horrible side effects. Within twenty-four hours, if I don't take it, I get horrifying brain zaps, nausea, all this sort of stuff. But I've noticed that if I literally forget that I haven't taken it, I will not experience those symptoms much at all. Whereas if I then become aware – Oh my God, I forgot to take my medication this morning –all of a sudden, like clockwork, by late afternoon I'm feeling the zaps, I'm feeling dizzy, I've becoming completely enslaved.

JD: I'm not trying to suggest that this stuff is going to change magically because of a different environment or anything…

MR: It's worth thinking about, though.

JD: I keep thinking about what you're talking about here in relation to bodies and ideal bodies and the discussion at the start of our conversation around the lie of happiness. That's fundamentally connected to the lie of the performance of a particular body, of a particularly valorised body, and the fact that that body is not achievable for many if not most of us.

MR: You'd have to say all of us, because the idea of the perfect body becomes a complete narrative, an orchestration. It has to. There's no possible way there can be a perfect body or perfect health or a perfect emotional state.

JD: So how does this all tie together the work in the book for you?

MR: The work in the book for me… I think that this does tie into the idea that I mentioned earlier about creating complete facsimiles. We talk about the whole idea of the perfect body — what would you do if you could literally pick and choose which bits of the body you want and then cobble them together like a collage? They are creating complete lies that are cherrypicked, which is exactly what you're talking about. The lie of perfection is a collage.

--

This text has been gently edited for relative clarity.

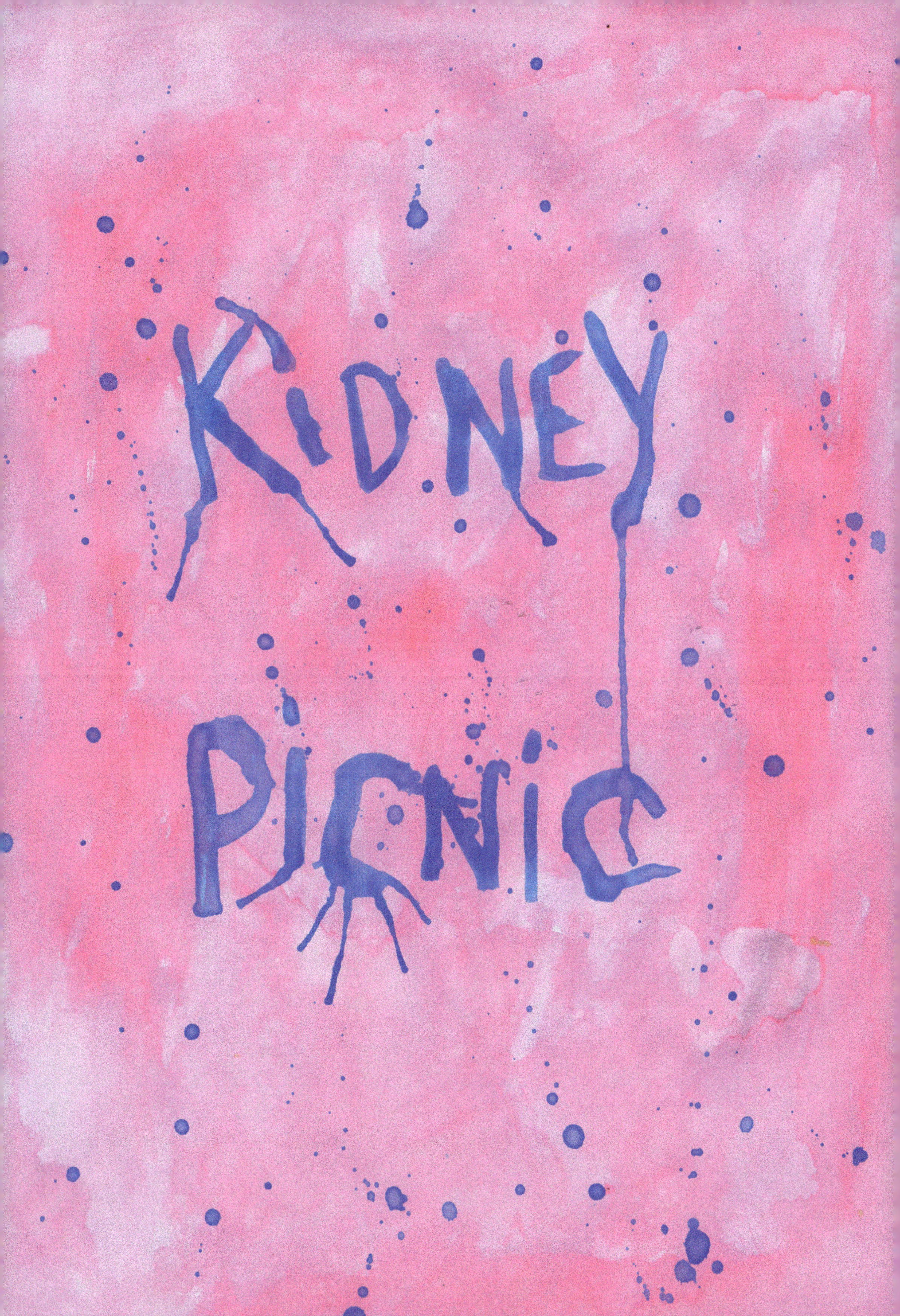

KIDNEY
PICNIC

Oh relax little cherub.
With your heart of hearts in the corner.
You didn't used to be this way Did you? Did you?

A confederacy of athletic losers

I went to school before the era of 'everyone gets a prize.' If you were bad at something, you were made aware of it. It seems near-anathema in our modern world to suggest a child may lack the necessary aptitude to succeed at certain tasks. When I was in high school, I vividly remember a ribbon one of my friends proudly displayed on his wall. It simply read, "I ran a race." This must have occurred during the primordial stages of the 'everyone gets a prize' evolution, because it marks the first time I had ever seen a ribbon like it. Initially I found it hysterical, but as I reflected further, it disturbed me a little. Why was it reasonable to produce some celebratory gimcrack for achieving nothing beyond a base level of participation? Was I somehow unreasonable for assuming reward was only warranted in exchange for achieving that reward? If I am demonstrably bad at something I wish to pursue, won't awareness of my inability provide important insight? Surely knowing you are bad at something is the first step toward becoming better? There is also the possibility that I am pursuing something that does not align with my natural aptitudes. Knowing you will never be good at something can be an important component toward understanding what you are good at.

Perhaps I'm merely a product of my time. I look at the life awaiting children as they journey toward adulthood with an intimate understanding of the many devastations to come. When a child's earned failures are orchestrated into achievements, their ability to process the inevitable failures to come will be under-developed. While the machinations responsible for this development are well intentioned, it's difficult to imagine these children are being adequately prepared for reality. Then again, I grew up in the 80s and may just be bitter. I can count many instances of failure in my childhood and maybe it will help to talk about one.

Once a year, an assortment of schools would converge at a sports oval to compete in a track and field competition. These were not days I looked forward to as my athletic prowess was only notable for its absence. I want to stress that this absence of prowess was very well deserved. I did nothing to improve it and received the outcomes one would expect. There was never a desire to excel athletically and I lived down to that without concern. It was only during these inter-school competitions any attention was placed on those of us without athletic prowess and for that reason they made for uncomfortable days.

I maintain a vivid memory of shitting myself mid-high jump one year. It occurred as I was colliding with the pole after a poorly executed scissor jump (I avoided the Fosbury Flop as the method appeared nothing more than a foolhardy shortcut to neck injury). The bowel evacuation was accompanied by a flatulent bark I'm sure many others heard and my flailing momentum rolled me off the landing mat entirely onto the gravel below. To say this was not one of my finer moments understates the totality of my failure and, as one would expect, I was not rewarded with any participatory ribbons or trophies. Instead, I sat crying in a toilet cubicle frantically trying to clean up the mess I had created and, upon failing to adequately do so, opting to tie a sweater around my waist for the rest of the contemptible day. I did not go to bed that night with unrealistic expectations of being a high jumper. No ribbons adorned my walls. This, to me, makes perfect sense.

During one of the athletic days in which I did not shit myself, I experienced a brief taste of undeserved reward. My performance during the various track and field events was uniformly unremarkable. Those sportier types who managed to place in the top three for any event were awarded a ribbon. First place was given a blue ribbon and second place a red, while those who scraped in third were presented with green. As the day progressed, I noticed the more accomplished child athletes with an ever-increasing collection of ribbons pinned to their shirts. As one of the ribbonless children, I definitely felt inferior, but it's important to remember that in the world of athletics, I was inferior. My lack of ribbons was in direct correlation to my lack of interest in the skills required to win one, but as more children around me received them, I felt such envy. Even as an adult it can be difficult to watch those around you succeed where you have not, but as a child, it feels like a cruel form of torture. I fully understood the ribbonless children who cried and felt a sense of solidarity with them - a confederacy of athletic losers.

It's strange how not having something is often the sole criteria required to want it. I sat in the grandstand with three others boys from the newly formed confederacy. We engaged in conversation unrelated to ribbons even though it was the topic screaming loudest in our minds. I remember talking about WWF wrestlers but upon picturing the championship belt winners received, quickly changed the subject to less victory-oriented topics.

I can't recall what we were discussing as a girl roughly our age approached us wearing an excited smile. We assumed she was celebrating a recent victory, but the smile was directed more toward us than herself. With an outstretched arm, we were presented with four red ribbons. "Congratulations," she said. "I was asked to give these to you." The four of us glanced at one another in silent surprise before smiles exploded on our faces. We accepted the ribbons with pride and danced about the grandstand in pure delight.

After an indulgent celebration, I decided to consider why we had been awarded to begin with. As far as I was aware, I had not come even close to second place in any of the events I participated in. I glanced at the ribbon and, in regal yellow font, was greeted with 'girls' 4x100 relay.' While my mind did a valiant job trying to convince me I participated in this race, I was rather sure I did not. The other boys were also beginning to notice the incongruity of the situation so, as a group, we attempted to understand what was happening. At no point in our efforts to understand did we consider the possibility of not having earned the ribbons. The most comfortable conclusion we agreed upon was having indeed placed second in some event we could not recall competing in. We earned the ribbon without question; we were merely given the wrong one - an administrative error. It should come as no surprise we had no intention of finding someone to correct the error. We agreed everyone was too busy to correct such a trifling problem. Each of us pinned our ribbons to our shirts and sat in the grandstand with cautious pride. It sure felt nice to be one of the winners - even if we hadn't actually won anything.

When a teacher approached the four of us a short while later, it was not a surprise. I hoped perhaps we were merely being congratulated rather than stripped of our title. As you can imagine, my hope was not the outcome. "I'm so sorry, boys," said the teacher. "Someone made a mistake. Those ribbons don't belong to you." We opted to remain silent before the teacher said, "I'll need to take them back." She held out her hand until each of us placed our ill-gotten gain into it. "Did you even read the ribbon? It's for the girls' relay," she said with a laugh. We remained silent as she walked away and presented the ribbons to their rightful owners and those rightful owners certainly looked overjoyed to receive them.

My favorite part of this episode is the distress that followed. The four of us somehow found it within to believe our treatment had been unjust. In our minds, we ran that race. In our minds we were, for a moment, four girls performing well in a relay and reaping the benefits. We didn't cry. We bypassed tears and settled on rage and shared passionate defenses of our position amongst one another. What world allows one to lose their rightful title and then forced to watch as that title is handed to another? Had any of us possessed an argument beyond our irrational moment, we'd have marched up to the teacher and demanded our ribbons back. We, of course, said nothing to anyone and arrived home that night with a justified absence of accolade. Each of us arrived home to parents who didn't bother asking how we had performed during the competition - they knew their children well enough to know the answer.

Now, in my mid-thirties, as I watch the shelves of my nephews fill with spurious trophies and medals, I lament. A trophy my eldest nephew has for soccer simply says "member of the team." My younger nephew has a medal for graduating kindergarten. I do wonder how they might cope when, later in life, they fail to get the job, or secure the home loan and receive nothing in return other than the cold reality of their failure. Understanding failure while young equips one with the wherewithal to endure the many instances to come and, most importantly, allows one to continue moving forward. It is easy to understand why a parent might want to protect their children from any sense they're not good enough, but no one can excel at every area of interest. We may lack the skill, no matter how much we apply ourselves, to achieve the things we want most. Sometimes, in our many failures, we stumble upon areas of natural aptitude we never considered. I, for instance, am still quite good at shitting myself.

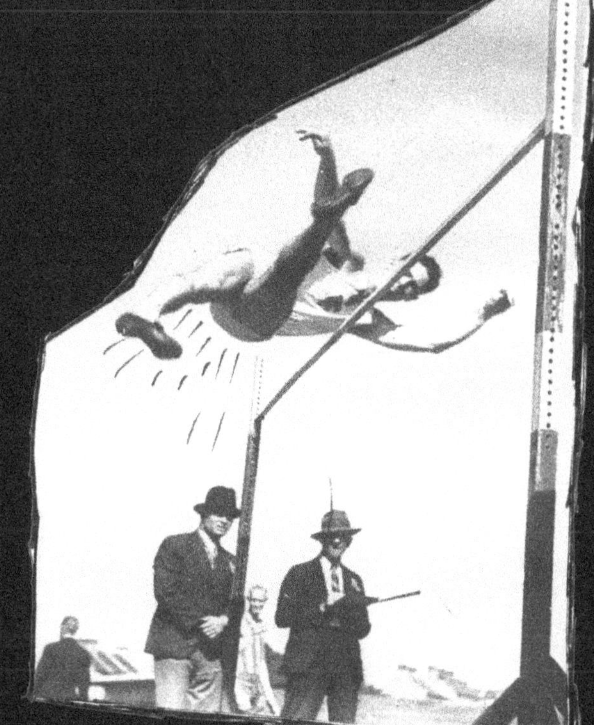

Contents

25	Whip paint
26	Rose-tinted looking glasses
27	Formal makeup
28	Politics of the playground
29	Baby's first word
30	Flamingo
31	Parents forced to sit through the recital
32	All alone
33	The Queen
34	Gym class shower redux
35	SPORTS
36	Team sports
38	Man problems
40	Lady three hands
41	Baby guts
42	Tummy ache
43	Kidney picnic
44	Tinder
45	If I die...
46	Captain anus
48	Appreciating Silver Surfer on the NES
49	Wedding day
50	Trauma shower

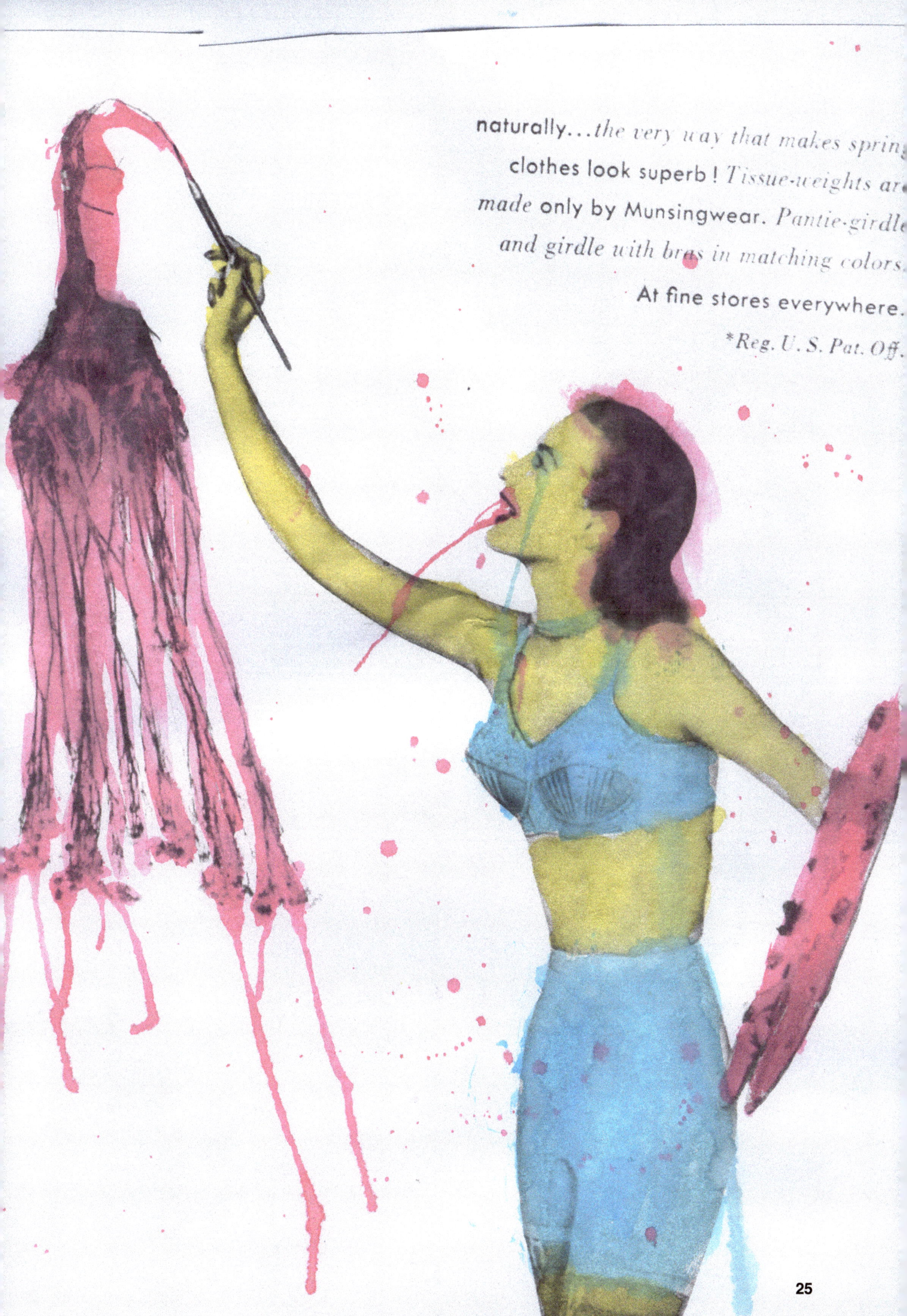

naturally...the very way that makes spring
clothes look superb! Tissue-weights are
made only by Munsingwear. Pantie-girdle
and girdle with bras in matching colors.
At fine stores everywhere.
*Reg. U.S. Pat. Off.

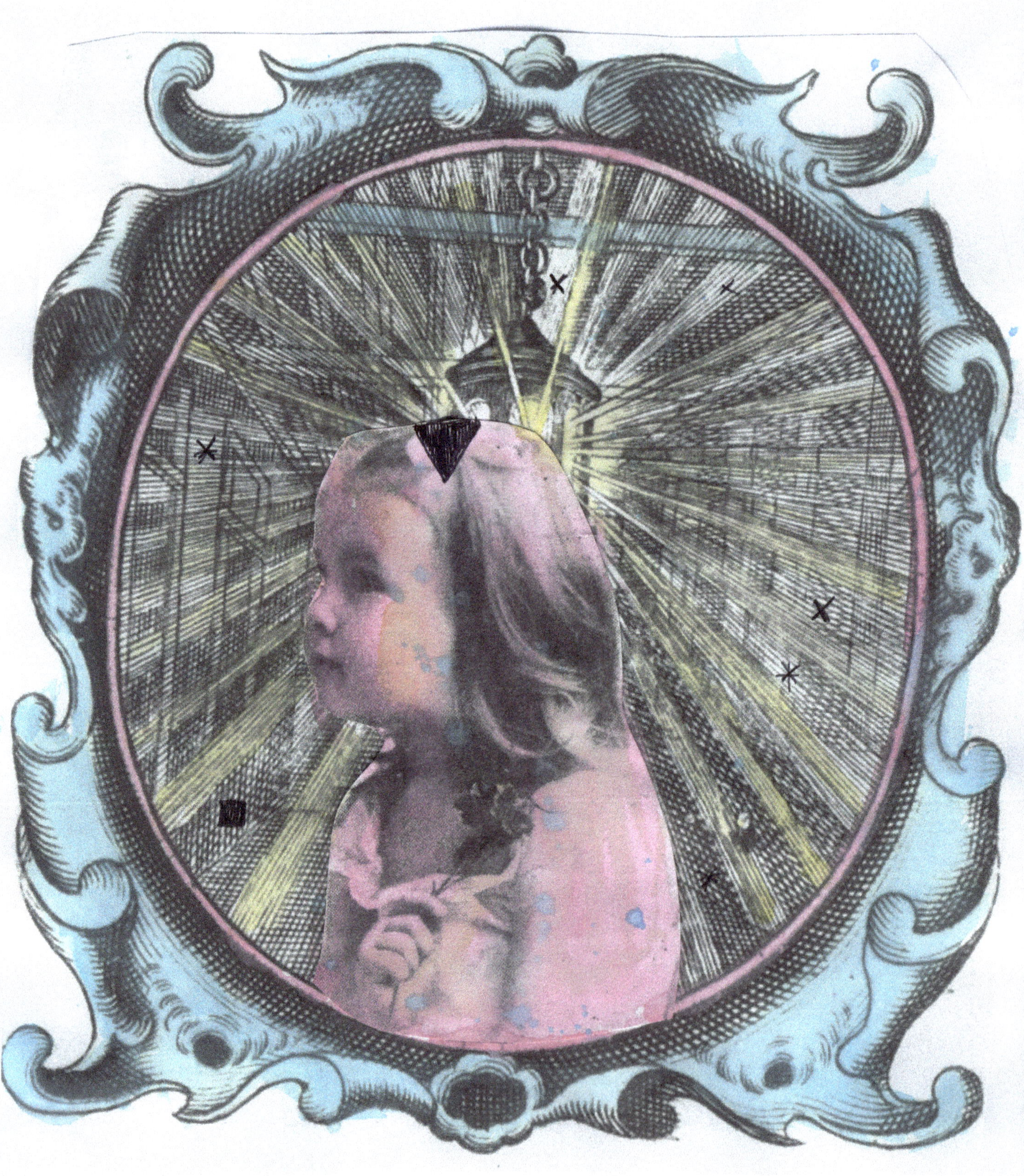

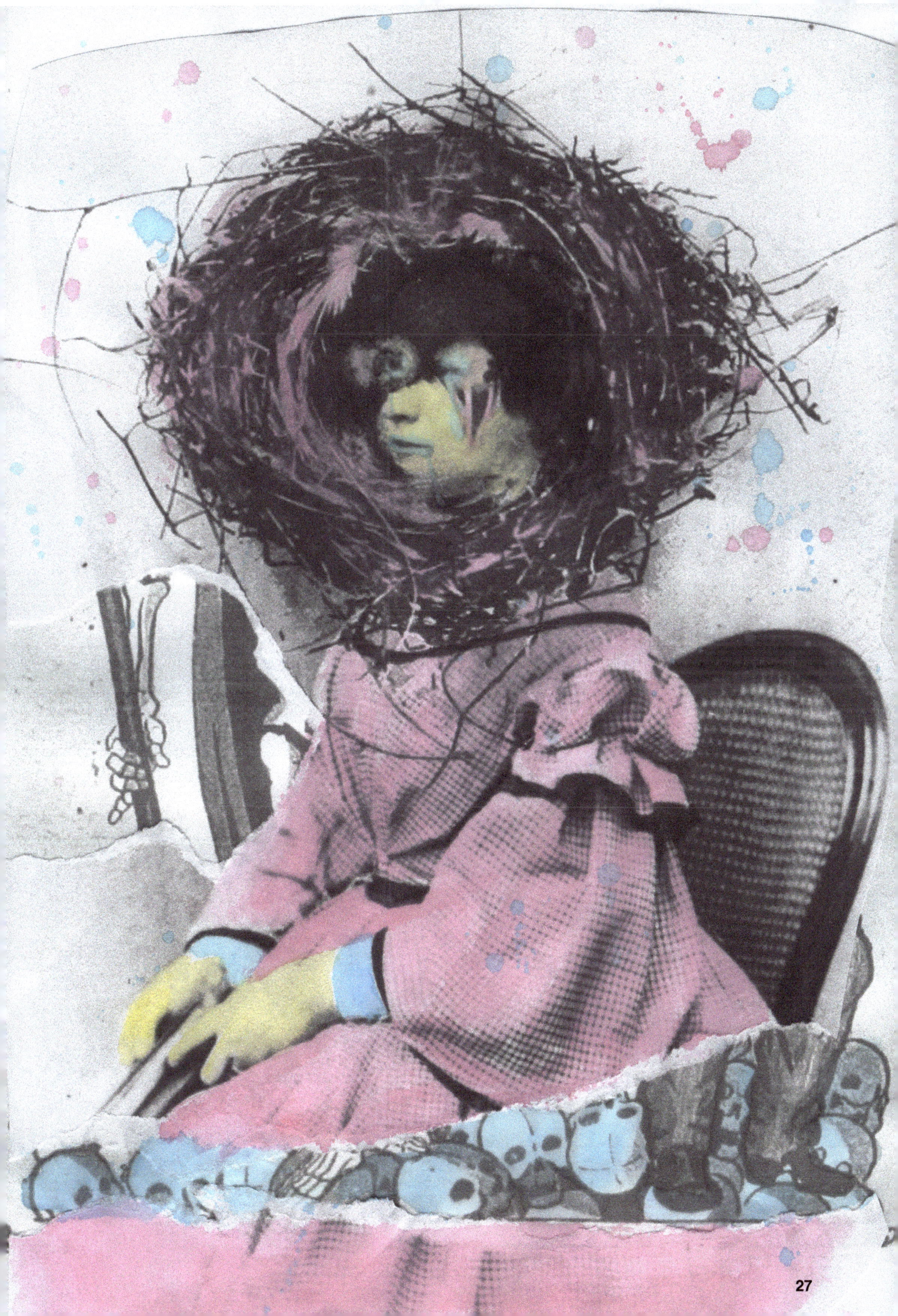

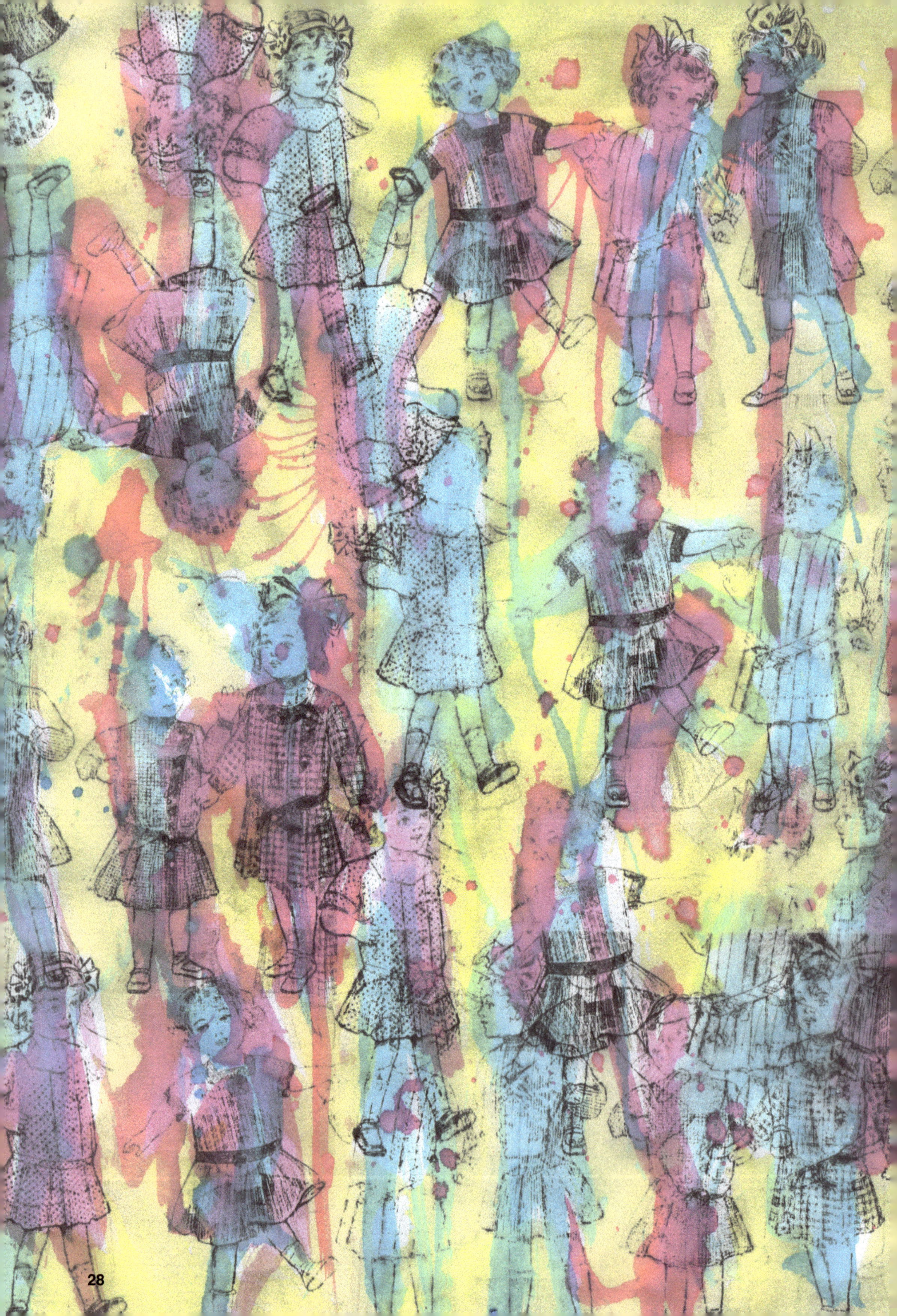

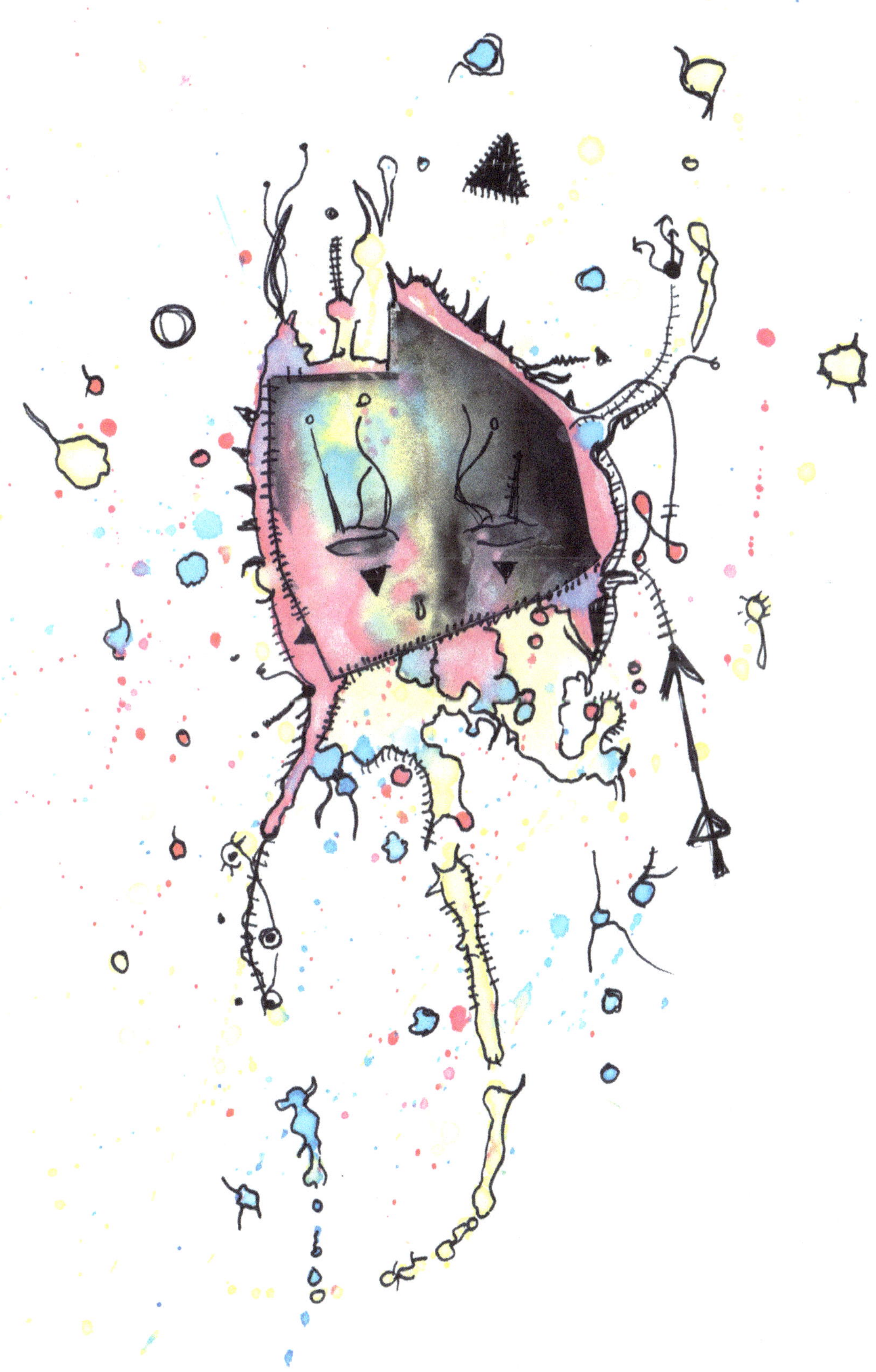

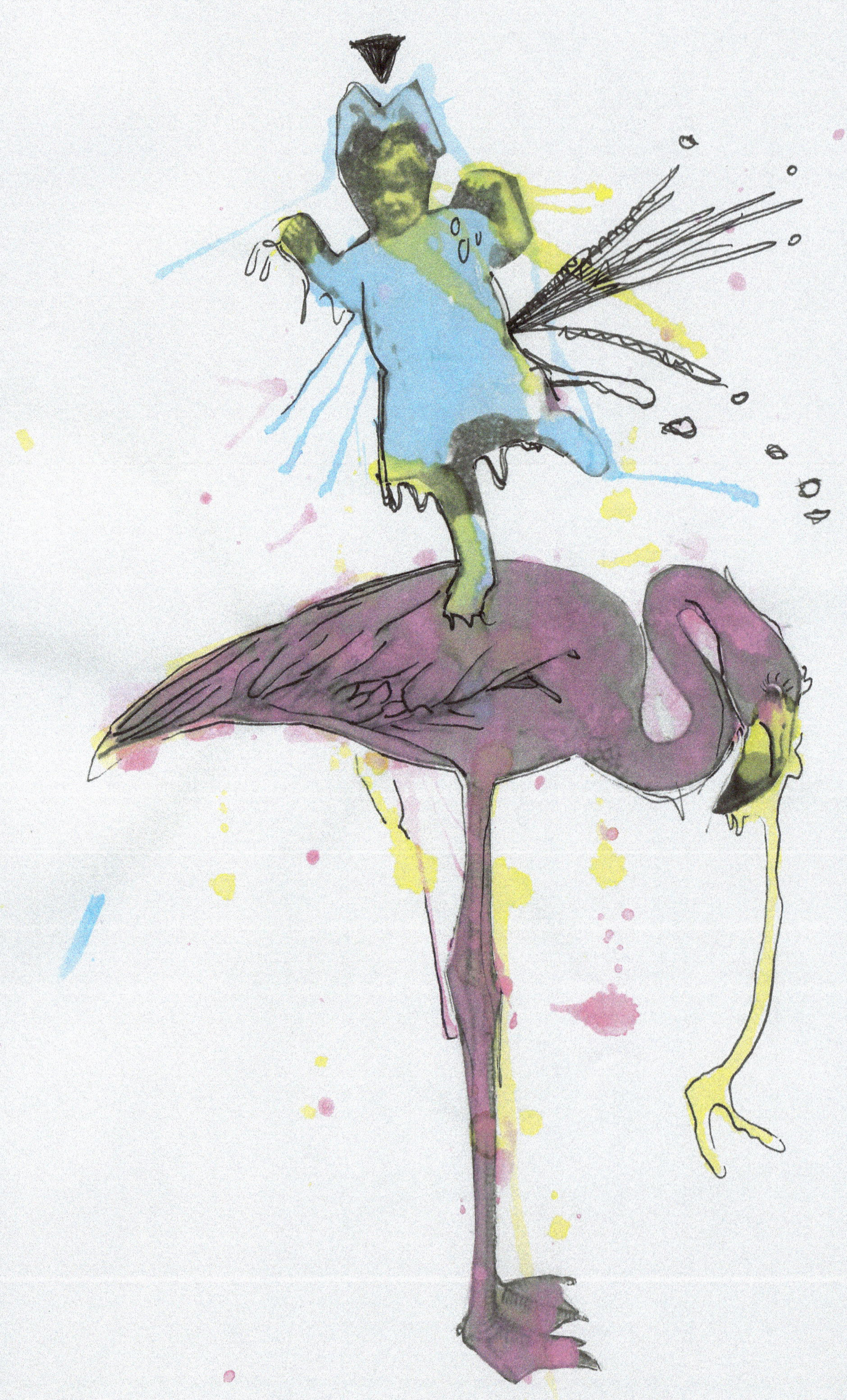

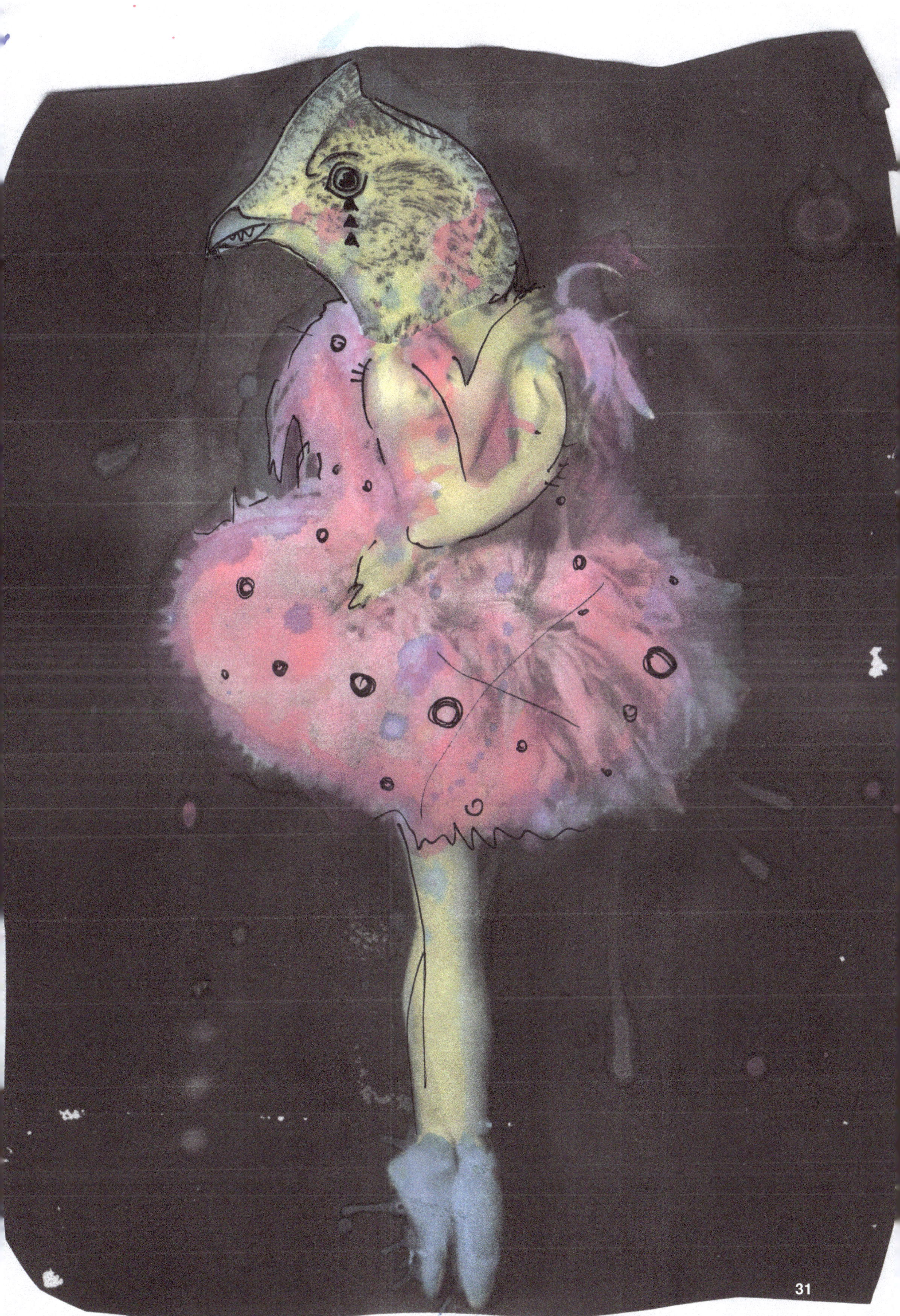

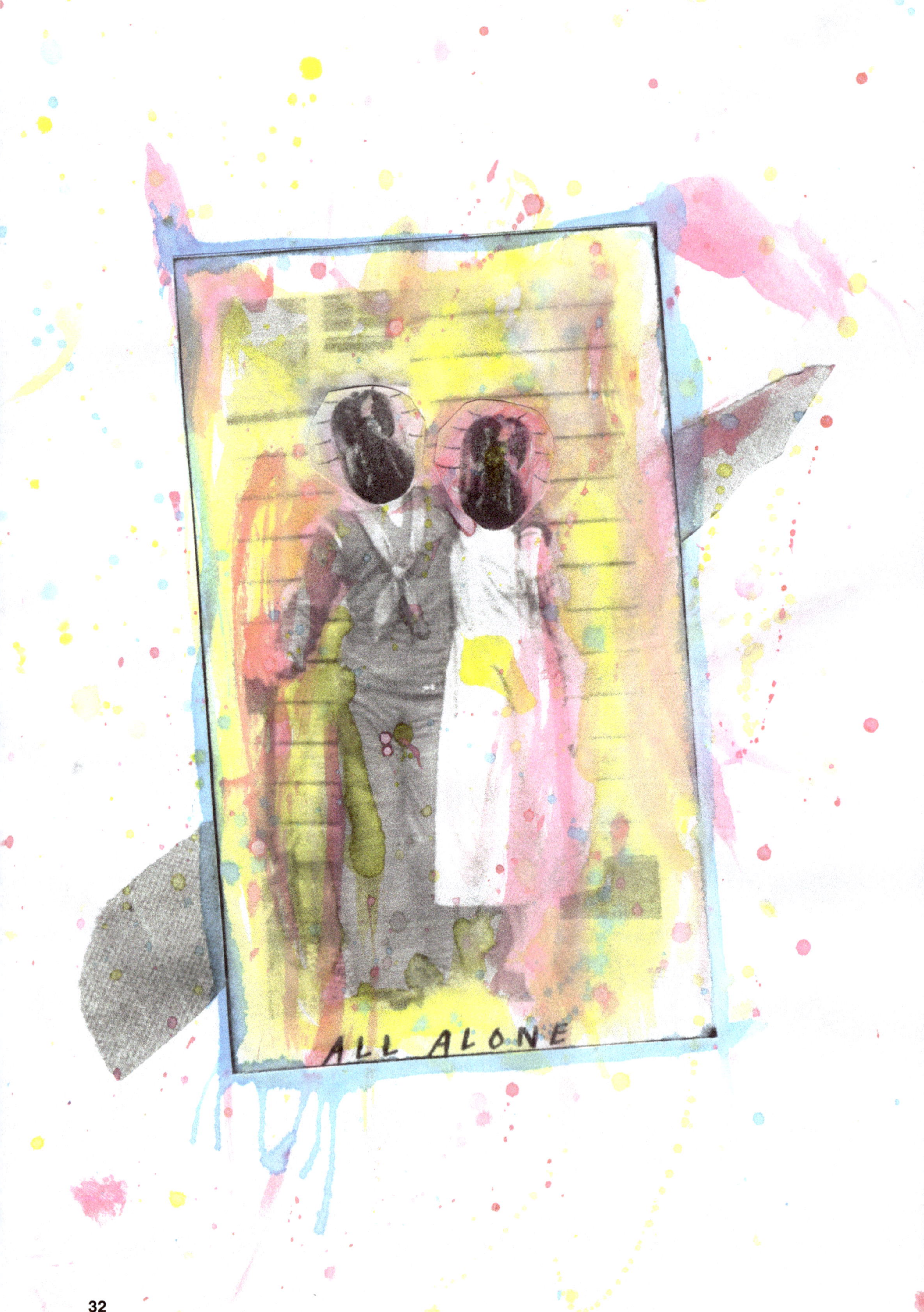

ALL ALONE

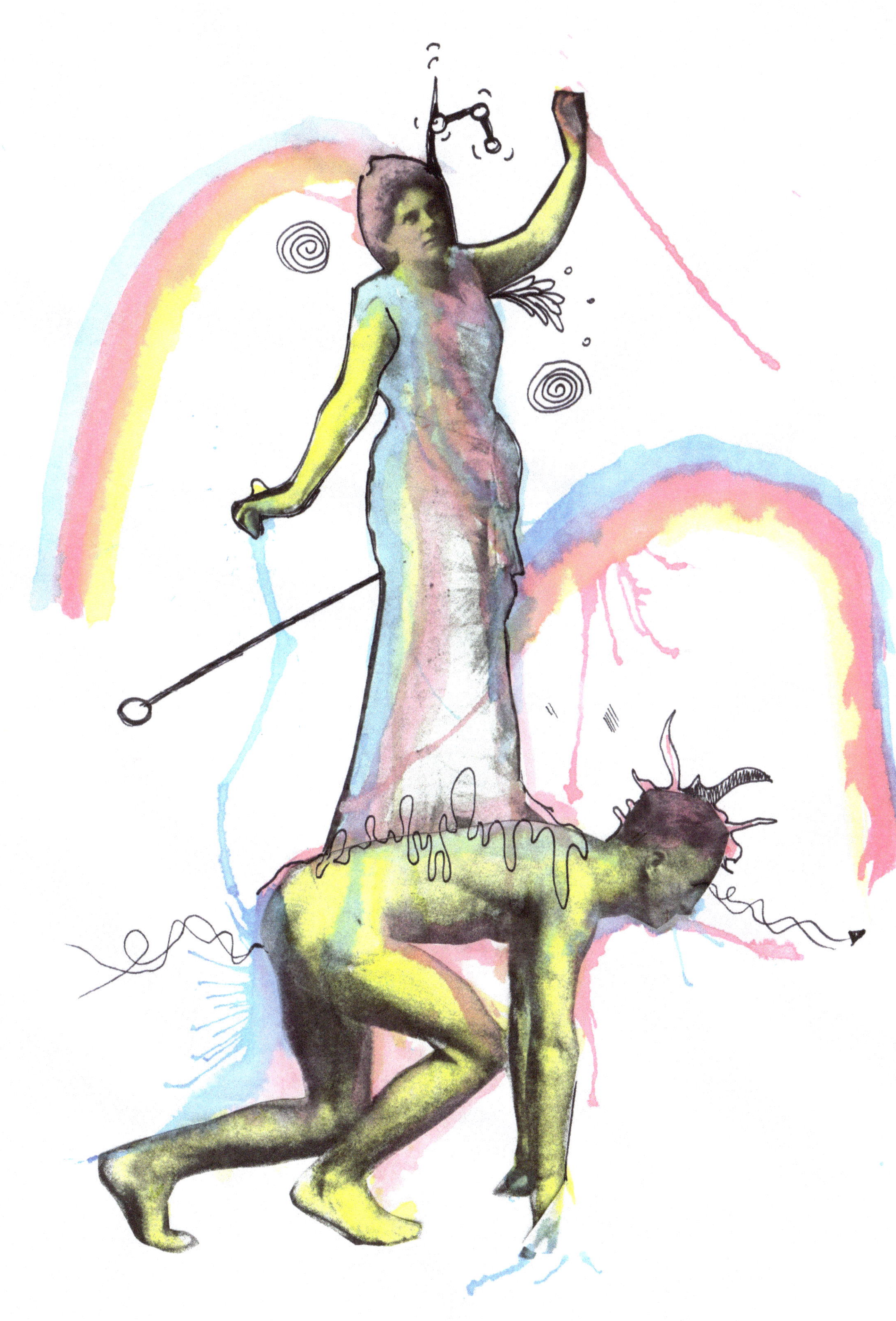

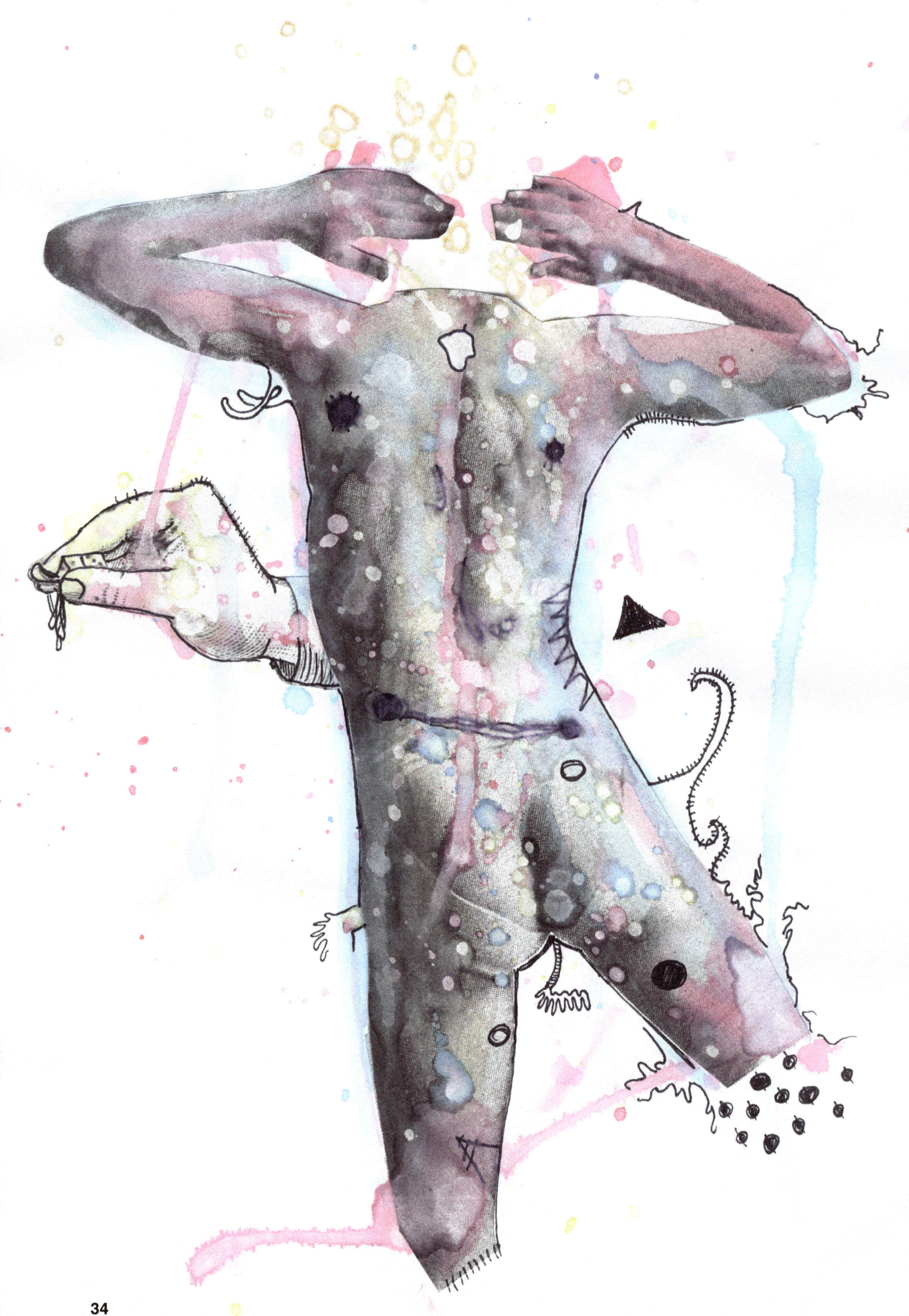

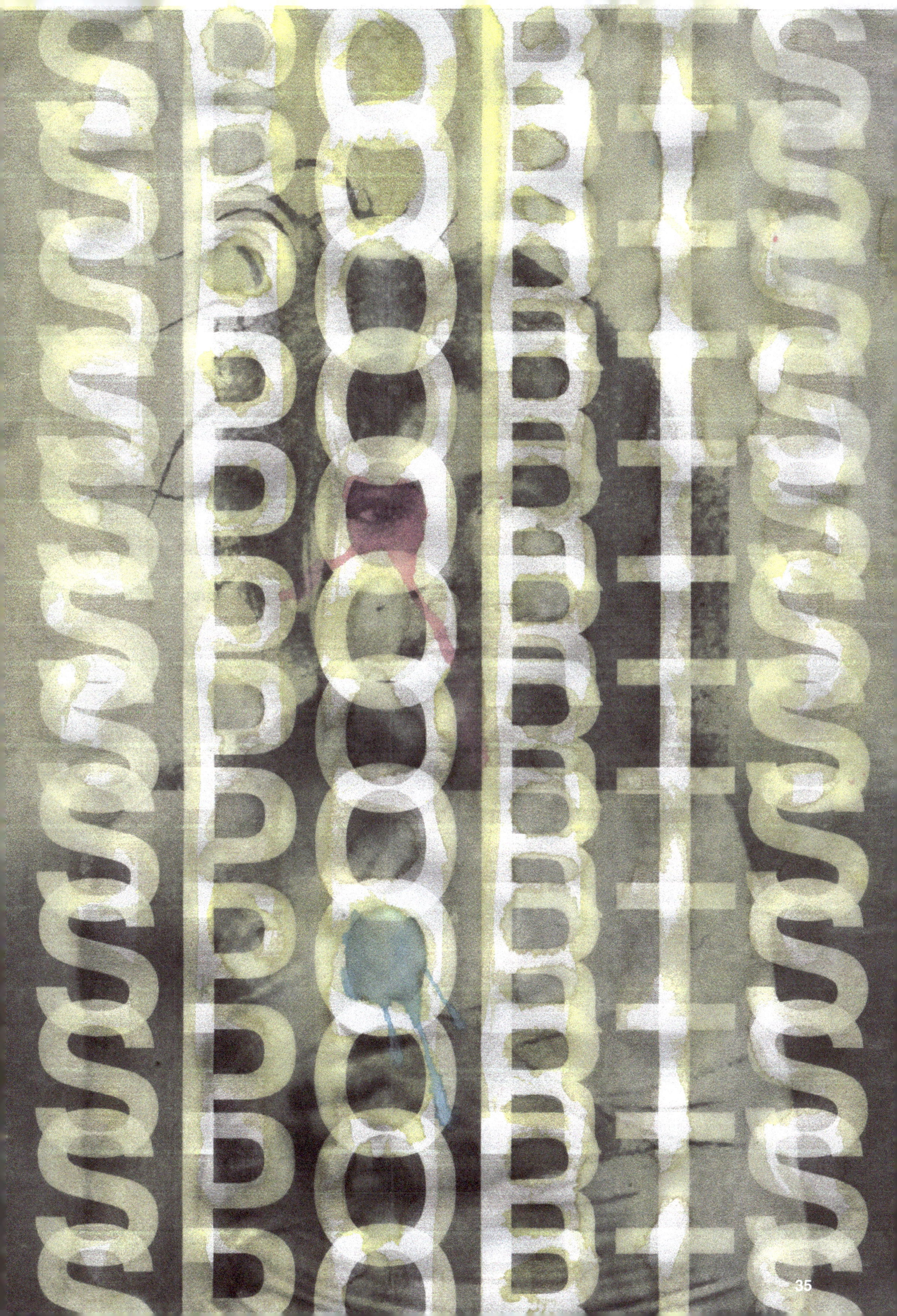

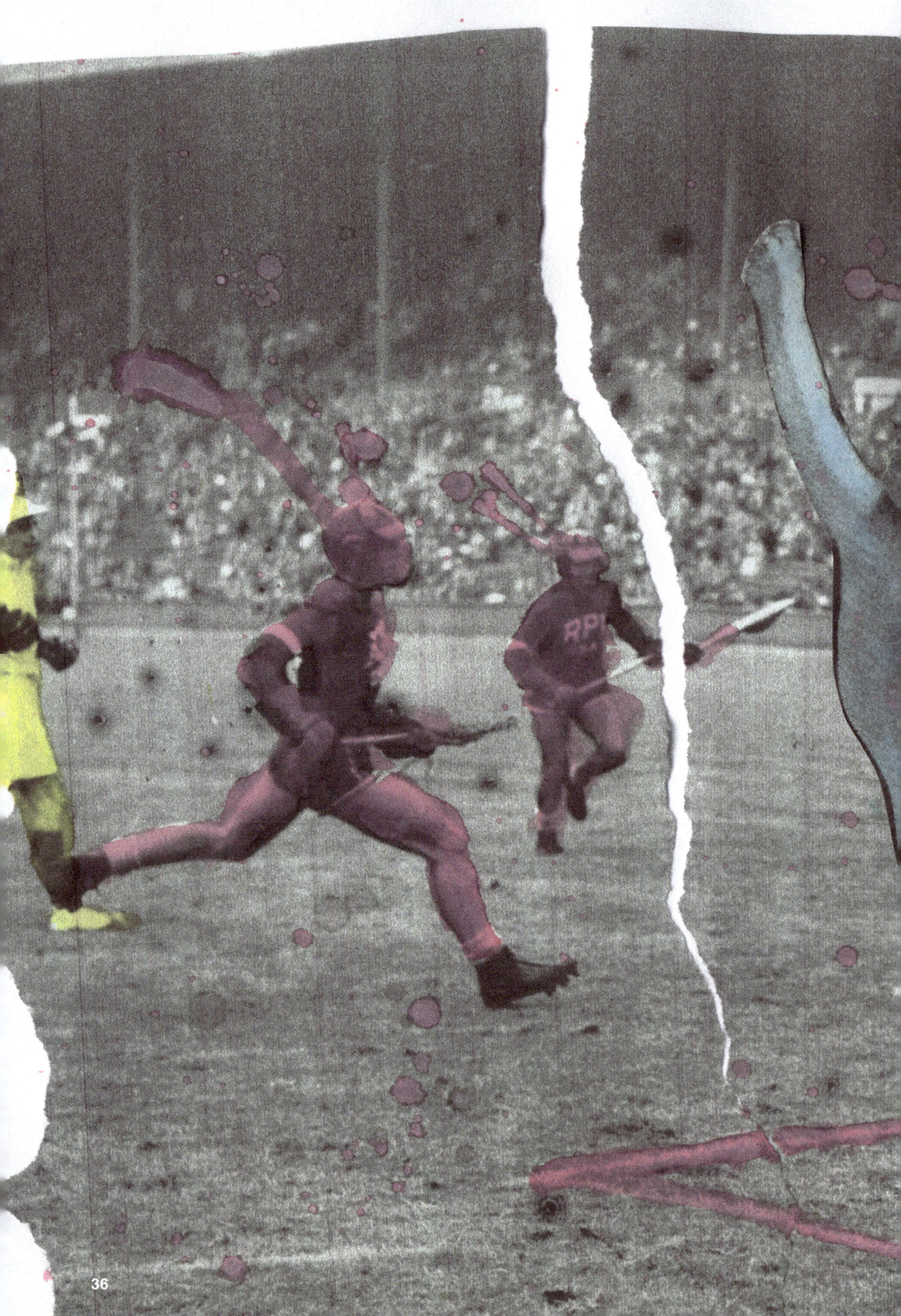

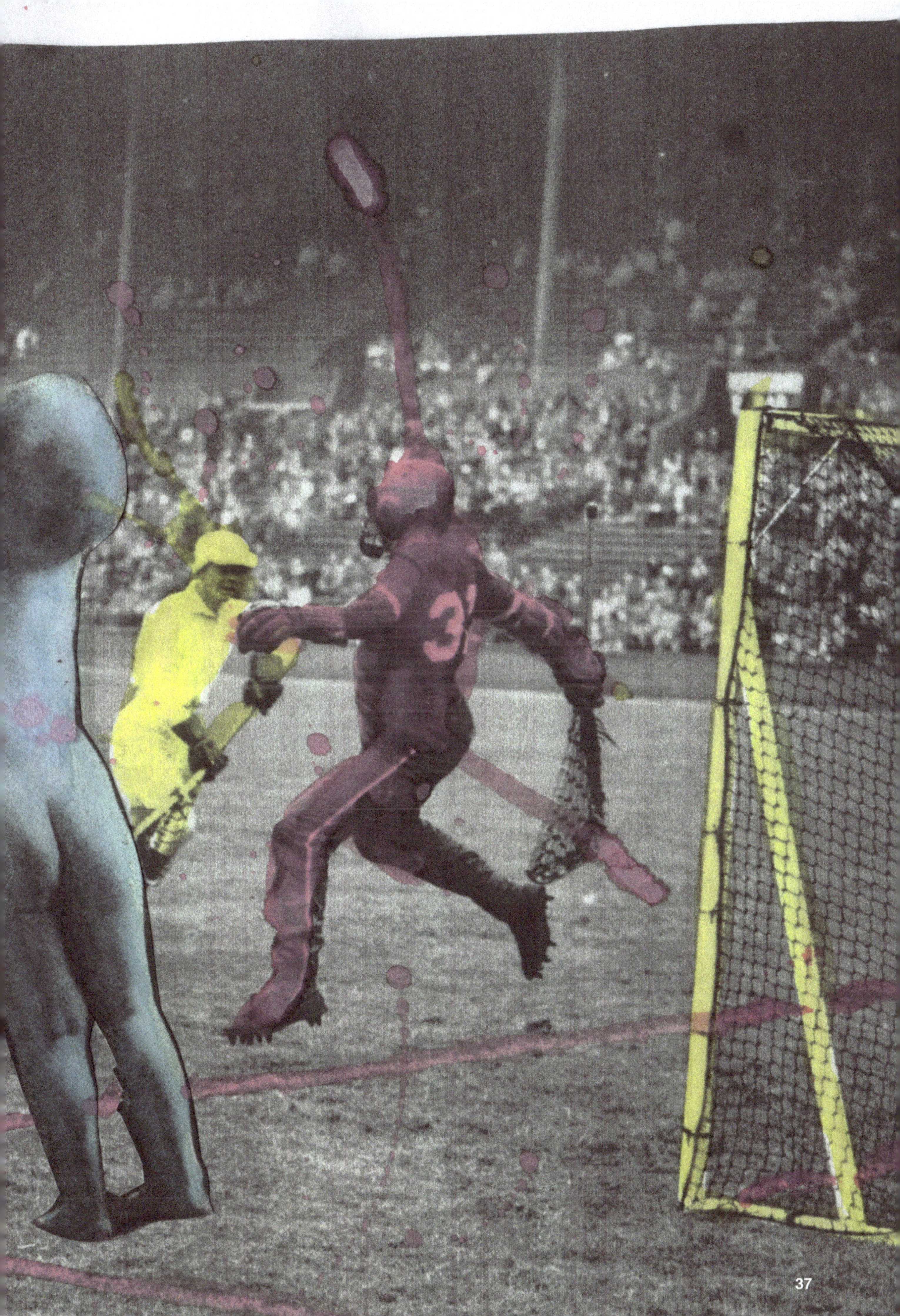

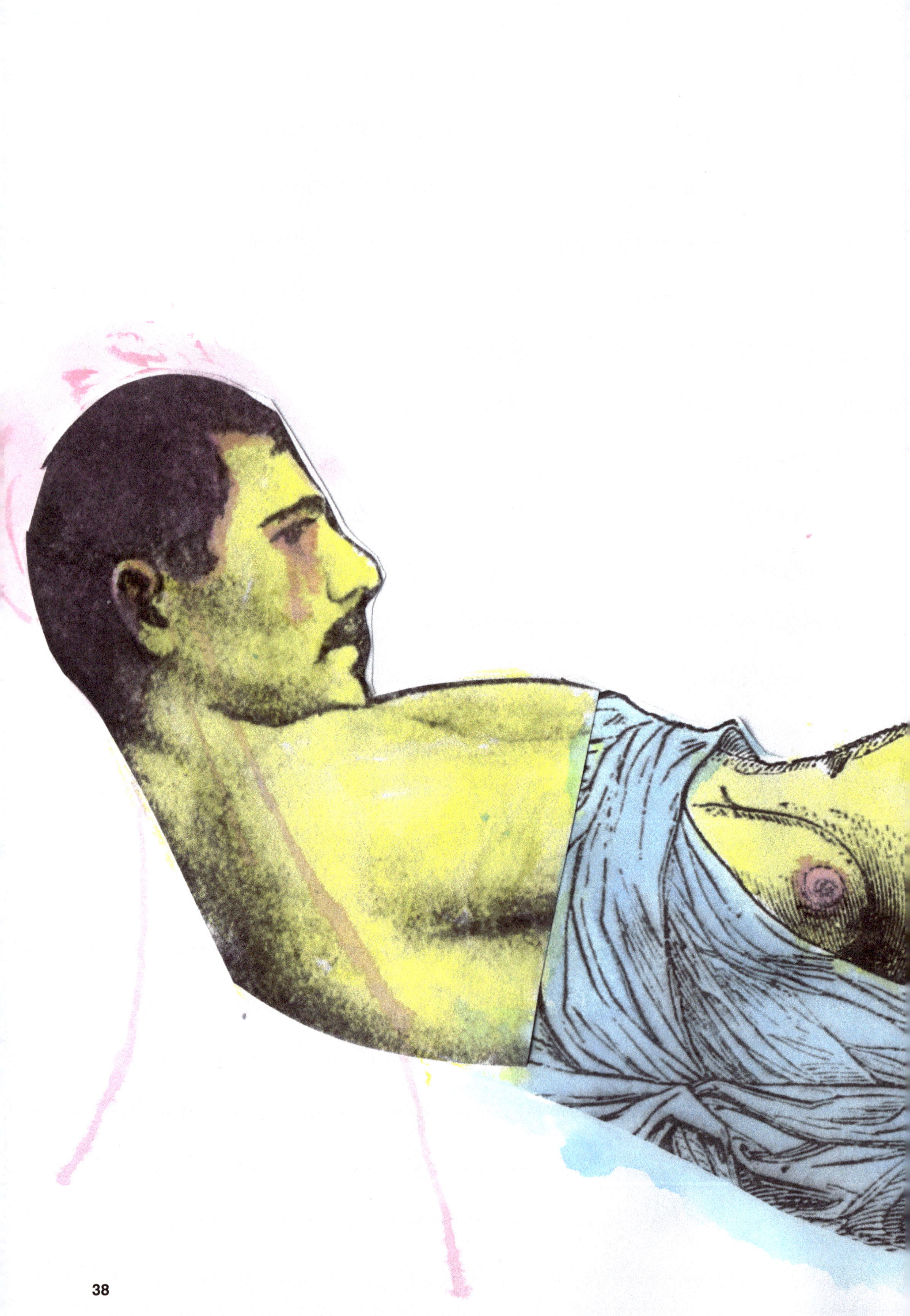

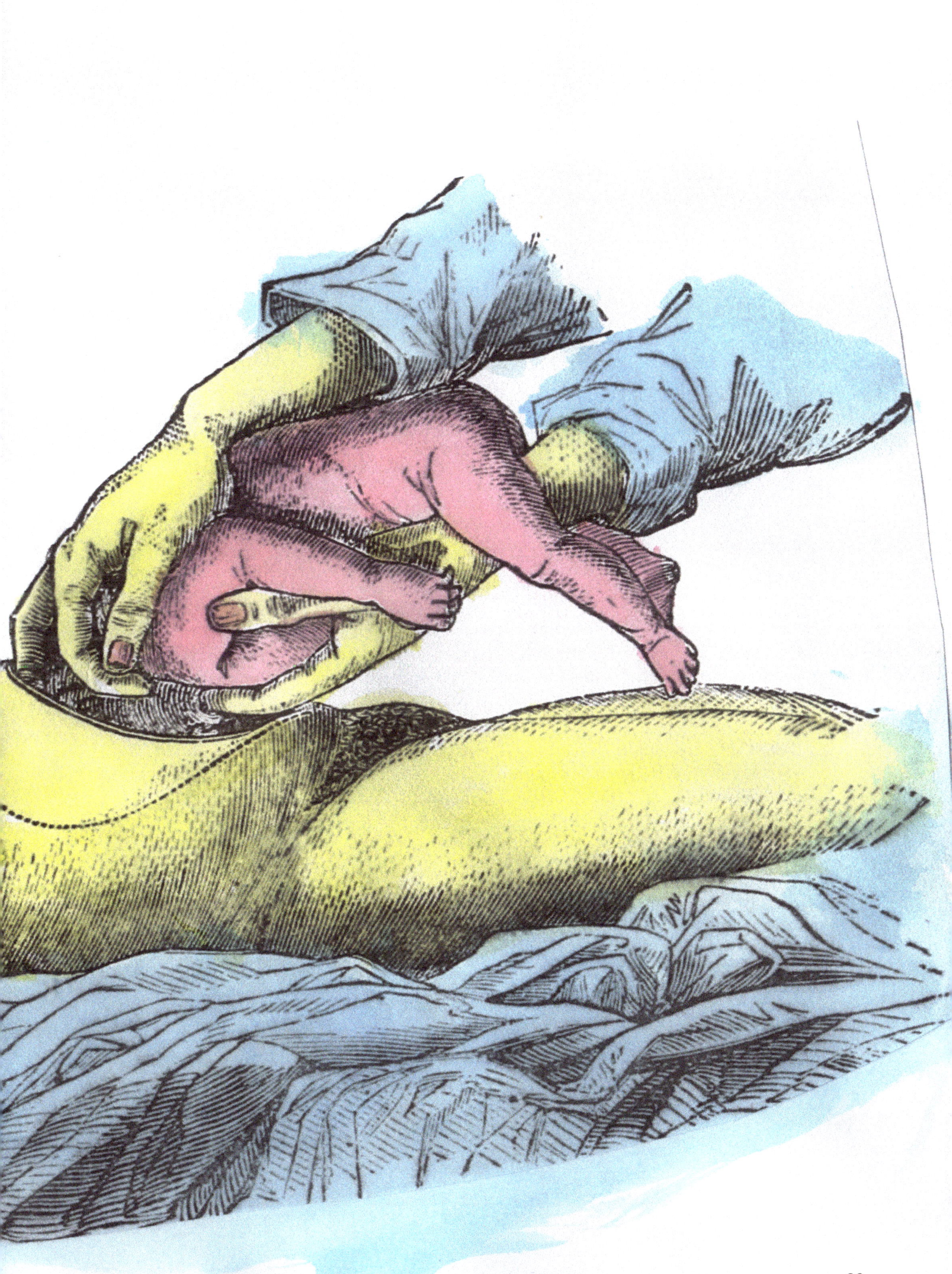

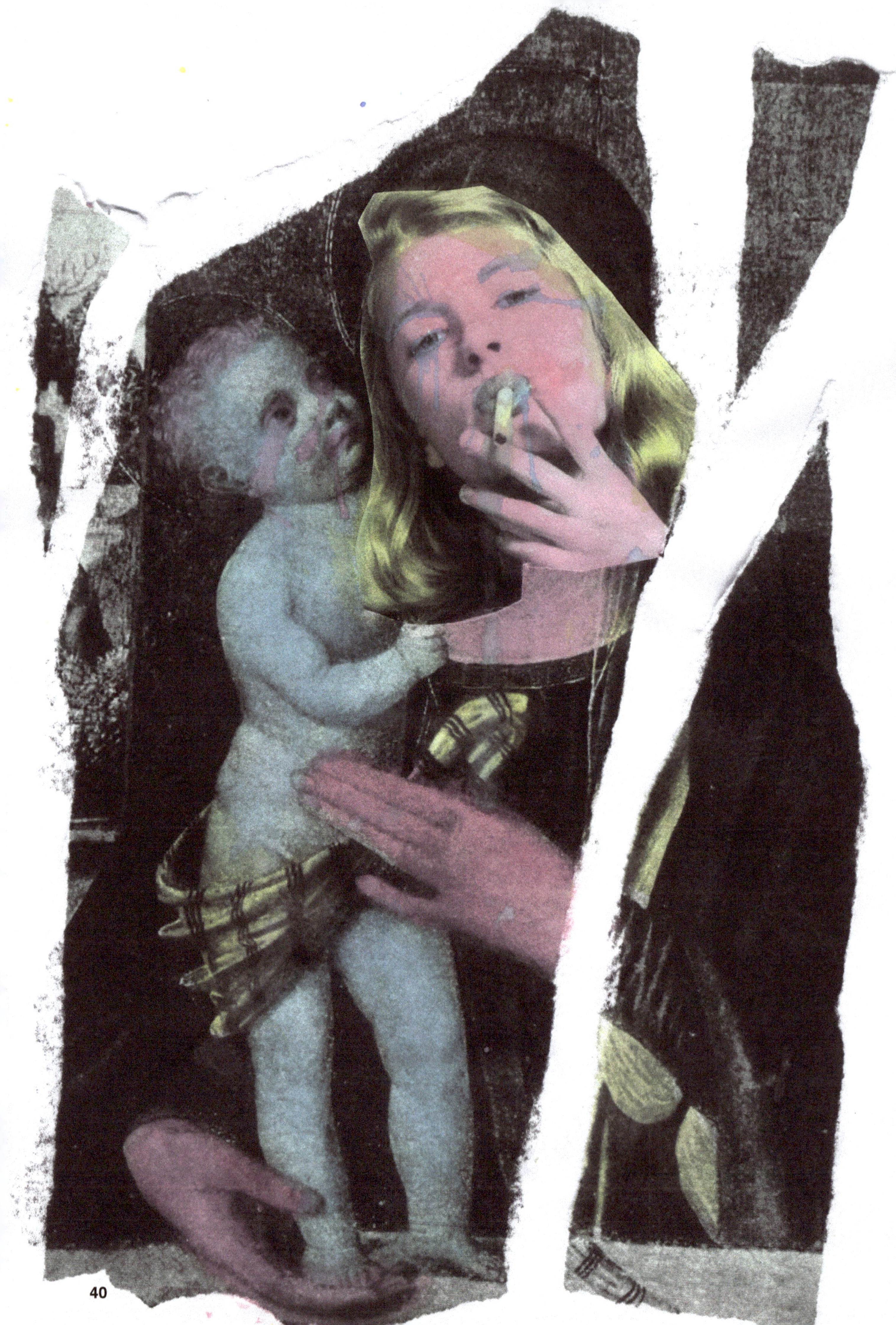

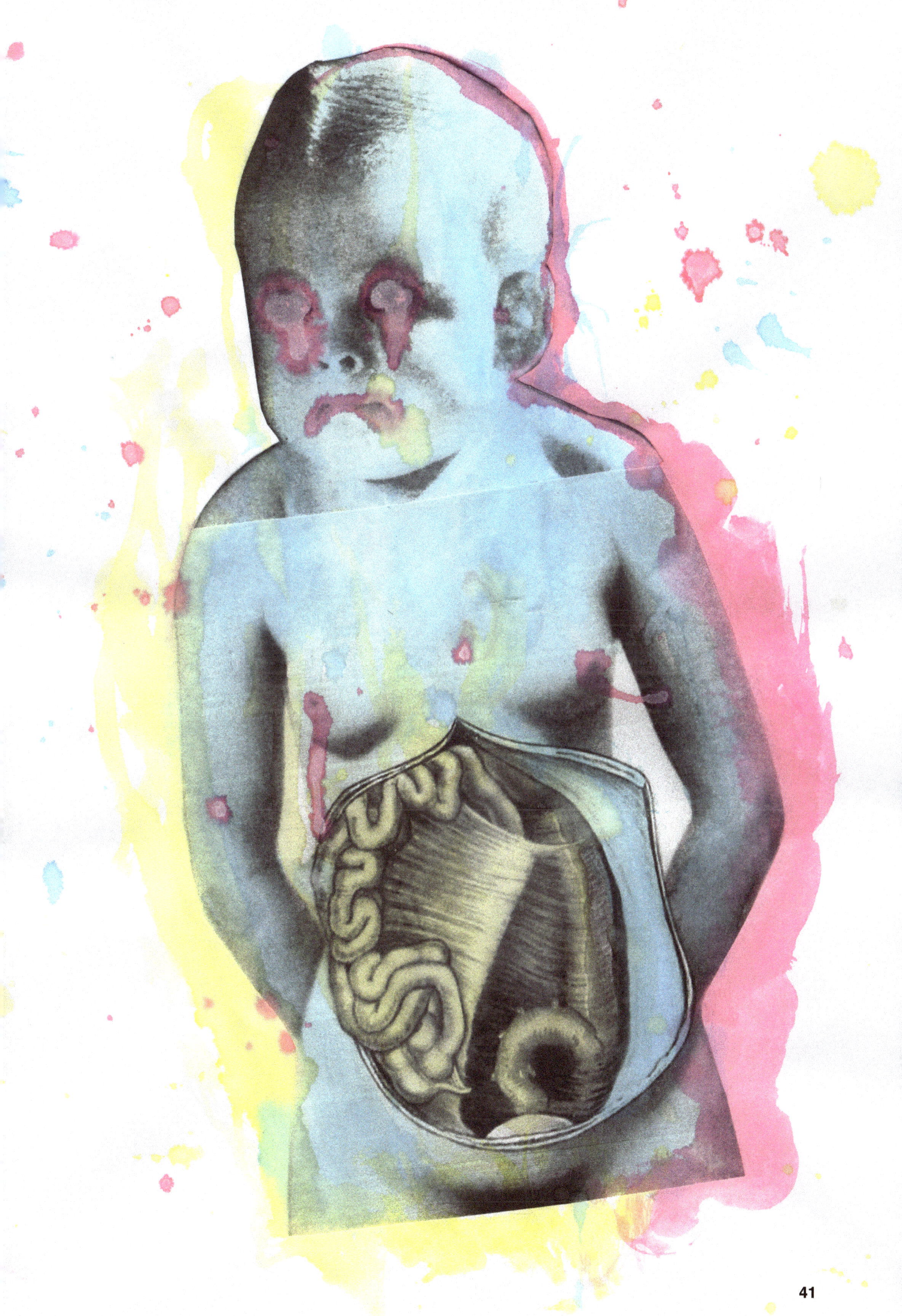

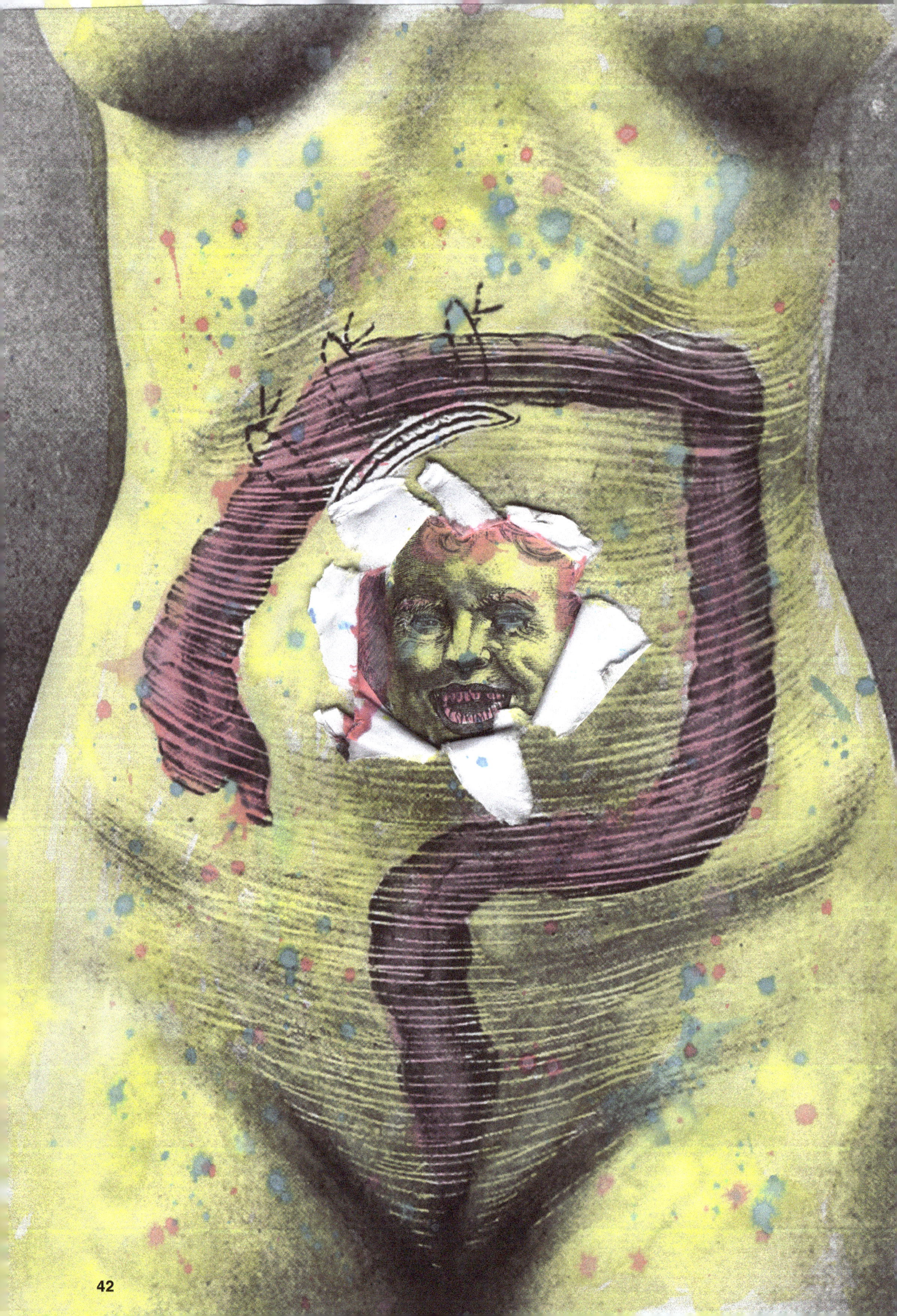

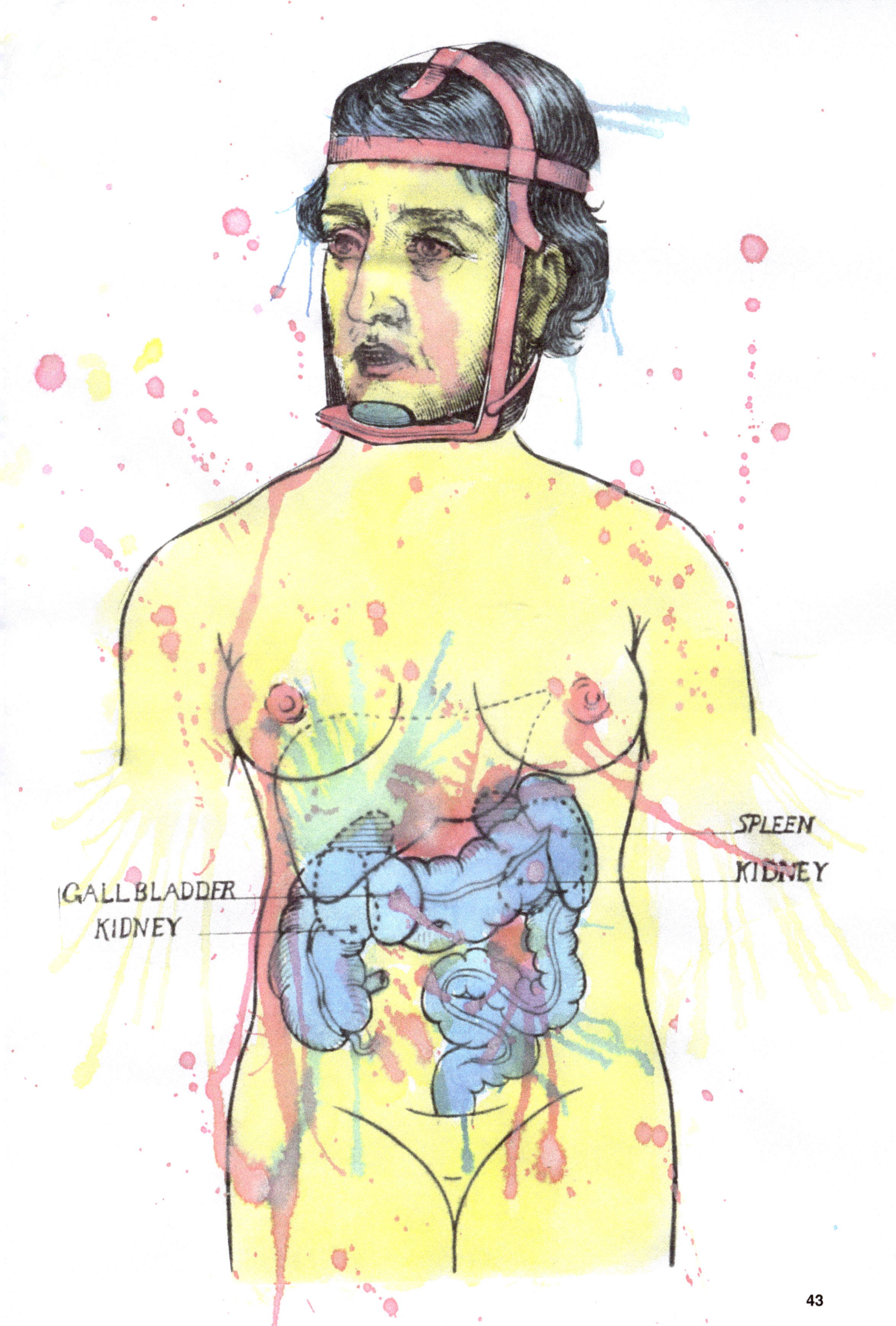

SPLEEN
KIDNEY
GALL BLADDER
KIDNEY

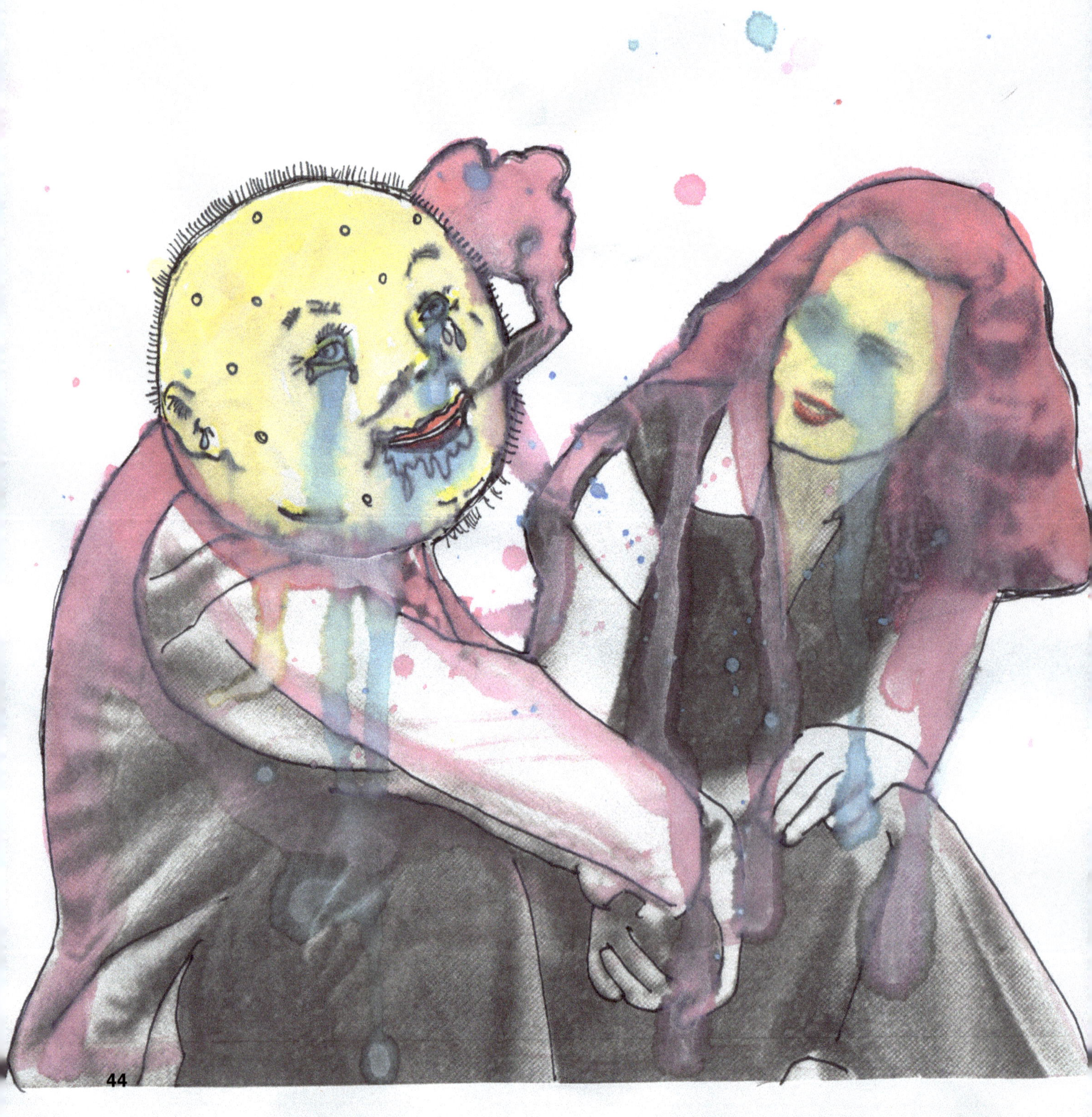

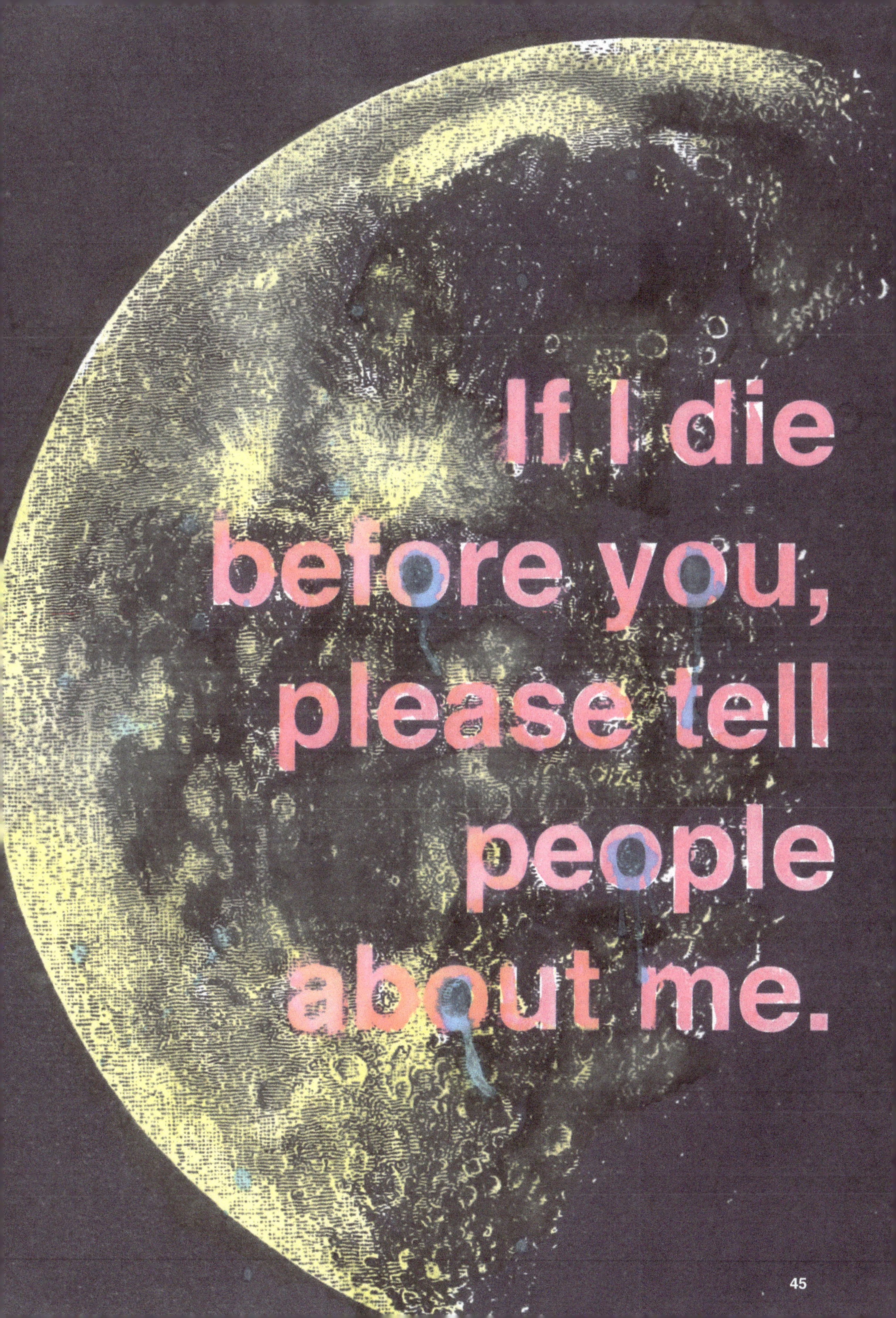

If I die
before you,
please tell
people
about me.

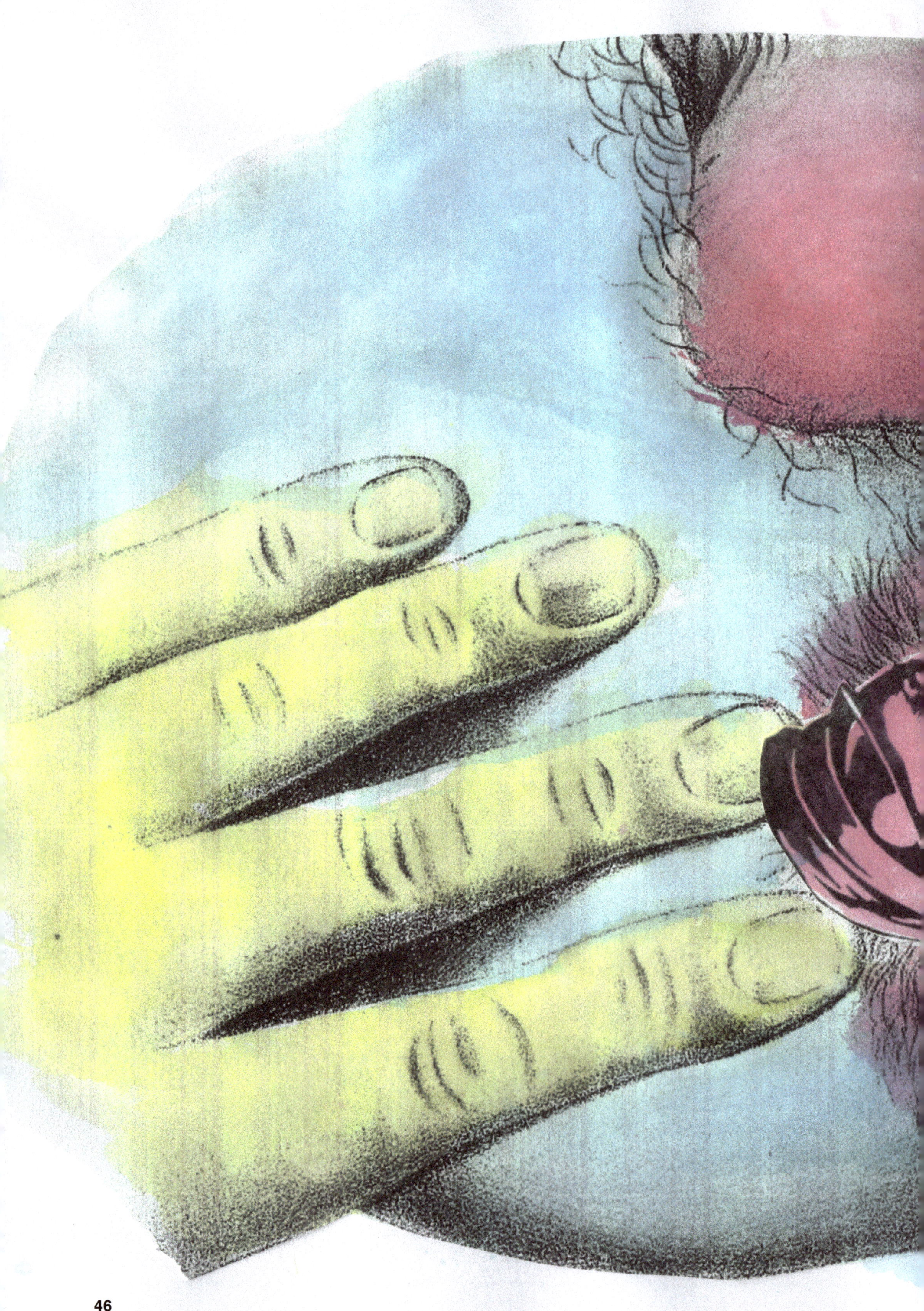

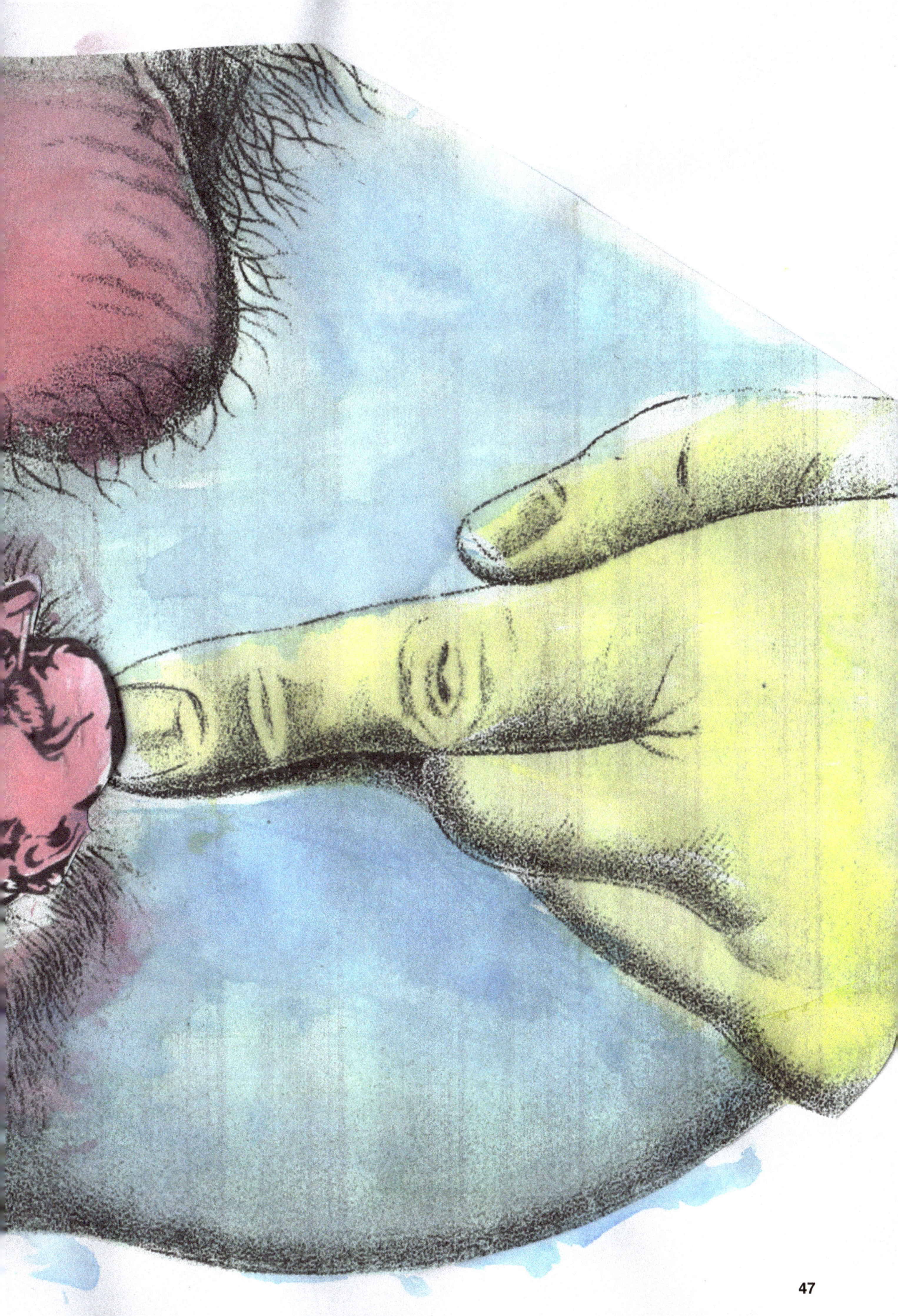

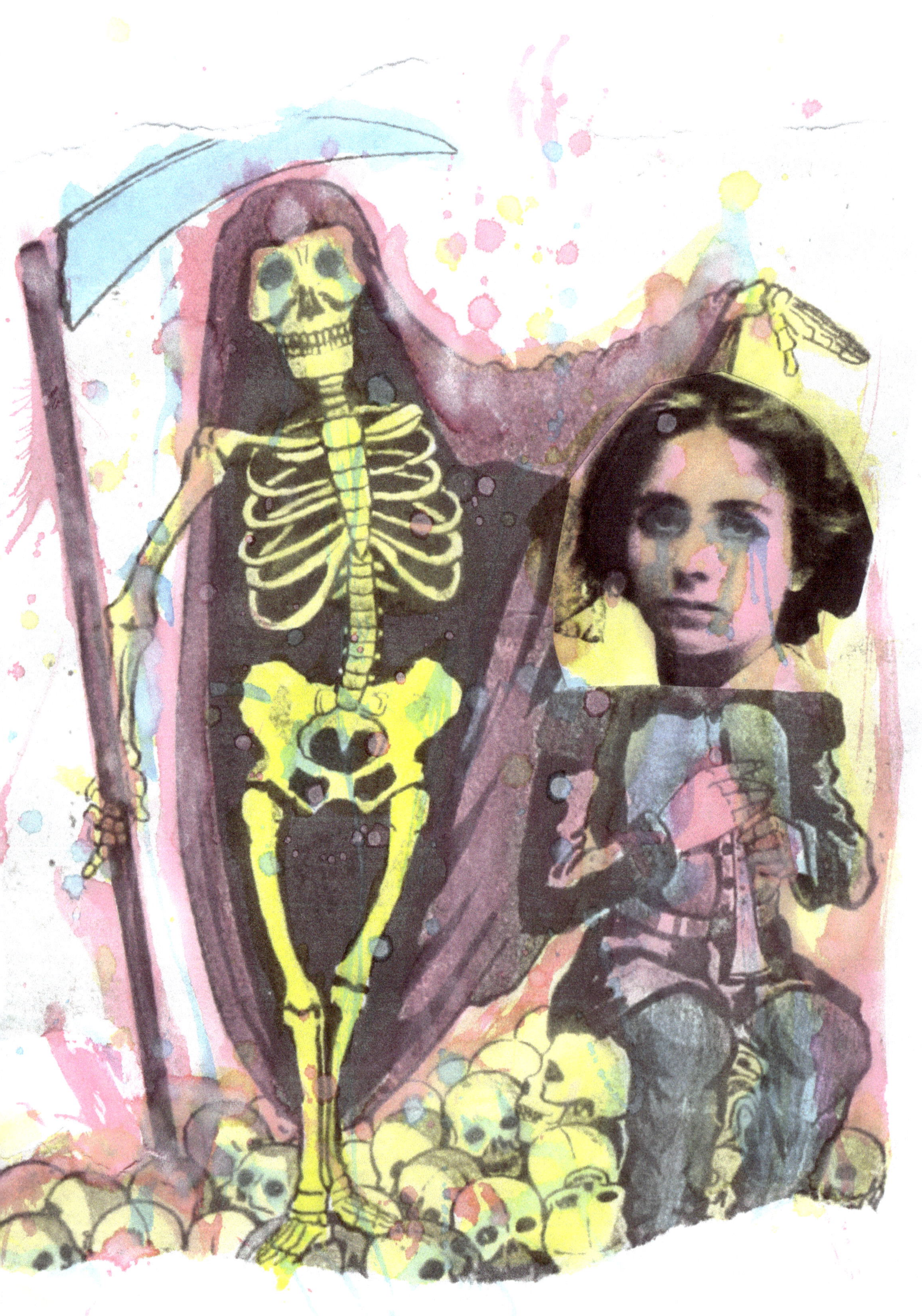

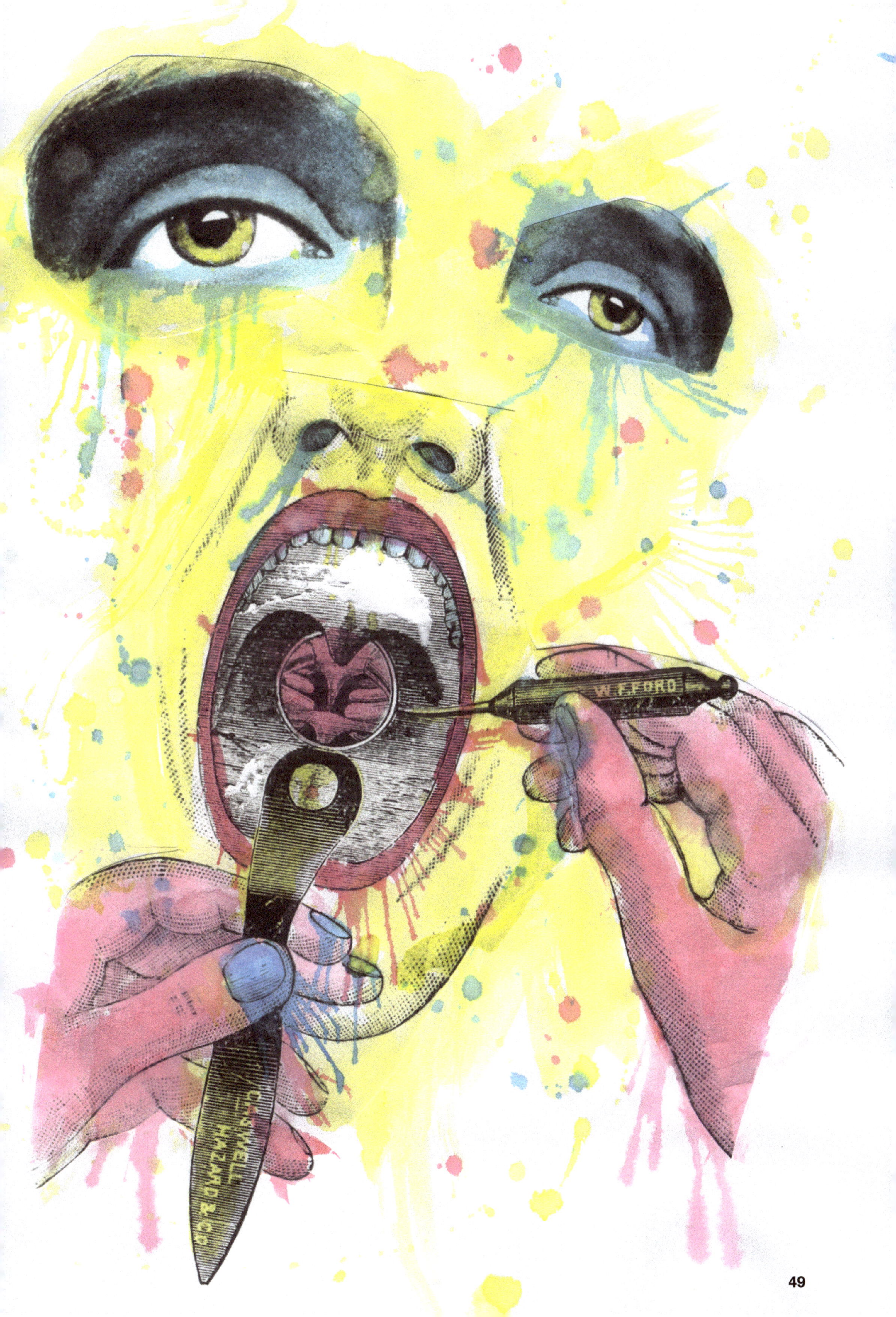
CRISWELL
HAZARD & CO
W.F.FORD

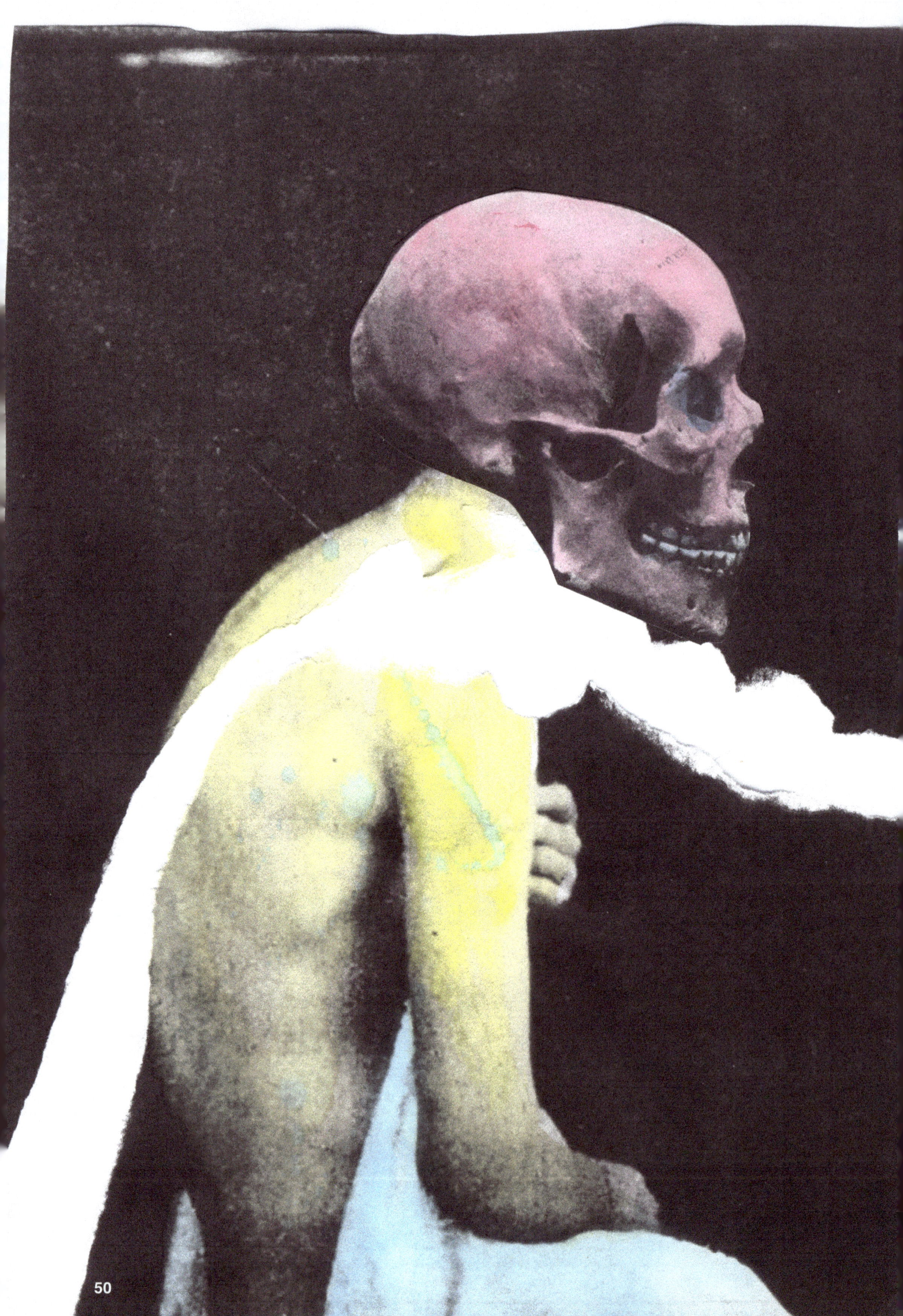

BAD THOUGHTS

We're stunning
in peach.
Did you know
every bird
belongs to you?
You can call
them down and
they'll massage
your shoulders.

Moments of unnecessary childhood nudity

As a child, when I would sit naked on a winter morning before the fireplace with the new day's clothes folded neatly beside me, I often felt perplexed. During this period of nudity between removing my pajamas and getting dressed in clean clothes, it struck me as implausible that everyone did this. Removing one's clothes completely until they were forcing every part of their skin upon the world seemed excessive. I conceded that on occasion it might be necessary to rotate certain items of clothing due to an accumulation of grime, but all of them? Every day? To what end did it make any sense? I'm not sure whether I was incapable of recognizing when I was dirty or if I simply didn't care if I was dirty.

Some mornings I would rush through the process of dressing in order to limit the amount of time my nudity lasted. Other mornings though, I became locked into that moment - sitting naked before the fireplace, my skin becoming unbearably warm - until my mother or father had to interrupt my reverie by warning I'd be late for school. These interruptions made me aware of my vulnerability and I rushed to get dressed in a panic that unfavorably colored my day.

At school, I would survey the students in my class and wonder if they experienced similar uncomfortable encounters with their own nudity. I reflected upon why I never had the same discomfort when I bathed and concluded it was because I was never naked when I bathed - my body wore the water. Then I wrapped it in a towel. The nudity between the towel and getting dressed made more sense to me because one would find discomfort dressing wet skin. Within the limitations of my five-year-old mind, this made sense. Why couldn't I have an outfit suitable for sleeping in and wearing the following day without break? Was it because I was actually 'dirty', or was I just led to believe I was dirty?

Socializing a child via the school experience is a war between the values enforced by the family unit and the values propagated by a constantly shifting and confused milieu. This milieu is a stew of often contradictory values instilled by countless family units each of which possesses their own faults and fractures. In essence, most of us, as children, are thrust into a cohabitation of confusion and status anxiety. This cohabitation may alter as our lives unfold, but the confusion and status anxiety tend to remain.

Thanks to the school experience, my relationship with nudity evolved from vulnerability to shame. In mid-80s Australia, a common 'prank' children (almost always boys) would play on one another was called 'dacking.' I've heard it referred to as 'pantsing' in the US and I'm sure other countries have their own names for it. As you may have guessed, 'dacking' is the act of pulling down the trousers of your target against their will. To consider a dacking successful, two criteria must be met. 1) The prank should occur before as large a crowd as possible and 2) Trousers and underwear should ideally be lowered in tandem.

Nothing instils shame in one's body as successfully as standing in a crowded playground with exposed genitals amid a sea of laughing peers. This only happened to me once, but I still have vivid imprints of the mocking expressions, which seemed to occupy every face I could see. It takes a moment to understand what's happened, like the elapsed time between burning oneself and feeling the burn. Once you become aware of your forced indecent exposure, the panic kicks in, which inhibits coordination, ensuring the act of restoring the position of your pants is executed in a slow and awkward way. In particularly aggressive bouts of dacking, the dacker will try and keep you from raising your pants. Thankfully my experience was not this aggressive. What undoubtedly takes mere seconds to remedy feels expansive like loneliness and indeed, in some ways it is. You remain exposed within yourself long after the genitals are covered and it becomes difficult to see your body without hearing that playground laughter and seeing those mocking faces.

I like my body now, but I want to admit something I don't think I'm allowed to openly celebrate - I also like the shame I feel for my body. Sometimes I will rush to cover up my nudity upon showering or changing clothes. Sometimes I will linger before the mirror, training my eyes over every collision of flesh. I tell my penis it looks ridiculous and poke at the fat adorning me with derision, but I like how ridiculous my penis looks and it's fun to poke at one's fat. I won't be me forever, so I'll enjoy it while I am.

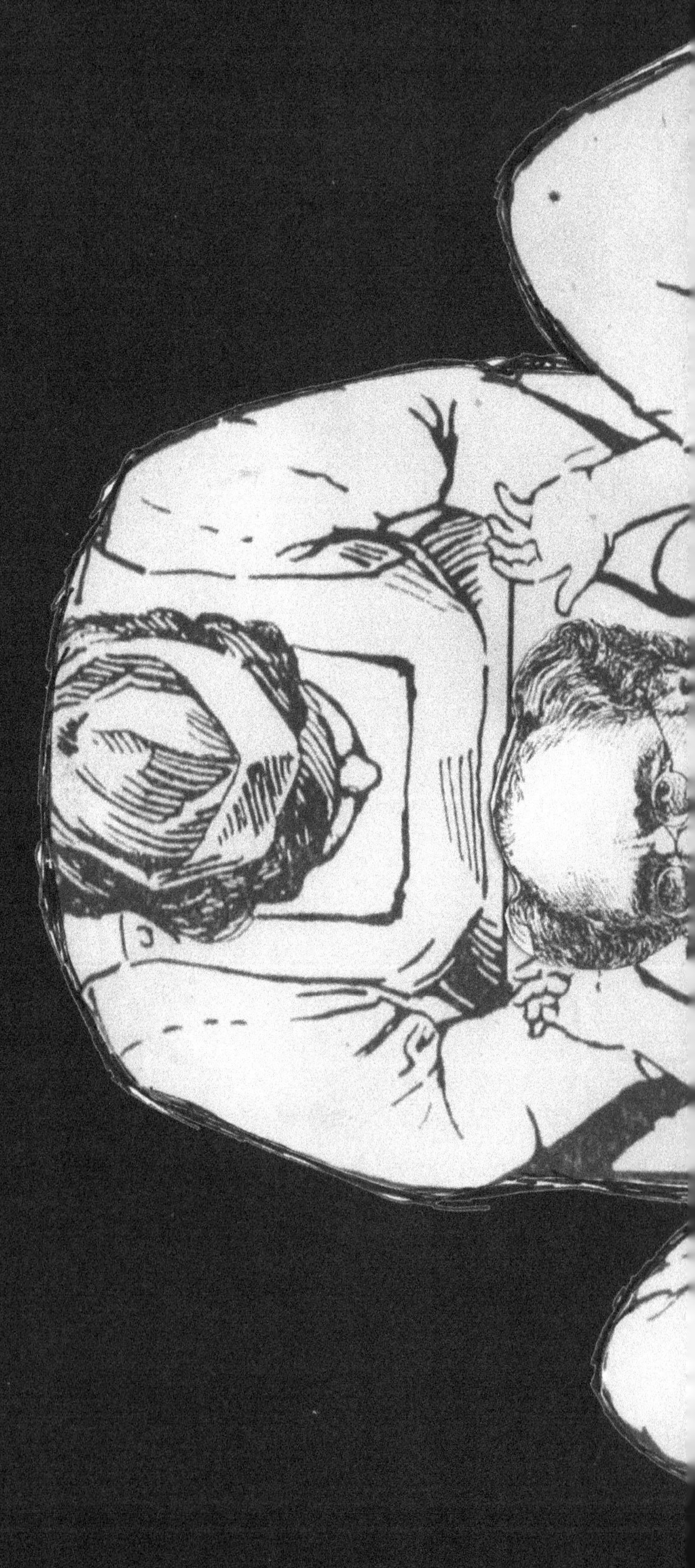

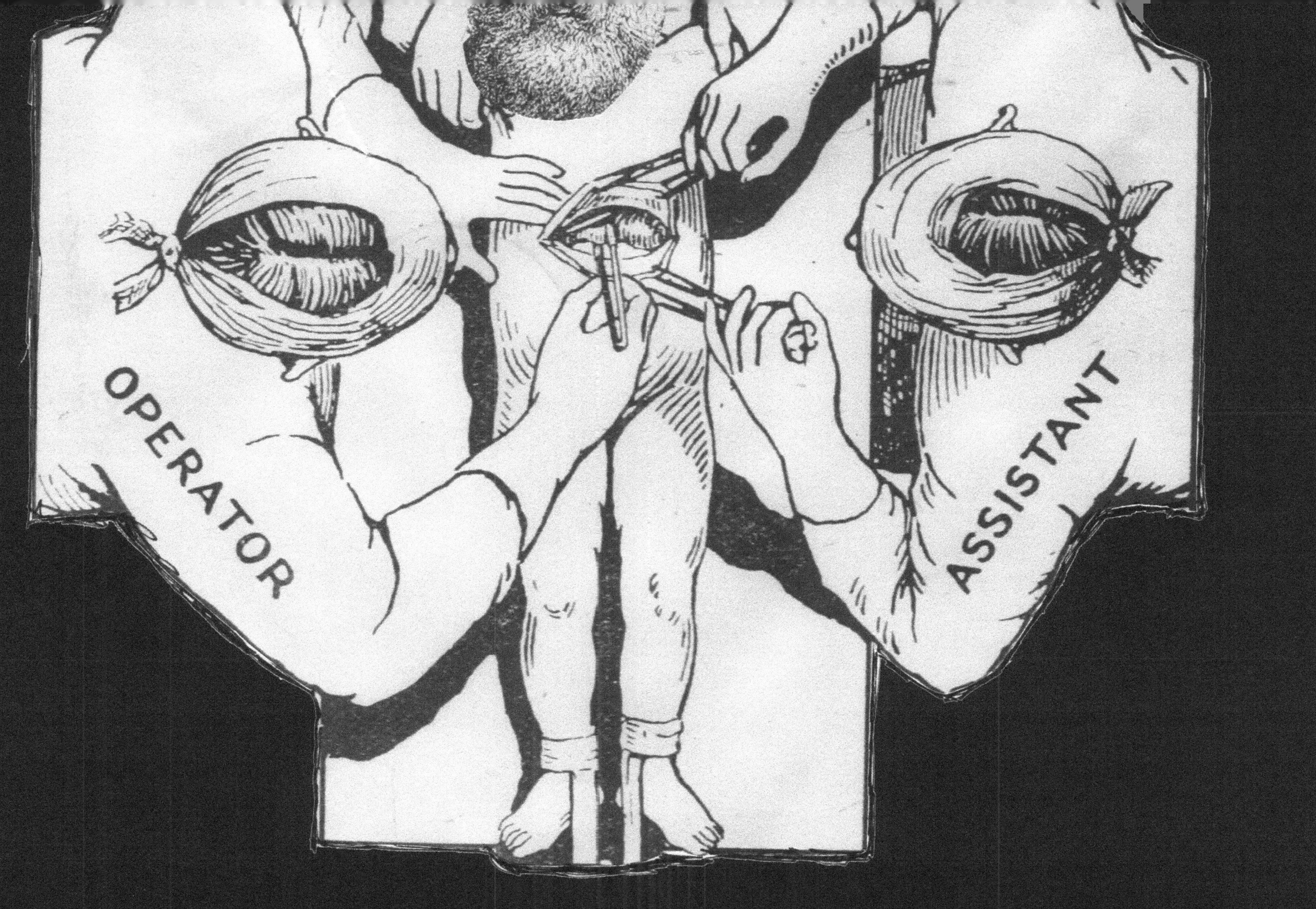

OPERATOR
ASSISTANT

Contents

57	Finding Nemo but with oil
58	Inventing Harrison
59	BANG
60	Sexting Henry
61	I can see me
62	Venus in birds
63	Piss scan
64	Private Polly
65	Community spirit
66	Heads
67	Jim's bedtime
68	Here comes the airplane
69	First date nerves
70	Bad thoughts
72	With love
74	Bruce's mother
75	Pride
76	Jesus girl hates her novel
77	Broken nun man
78	Cock climb
80	Palm psalm
81	Ram man
82	Now I see me, now I don't

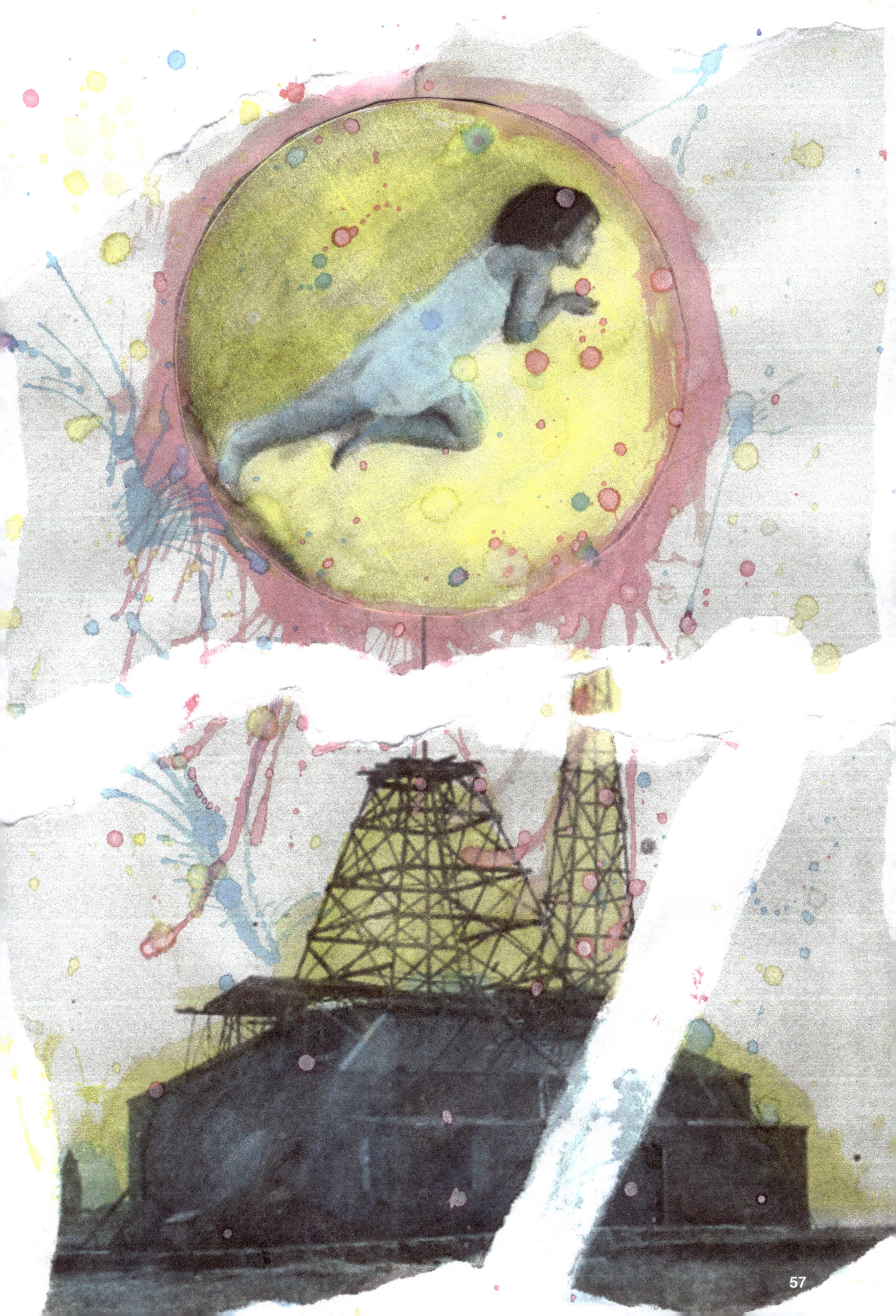

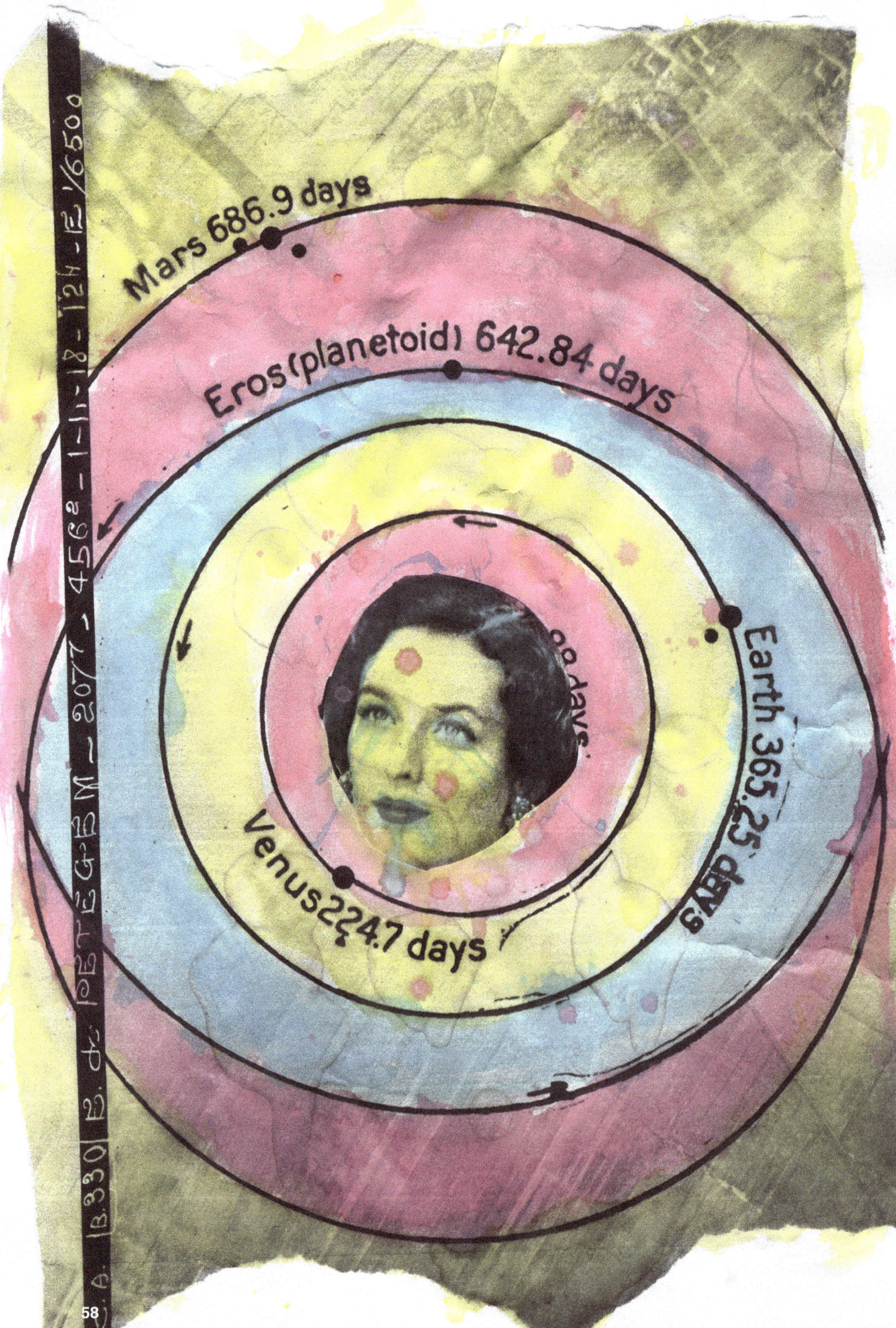

Mars 686.9 days
Eros (planetoid) 642.84 days
Earth 365.25 days
Venus 224.7 days
88 days

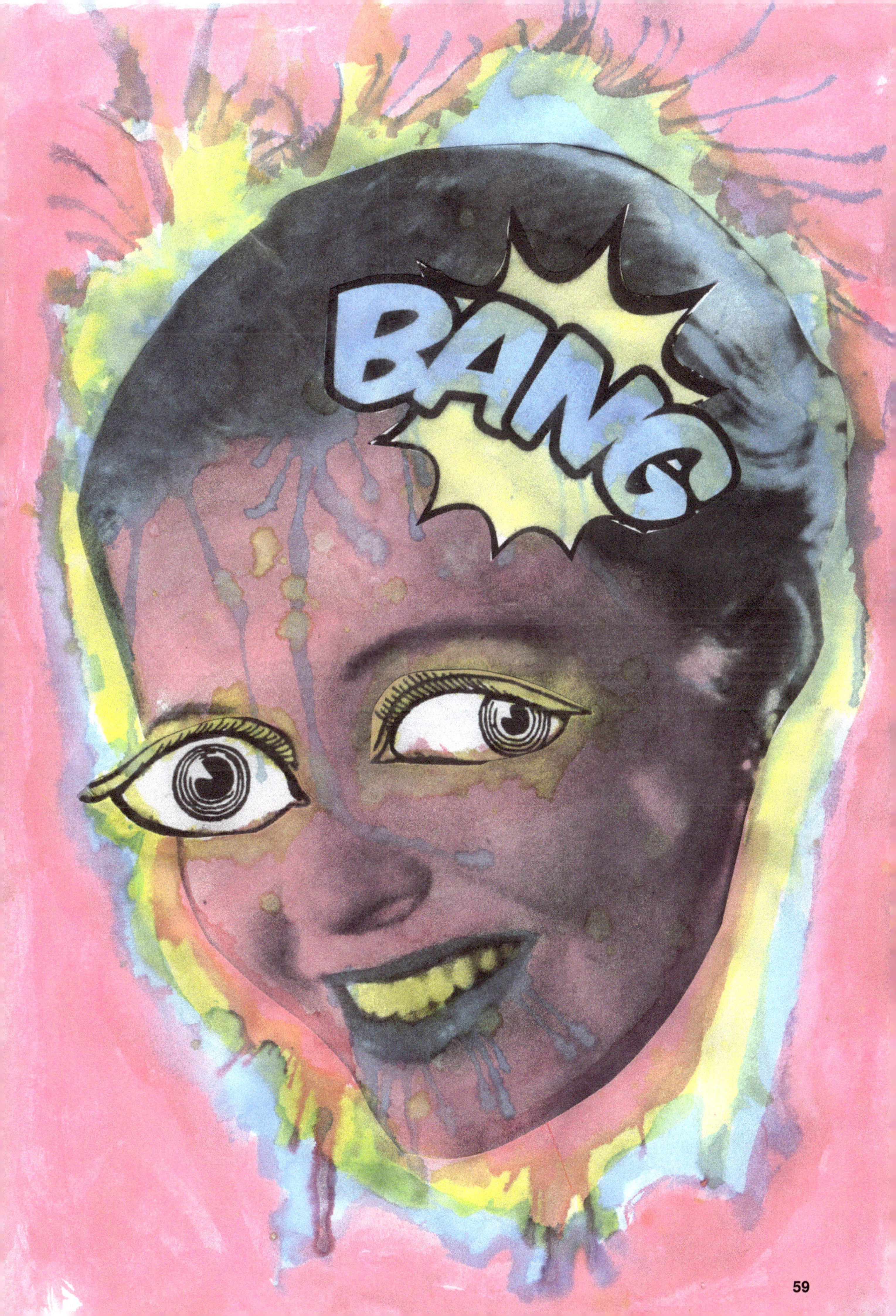
BANG

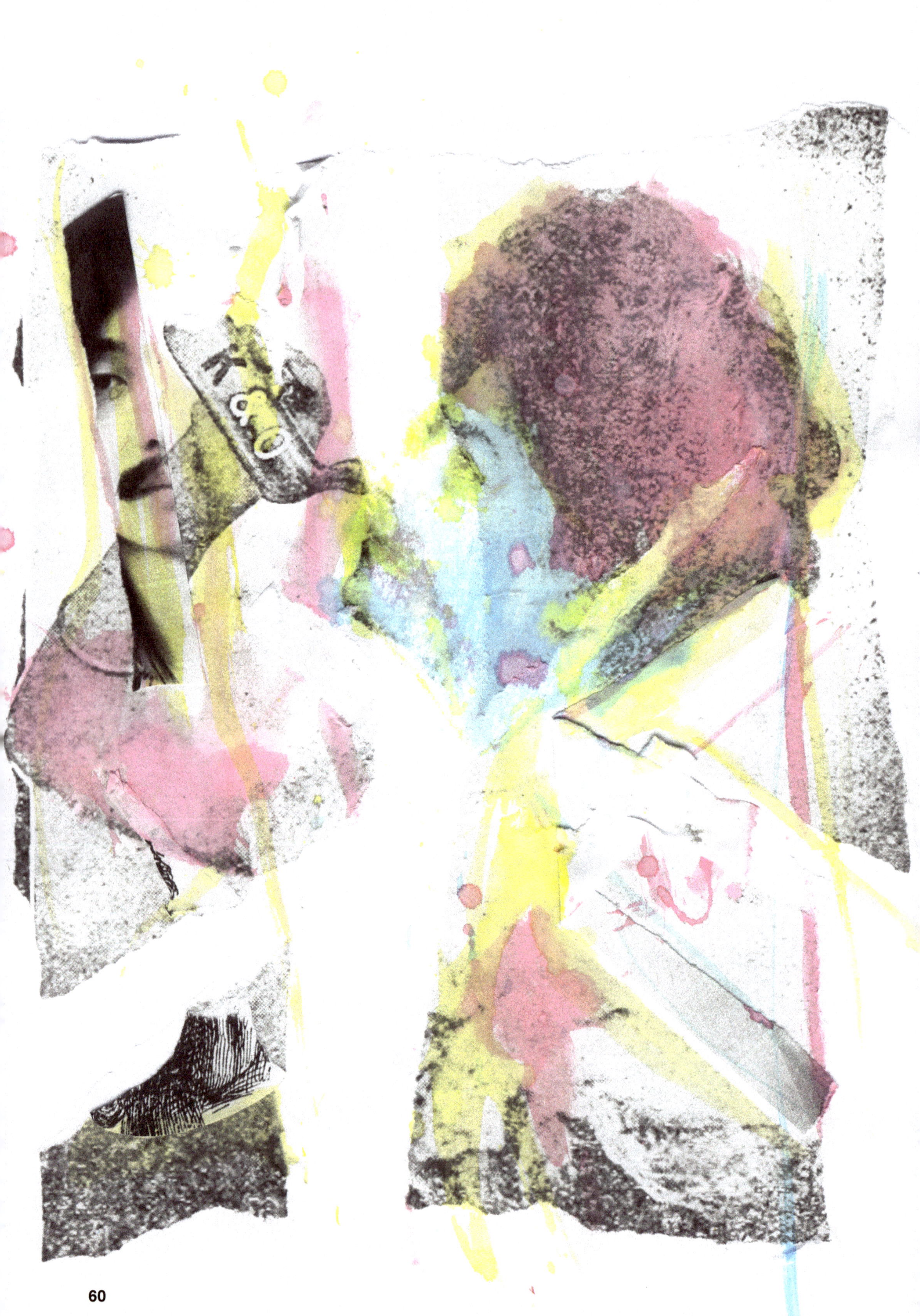

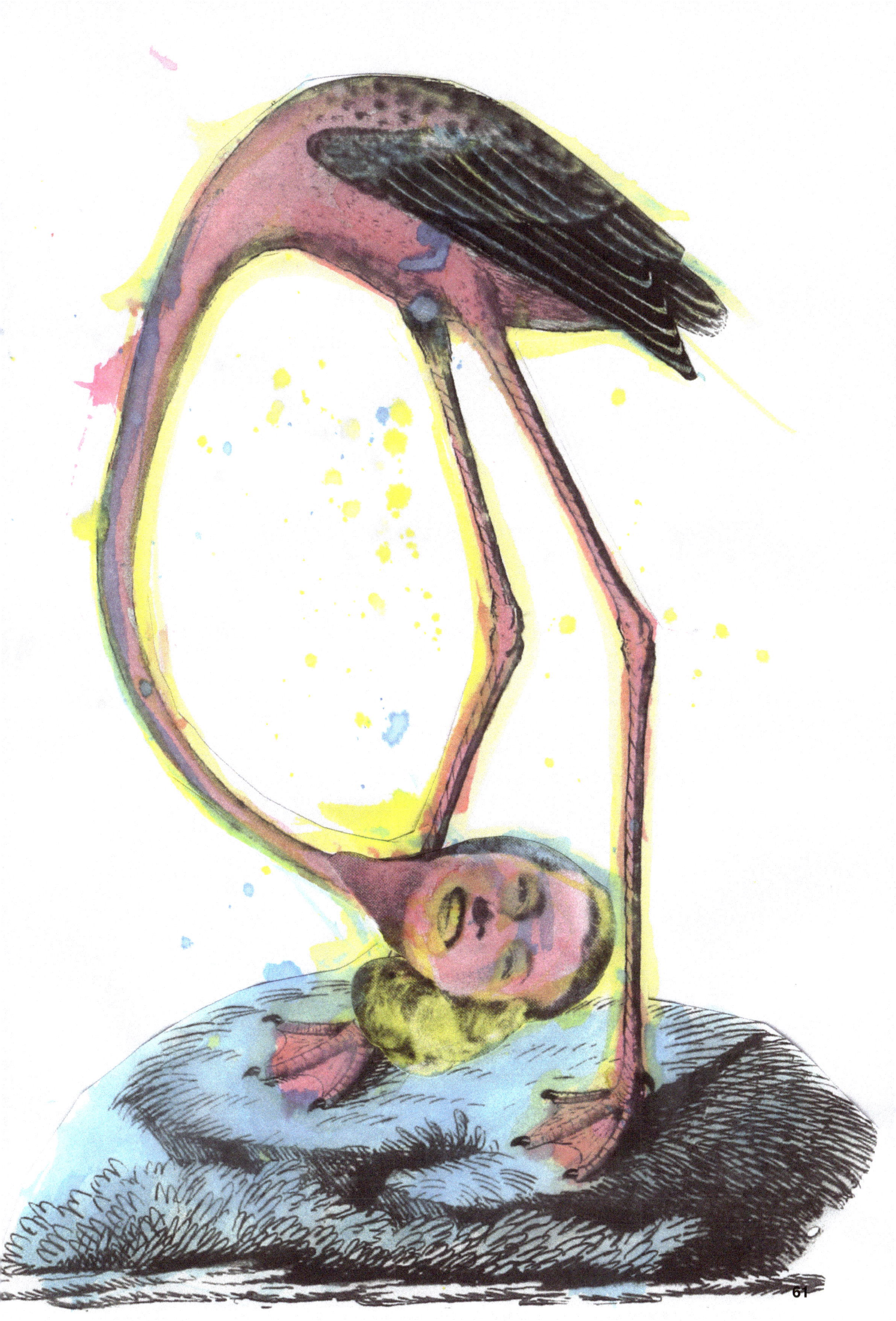

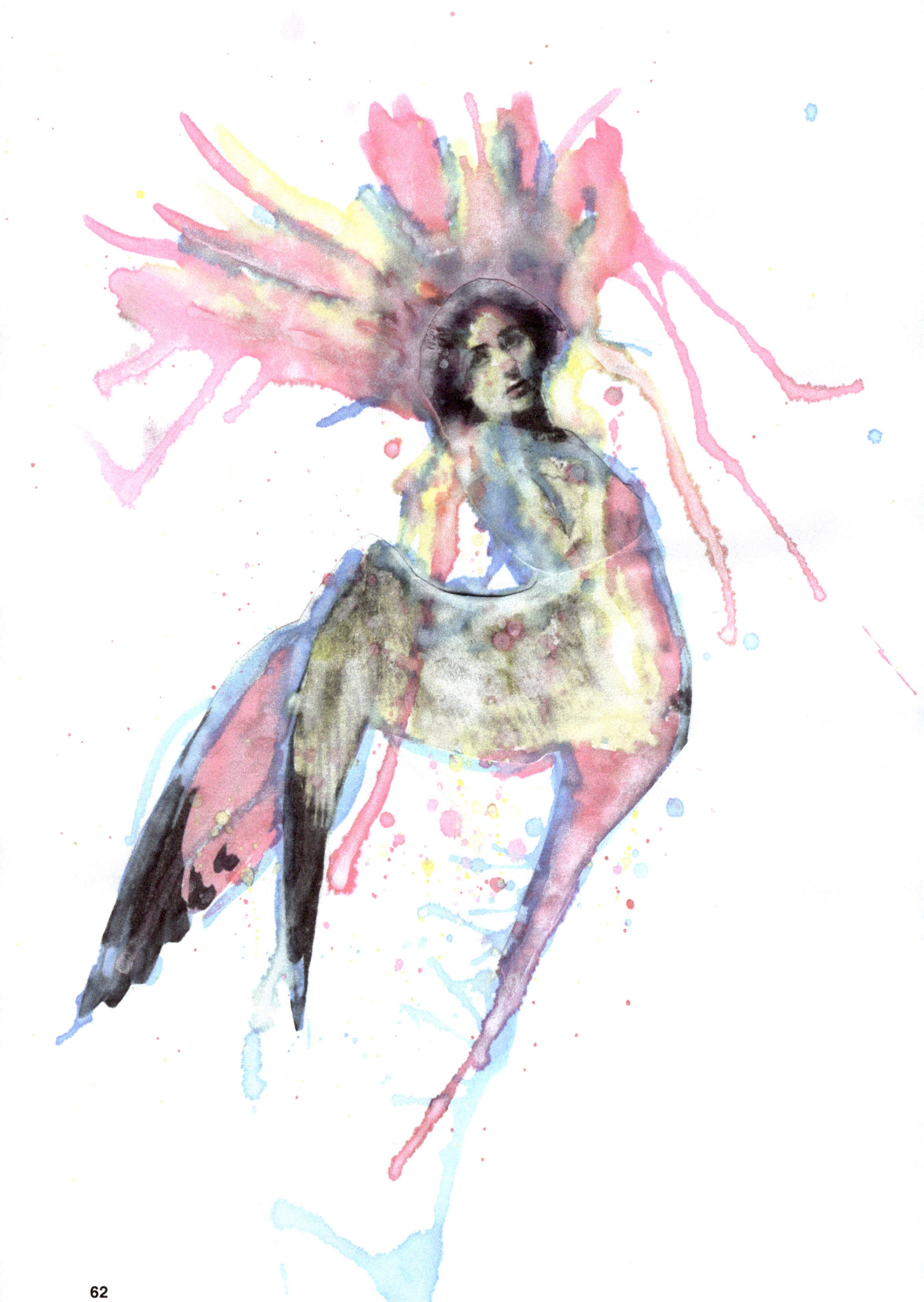

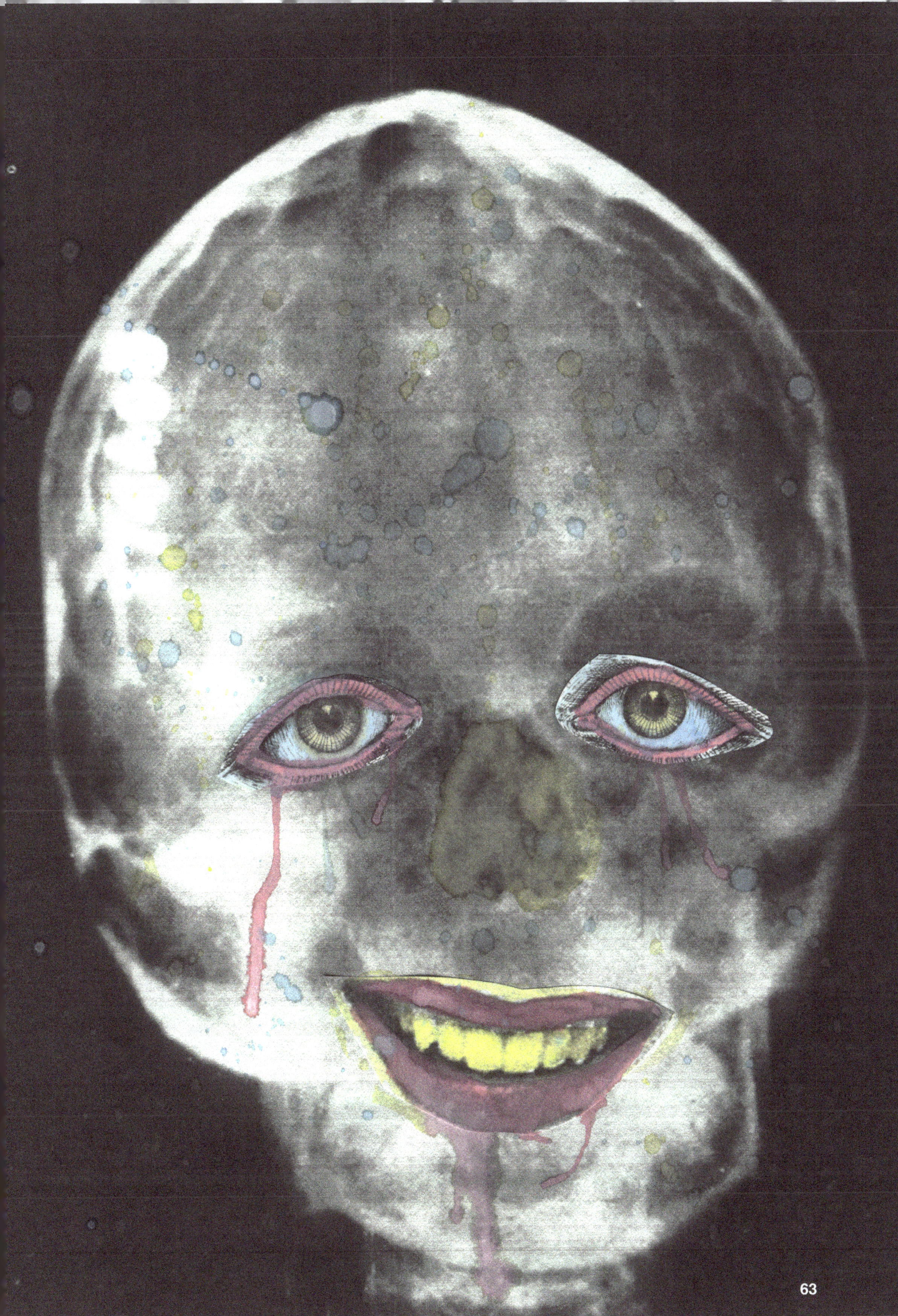

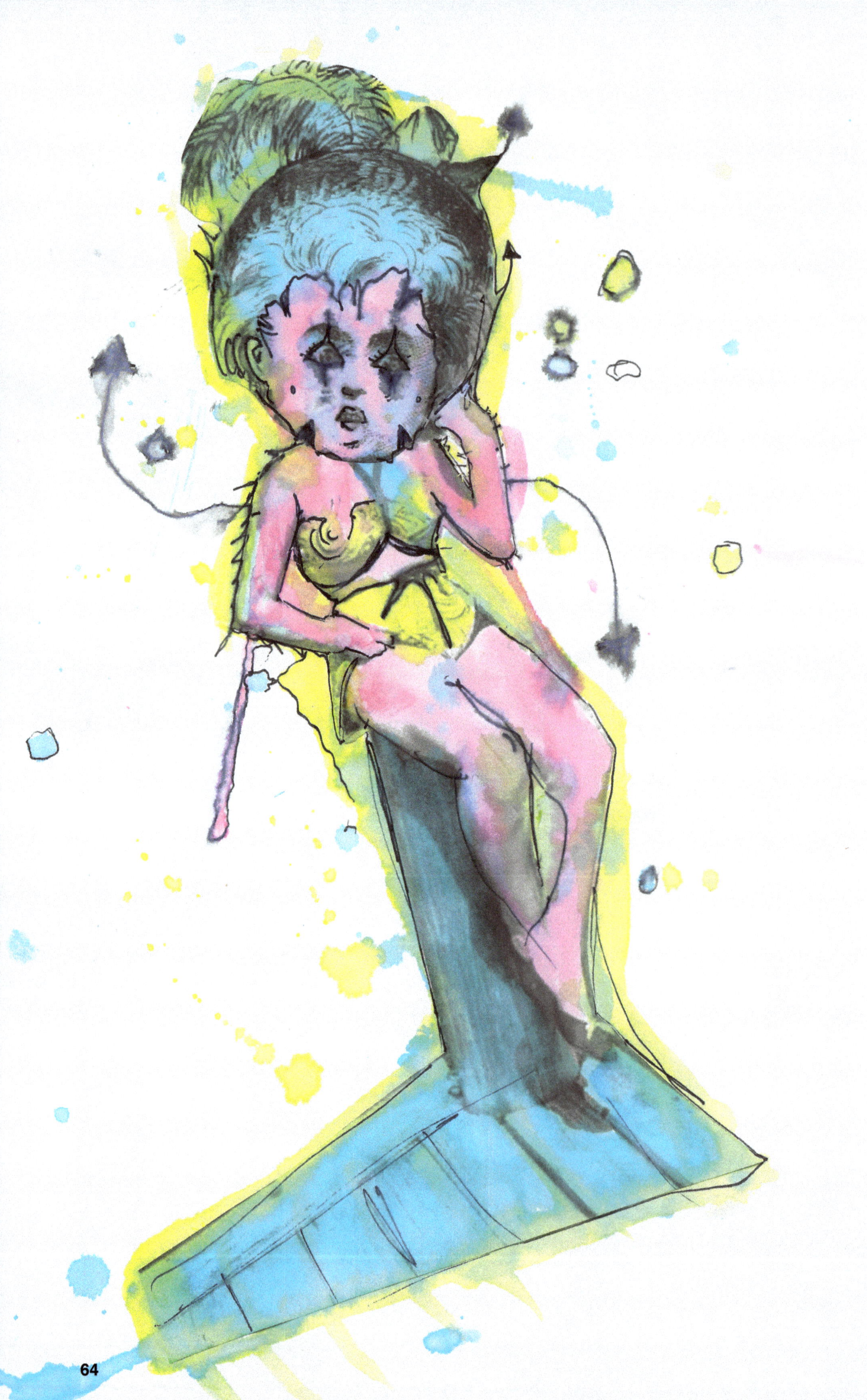

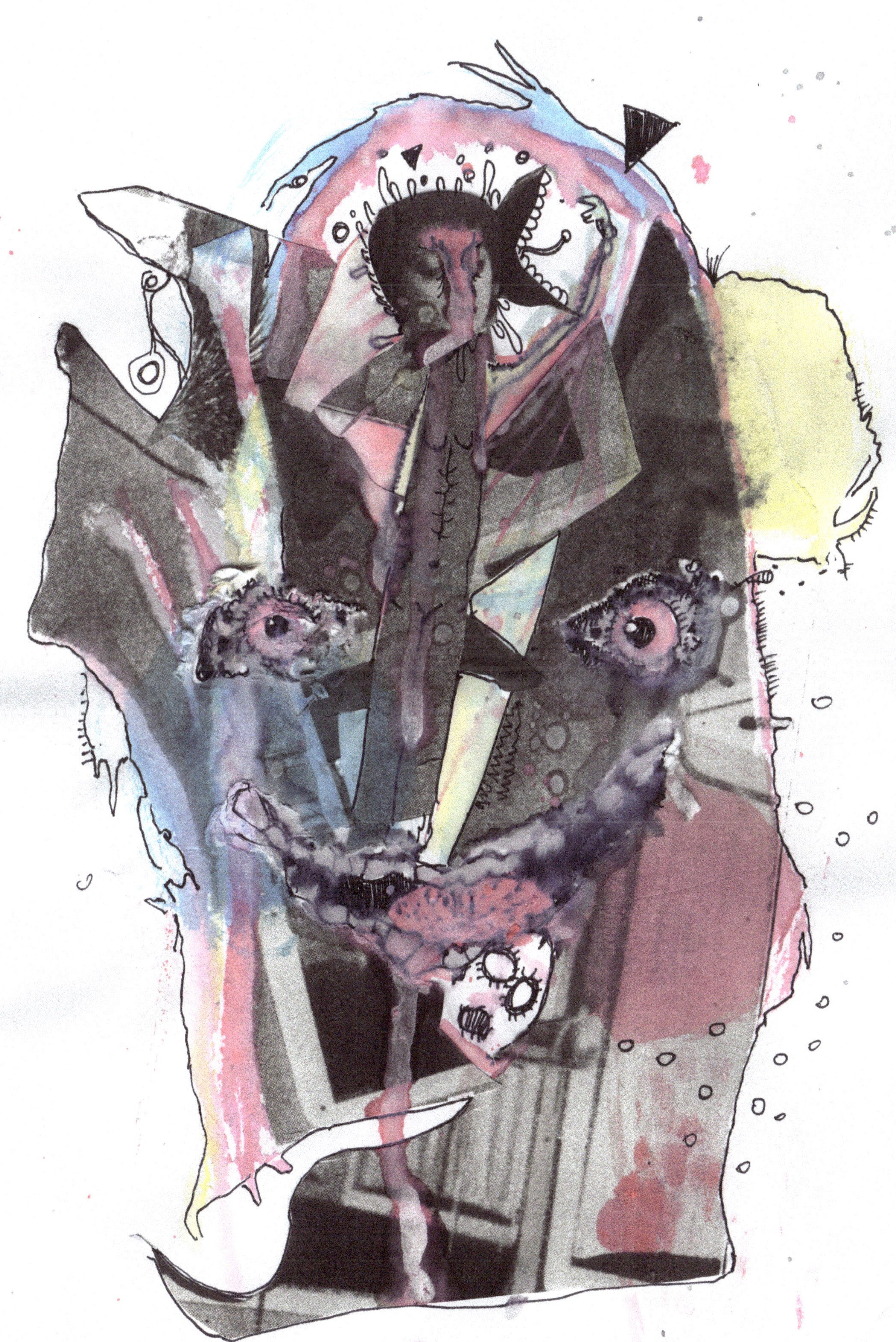

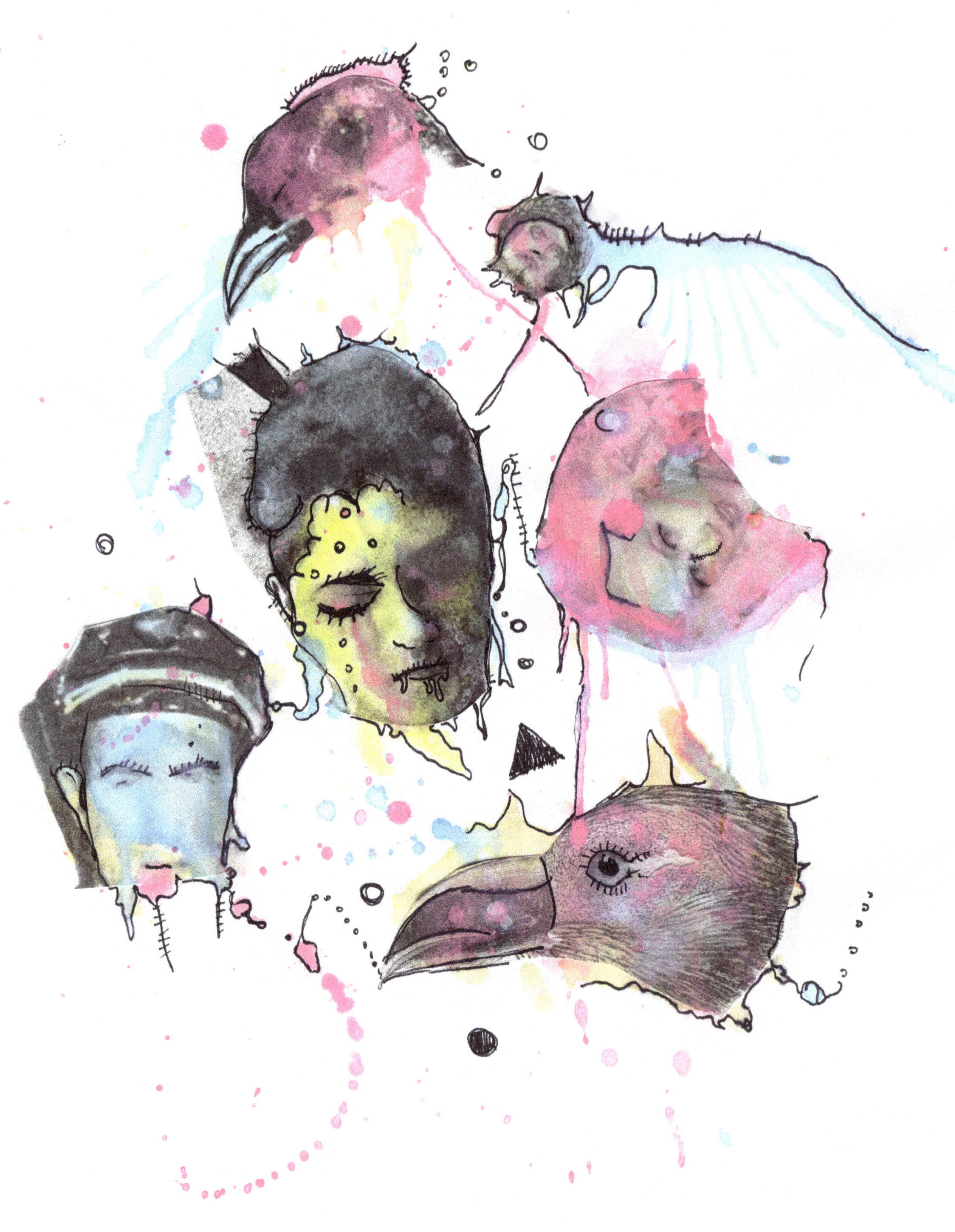

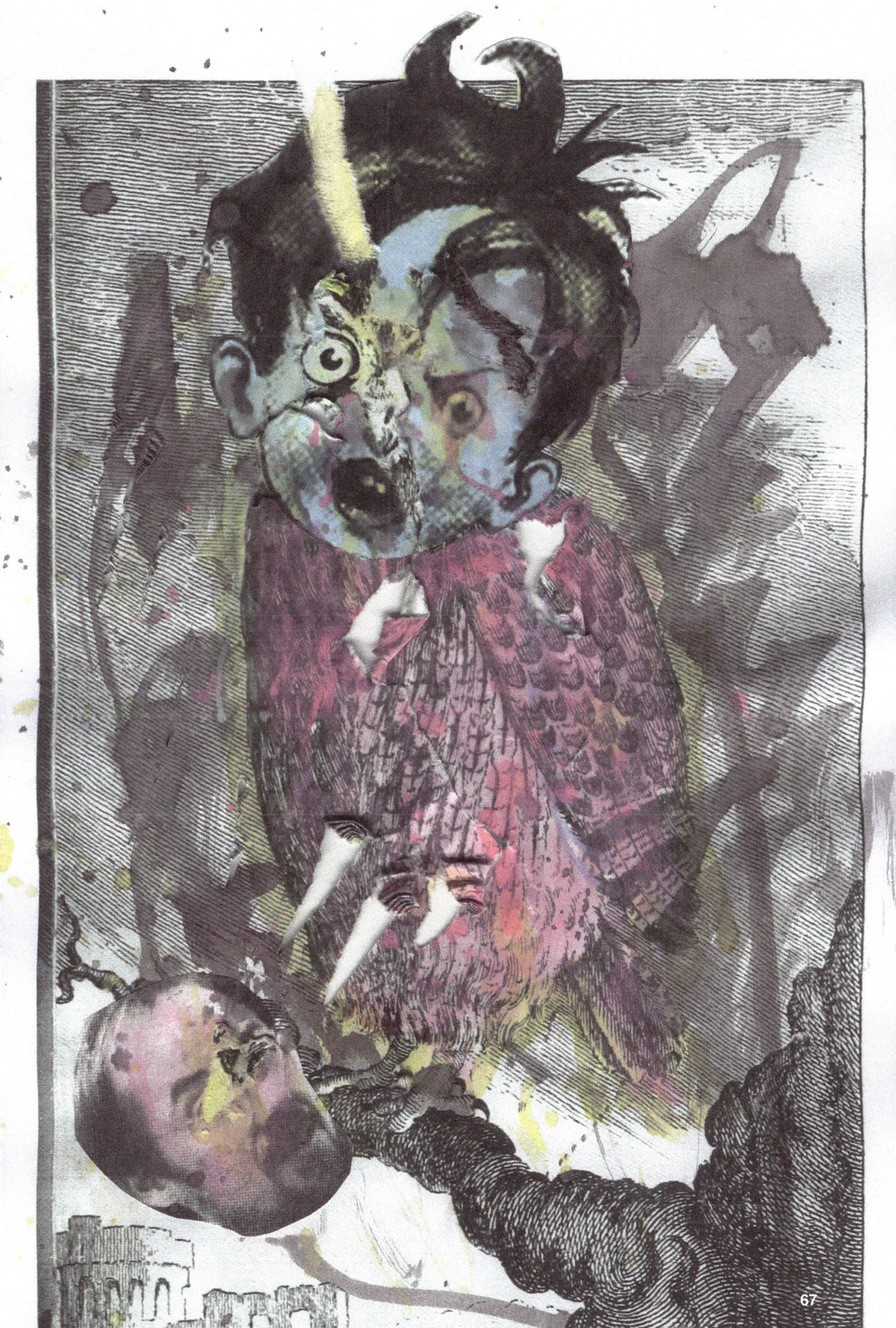

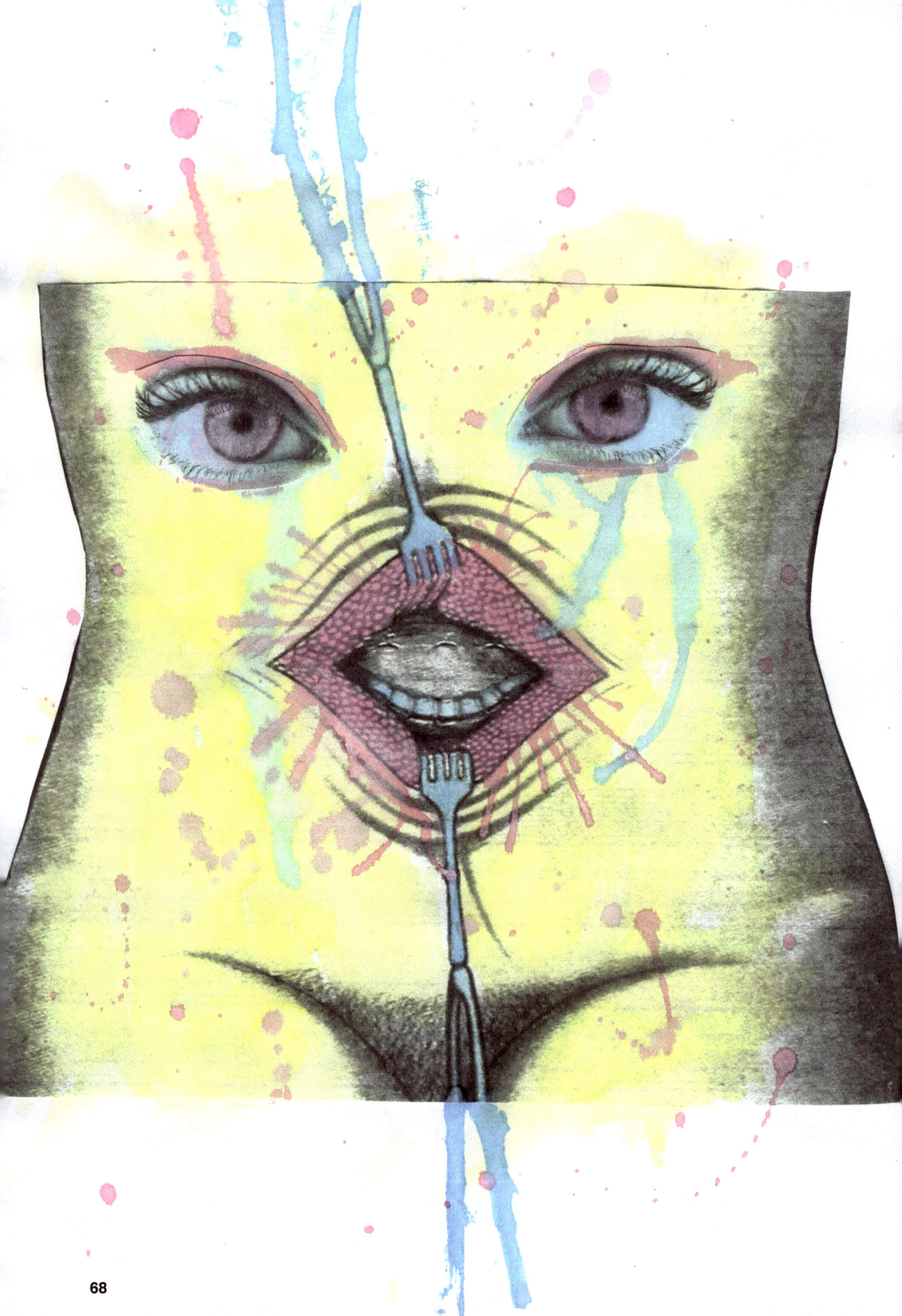

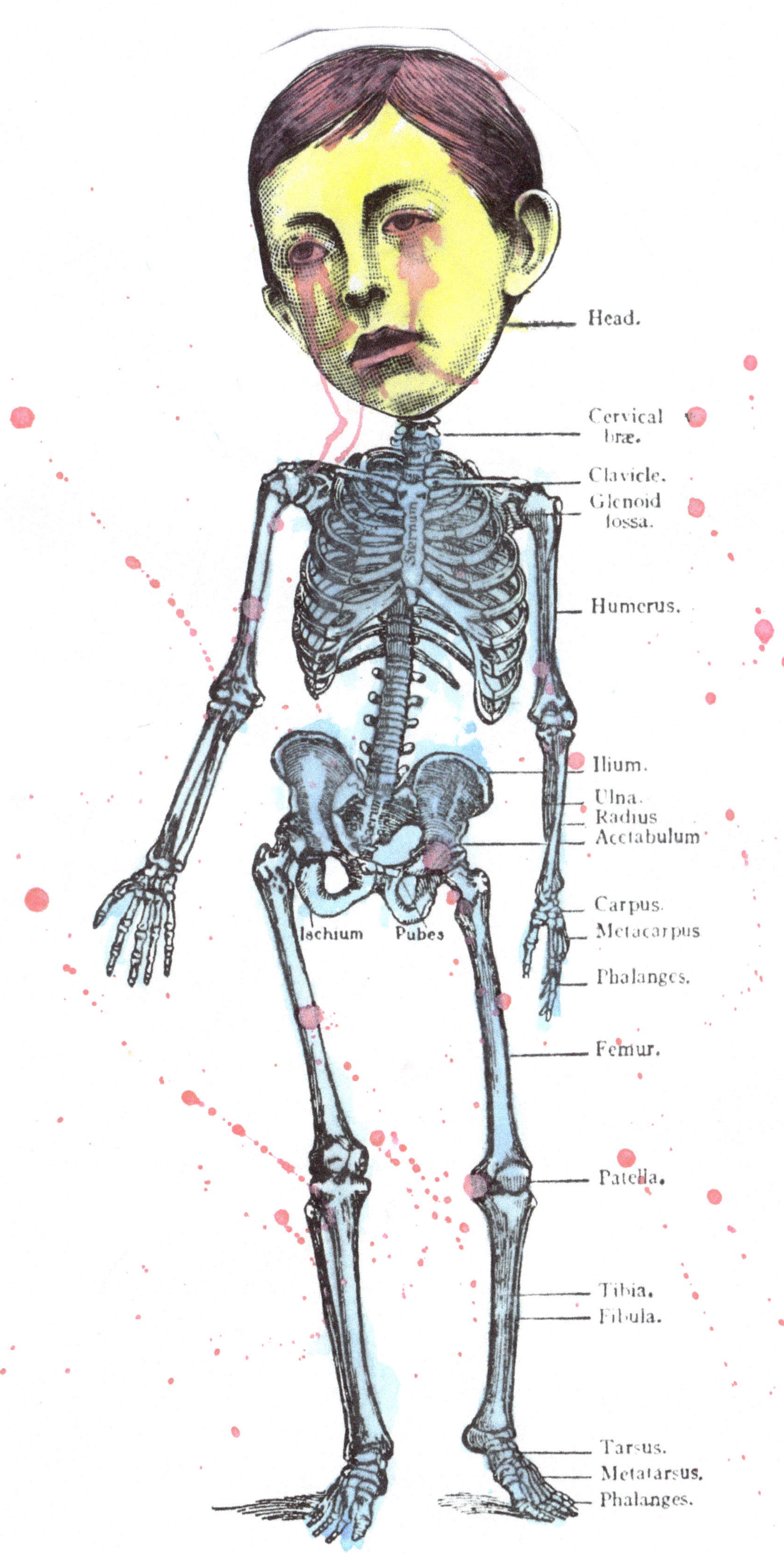

Head.
Cervical
bræ.
Clavicle.
Glenoid
fossa.
Sternum
Humerus.
Ilium.
Ulna.
Radius
Acetabulum
Carpus.
Metacarpus
Phalanges.
Ischium
Pubes
Femur.
Patella.
Tibia.
Fibula.
Tarsus.
Metatarsus.
Phalanges.

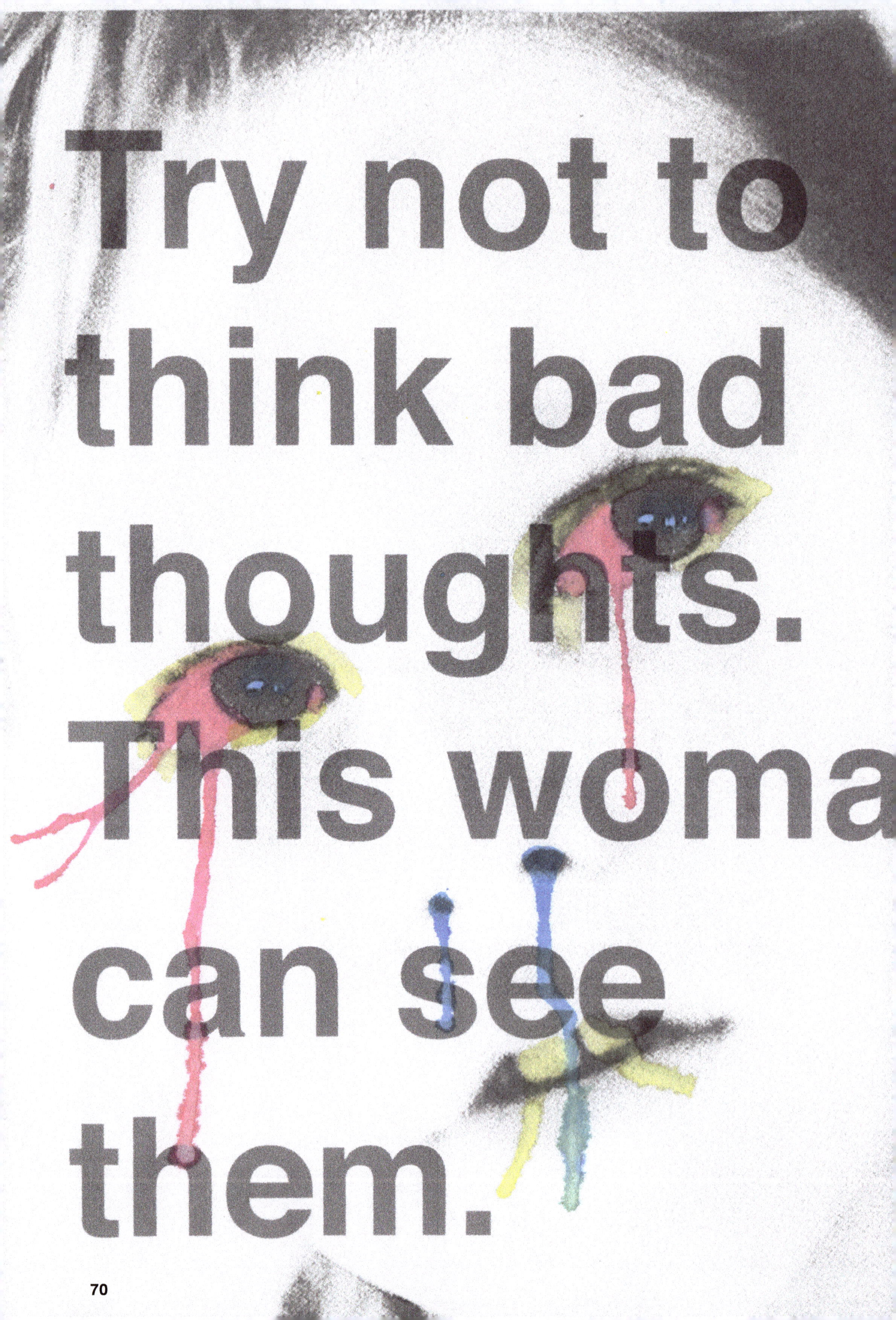

Try not to think bad thoughts. This woma can see them.

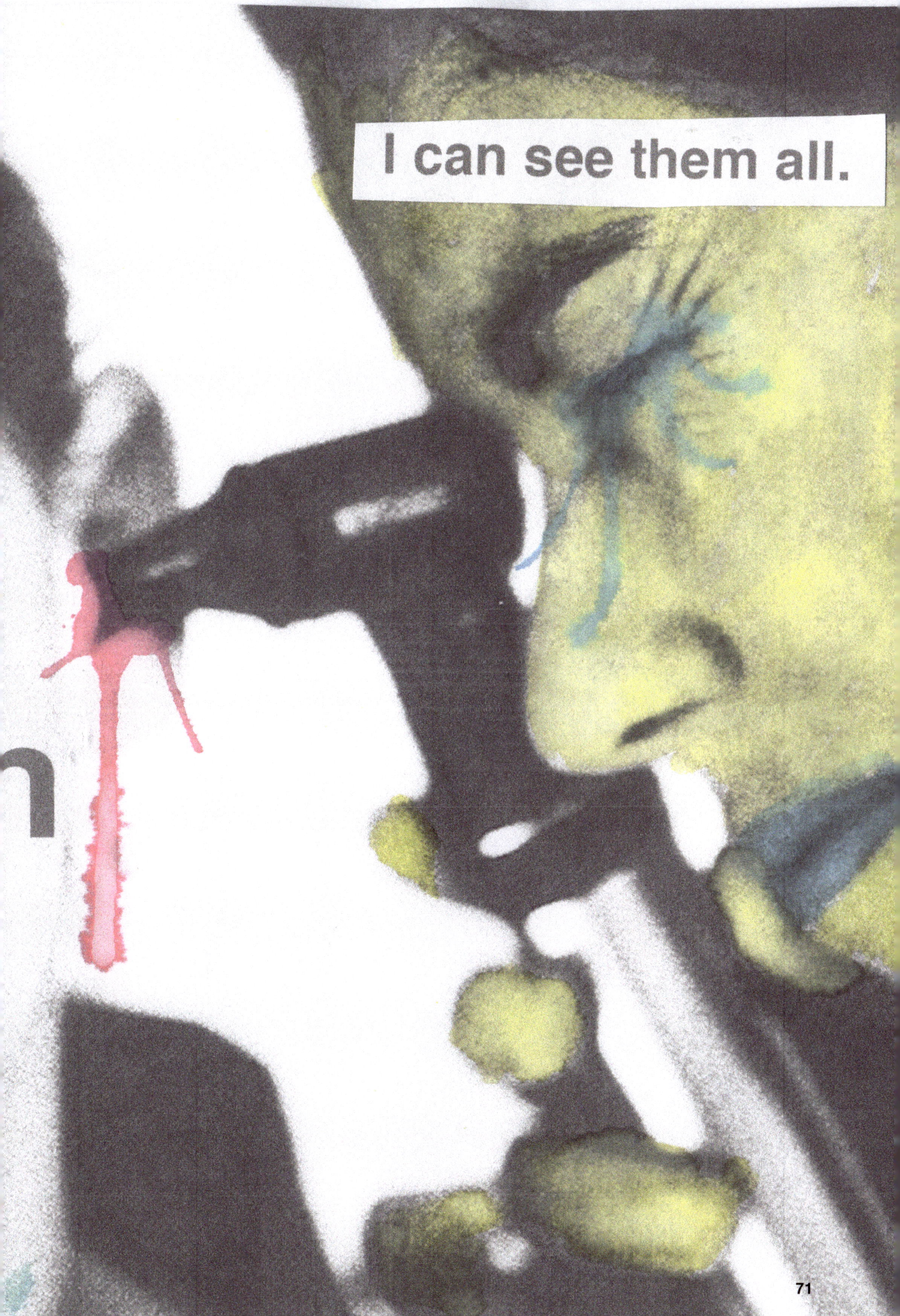

I can see them all.

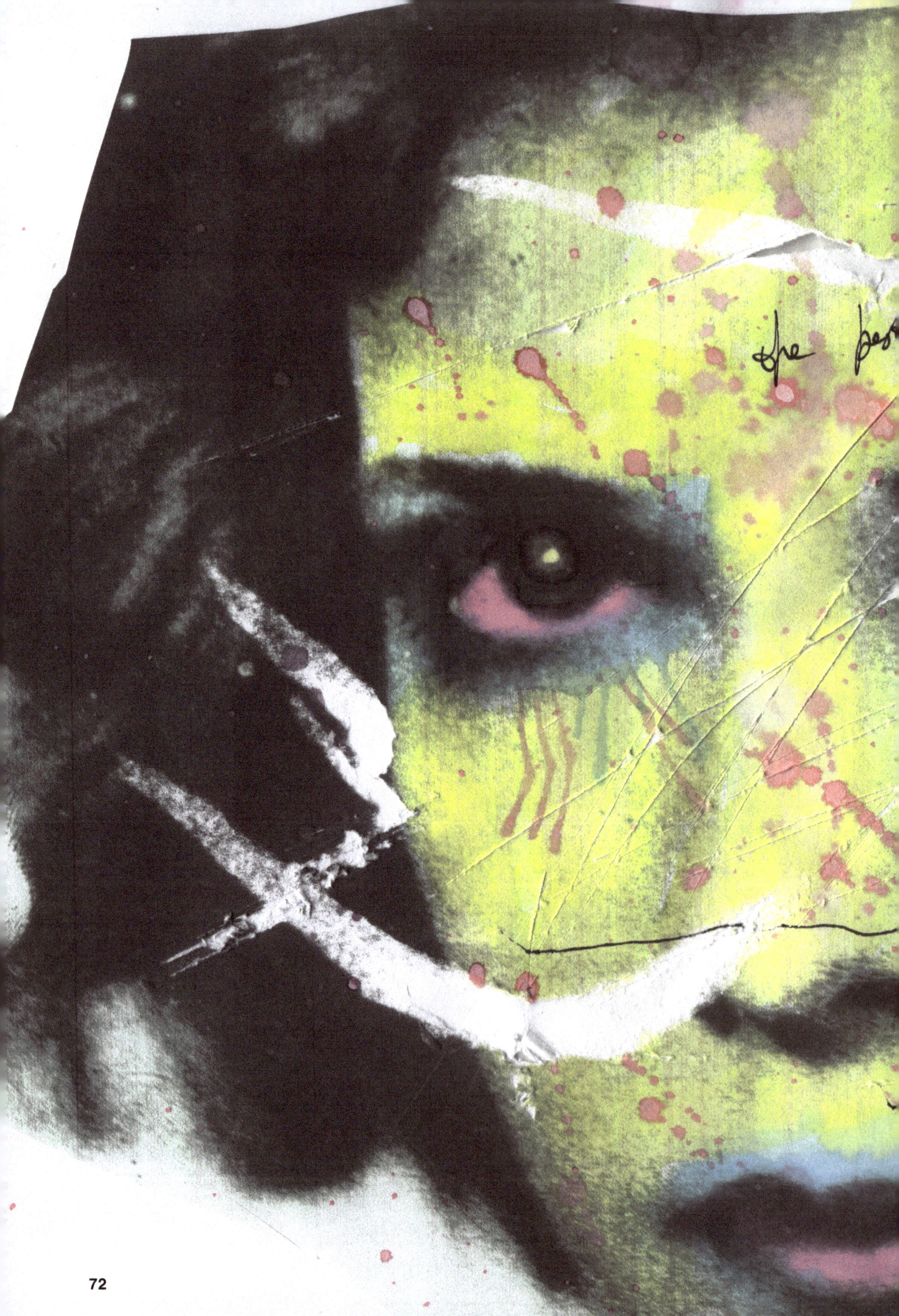

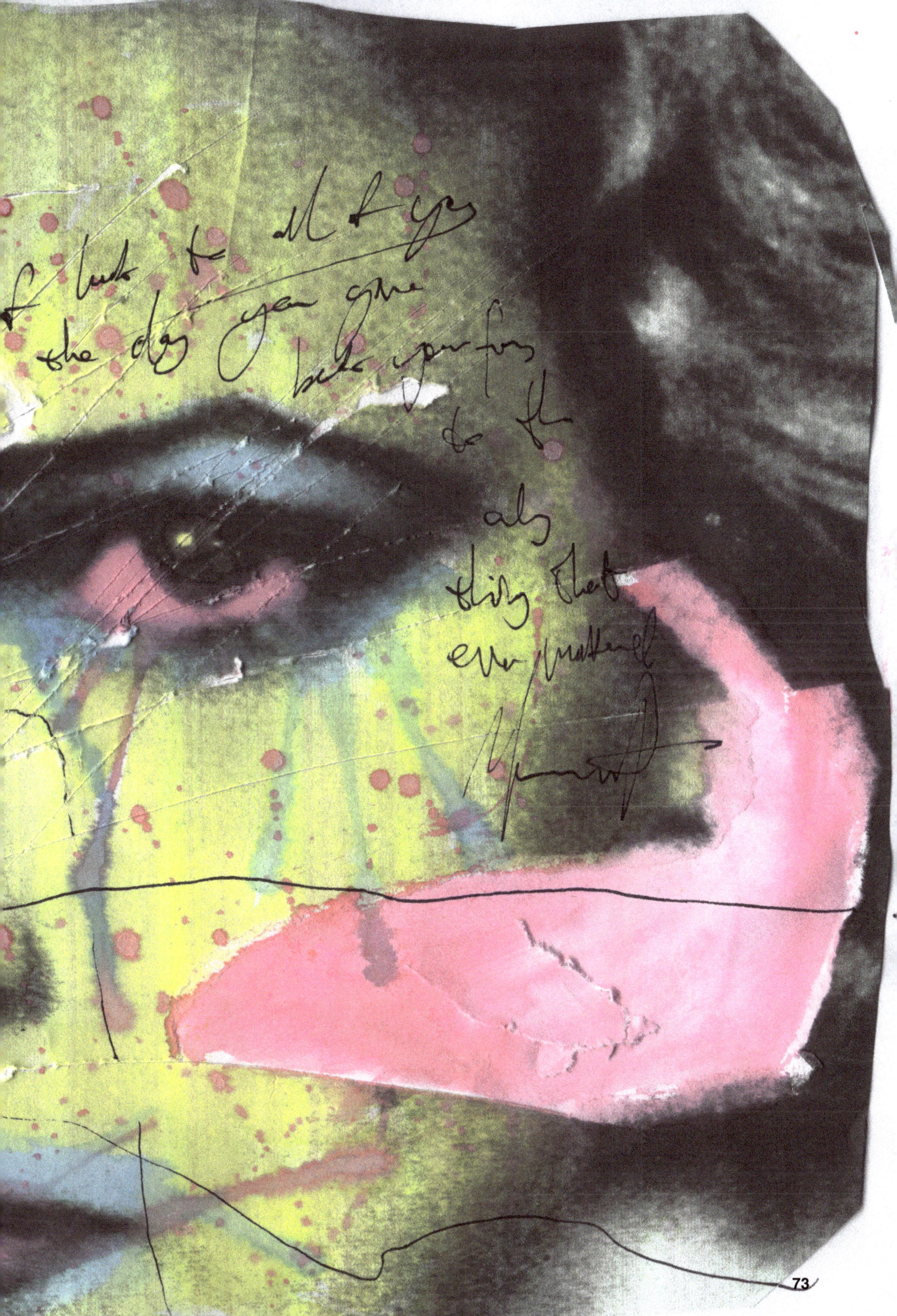

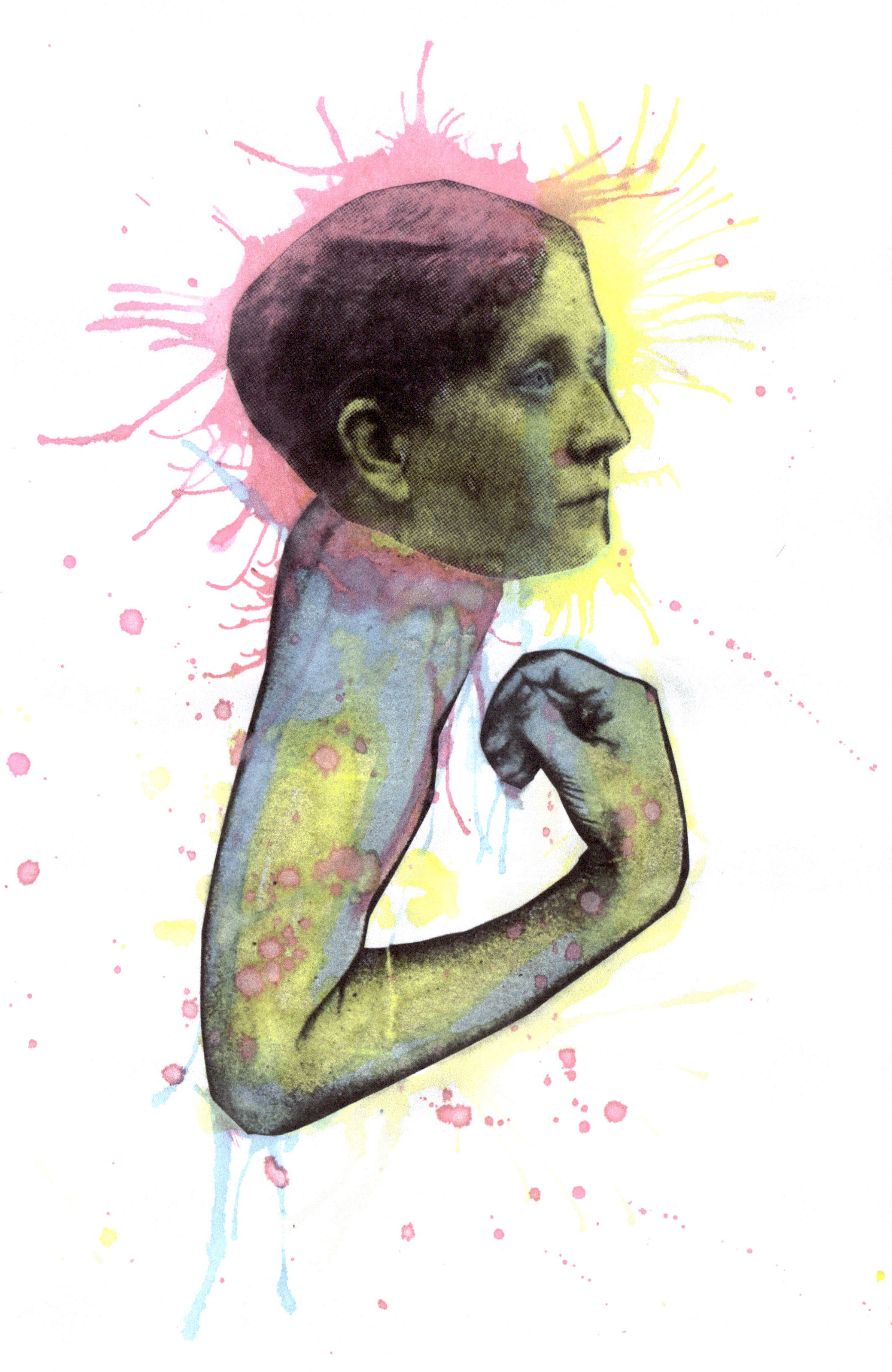

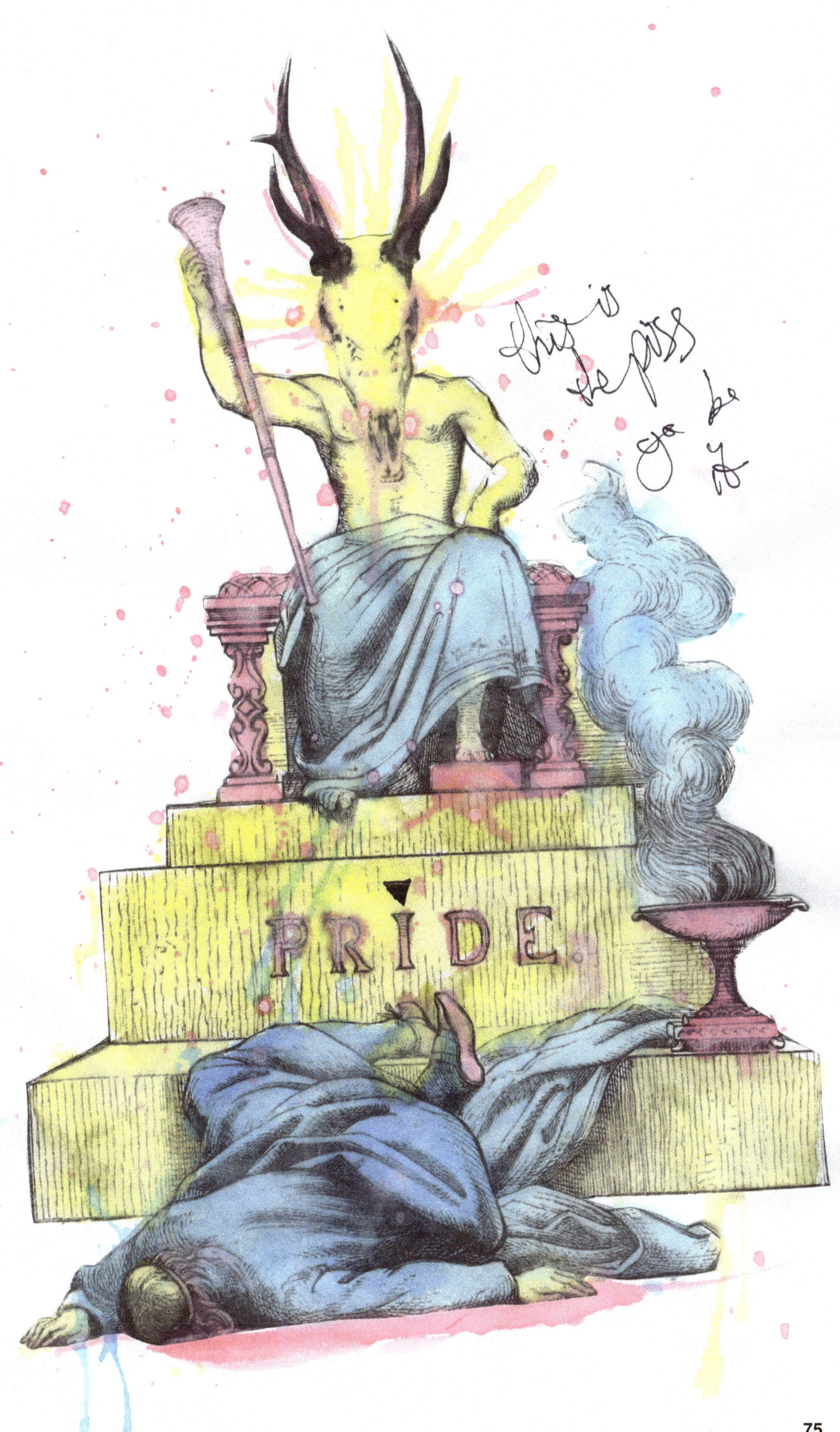

PRIDE.

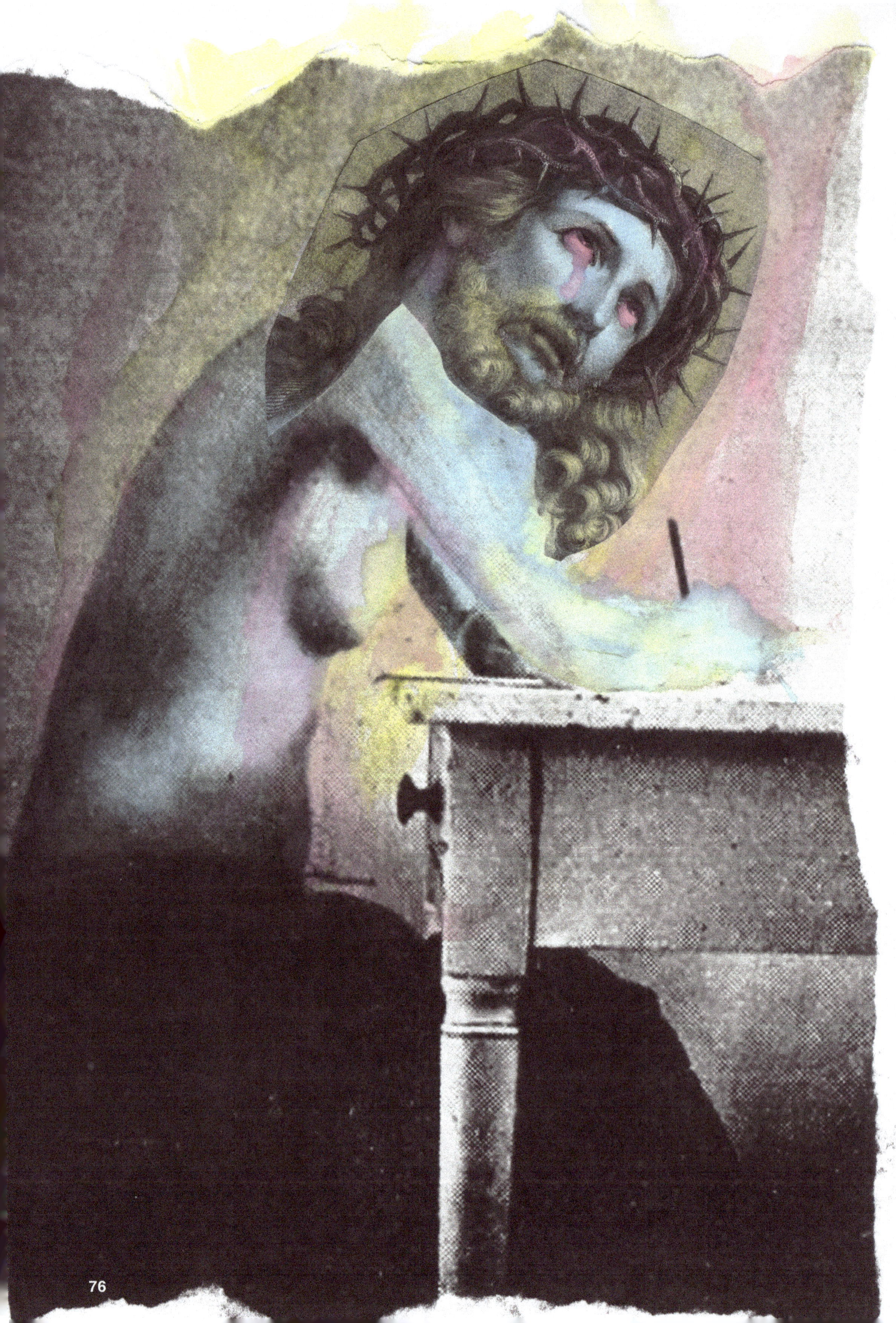

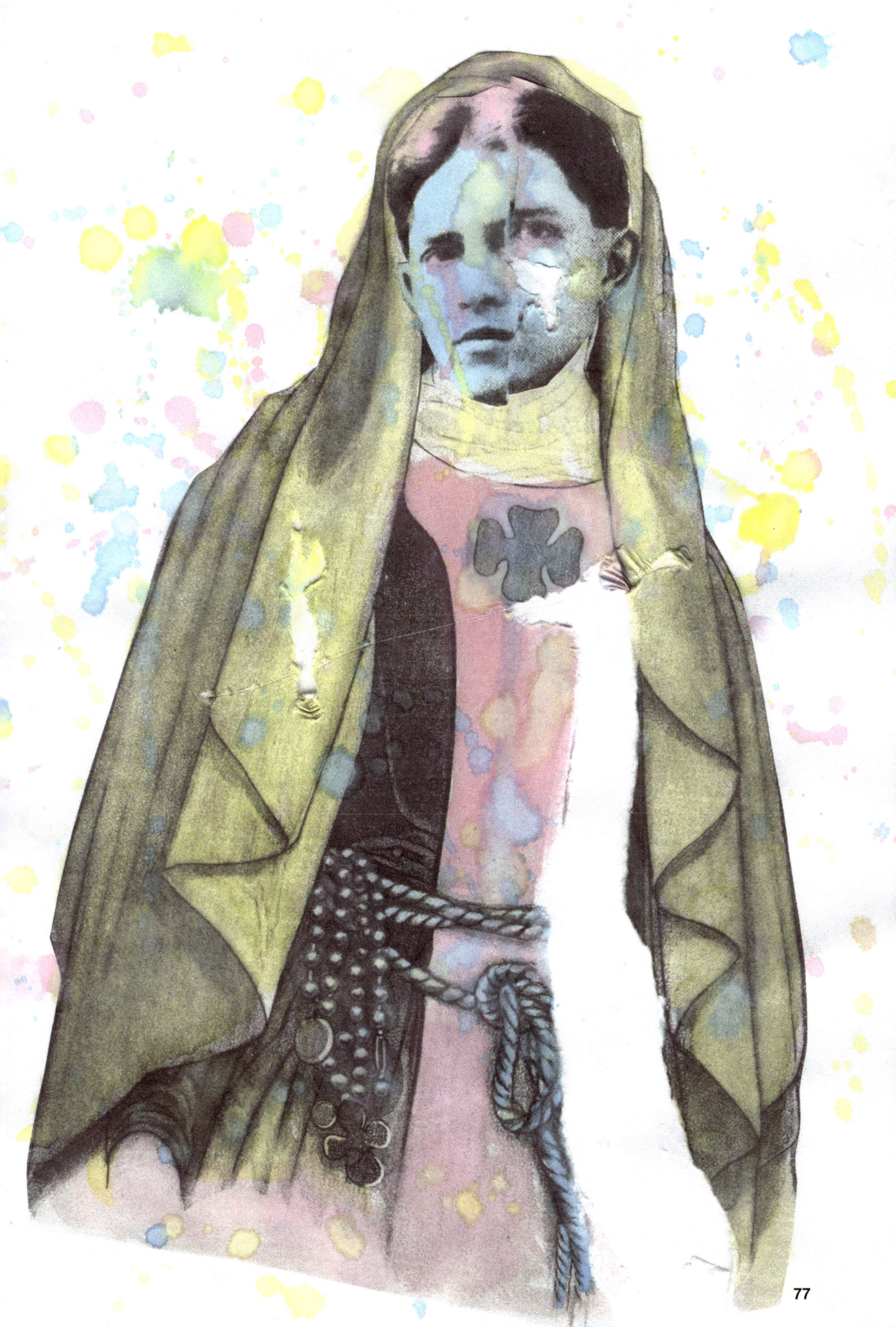

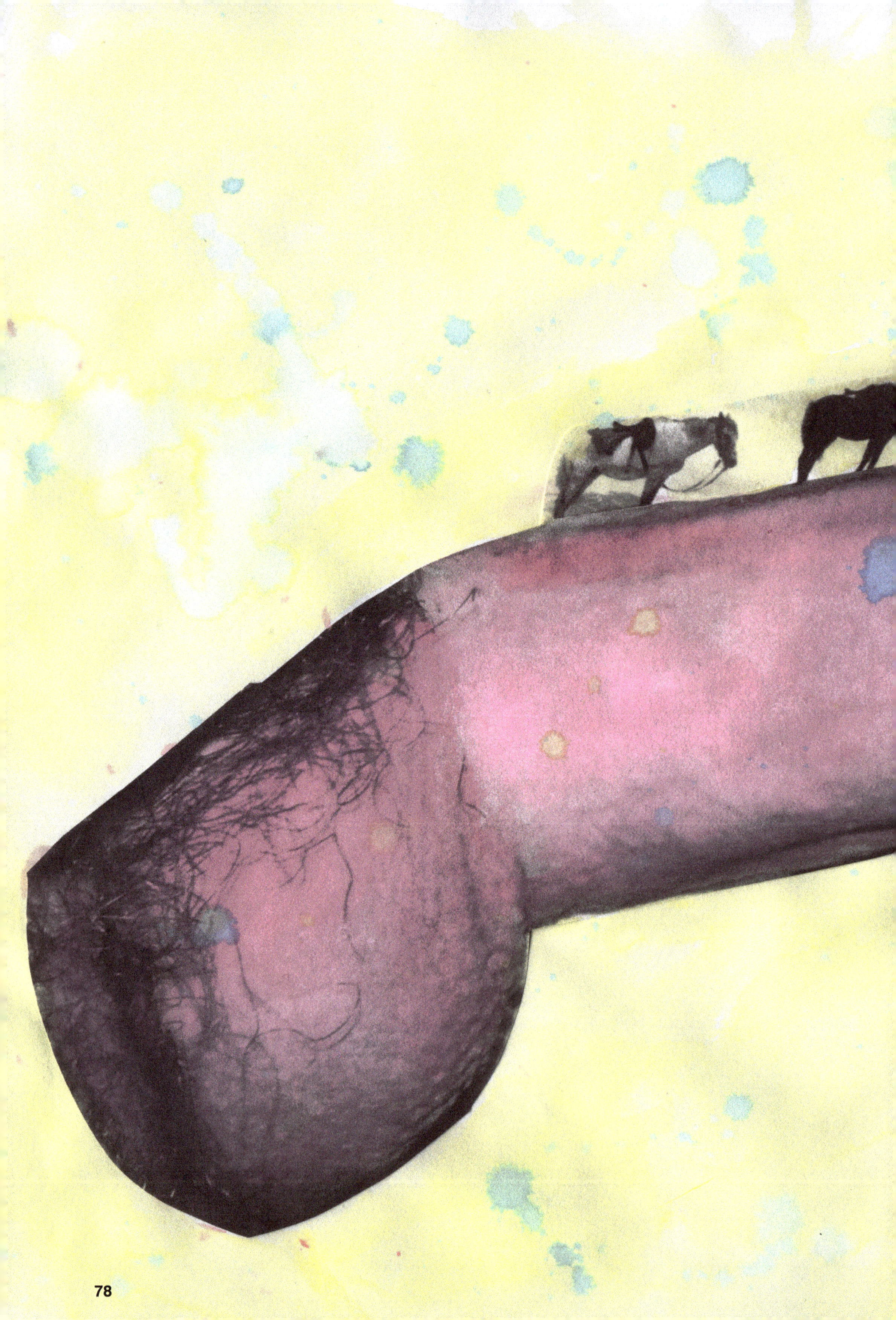

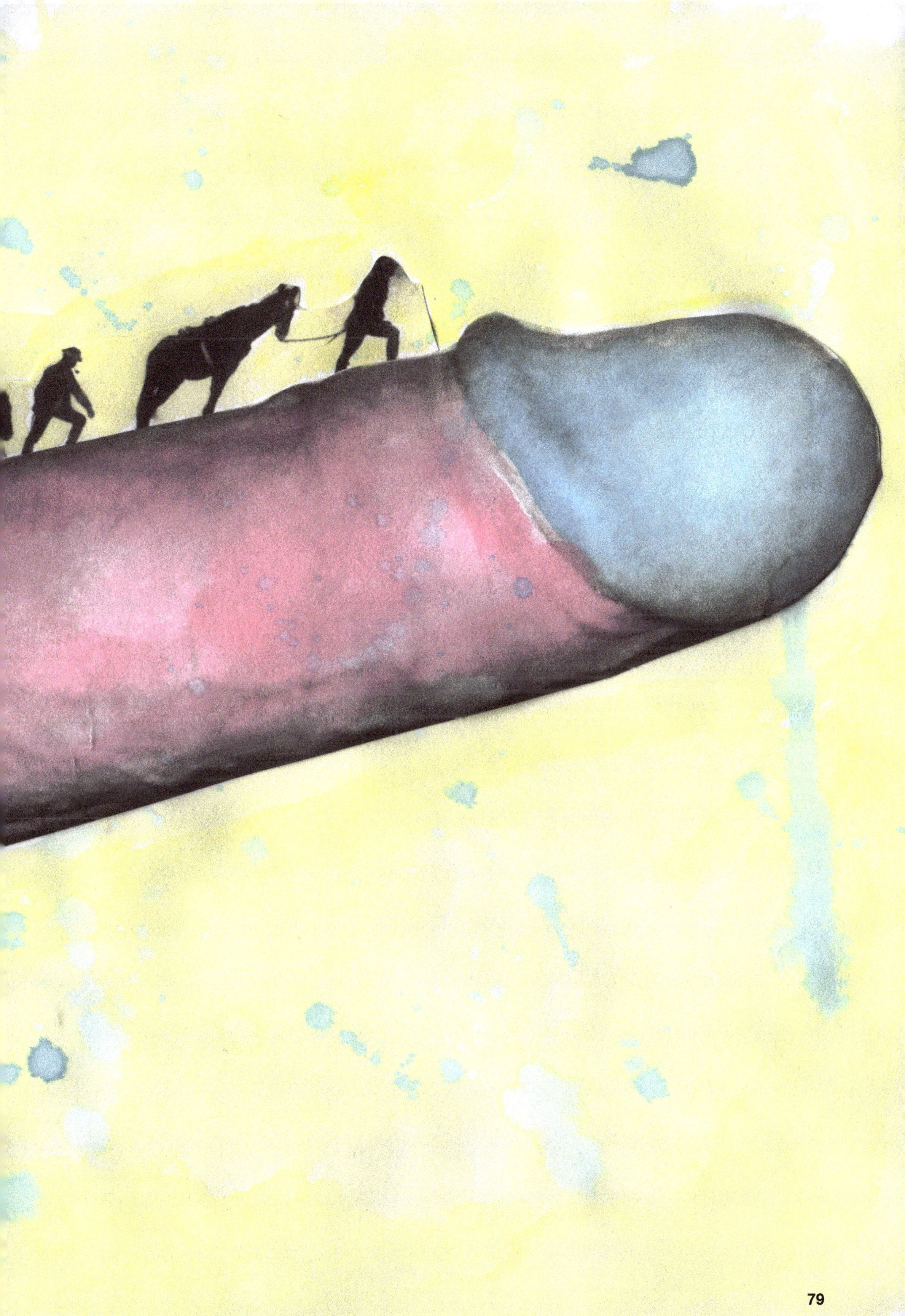

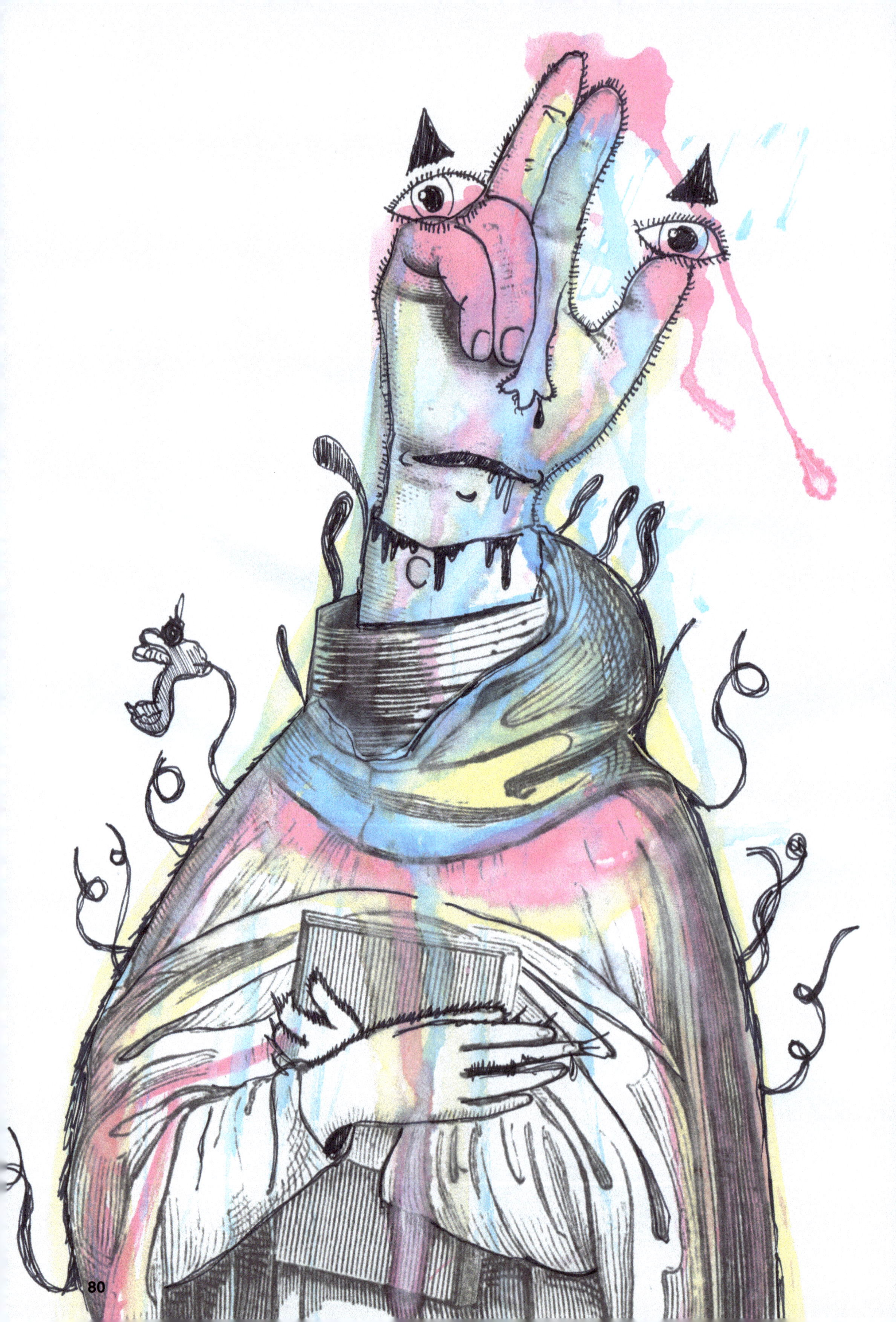

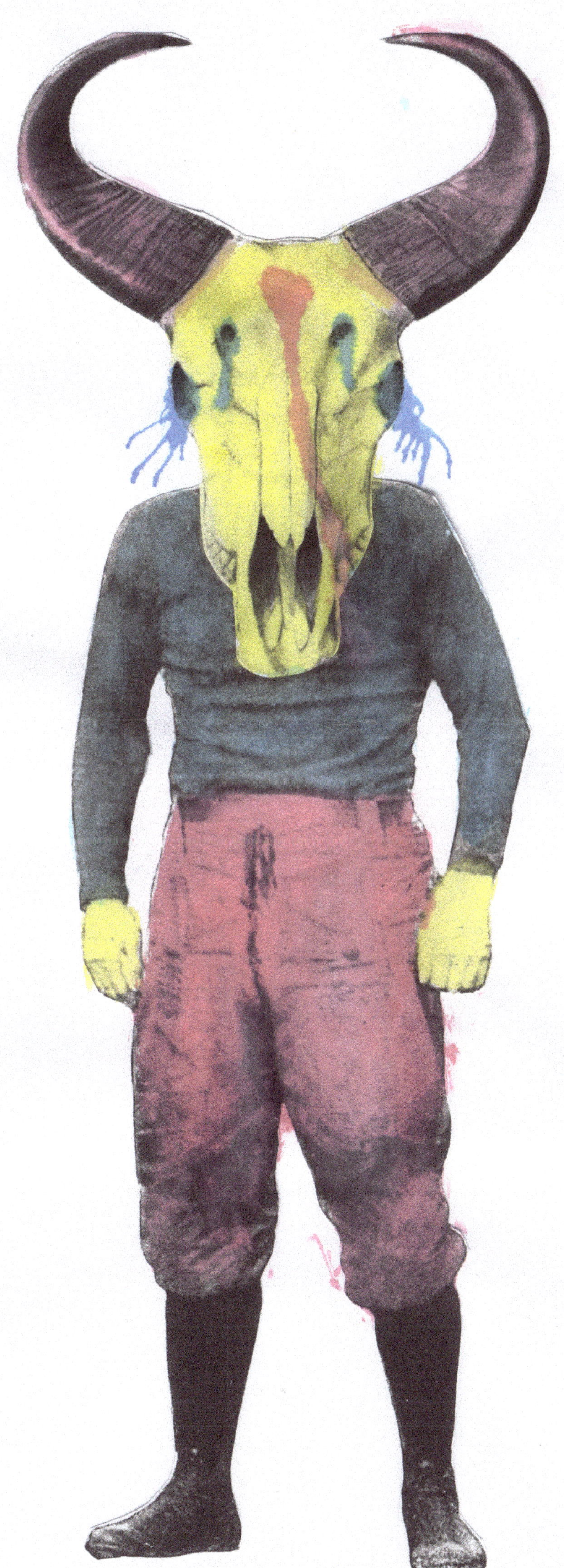

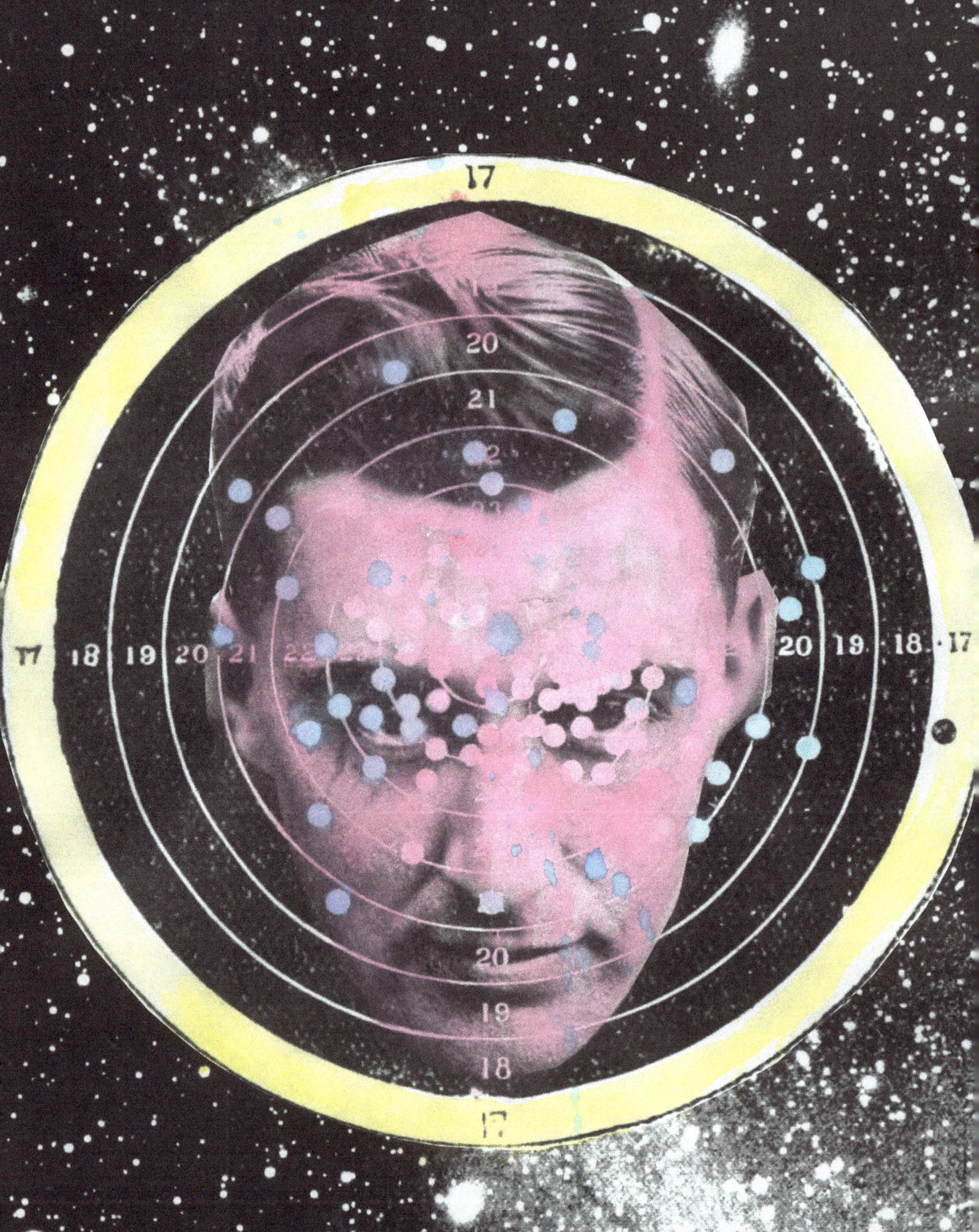
17
20
21
2
17 18 19 20 21 22   20 19 18 17
20
19
18
17

GIRAFFE
BOY
CAUGHT
A FISH

Good morning. Your voice is barely there. More like the promise of a voice.

Whatever that promise is.

Secretly playing Mortal Kombat II

The attitude my parents adopted toward censoring the media I consumed was mild. There didn't appear to be limitations placed upon the movies I desired to watch and dad would frequently rent decidedly un-family friendly films for the family to watch (thanks to Pulp Fiction, I discovered what a gimp was at a very early age). I remember my father providing help when a music store forbade me from purchasing 'Butchered at Birth' by Cannibal Corpse in the early nineties. My father had me wait outside while he obtained the forbidden music on my behalf. Other than chastising my musical taste as 'utter rubbish,' he was happy to do this for me. This lax attitude toward censorship was so commonplace that I wasn't capable of feeling grateful - it was just the way things were.

It's for these reasons my brother and I were baffled when our parents took an active role in determining what video games we were permitted to play. When Midway released Mortal Kombat II on home consoles in 1994, my twelve-year-old brain could barely process the excitement. I had researched it exhaustively and watched others play the arcade version with quiet reverence. The thought of sitting down to play it myself was overwhelming. My Super Nintendo was thirsty for me to feed its slot with this gore-soaked cartridge. My family's financial situation ensured no possibility of purchasing the game outright, but for a few dollars, my brother and I could rent it from our local video store, which is exactly what we planned to do.

Thursday evenings were exciting for us. It coincided with my father getting paid. This meant we enjoyed fast food for dinner and, more importantly, renting our weekly videogame. We knew Mortal Kombat II had been released days earlier and we knew without doubt our video store would stock it. The game's popularity was such that it was already out on loan, but we anticipated this. Our goal was merely to have our names added to the queue so we may enjoy it later. We informed our father of our intentions and a most unlikely thing occurred - he refused. Assuming he maybe misunderstood, I repeated our intentions and, once more, he refused. With each repetition of the intention, the same refusal occurred with increasing assertion. This bypassed so many of the patterns I relied upon to navigate life with understanding and, for an irrational moment, I wondered if perhaps my father had fallen victim to mind control. I asked him why he was refusing and he told me we were both too young while pointing out that those below 15 were not permitted to play the game. He then explained he didn't want us playing 'that rubbish.' I'm not proud of it, but I stormed out of the video store in quite an embarrassing huff. We didn't even rent our weekly game. There were tears that night.

The impasse persisted for weeks. My brother and I concocted methods of manipulating our father into capitulation, all of which he would shut down. No argument made it beyond his initial wall of refusal and we felt utterly defeated. It soon became apparent that, if we were to enjoy this game, it would have to happen beyond permission granted to do so.

My mother had multiple sclerosis and by the time I was twelve, she was unable to walk. While this is sad, it's also pertinent to the story. Due to my mother's inability to walk, she was unable to move about the house without my father's assistance. While he was my mother's caregiver, he also worked full time, which meant during the week my mother was immobilized except for a brief window around lunchtime when my father would drive from work to help her with anything she required. This created a situation whereby, should one be quiet enough, they could quite easily escape going to school while avoiding detection.

The plan was quite simple. My brother and I would dress in our school uniforms and make a show of leaving for the day. Our father had already left for work and our mother showed no signs of suspicion as we kissed her goodbye. We started our walk to school as we normally would, but rather than doing so, we simply took ourselves around the block until we were back at our house. If we crept up the driveway, there was no possibility of mum spotting us from her vantage on the couch. As though dropped into enemy territory, we skulked into the back garden and through the backdoor (which I had unlocked upon waking).

The video store would not open for another two hours, so we passed that time obsessing over the reality of playing Mortal Kombat II. For those who don't know, the Mortal Kombat games are famous for their 'fatalities,' which allowed the winner of a fight to kill their opponent in grisly cartoonish ways. Each fatality required the input of a button combination not included in the instruction manual. In a pre-internet era, we relied on magazines to provide such codes, but we were unable to afford these. This combination of factors placed me in a news agency one morning with pen and paper, hurriedly writing down the button input for every fatality and leaving before a staff member caught me. It was these hastily scrawled button combinations my brother and I stared at while waiting for the video store to open. We memorized as many as we could and quizzed one another to ensure our powers of recollection were honed. Our window to play this game would be comparatively small and we wanted to ensure our time was well spent.

With the requisite time whiled away, we prepared to enact the most crucial component of our plan. As we walked to the video store, we were aware of the potential roadblocks. Although the game was no longer new, there was still a possibility it would not be available when we arrived. If it was available, we didn't even know if the woman who worked there would allow us to have it. I had spent enough of my life within this video store to forge a friendship with this woman, but she knew my father. Had she refused, there would be little I could do. Perhaps she would let us have it and tell our father at a later date. This was a bullet we were prepared to absorb because it involved playing Mortal Kombat II first.

We arrived at the store and immediately spotted Mortal Kombat II was available. I remember the anxiety I felt as I approached the desk with the game my hands. The entire fate of this plan (and our happiness) rested in the hands of this kind woman who greeted us with a smile. She asked me why we weren't at school and I immediately lied, explaining that our mother was particularly unwell and we were helping care for her. This excuse was not only intended to give us irrefutable cause to miss school, but also imbue the situation with sympathy, which would hopefully increase our chances of renting a game we were clearly too young for. As I handed her the game she looked at me with suspicion and asked if our father would be ok with us playing something so violent. I assured her it was dad's way of thanking us for helping our mother. She hesitated once more before processing the transaction and giving us the game.

We had Mortal Kombat II.

It's interesting to experience the atmosphere silent excitement creates. We sat in the dining room before an old television with our mother immobile in the next room. We ensured the game sat at a volume barely perceptible and exploded with a pure joy we could not convey with sound. We had roughly two hours before our father would check in on mum and we made use of every second. There is no way the reality of playing Mortal Kombat II can compare with the anticipation of doing so, but it was still a sacred gaming experience. Whenever one of us made a sound, the other would throw a stern look and nod their head toward the lounge room in case our mother's close proximity was forgotten.

As noon approached, we turned off the television and snuck out the back door. Dad would be arriving soon and it was imperative we were hidden from view. We could have sought sanctuary in the back garden, but it didn't feel secure enough. At the time, we lived in a sparsely populated area and rather than a neighbor to our right, there was a large field, which no longer held the cows it used to. We scrambled over the fence and found cover, choosing to hide in a large section of head-high grass. From here we peeked toward our driveway until we saw our father's car approach. We ducked into the heart of this grass and laughed with nervous excitement. This is where we remained for the ten or so minutes our father's lunchtime visits lasted. When we emerged back into our garden, we were wet and dirty, but also elated.

We continued to silently absorb ourselves in every cell of the game until it was time to perform the act of arriving home from school. I had prepared some stories regarding events experienced at school and my brother did the same. We were careful to make the events banal, but not so banal that relaying them came across as odd.

The game was returned the next day and we forever felt the resonance of how successfully we executed our plan. A short while later, dad stopped policing the videogames we played, but I am happy he withheld this right long enough for us to experience entertainment as contraband. Children learn who they are by virtue of what they disobey and what can be manipulated to their advantage.

Horrible, isn't it, to consider how easily two children could take advantage of their mother's illness? How, without guilt, we so easily evaded her as a means of disobeying our father. Horrible, that two children should have to wrestle with the ethics surrounding their mother's disability and the ways in which it could be used to for their gain? A part of any child's development is learning how to push the limits of their parents' discipline and in essence, that is all we did. In so doing, I now, as an adult, must forgive the child I was for turning my mother's unfair predicament into an opportunity. I must learn to acknowledge the ways in which that same child provided care no child should be asked to provide.

I continue to allude to how sad my mother's disability was, but that is not the total truth. The sadness only arrives by way of hindsight and it's easy to forget that we take the persistence of any situation and weave that persistence into normalcy. It was normal to brush my mother's teeth before leaving for school. It was normal to help her eat and provide assistance when she needed the toilet. It was normal to perform mischief knowing our mother would never appear at the doorway to punish us. What an insult it would be to my mother if I enforced sadness upon that normalcy - to suggest that she was a harbinger of something ugly. There is joy in the way my brother and I had to stifle our expressions of excitement while we played our forbidden game. It was a thrill to hide in the field next to our house to avoid our father's attention. Every careful step we took was a game even better than Mortal Kombat II.

There is nothing horrible about the true joy we found in such abundance. Sadness will never negate happiness and happiness, by embracing sadness, will only grow stronger for having done so.

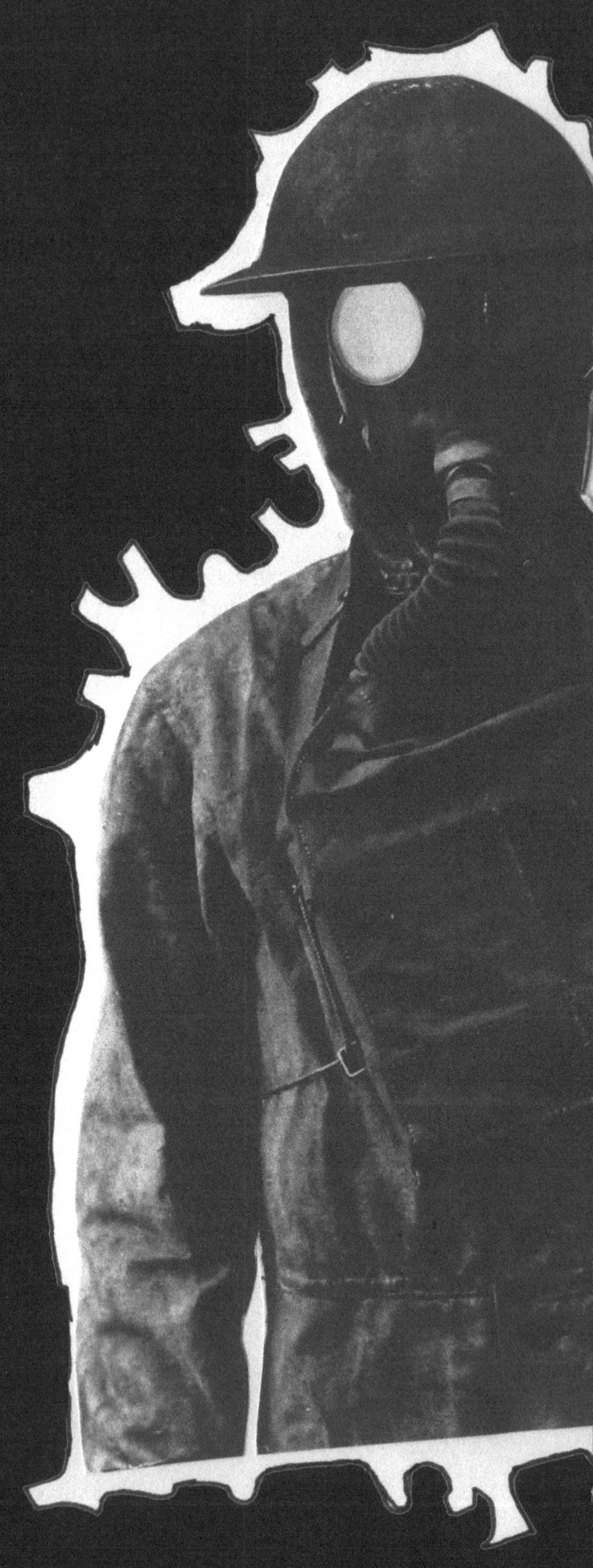

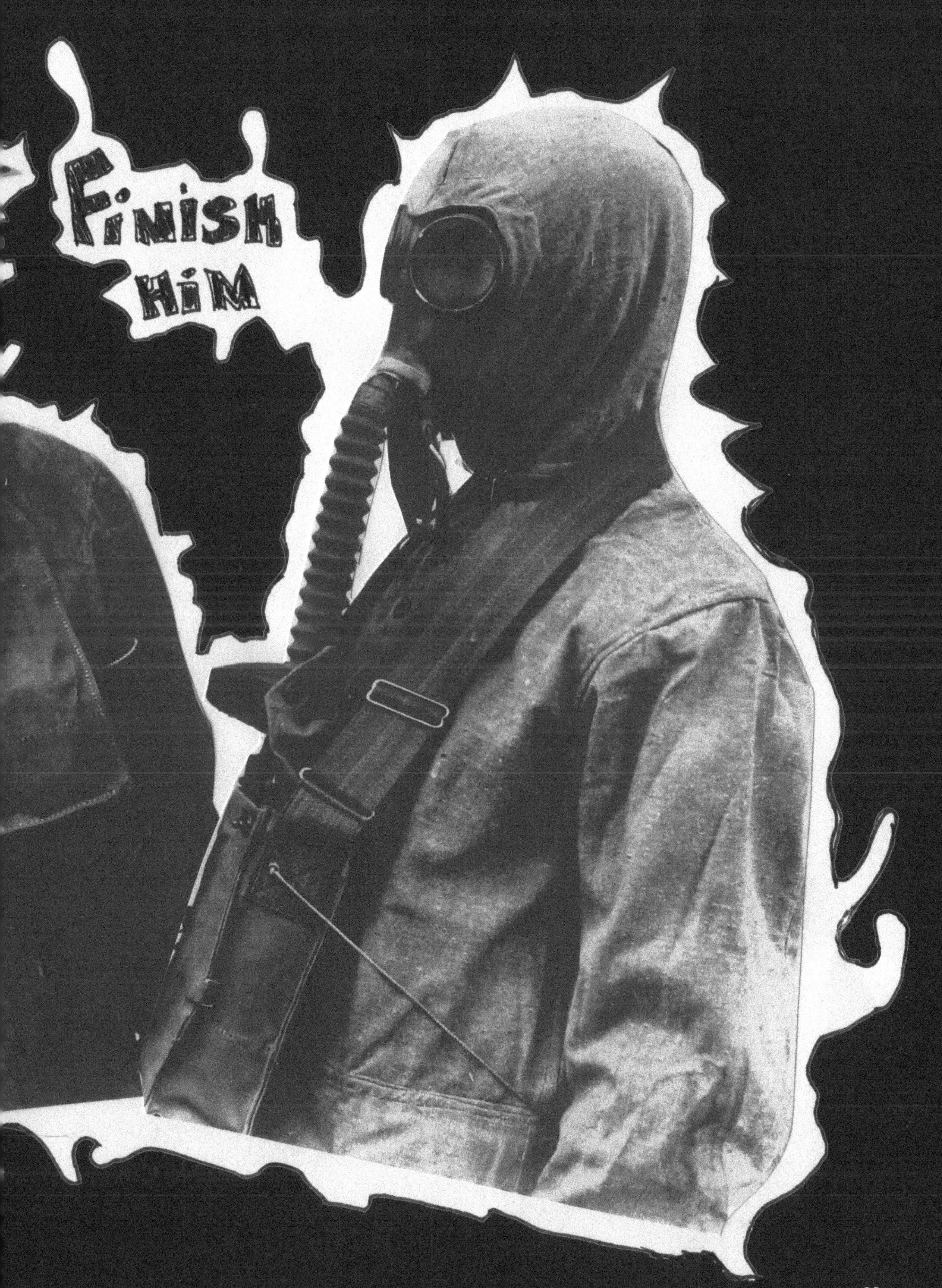

FiNiSH
HiM

Contents

91	The solemn urge to piss
92	Clancy's folly
93	Giraffe boy caught a fish
94	Swanning about
95	Shards of Margaret
96	Fancy the goat
97	Space goat that is actually a ram
98	County fair for introverts
100	Mortal Kombat -1
101	Sneaky brojob
102	The pisswick fingers
103	F.R.I.E.N.D.S season 5
104	Cat
105	Making a sex
106	Painted hair
107	Let's talk about us
108	You exist
109	Carry me, daddy
110	The puppets
112	Shhh... the forest needs me
113	Modesty patch
114	Trustworthy fellow
115	Give artists less credit
116	The travelling cockhead

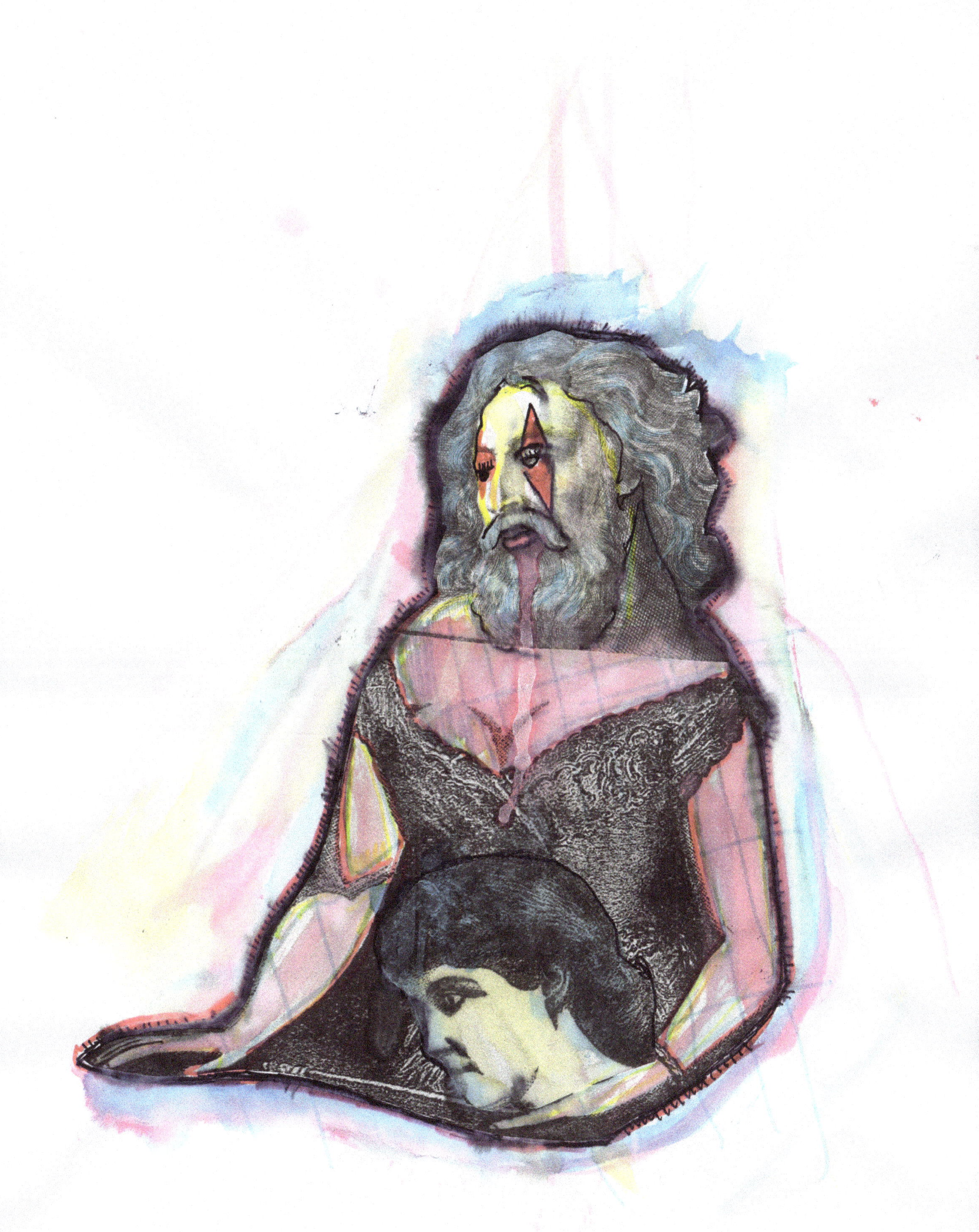

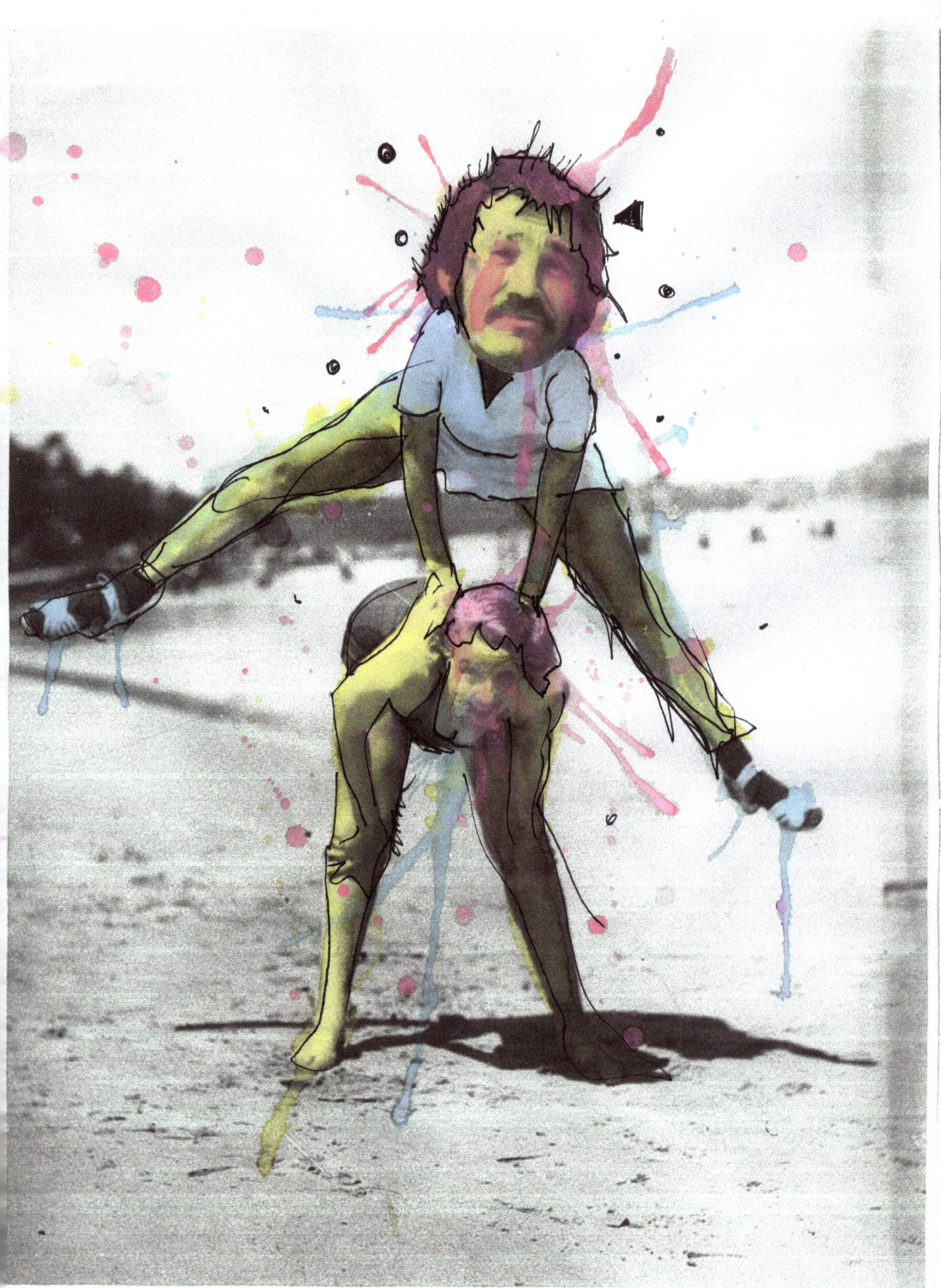

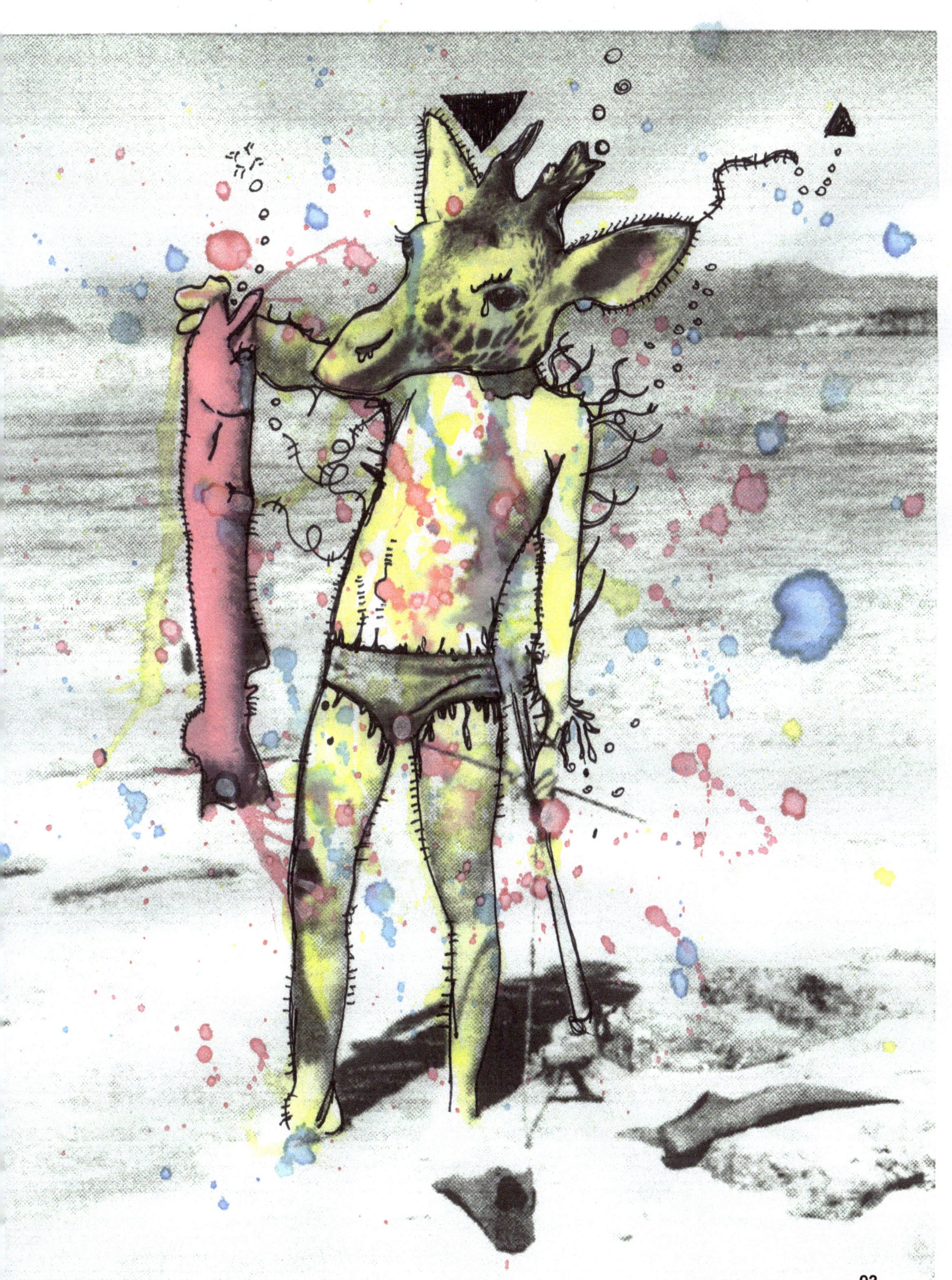

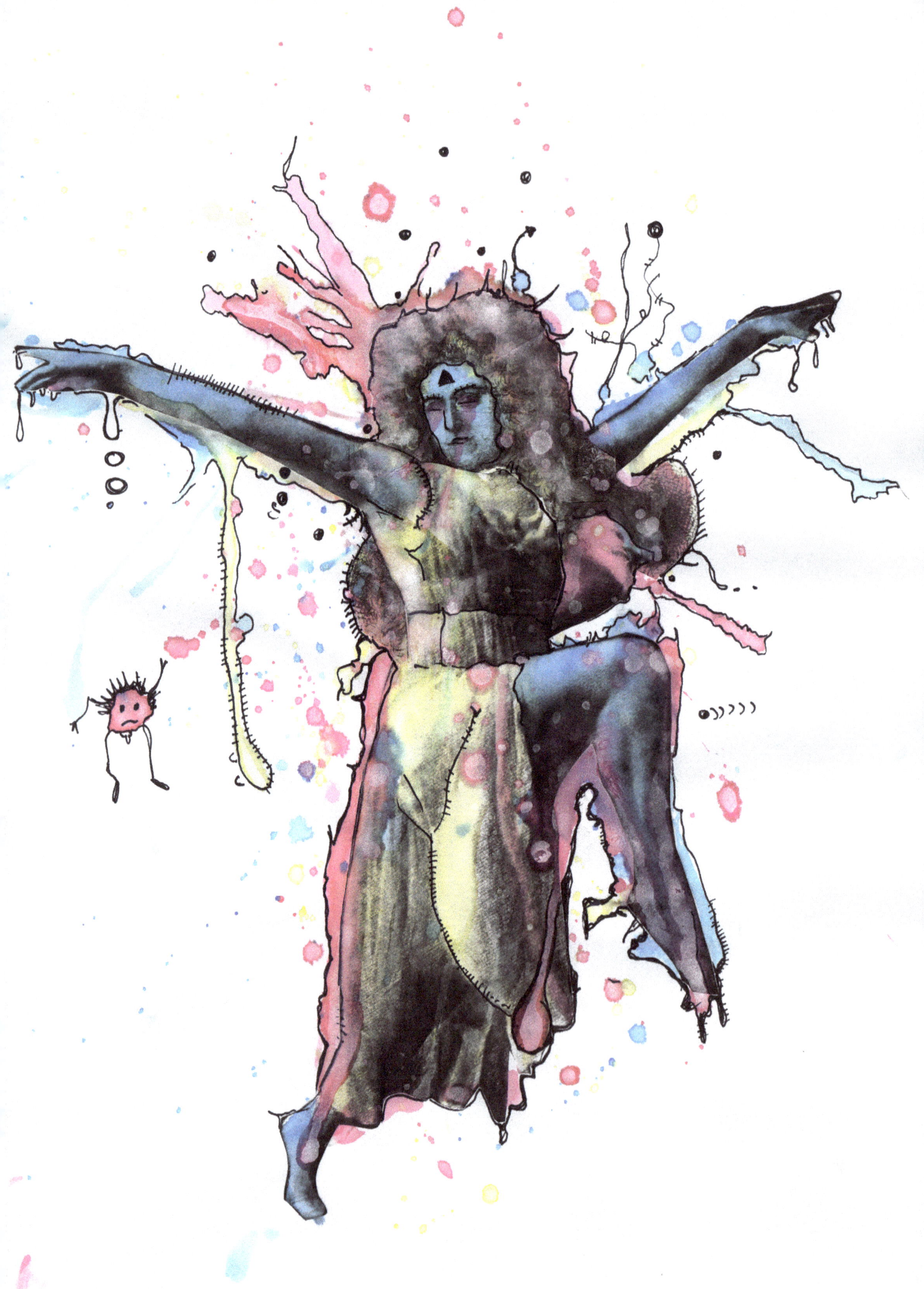

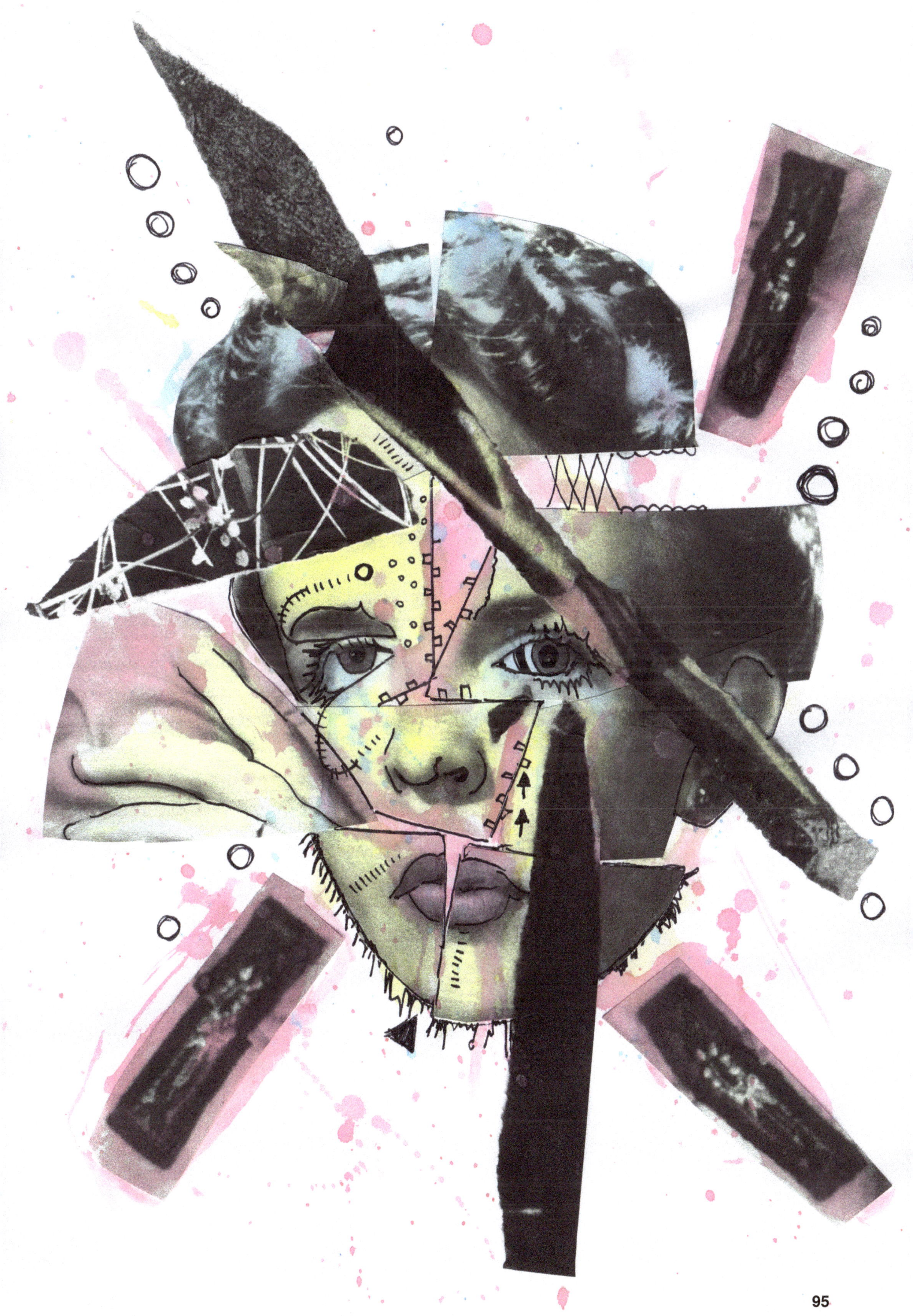

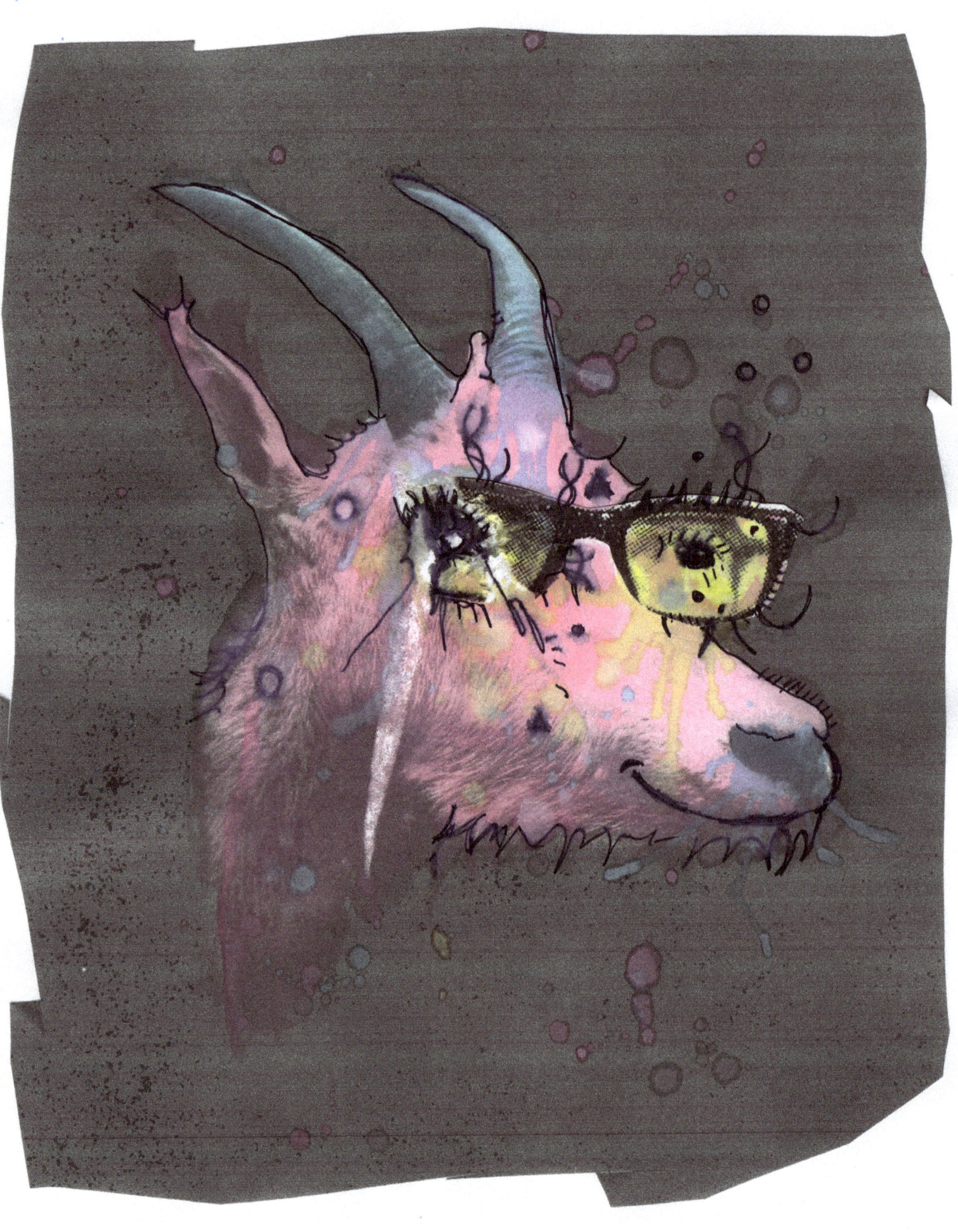

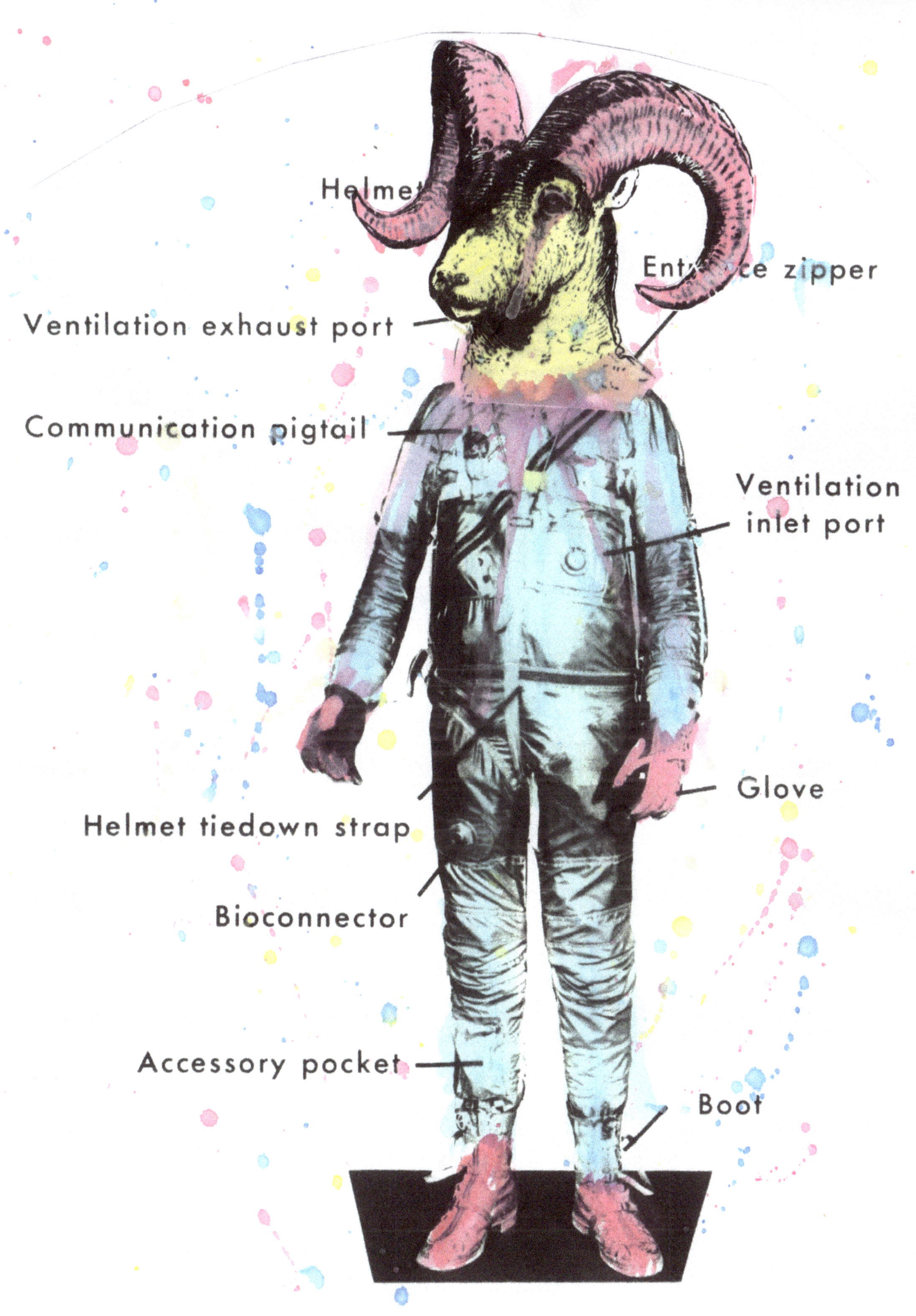

Figure #1 Mercury pressure suit

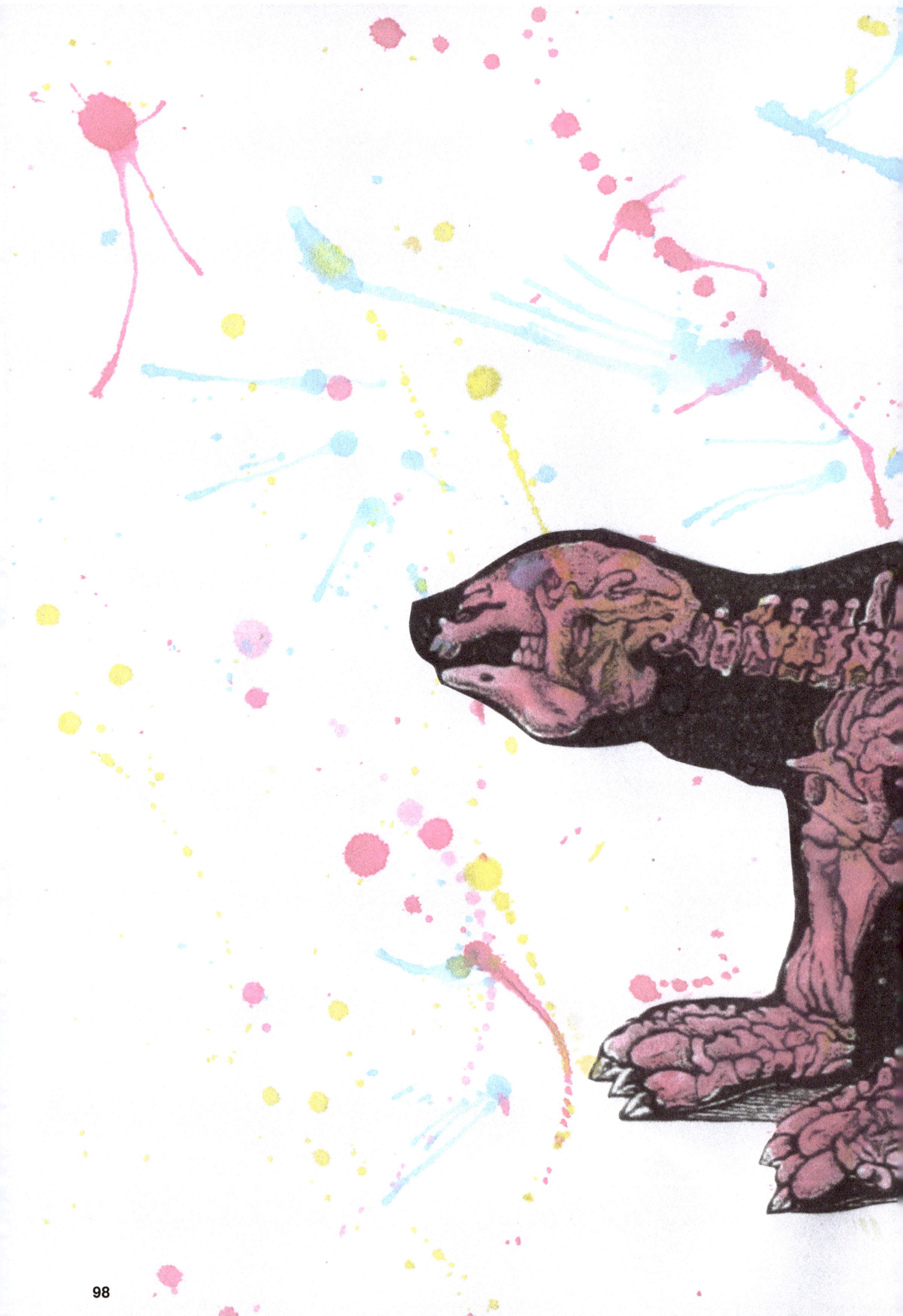

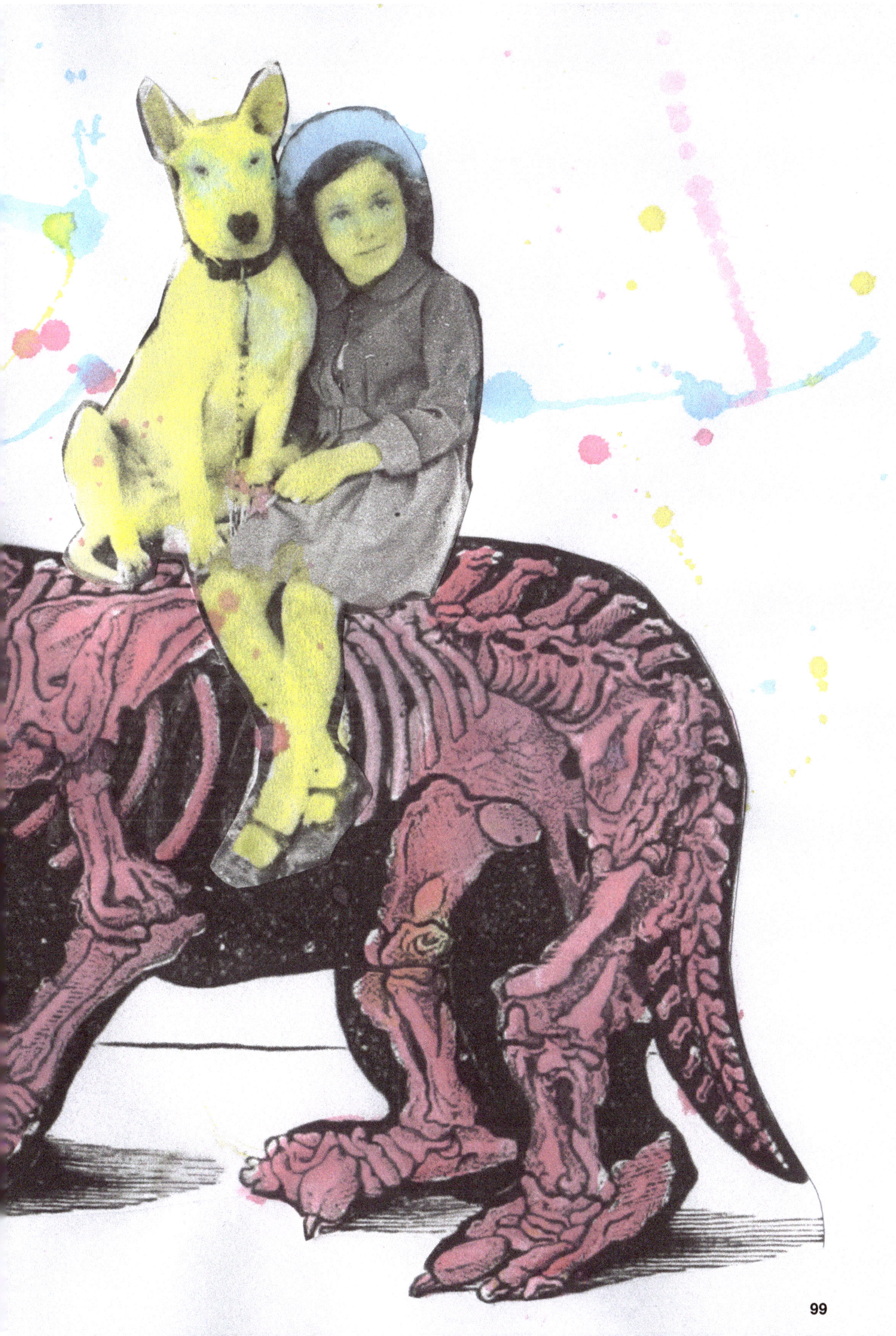

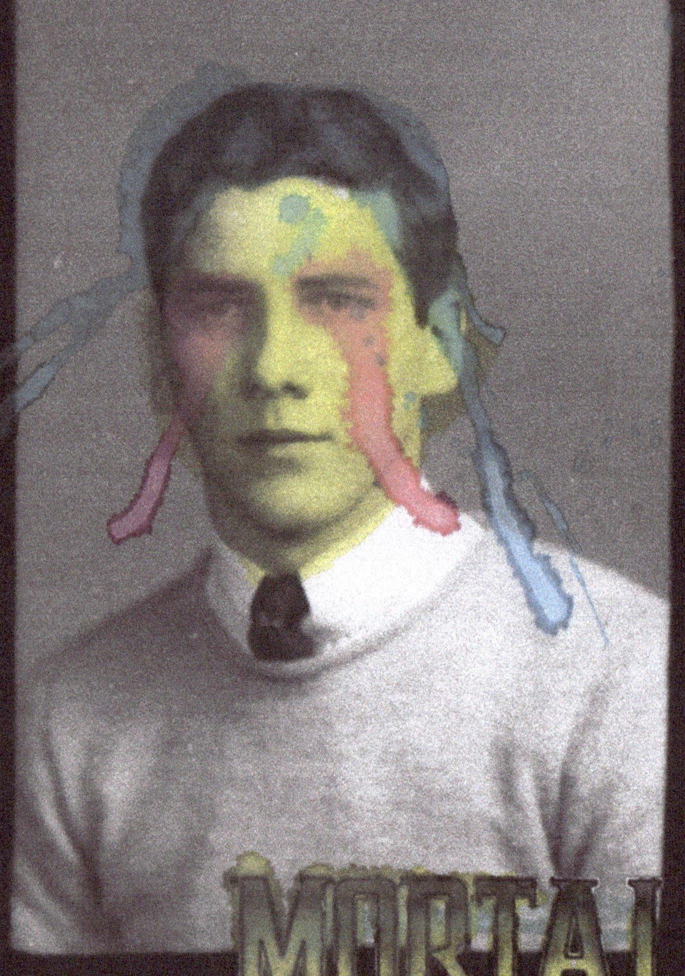

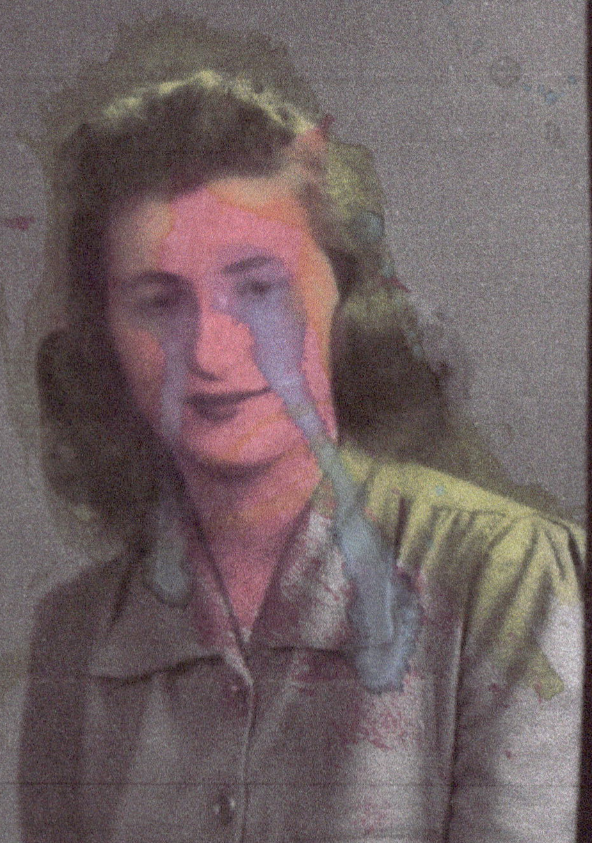

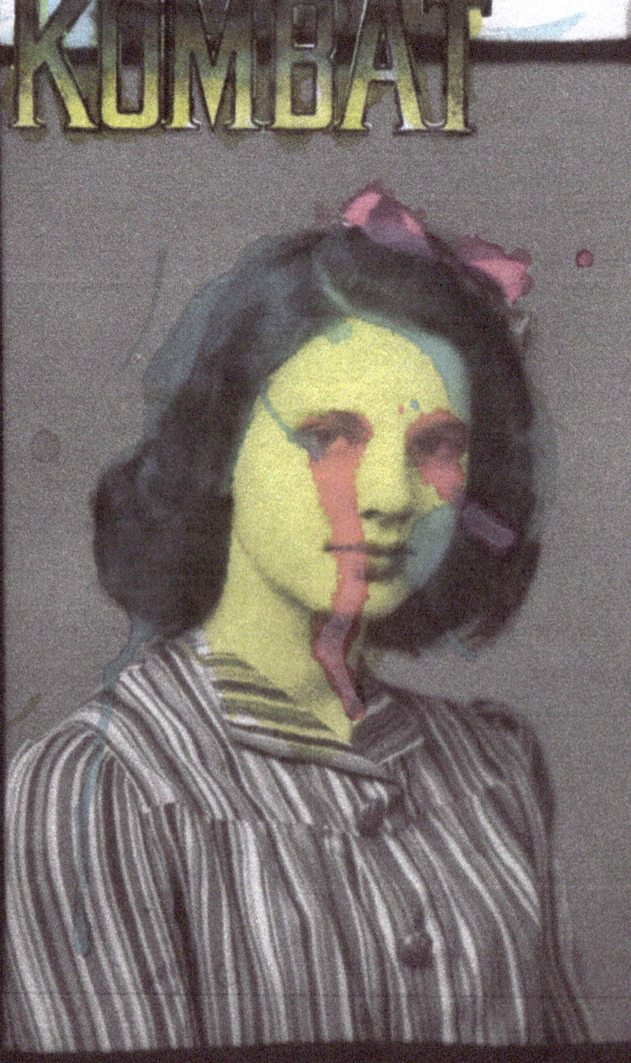

MORTAL KOMBAT

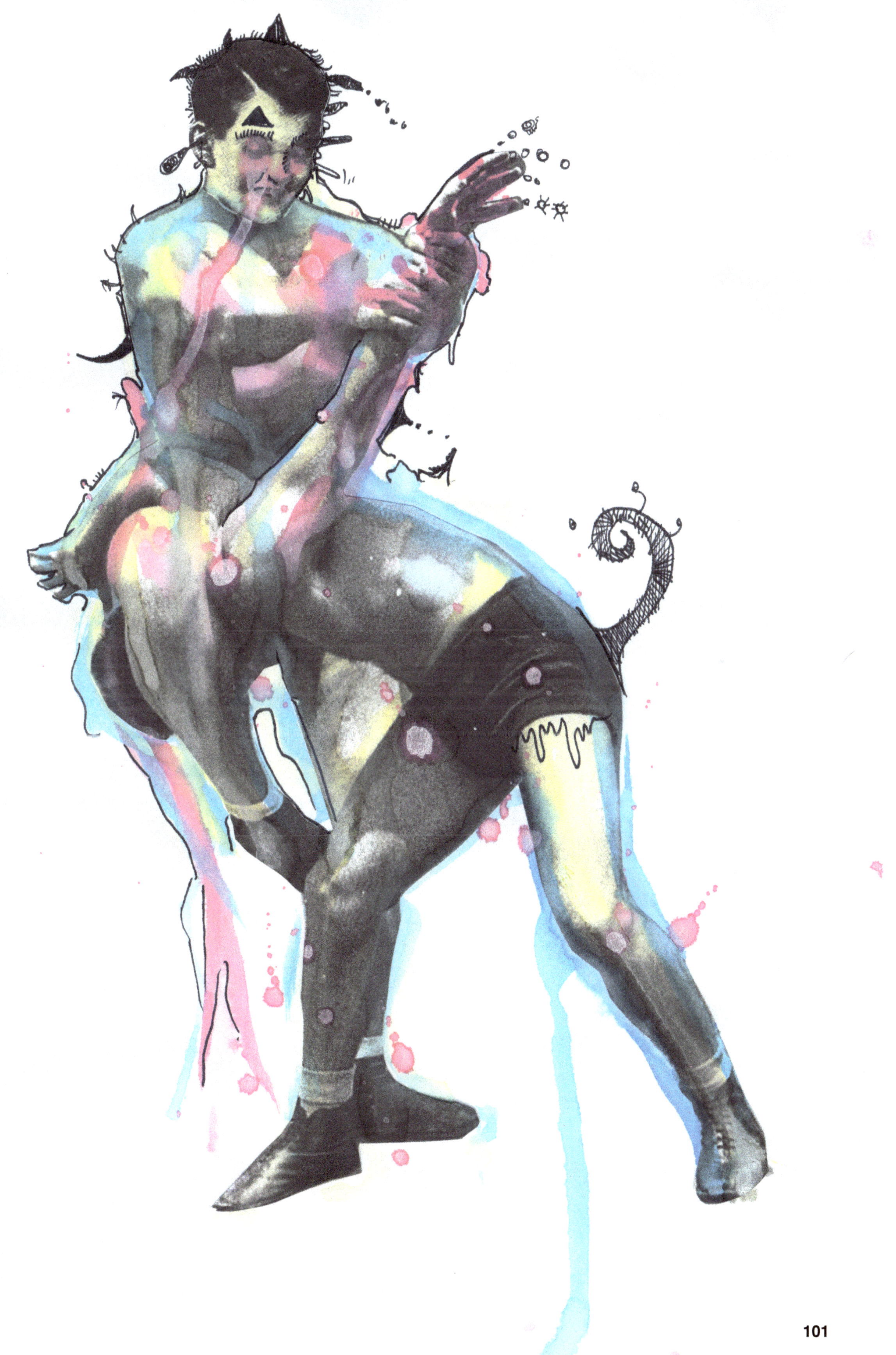

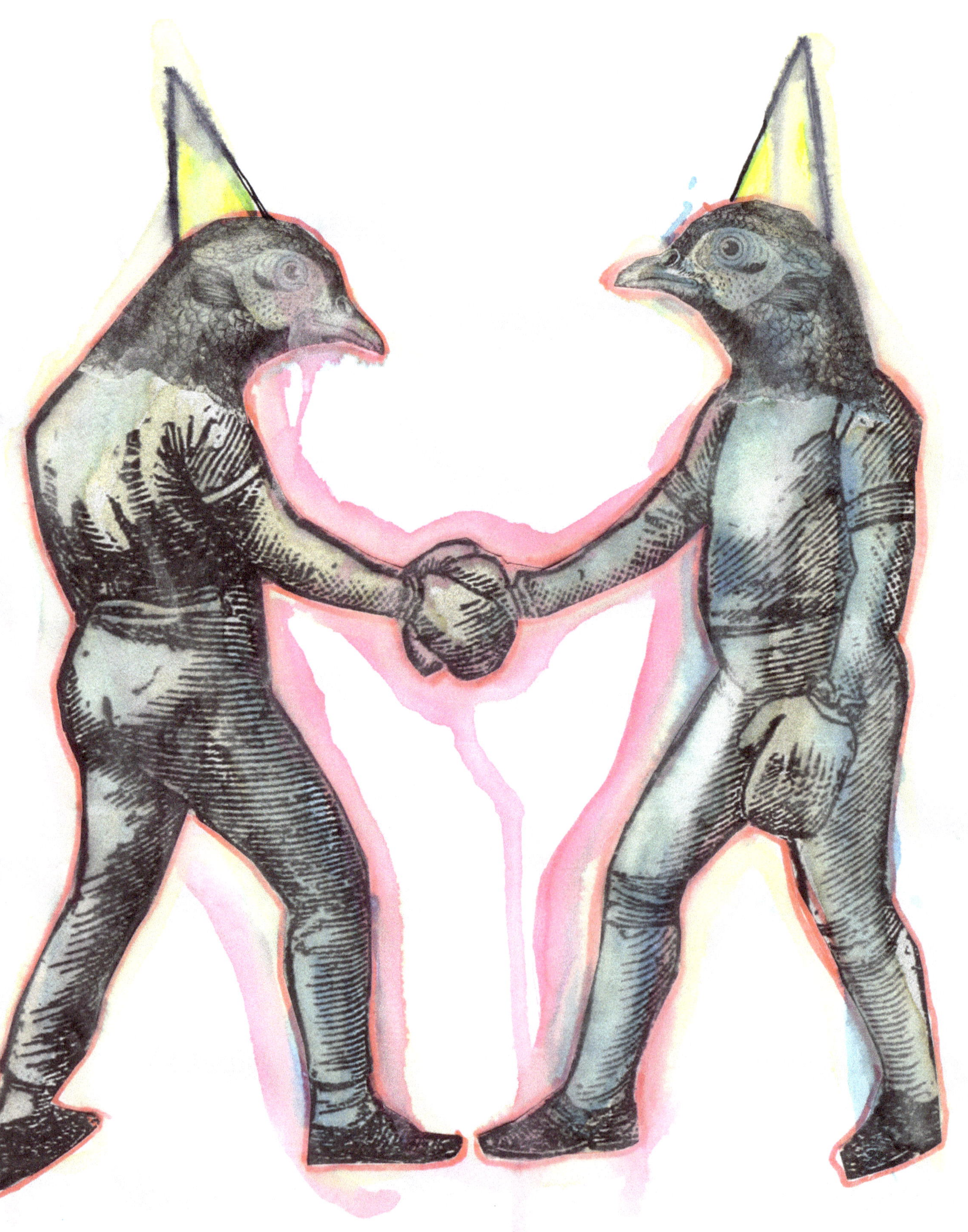

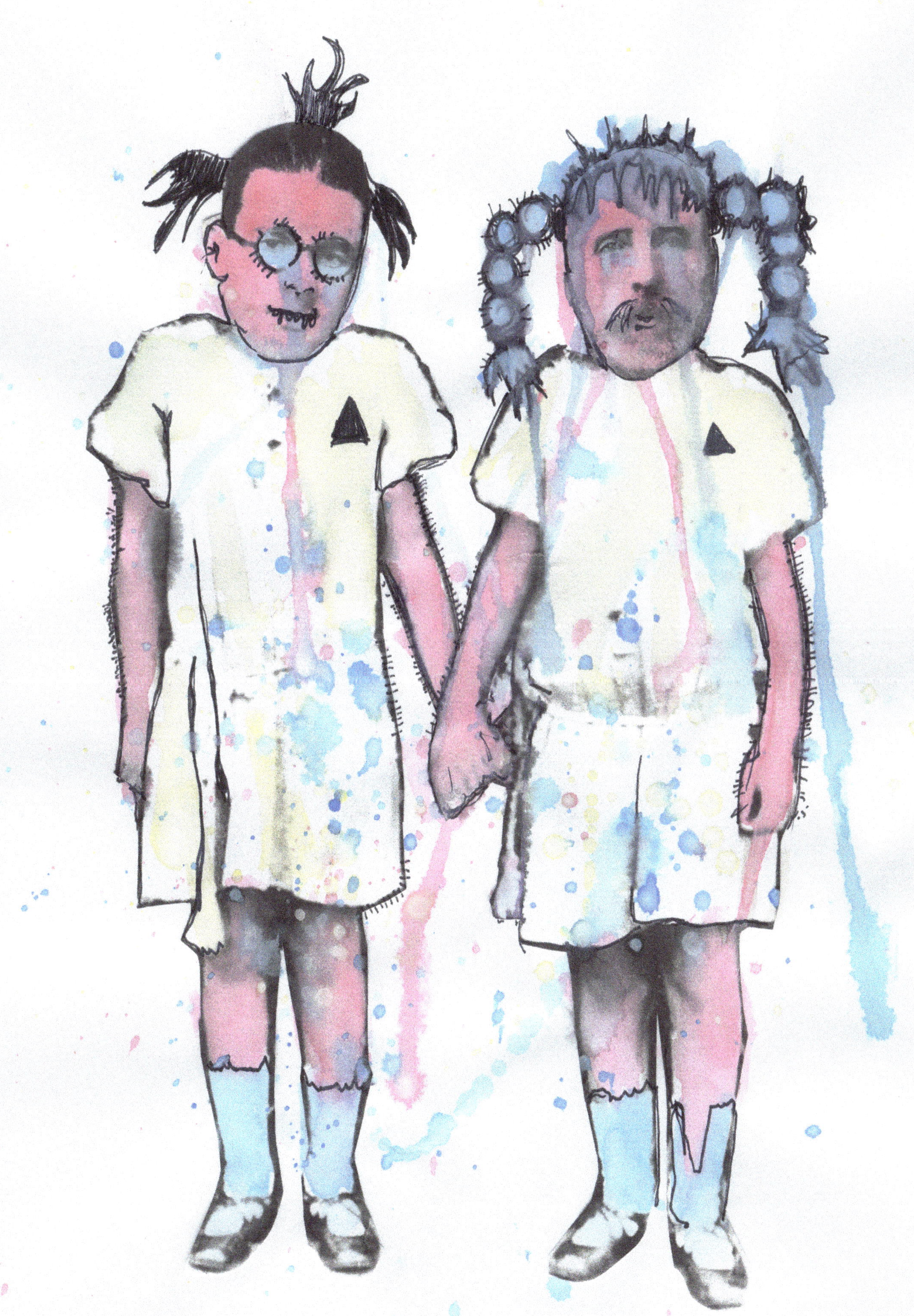

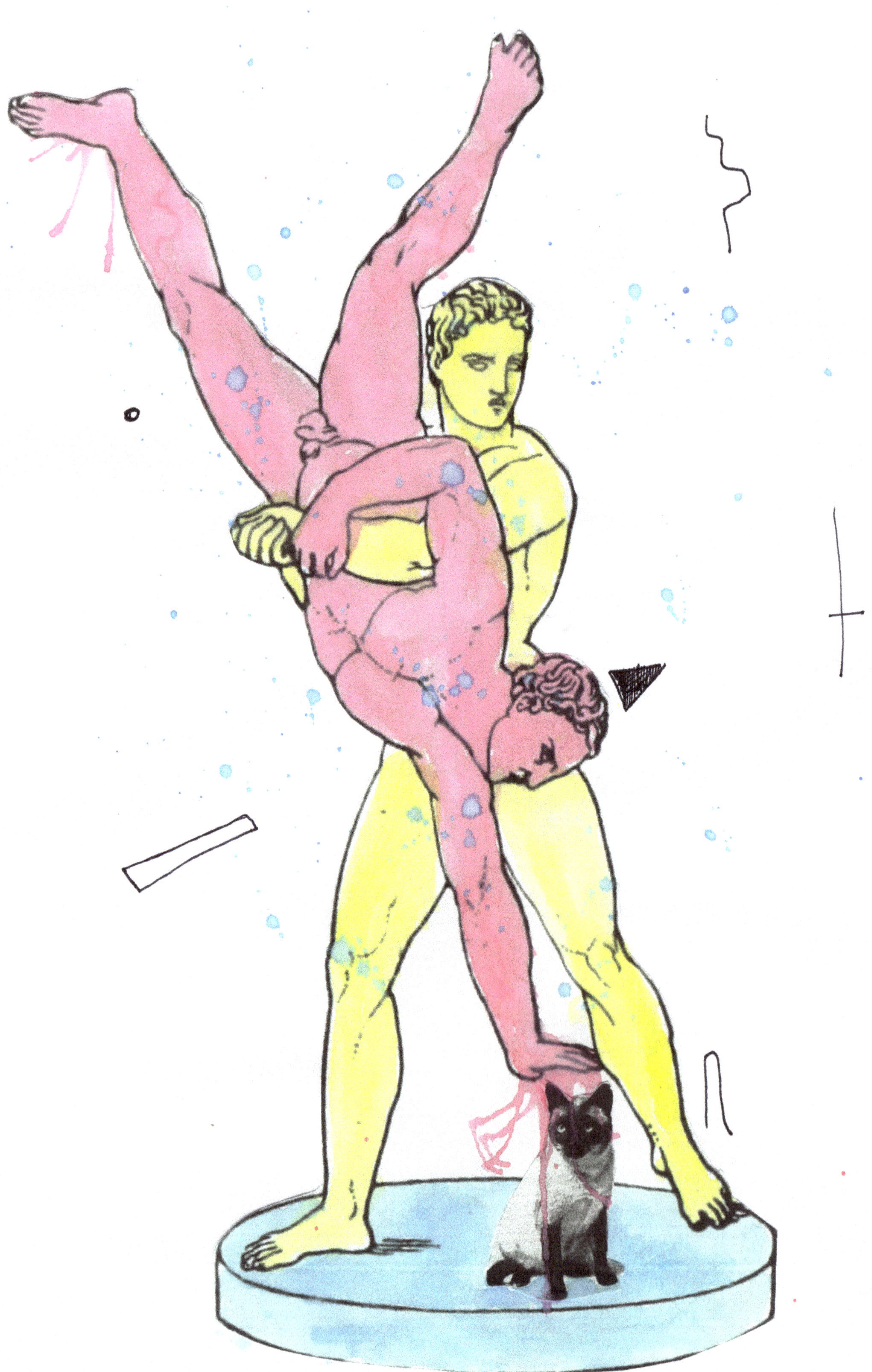

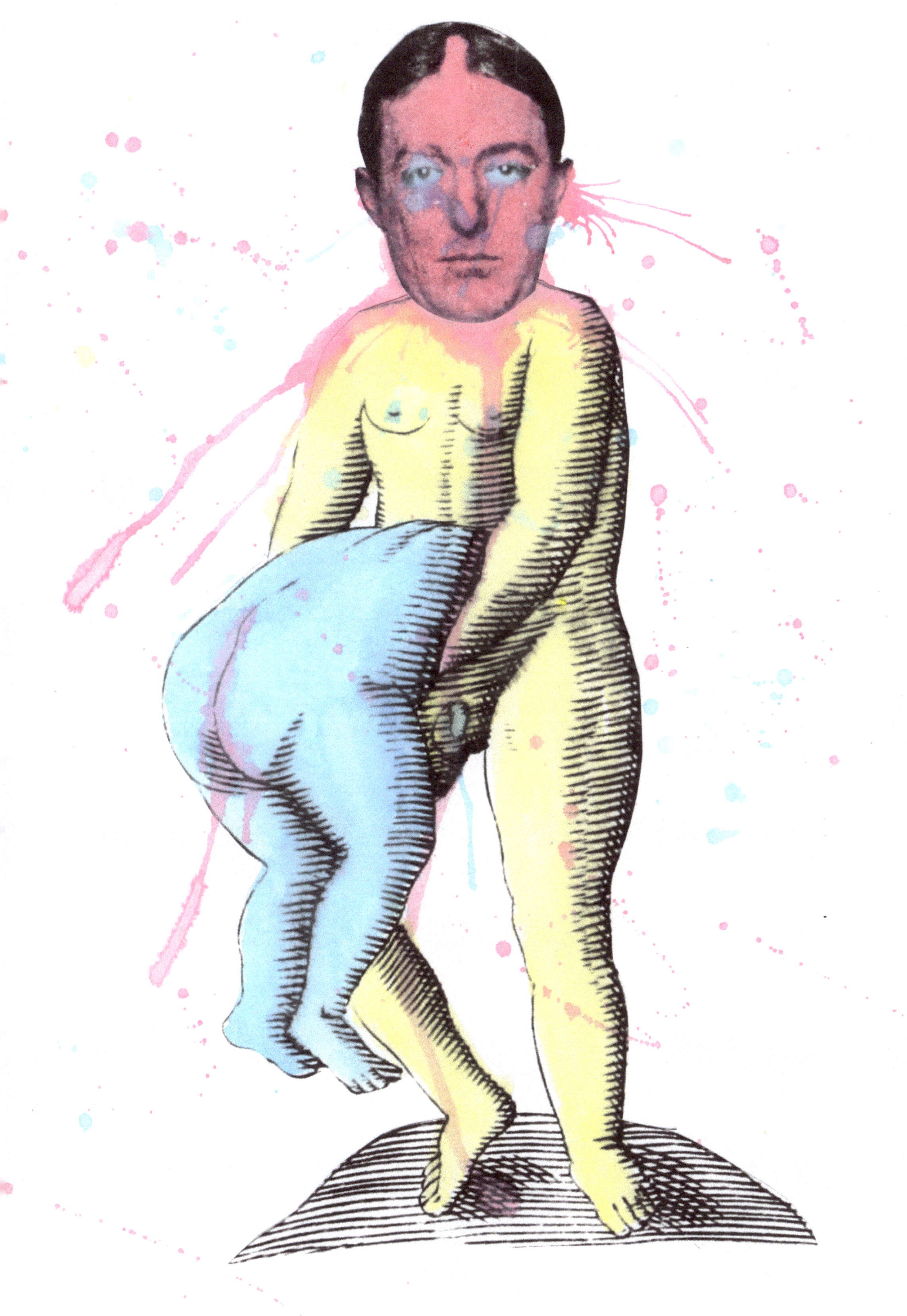

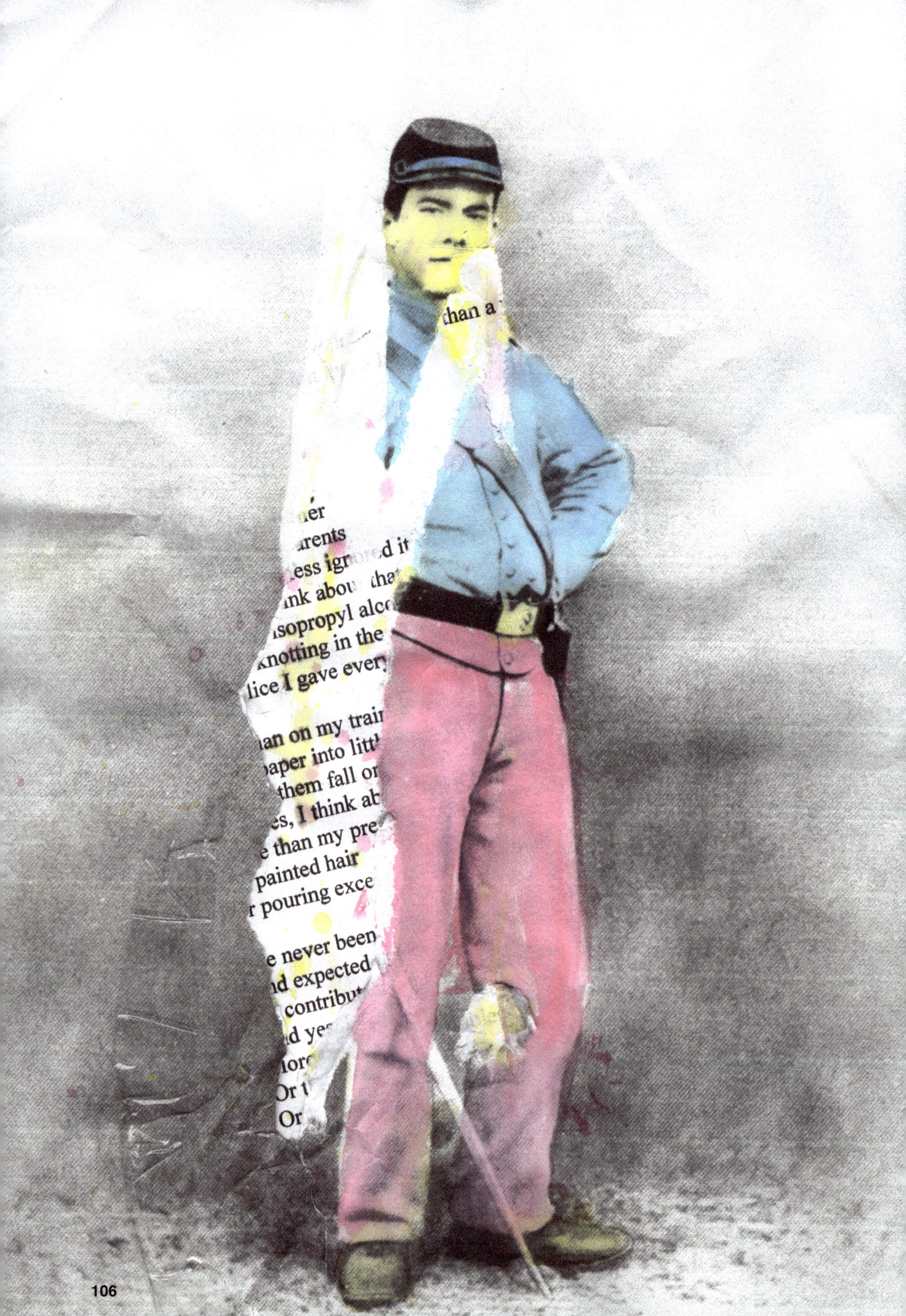
than a
her
rents
ess ignored it
nk about that
sopropyl alco
knotting in the
lice I gave ever
an on my train
aper into littl
them fall o
es, I think ab
e than my pre
painted hair
r pouring exce
e never been
d expected
contribu
d ye
lor
Or t
Or

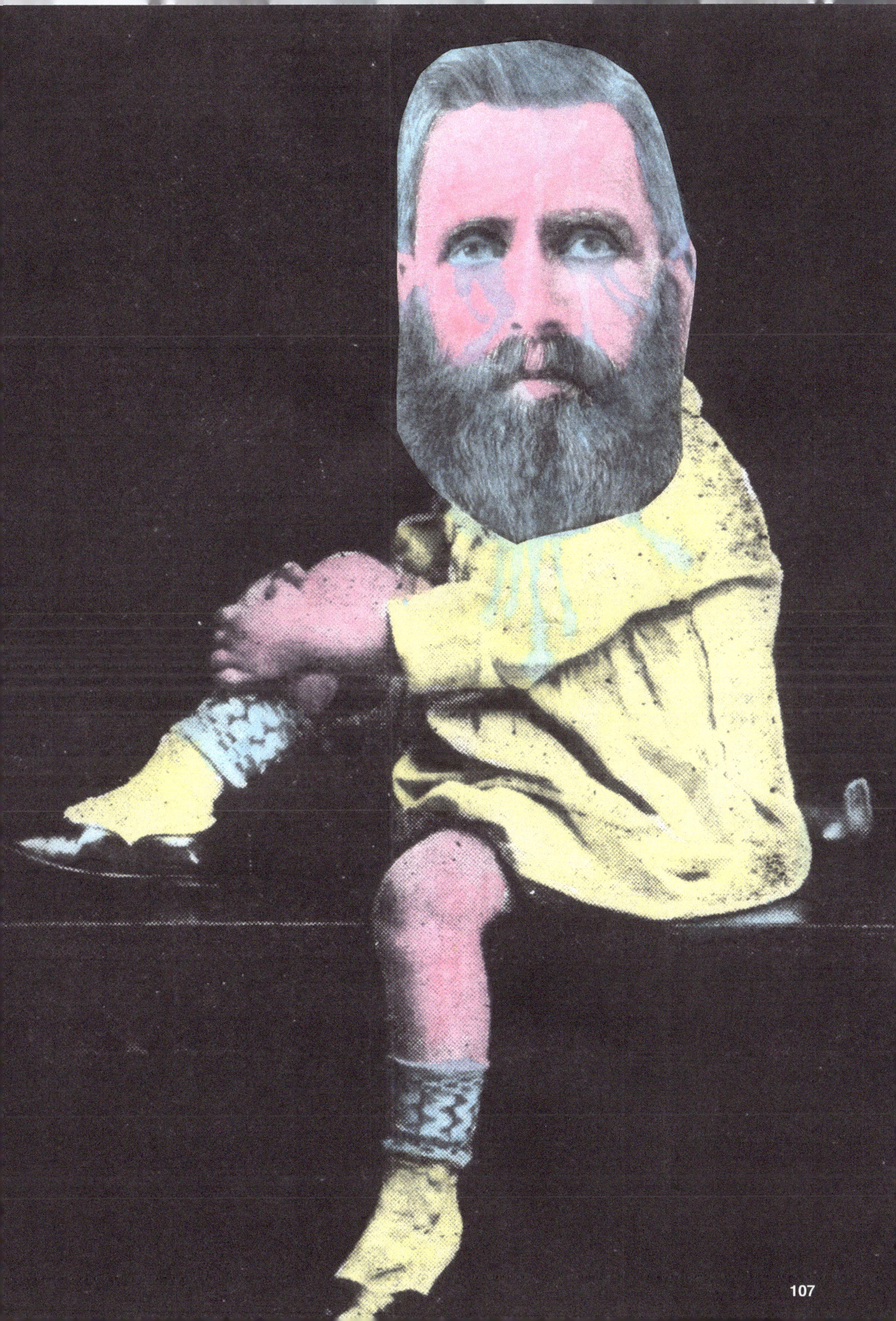

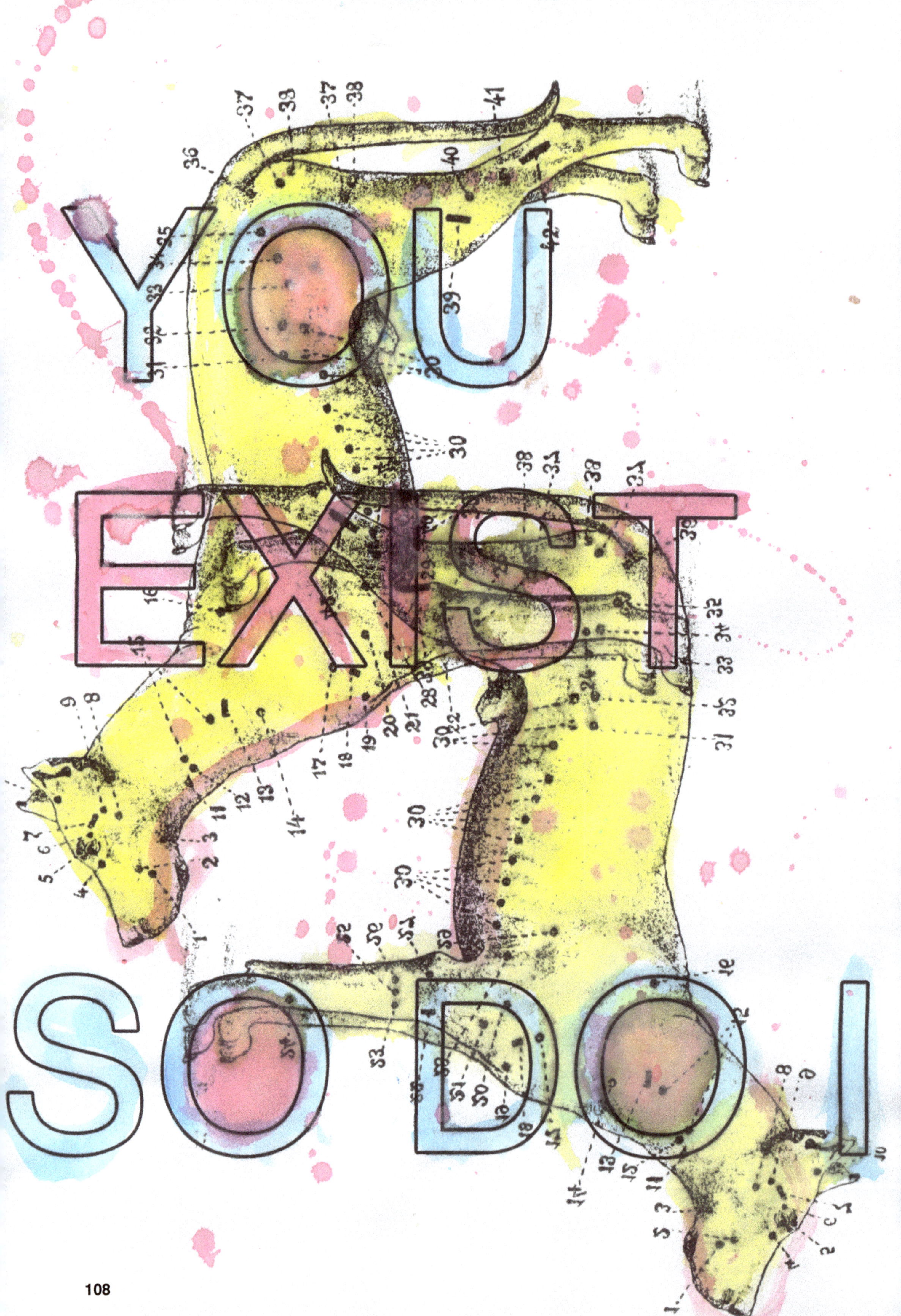

YOU
EXIST
SO DO I

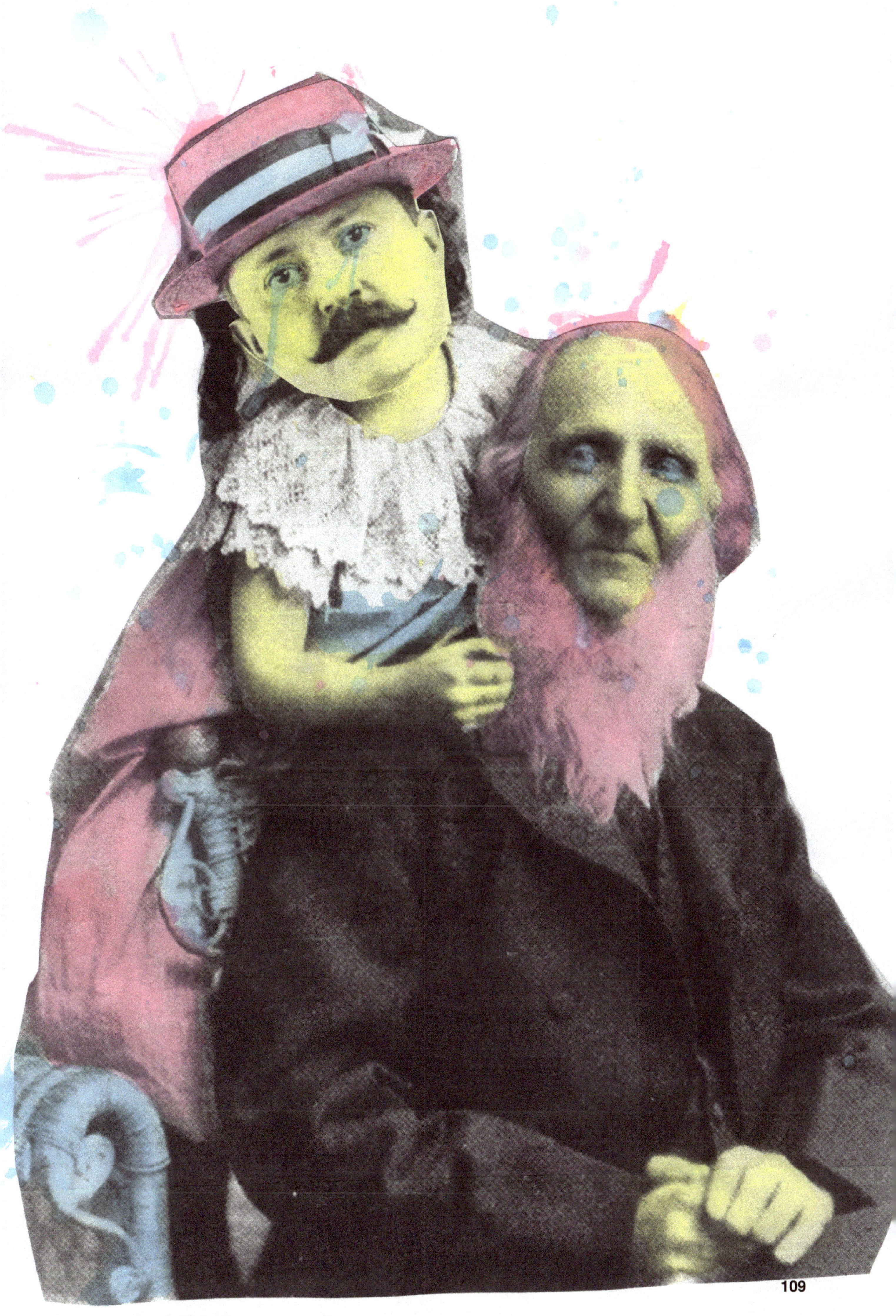

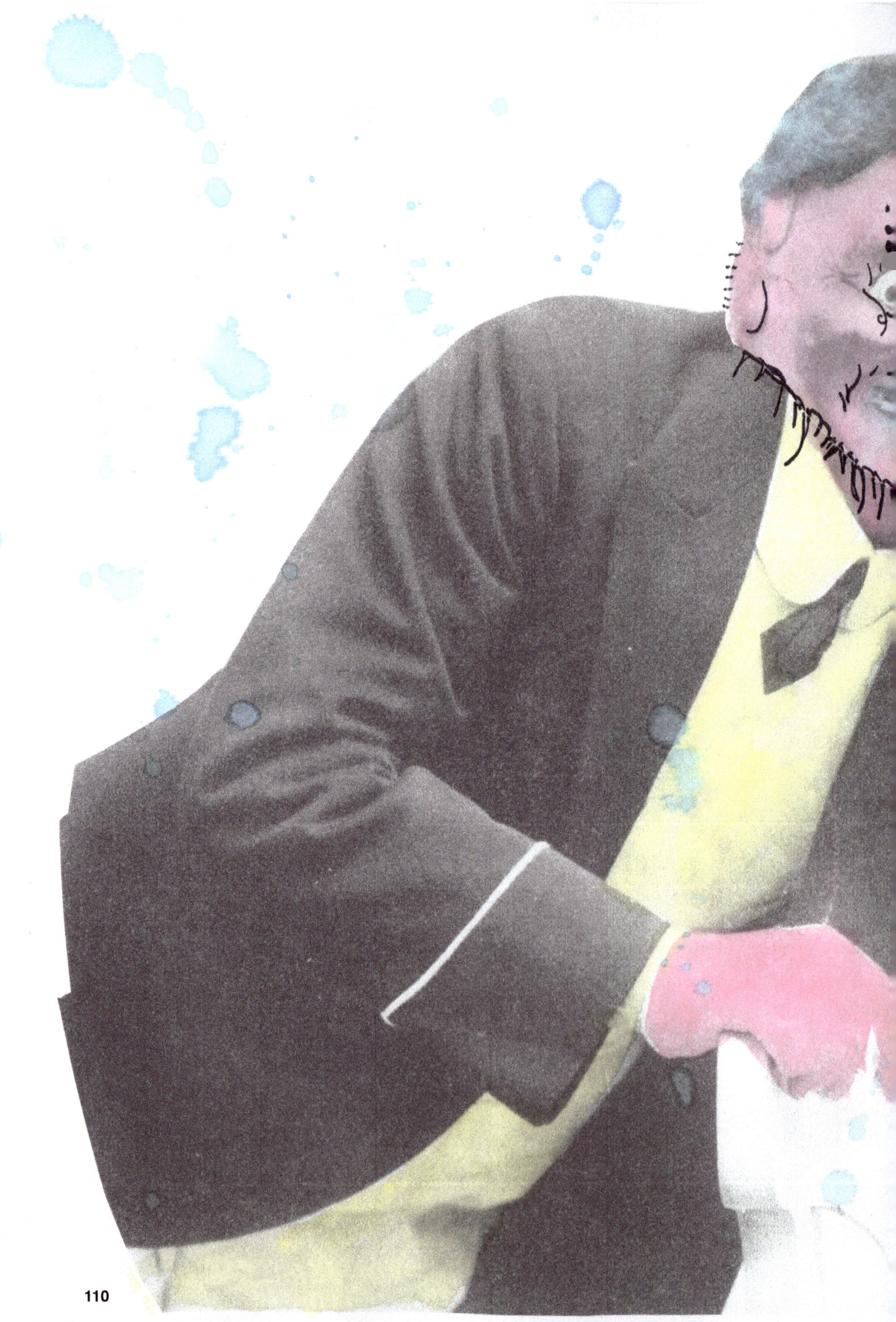

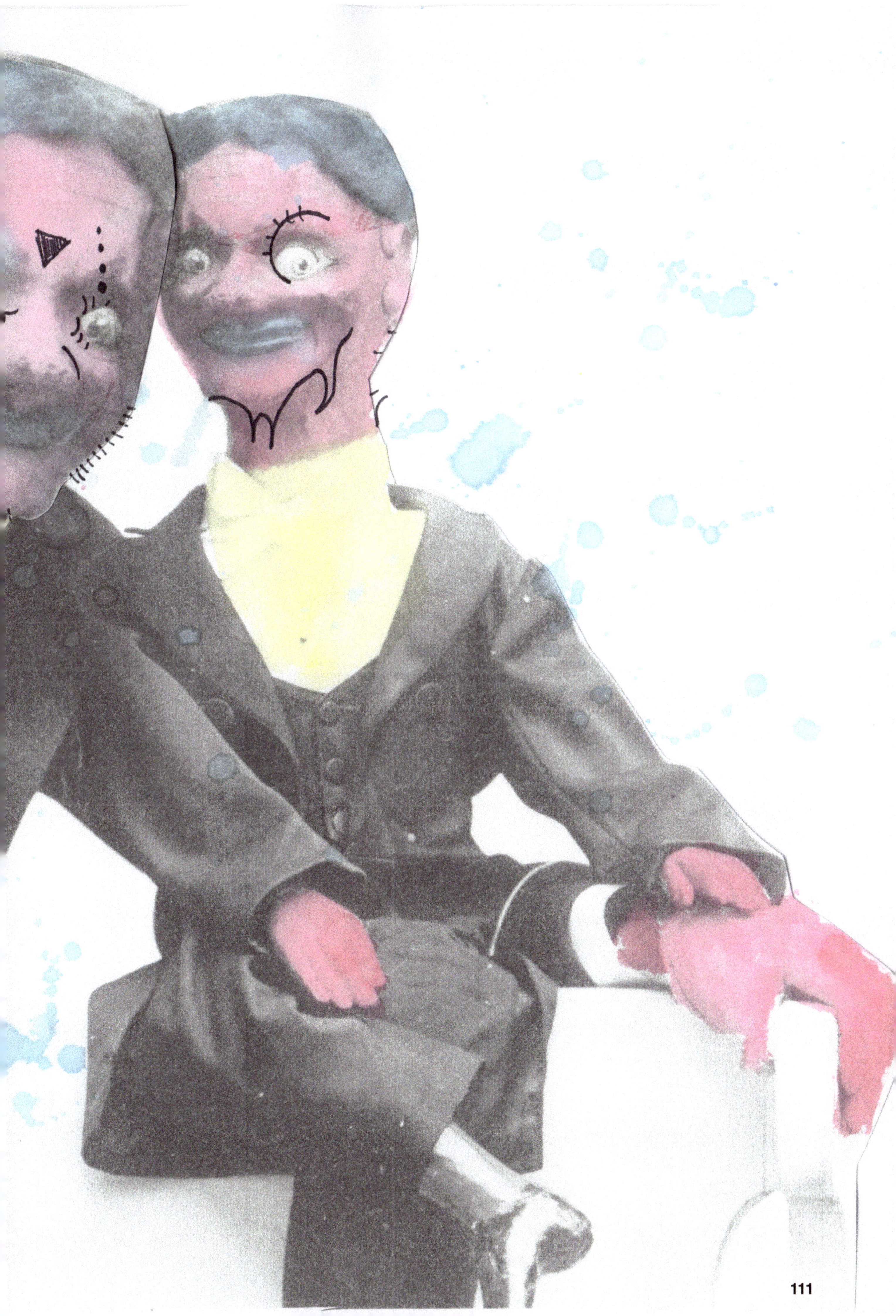

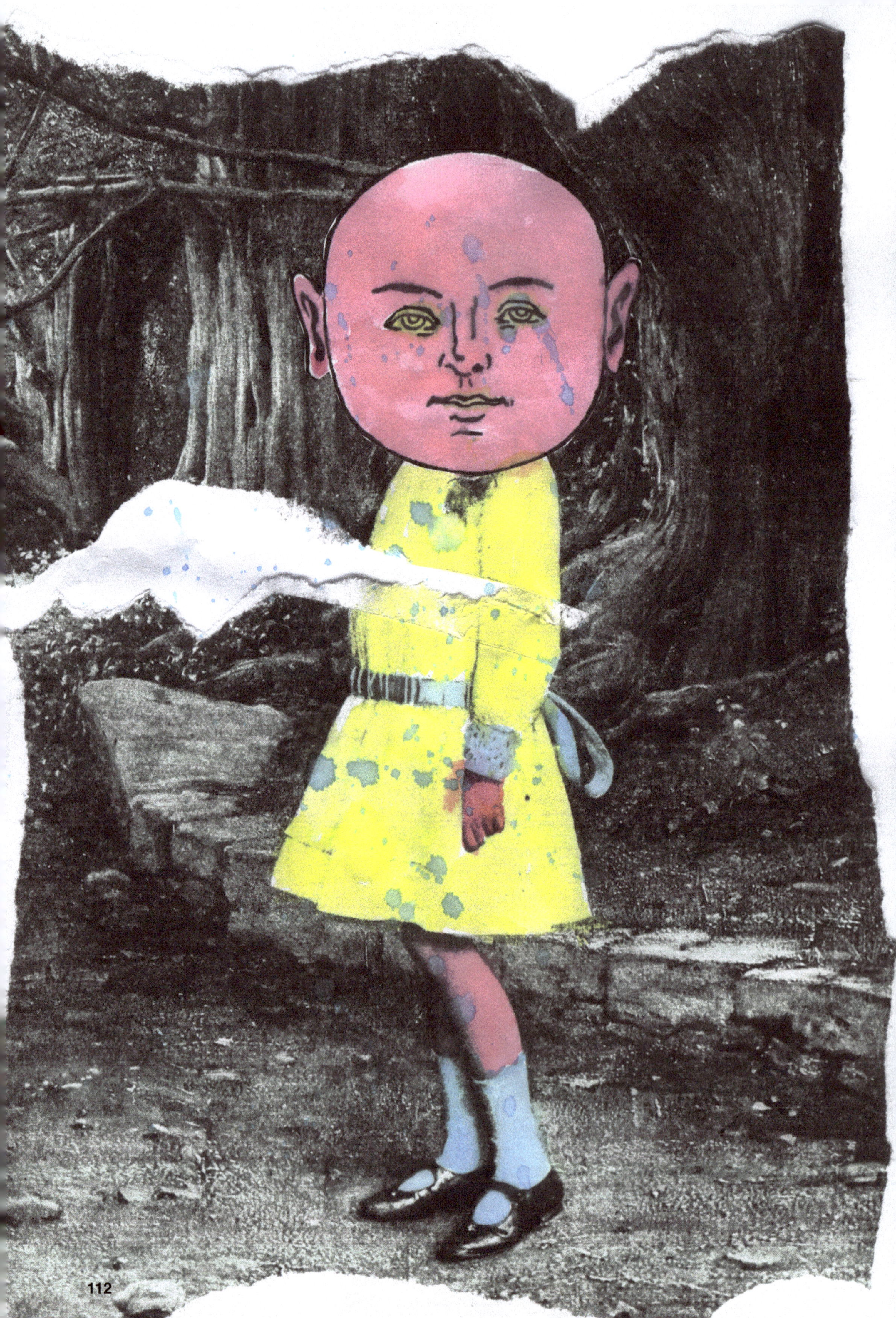

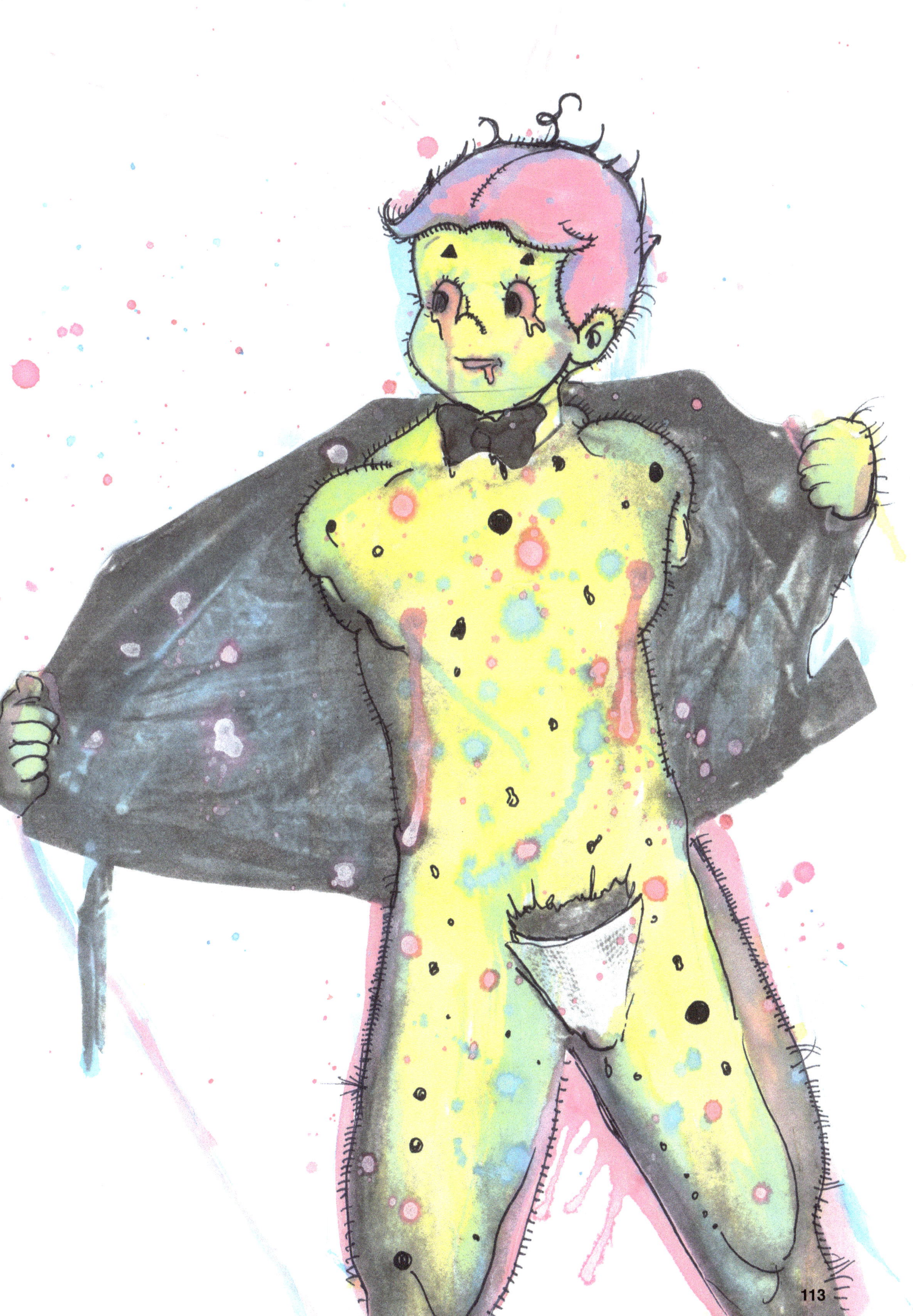

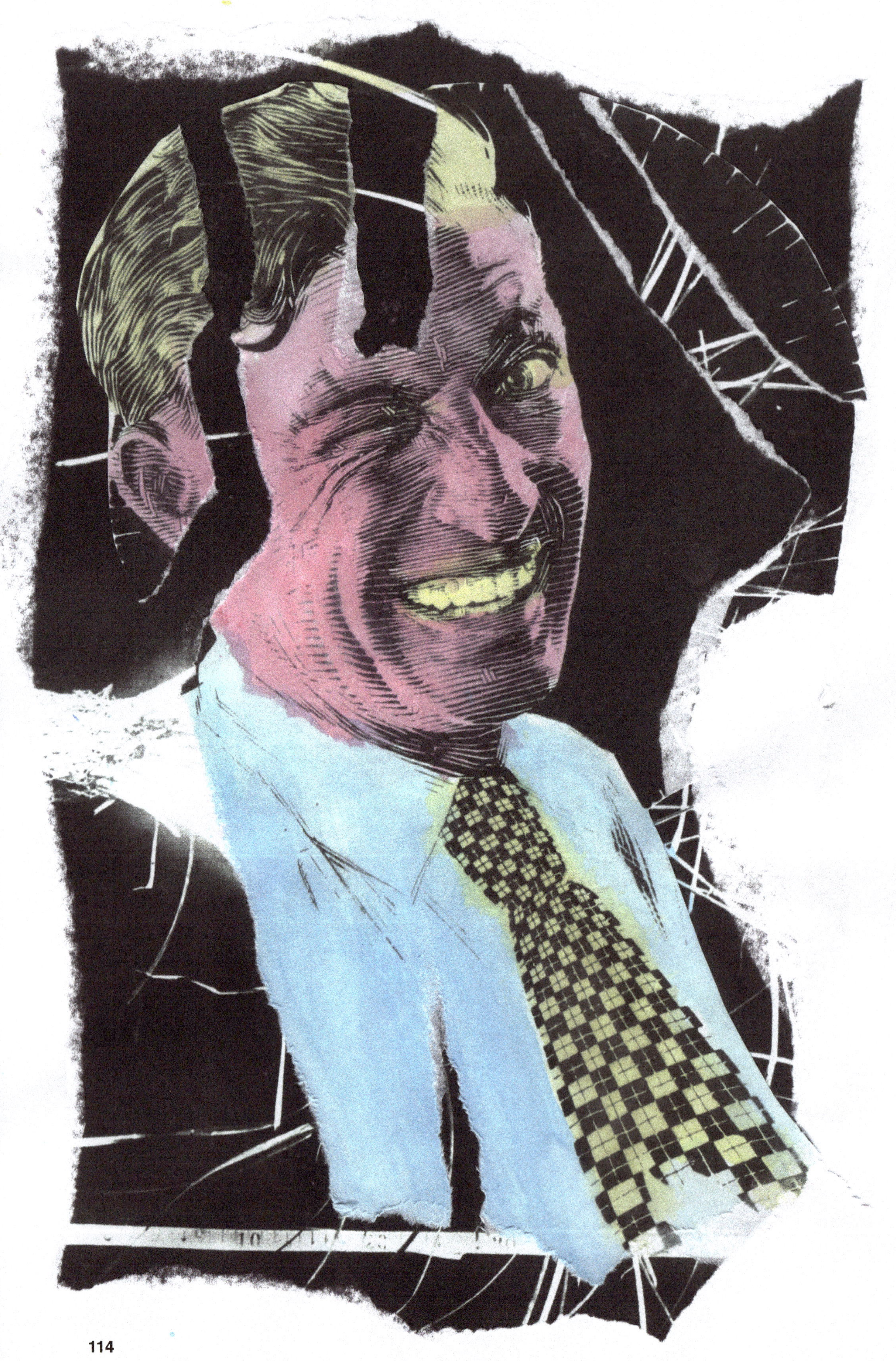

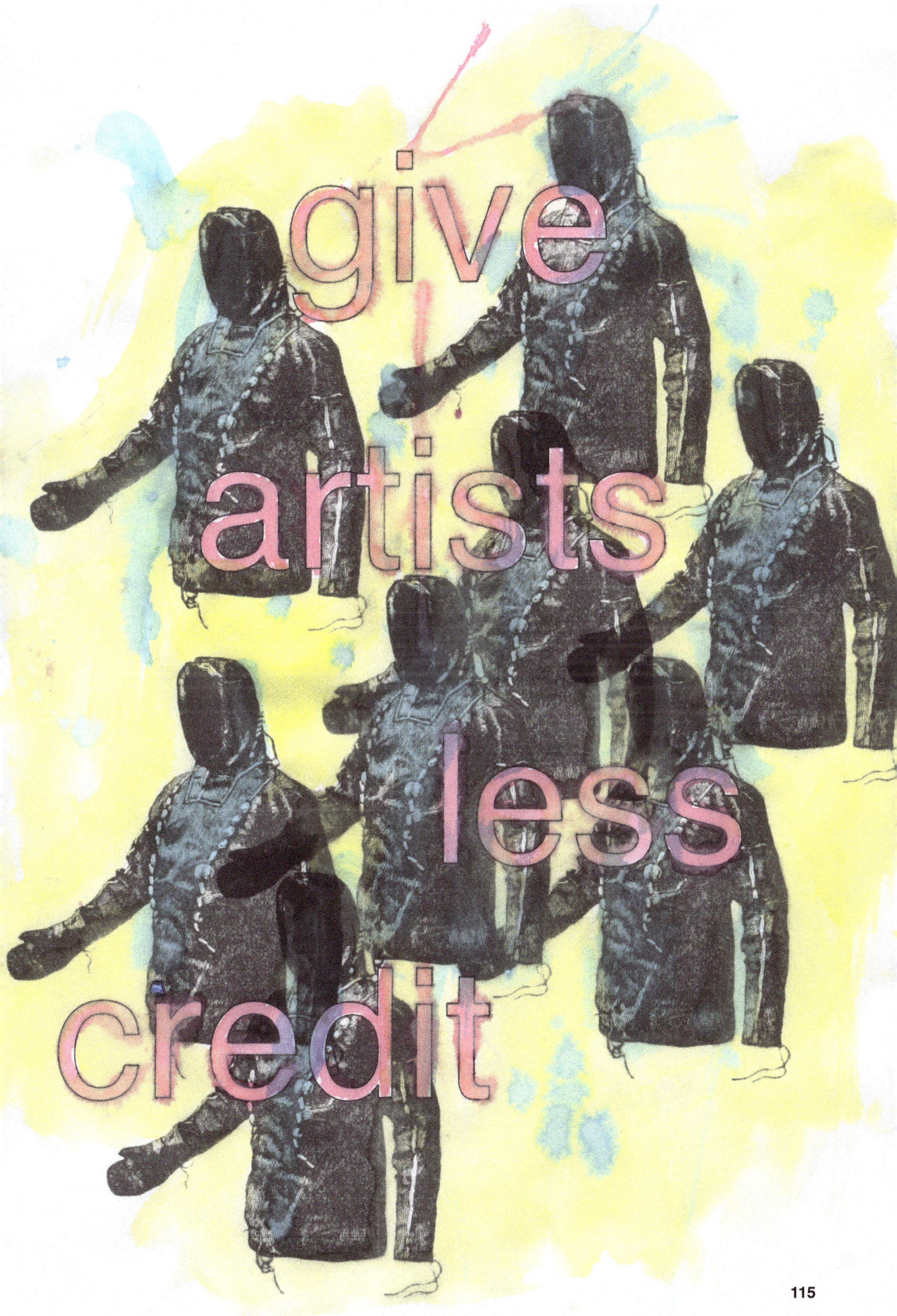

give
artists
less
credit

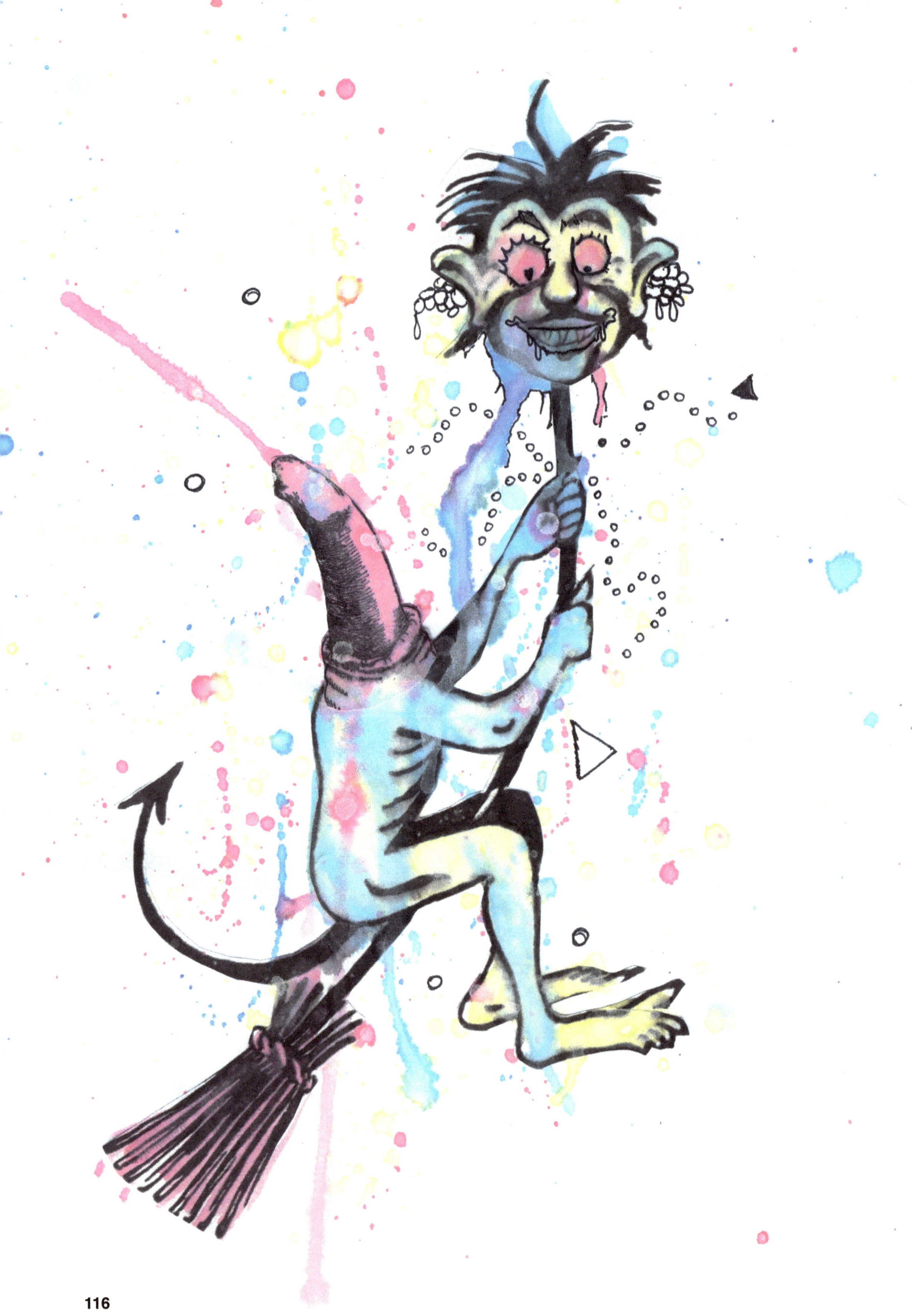

THE INTERNET
JUSTIFIES
ME

In the wispy shiny sad of your halfway house. The mondegreen of your mother's ears. Turning your complaints into famous songs.

O' ho ho ho. Shhhhhhhh.

Refuting my Childhood Amnesia

Childhood Amnesia is the process by which we literally forget our childhoods. It is said that those who claim to possess memories prior to age four are likely experiencing false memories predicated on knowledge of an event rather than recollection of the event itself. When I consider this, I am overcome by a sense of death whereby who we were ceases projecting any form of resonance. When I stare at childhood photos, I feel myself within them and experience the frozen moment as something imbued with life - my own life. Research suggests this experience of myself is a lie. For this reason, you have scientific evidence to disbelieve the following as it occurred before I was four. No photos of the moment exist and I experienced it alone, which limits the possibility I learned the memory from another. I think I enjoy the probability you will disbelieve me. The uncertain relationships we form with truth are a celebration of life.

I was two years old when the following occurred or did not occur or half-occurred. In my infancy, I was terribly unwell and while the memory in question doesn't relate to the perilous nature of my health, everything at that stage enjoyed a parenthetical relationship. Reportedly I nearly died upon tasting my mother's breast milk for the first time. This is not the memory I remember. To me it exists as a myth handed down, which I am unable to associate myself with. The memory I am going to share is far less dramatic than flirtations with death.

Infants are required to nap regularly and I was no different. The time of day escapes me beyond a general understanding that it was afternoon. My cot was in my parents' bedroom. This was an age before baby monitors allowed one to observe every movement and utterance from anywhere in the world. The only way to obsessively survey an infant in those technologically primitive times was to remain by their side. I assume this is why I shared a room with my parents. According to this memory, daytime naps did not enjoy any surveillance because although in my parents' bedroom, I was alone. This is my first memory of loneliness.

An awful lot of my context surrounding this memory is assumption. For instance, I assume I was put down to nap around the same time every day. Sleeping is not something that comes easy to me and I also assume this was the case in my infancy. The cot I slept in was made of wood. The dark brown color makes me think it was a richly stained mahogany, but I doubt my parents could afford that. At the very least, it looked like a dark mahogany. It was through these mahogany bars that I am entrapped in this memory.

Perhaps childhood amnesia is a blessing

that allows us to forget the helplessness of our infancy - the knowledge we survive only because caregivers allow it. Two-year-old me, in my cot, staring through mahogany-like bars was at the mercy of my parents. Without them, I would have died in that cot of starvation or perhaps suffocating after rolling my face into a pillow. It is with concern that this sliver of childhood helplessness is granted access to my cognition - whether it is a memory based on truth or not.

The light in the room is always my first impression. The blinds were drawn, framed by a rectangle of feathered daylight bleeding around its edges. A lamp on a dresser threw a dirty yellow light throughout the room, casting unnatural shadows and imbuing every object with pernicious intent. Were something to attack me, how loud would I have to scream before my parents came to my rescue? Would my screaming only encourage the nameless ubiquity of my terror to dispatch me with greater haste? Passing time has allowed me to translate my childhood mind into something communicable beyond screams and tears. I can give form to the moment, which allows your understanding, which my two-year-old self could not. This only feeds the memory with more dread, reminding me how truly alone I was.

While the room's light guides me back into the memory, it is the closed door that occupies every other facet. A closed door I could not open viewed from behind wooden bars I could not break. I stared with the understanding that everything capable of ensuring my safety existed beyond that door - a door actively closed by the keepers of my safety. I was supposed to be asleep. I was not meant to see this. What would my parents have thought had they known how abandoned I felt? Staring into the essence of that closed door lacked the visceral fear of the ominous shadows, but

became something so much worse - an understanding of my loneliness and how it never truly leaves us alone.

I chuckle slightly as I read back over these words with the knowledge it may be false. It is easy to picture the person I'm told is me in photos from my childhood and place that representation of me into so many different scenarios and, over time, allow those scenarios to become real. This is different. This is not a fabrication - at least, I don't think it is.

Do you believe me?

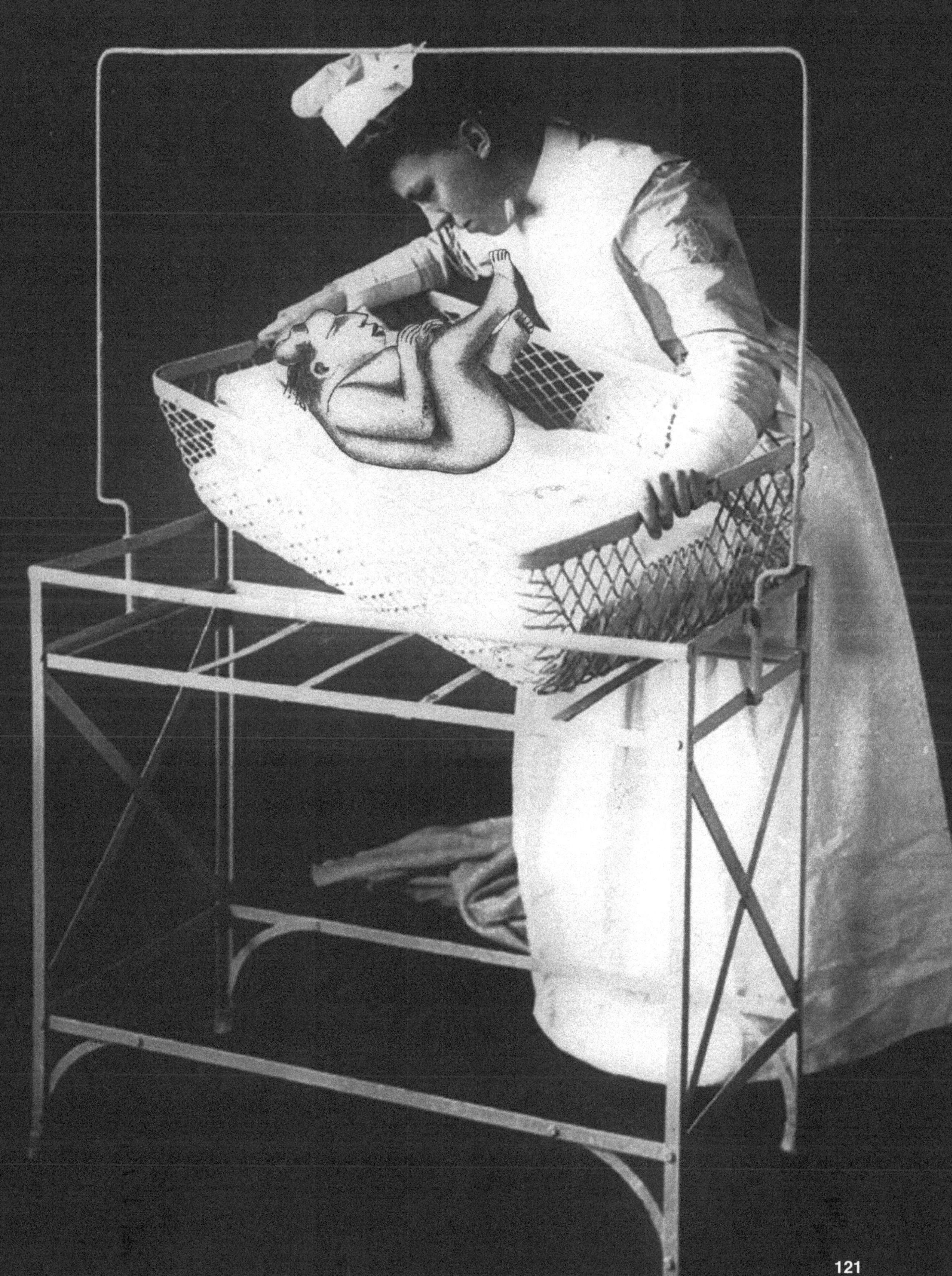

Contents

123	Footsies
124	Hermin's debut
125	Imprison the doves
126	Edna's quandary
127	Zachary's trike
128	Work for sand
129	Approaching shore leave
130	Crup of trea
132	The professor who destroyed science
133	Balance
134	This is why she left you
136	YOU
137	Hi there
138	Substitute teacher
140	Druce yearbook
141	Dainty skull
142	The Internet justifies me
143	Online strategy
144	Measurement lad
146	Xerox over Manhattan

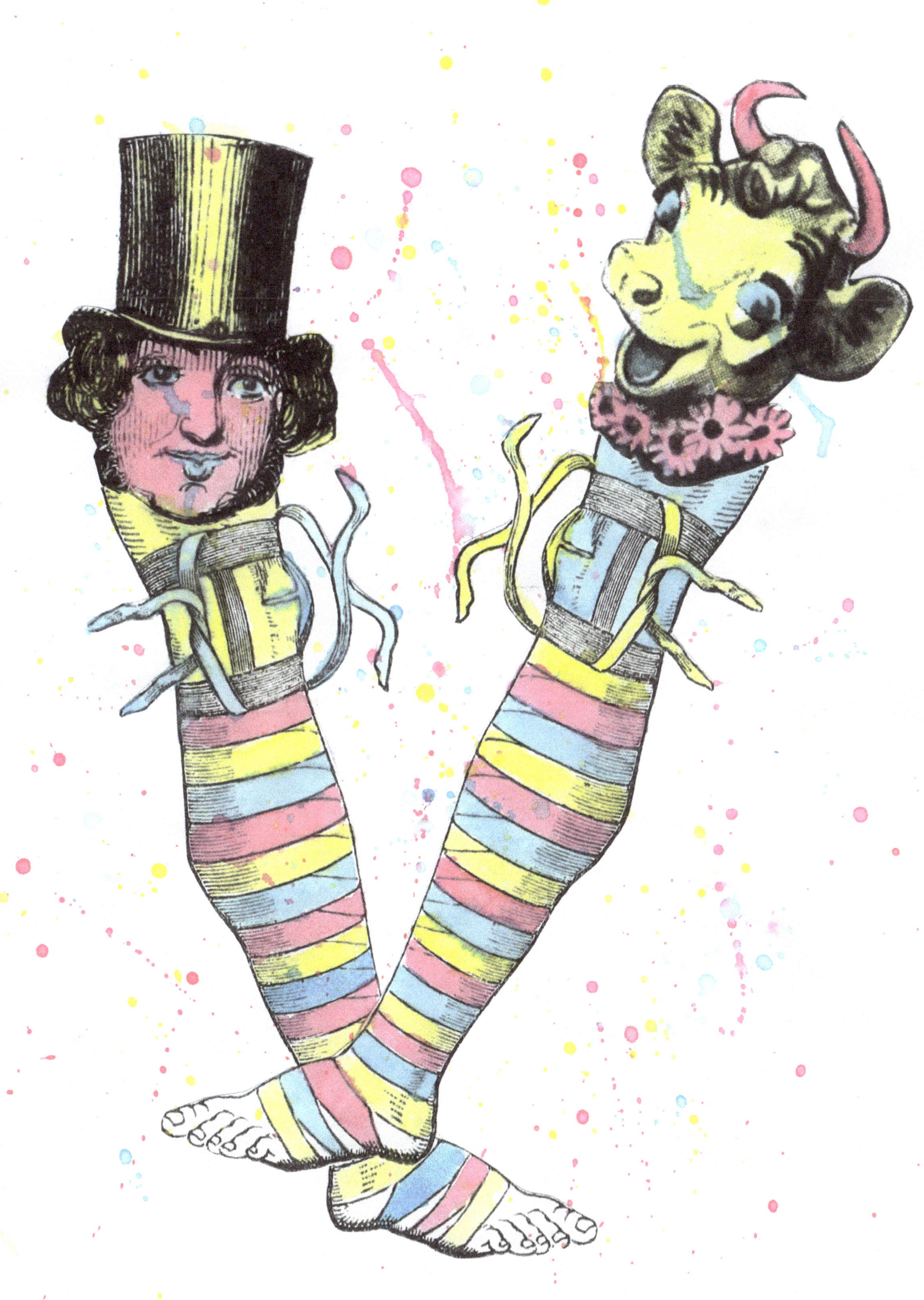

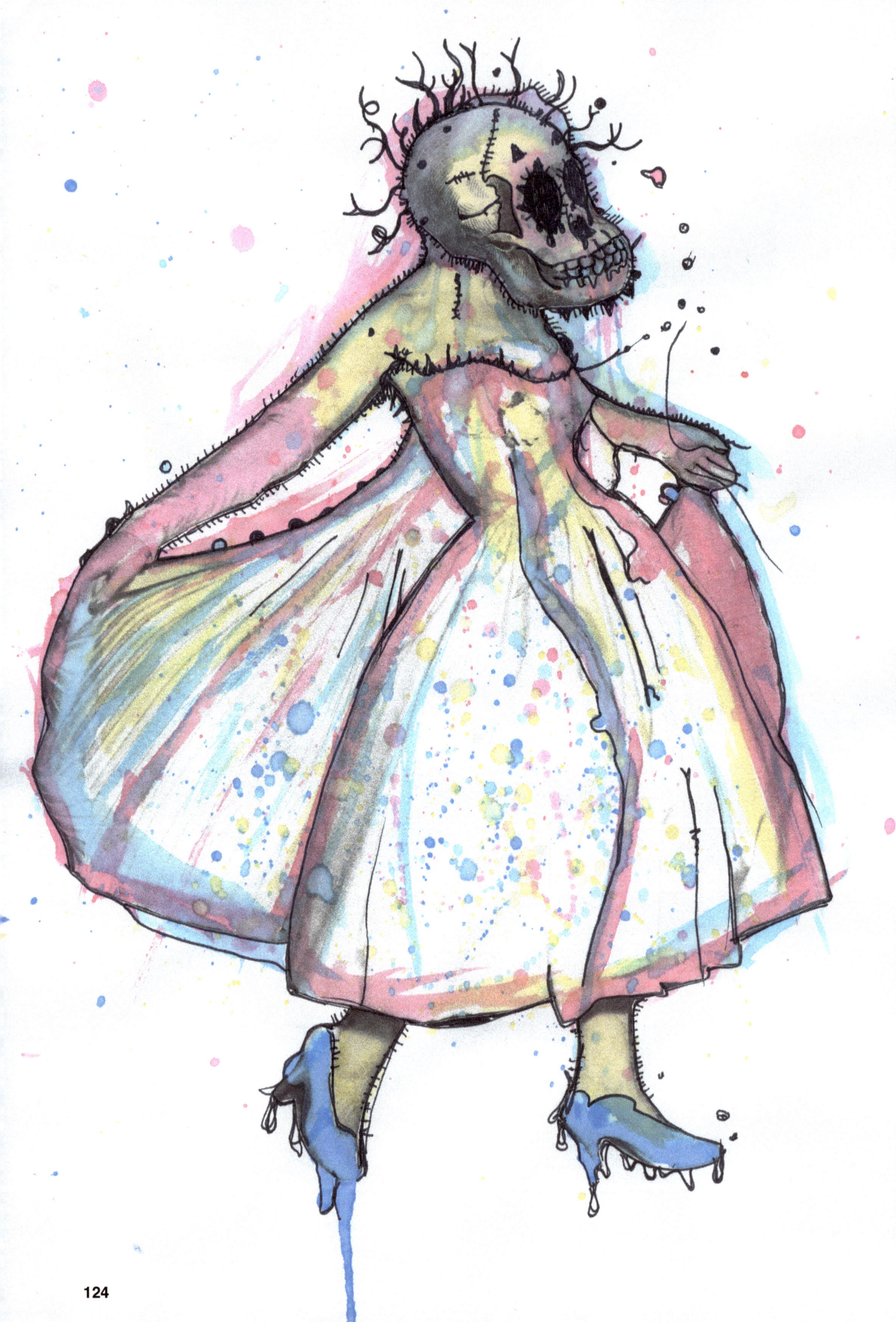

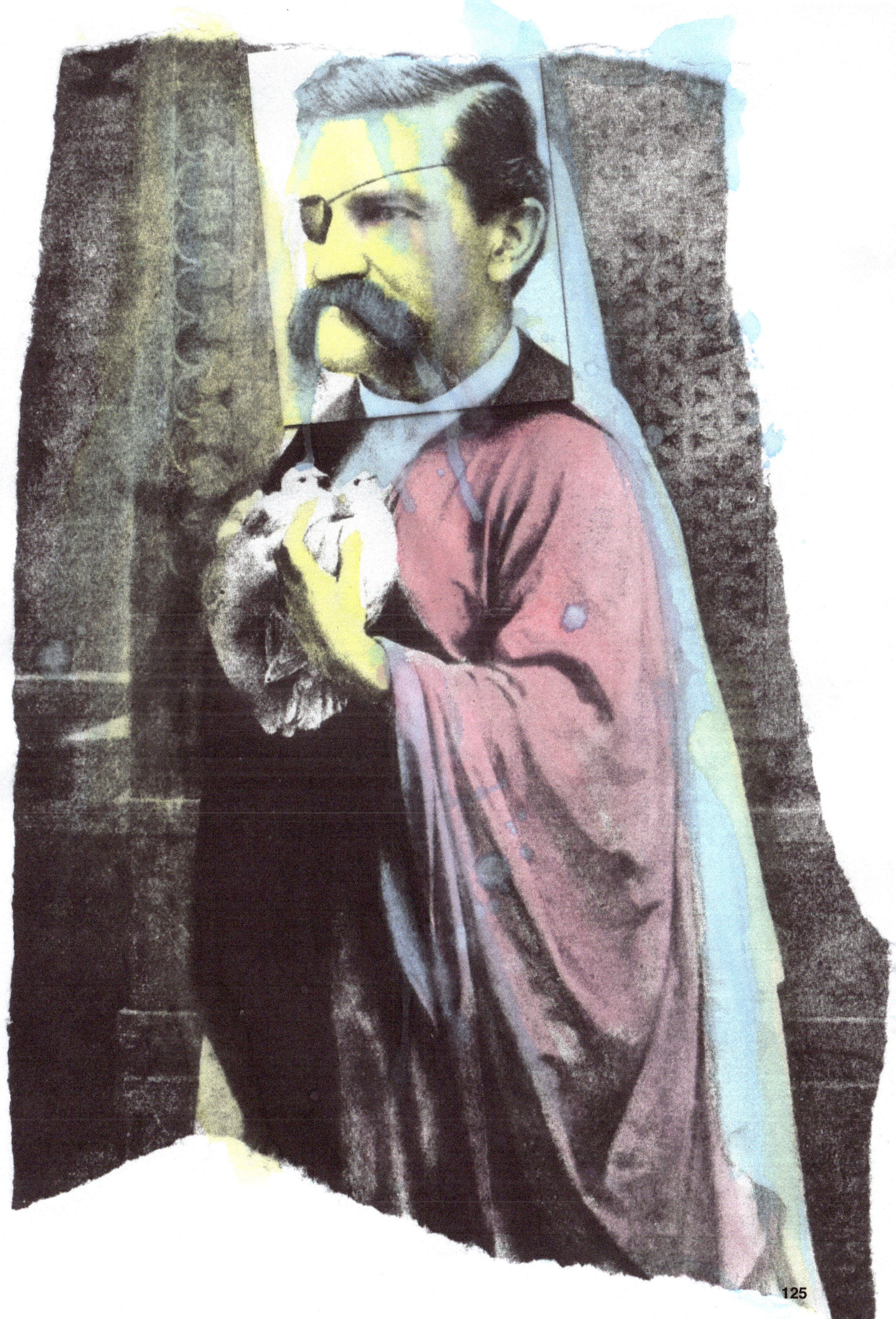

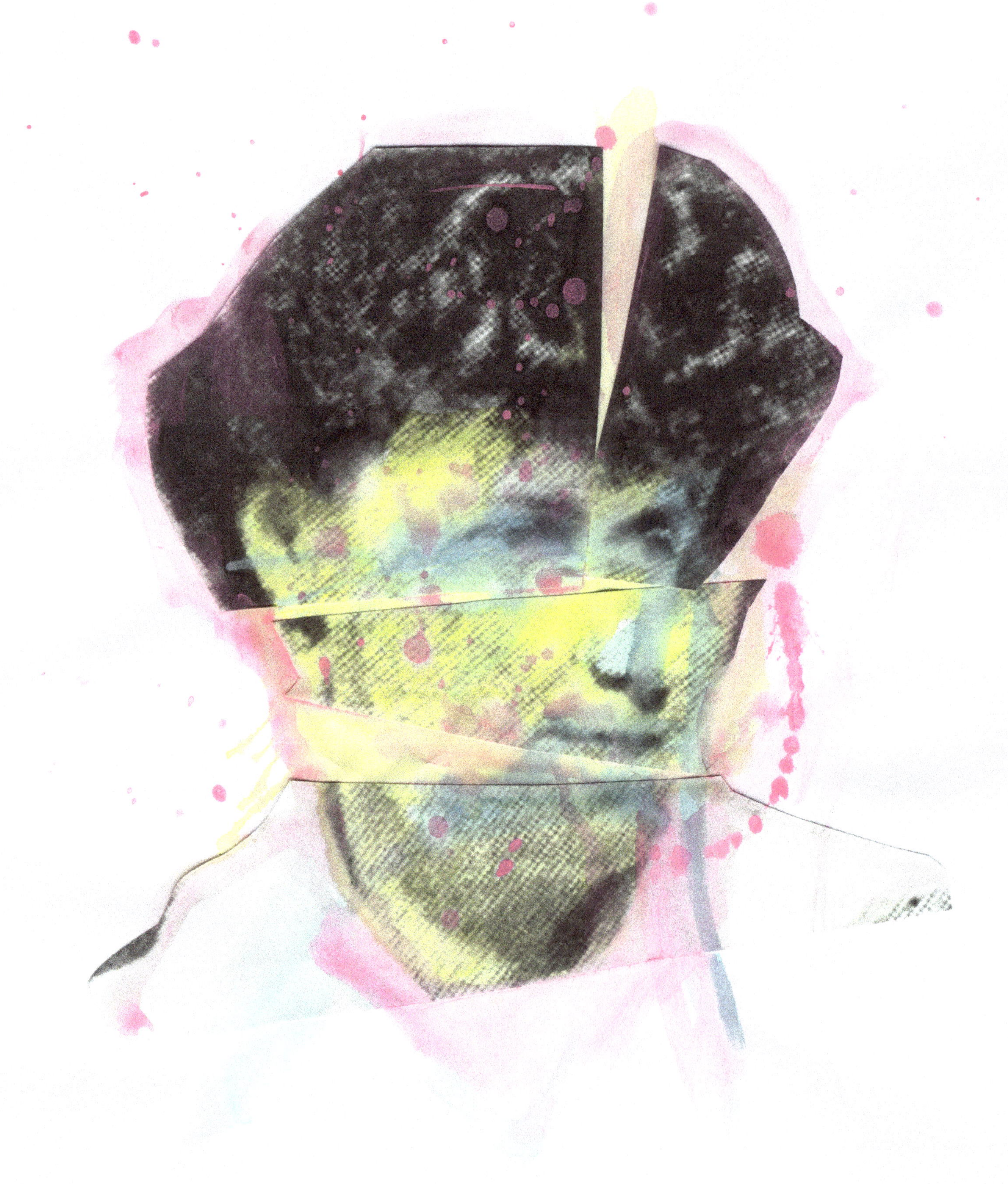

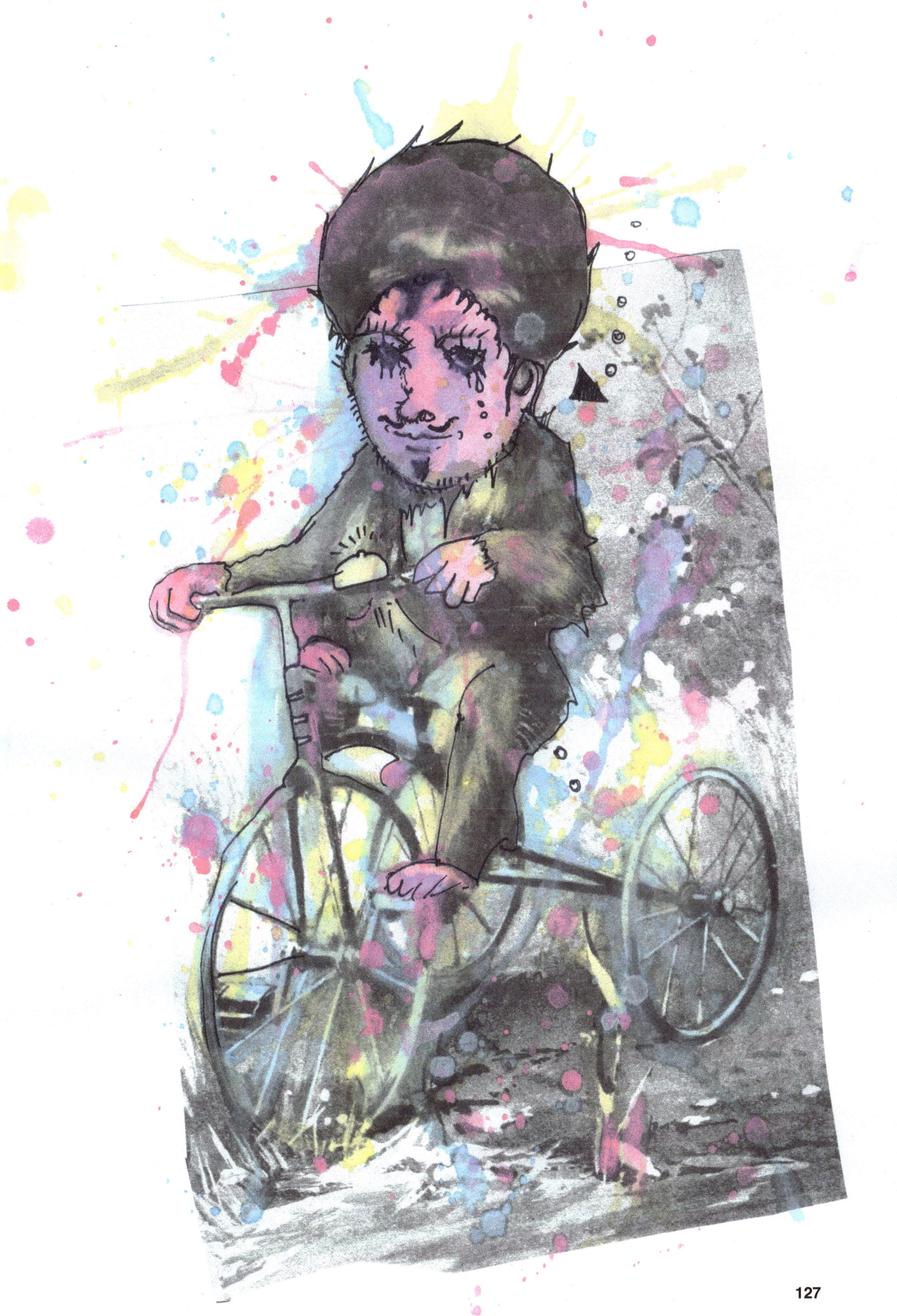

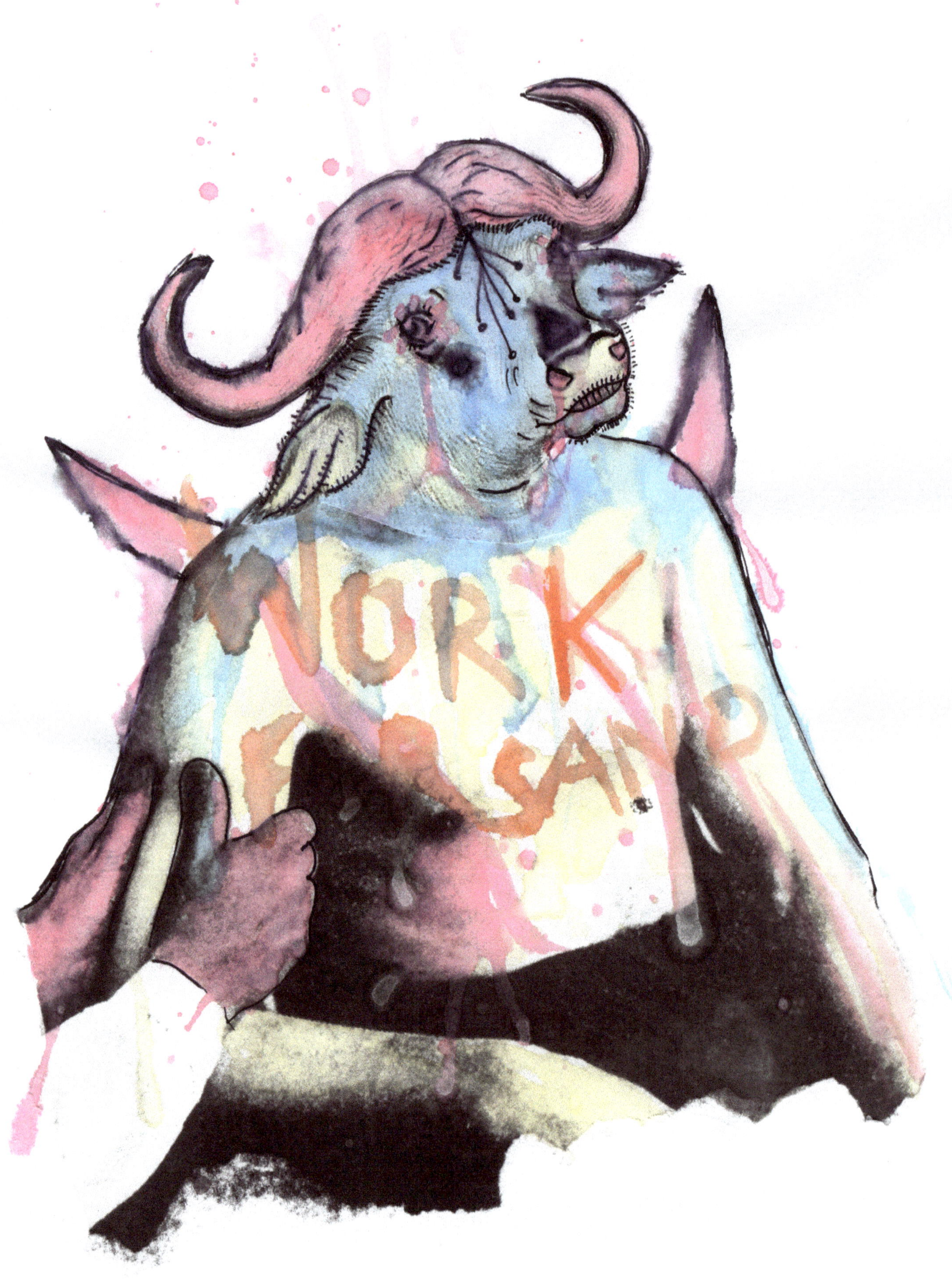
WORK
SAND

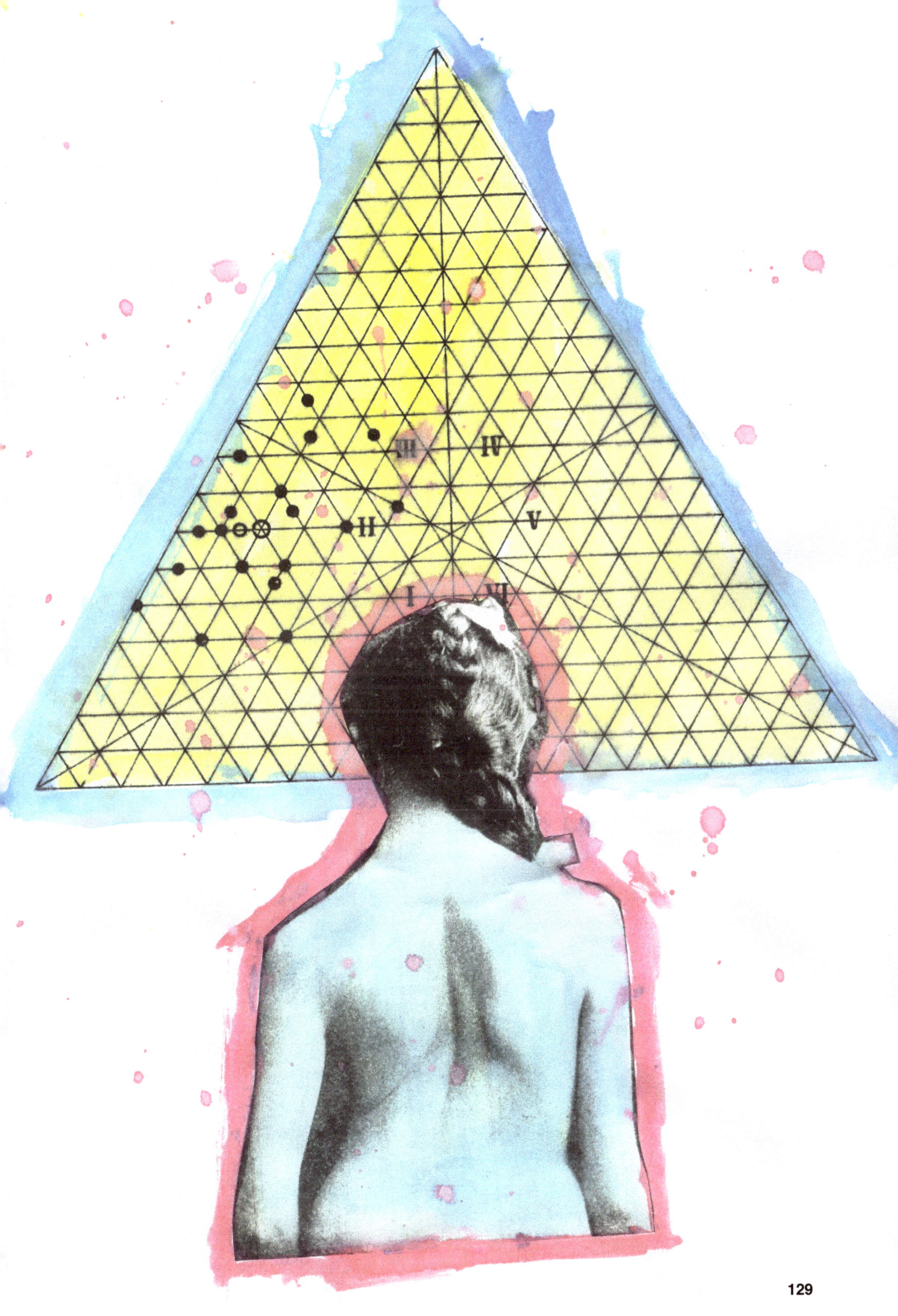

III
IV
II
V
I
VI

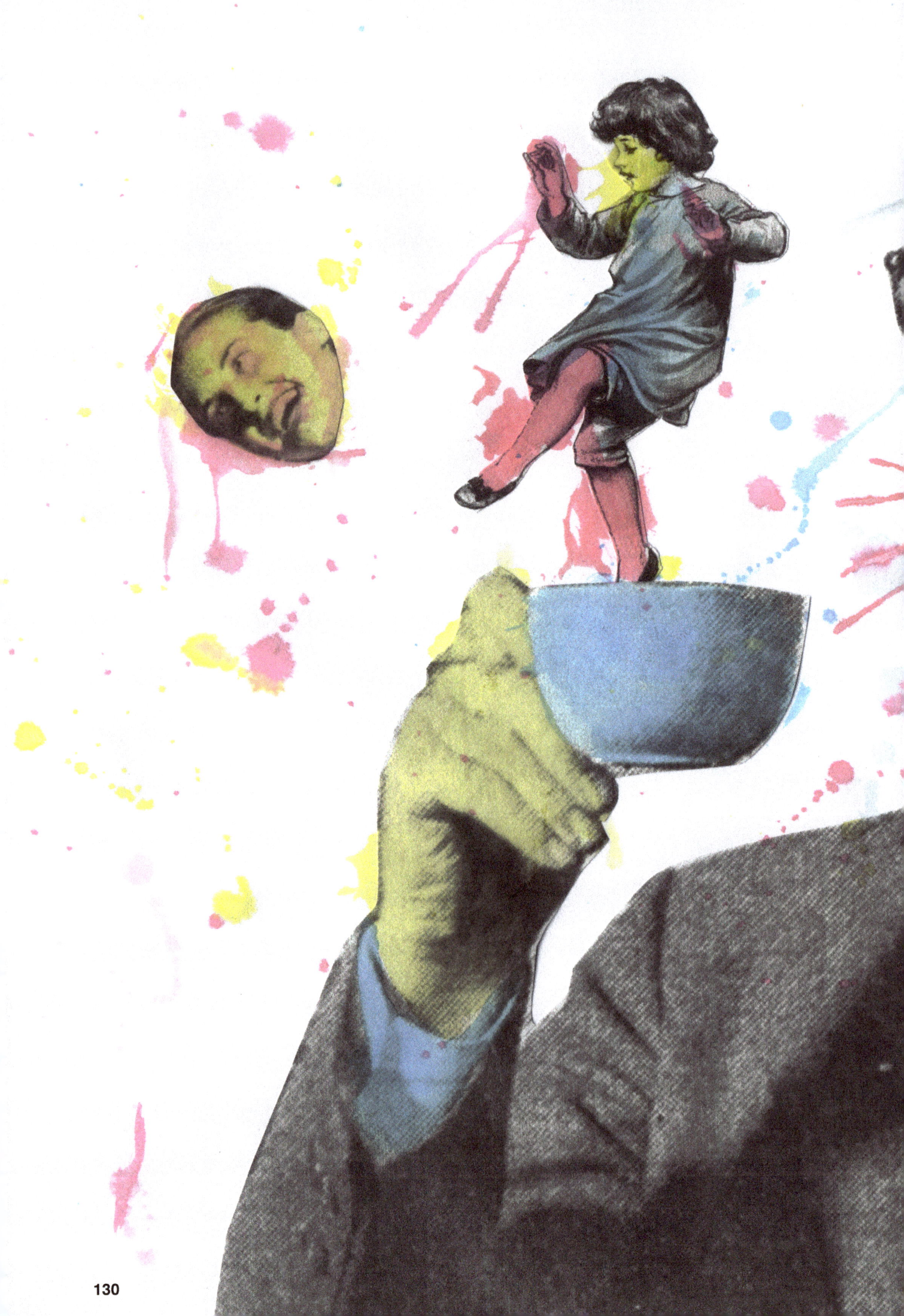

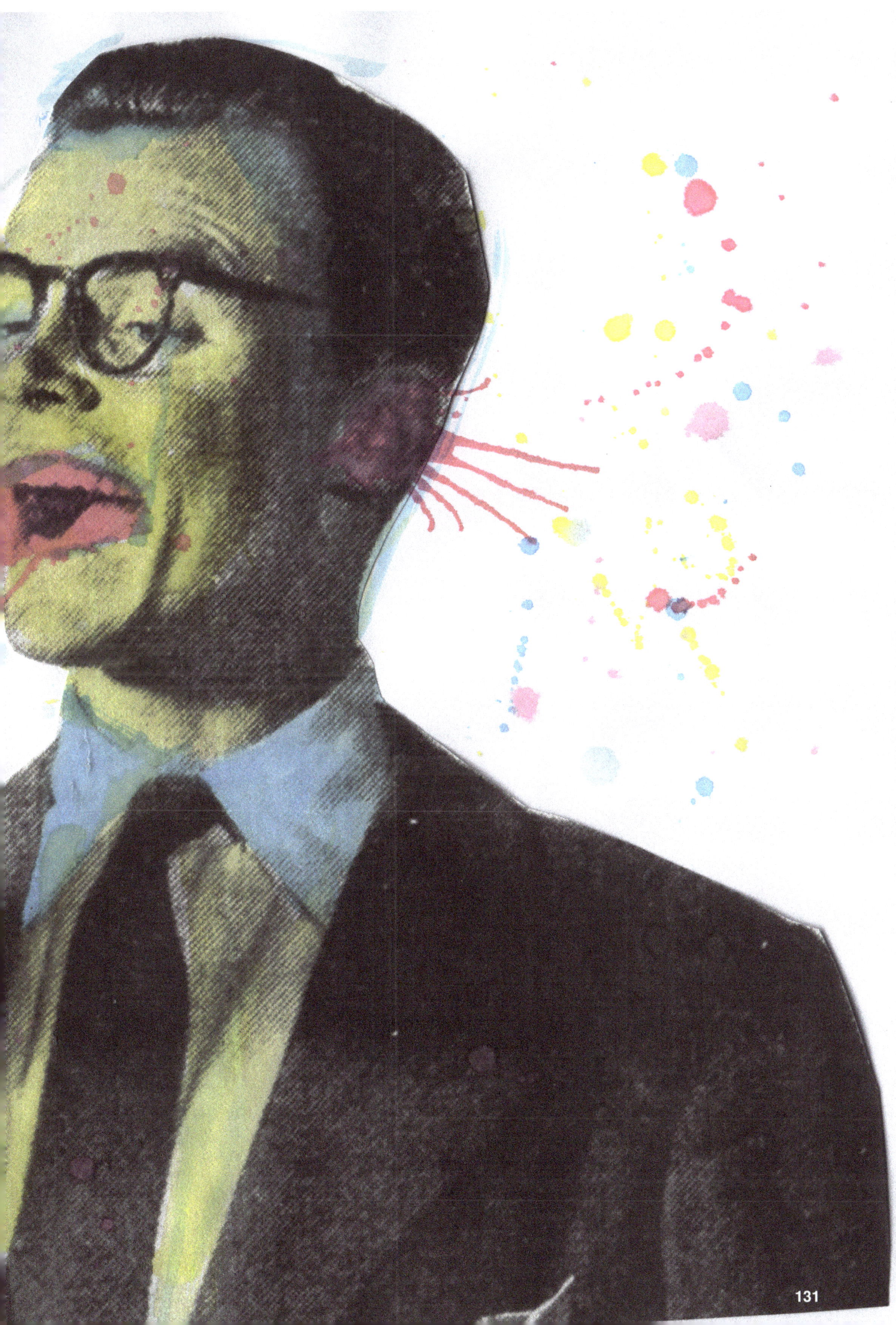

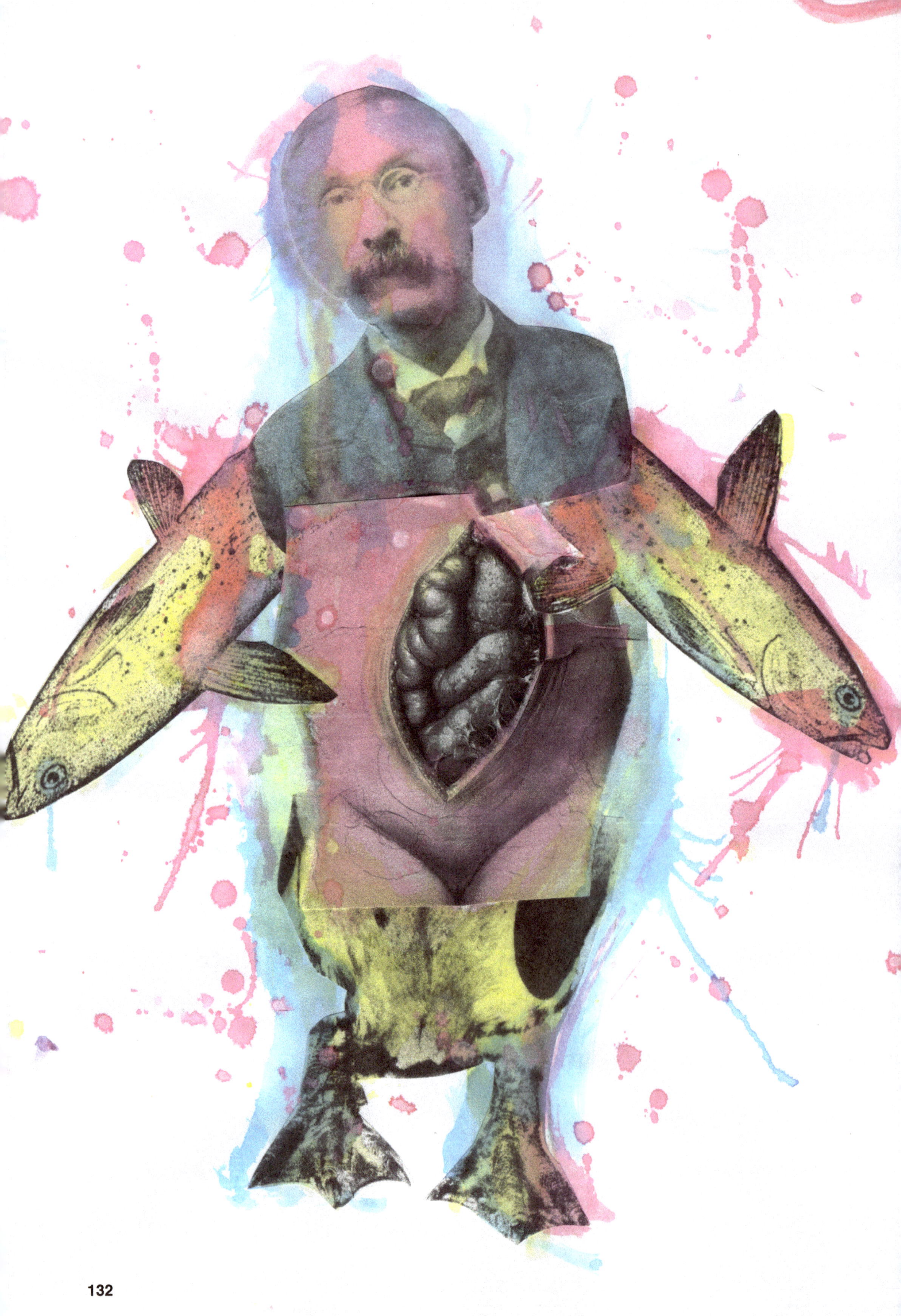

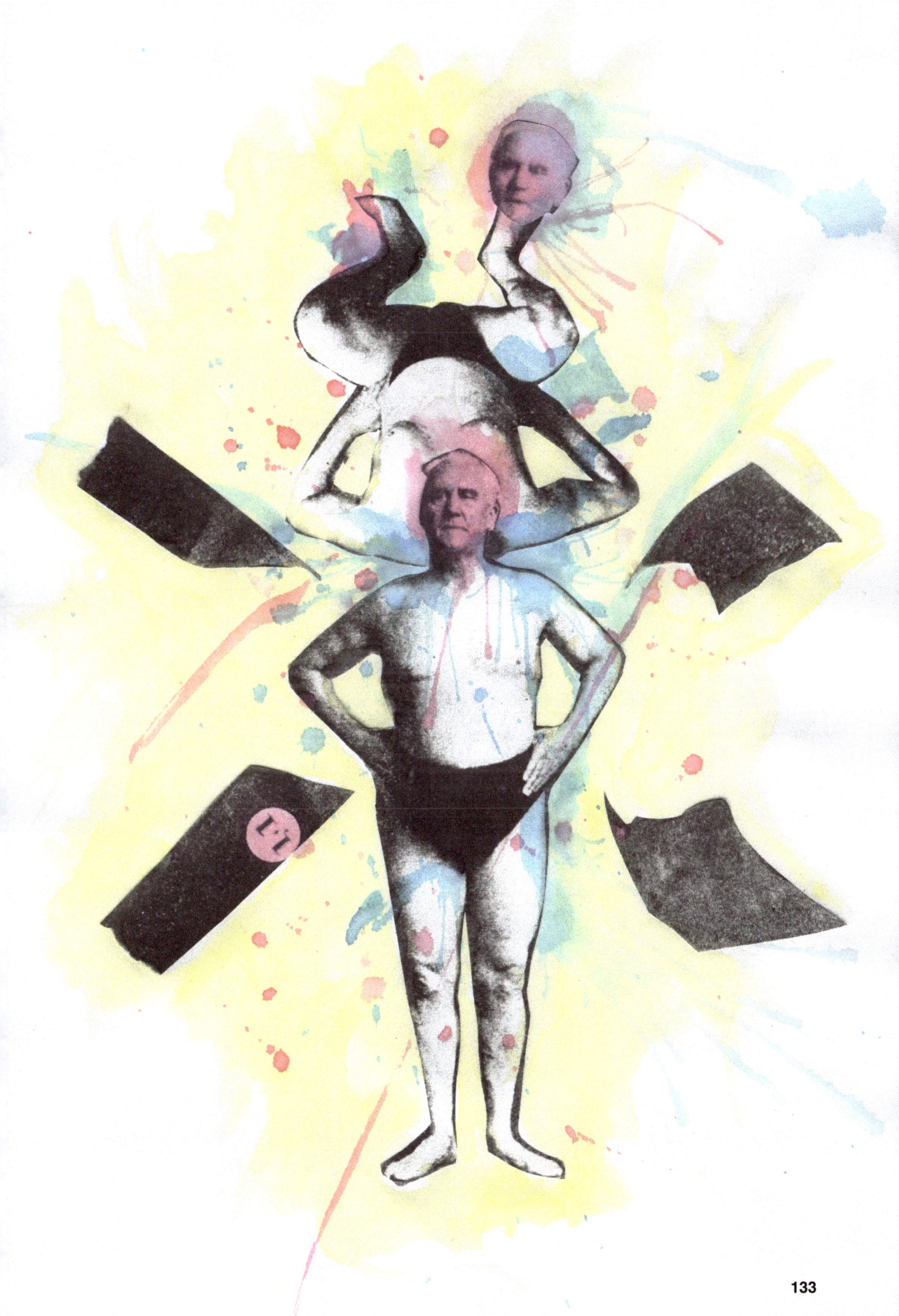

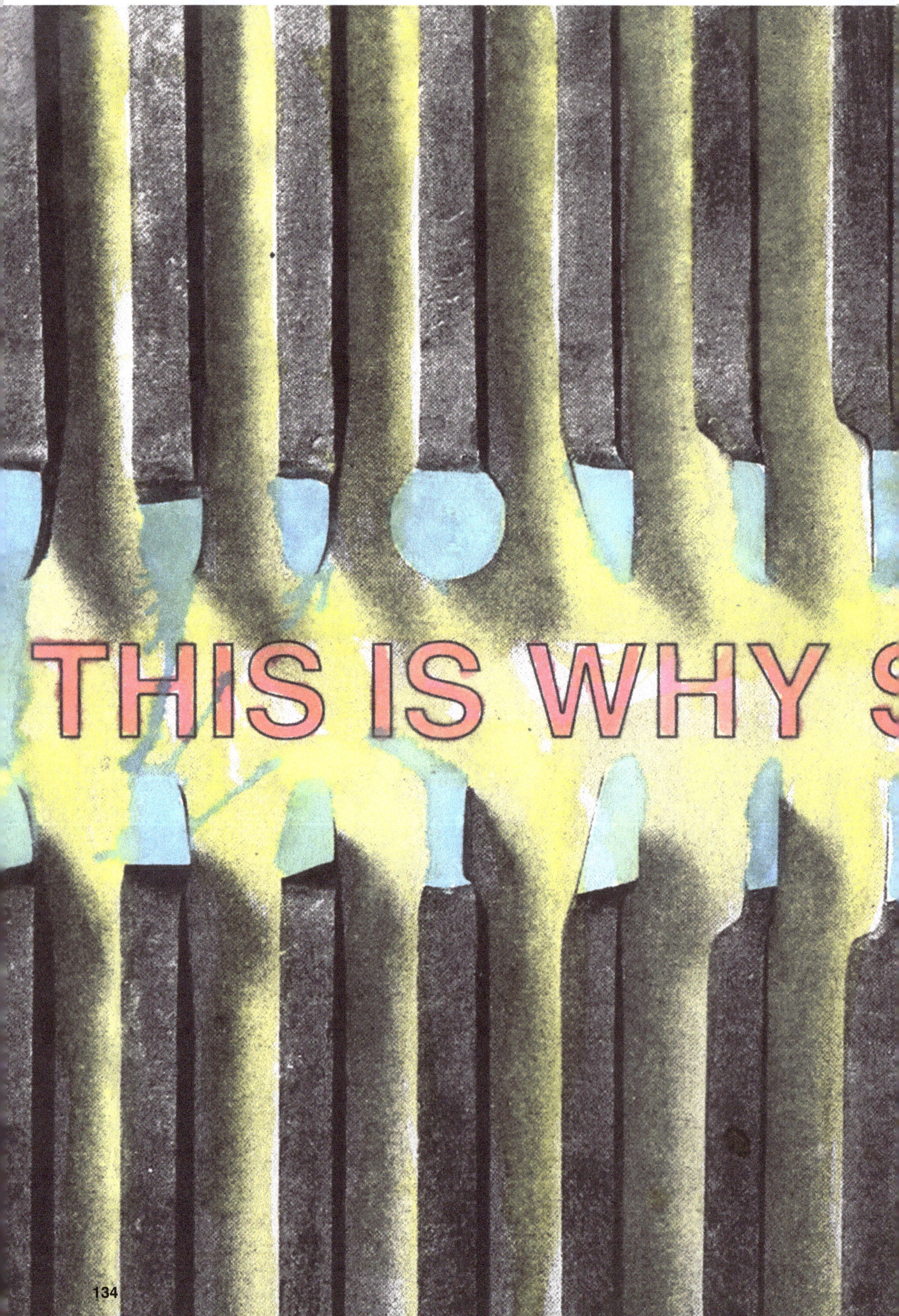
THIS IS WHY S

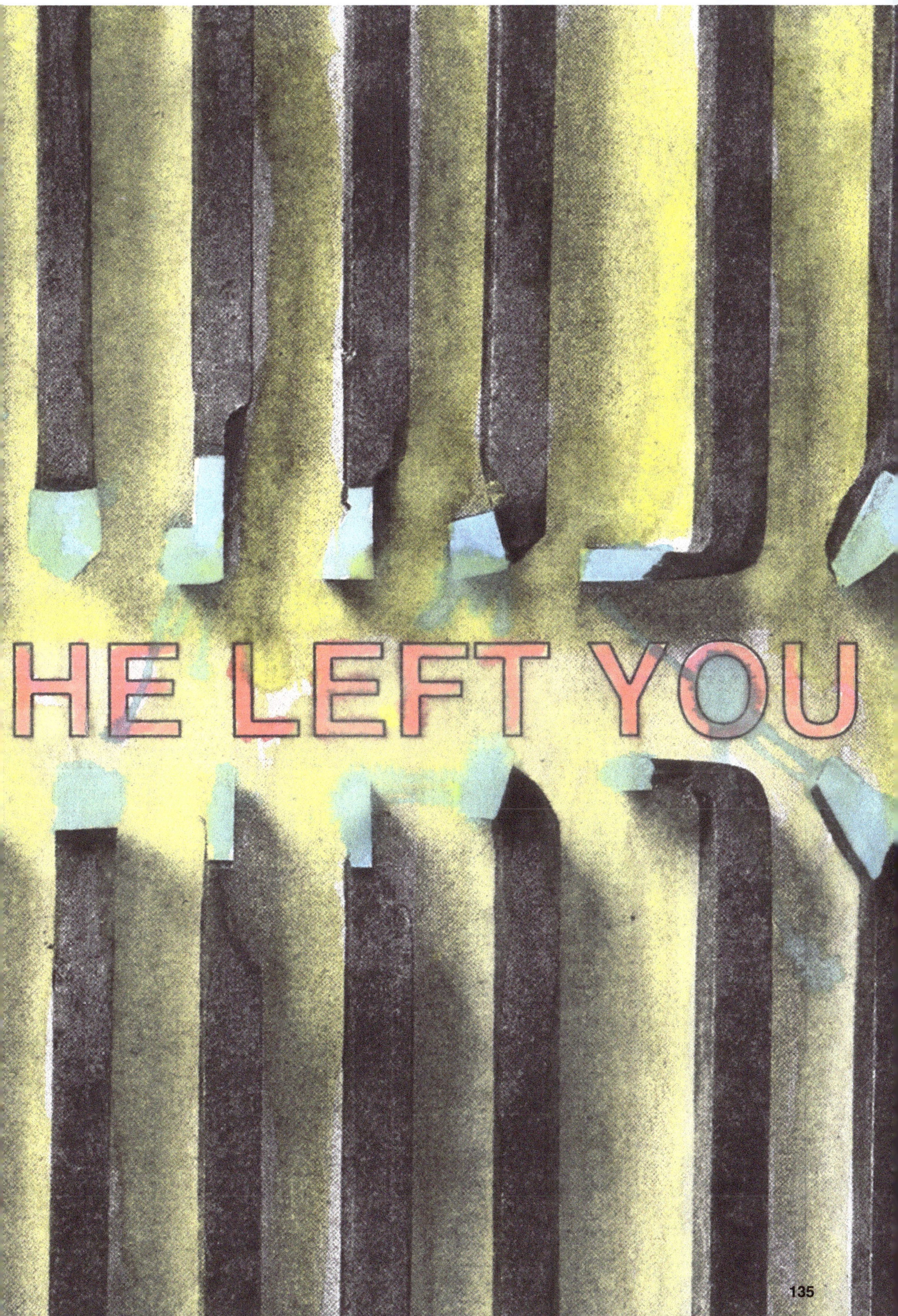
HE LEFT YOU

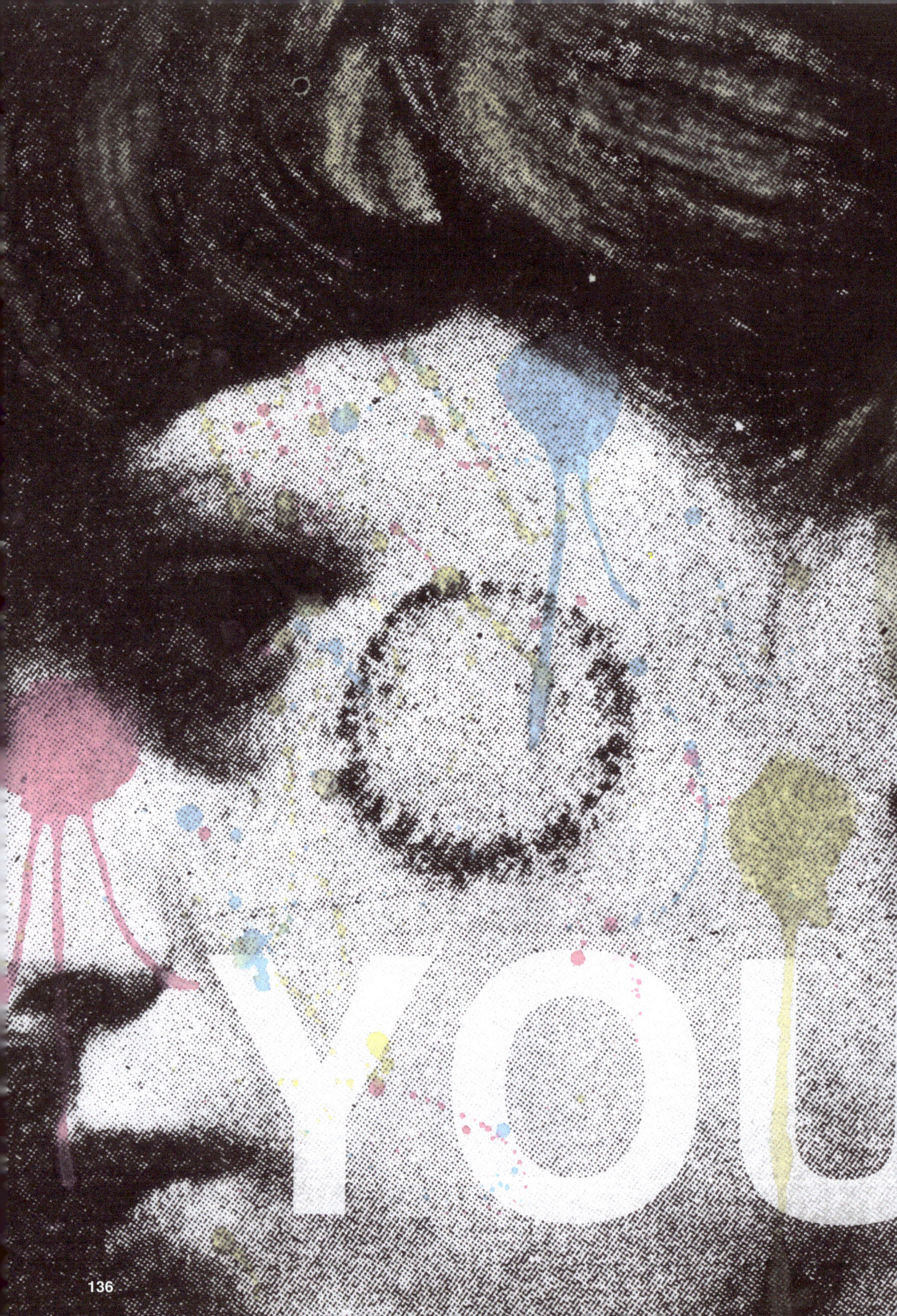

YOU

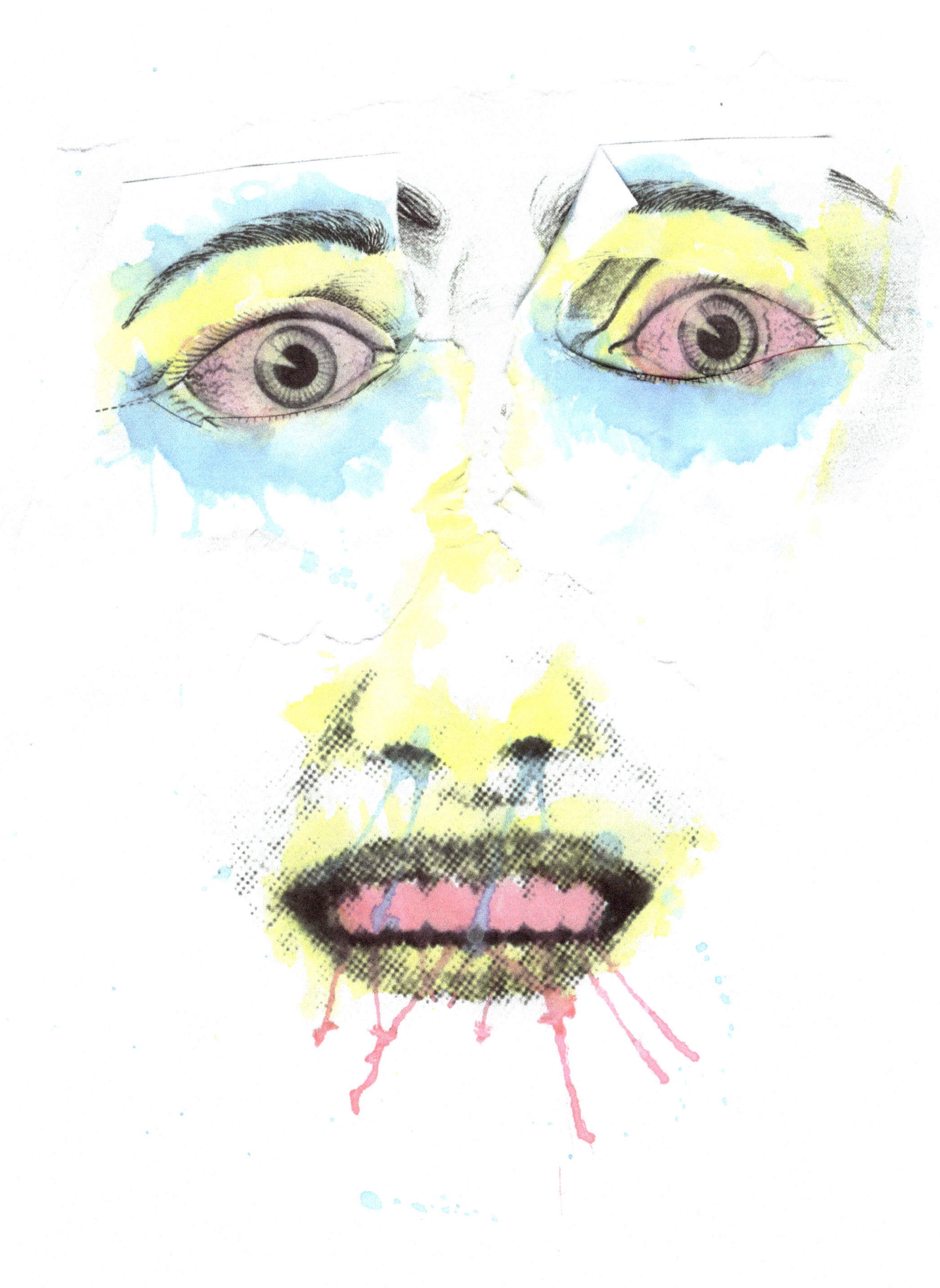

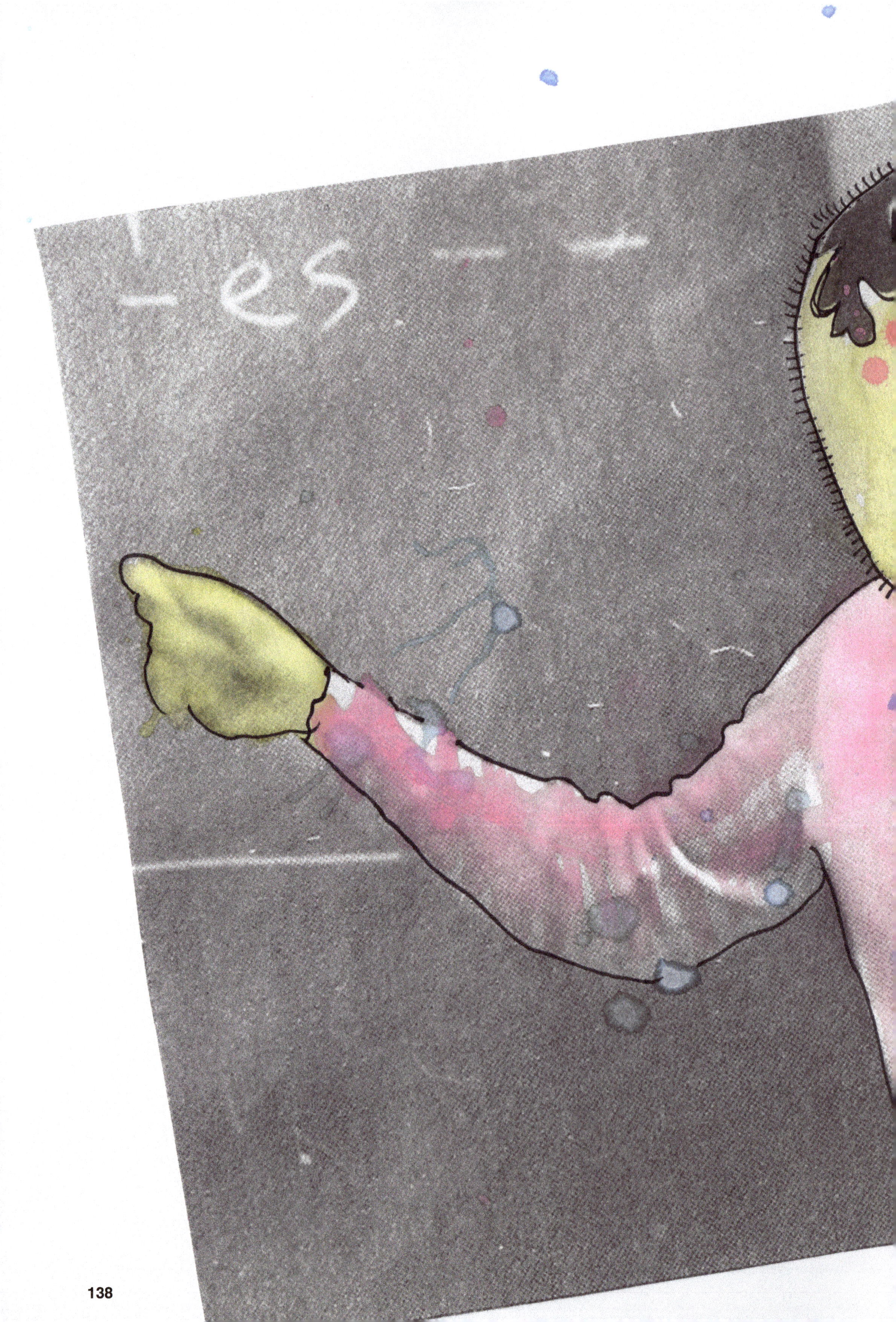

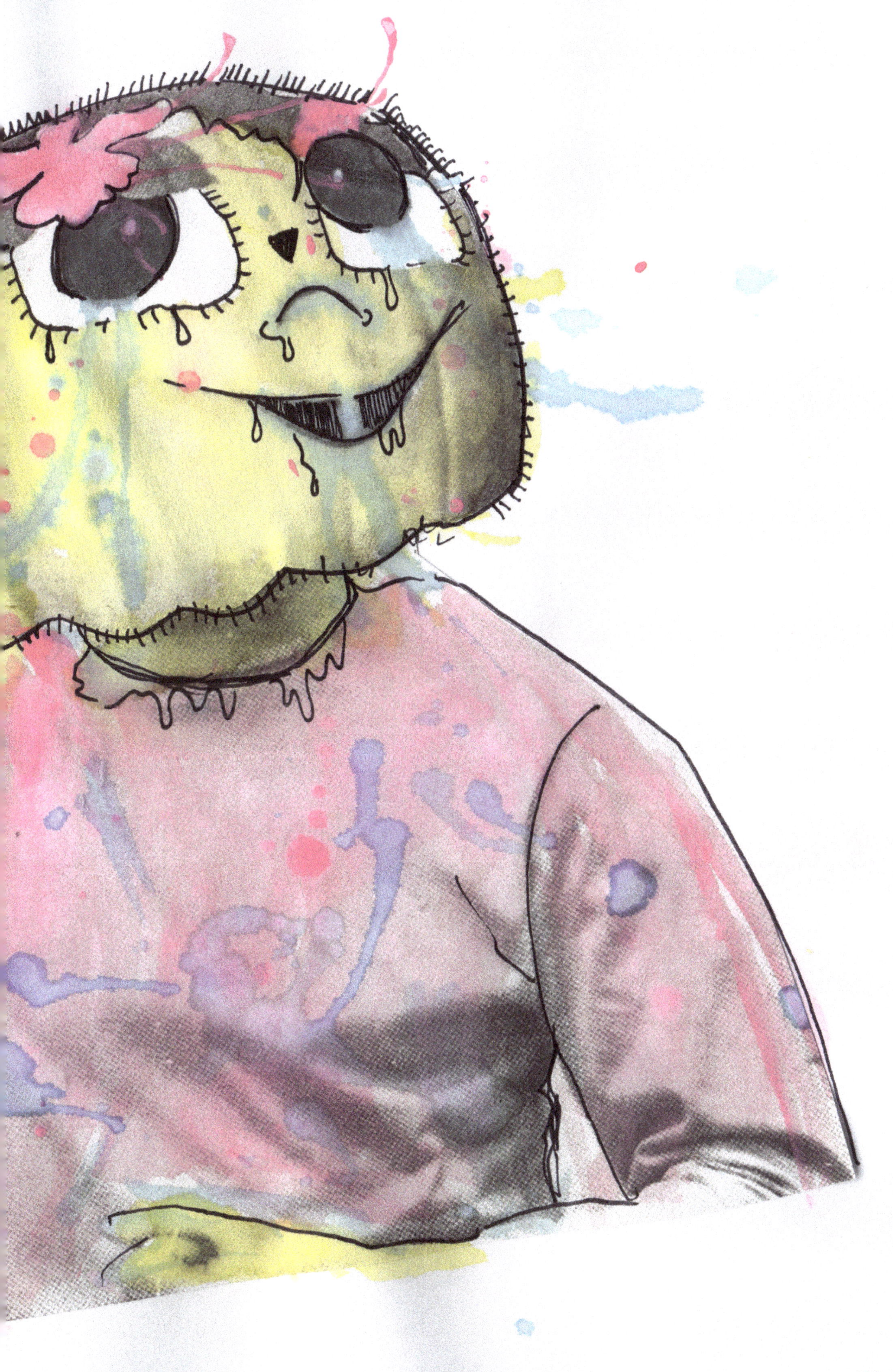

DRUCE YEARBOOK

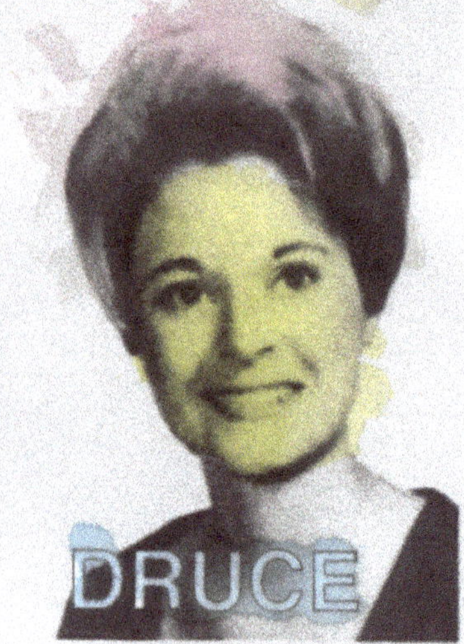

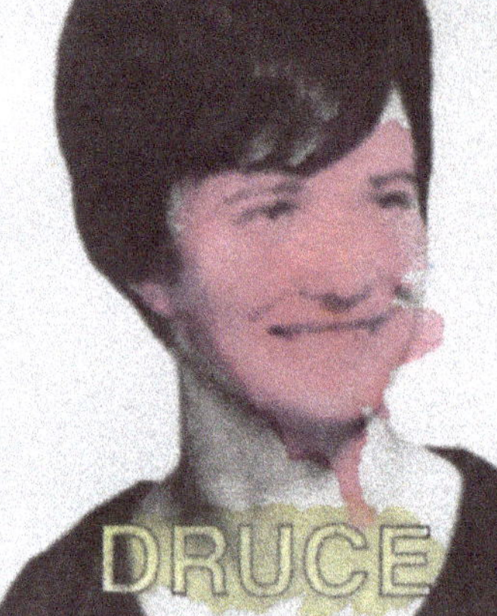

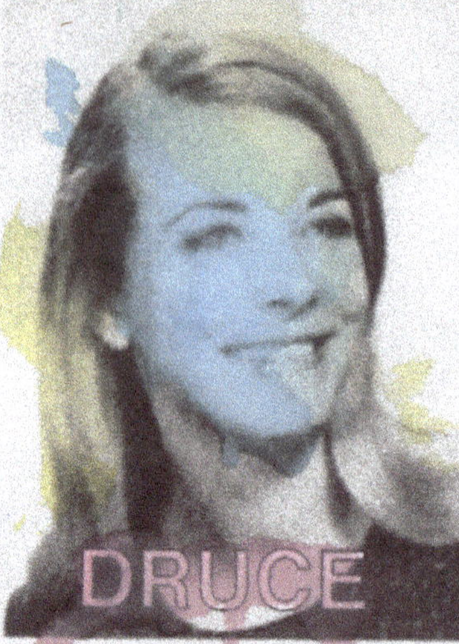

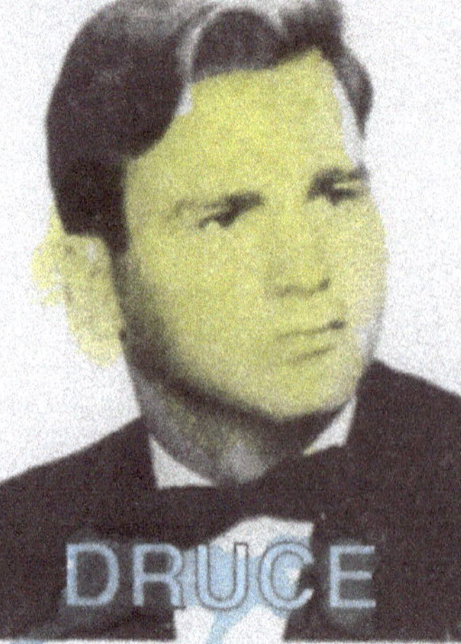

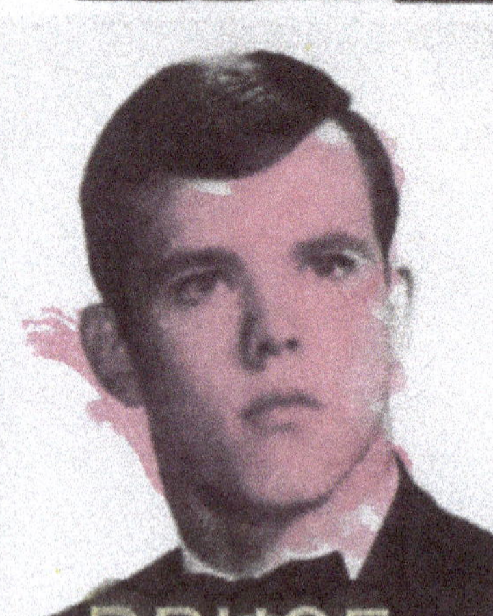

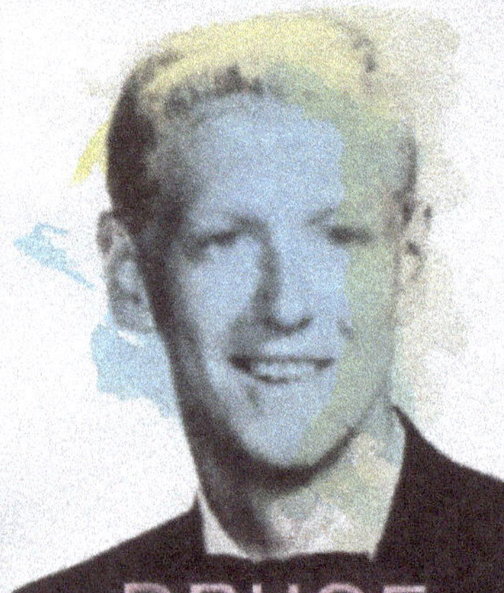

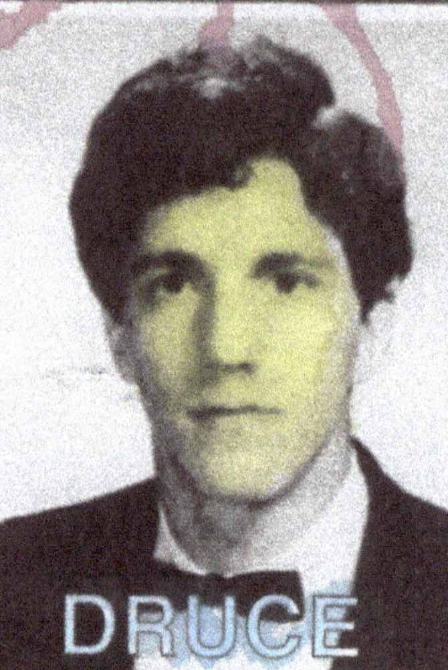

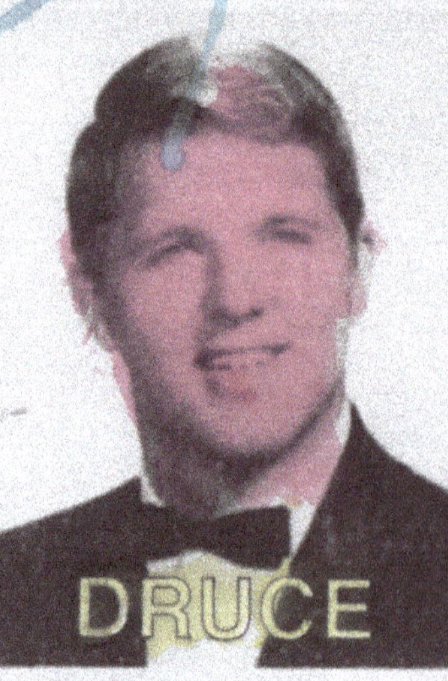

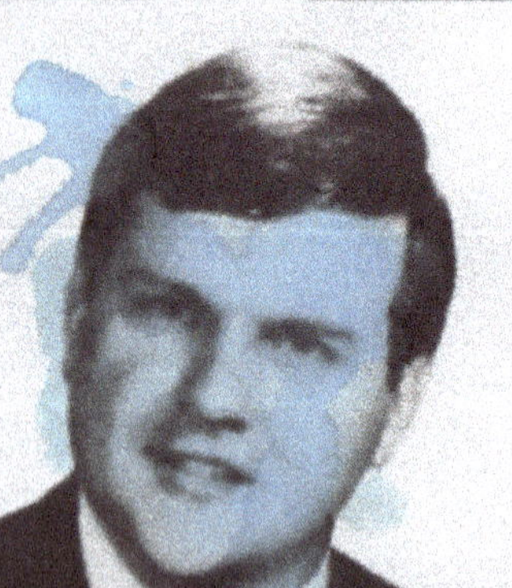

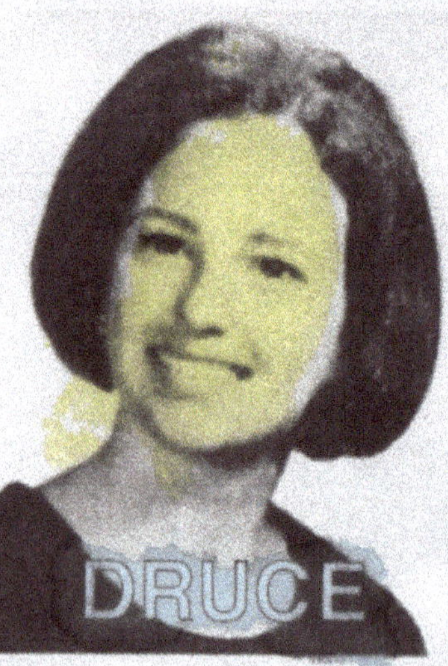

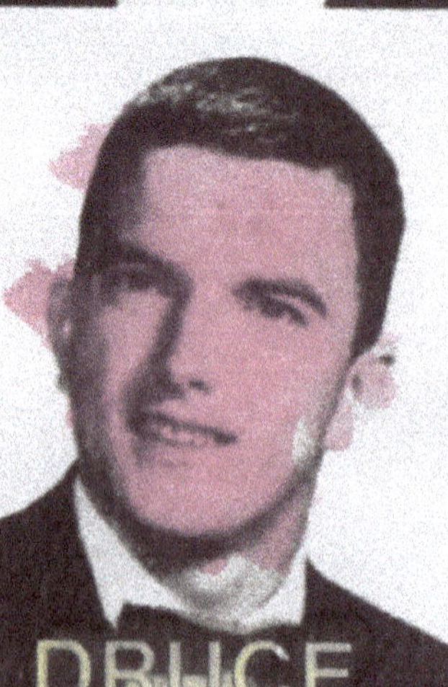

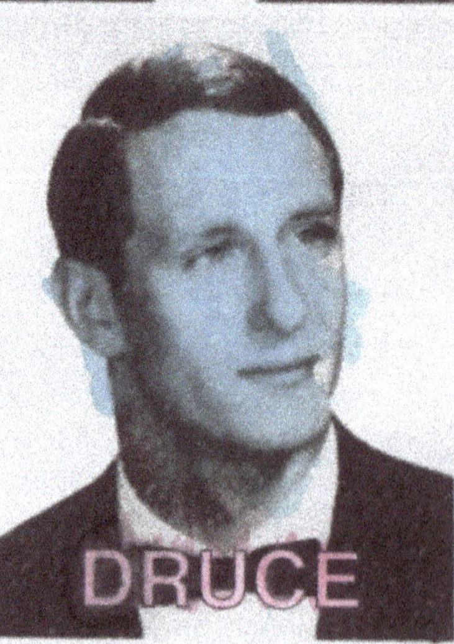

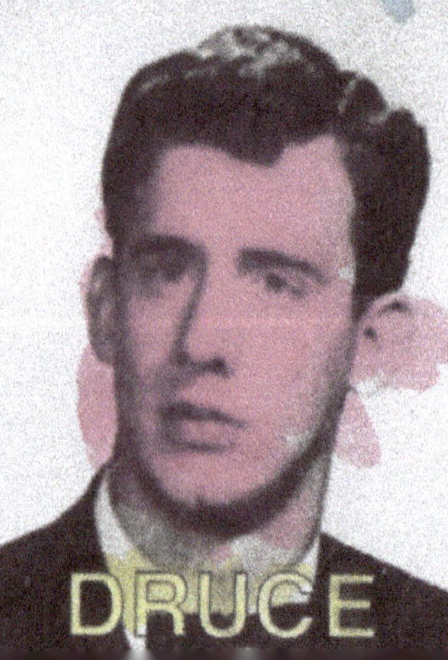

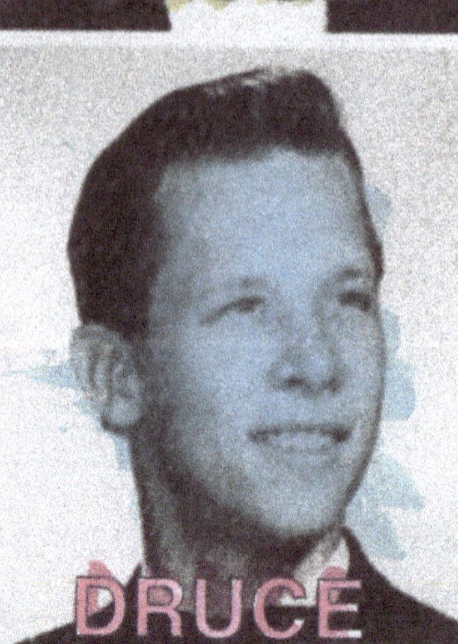

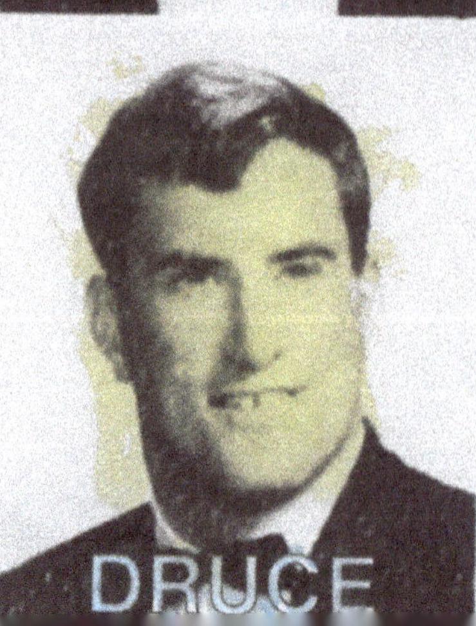

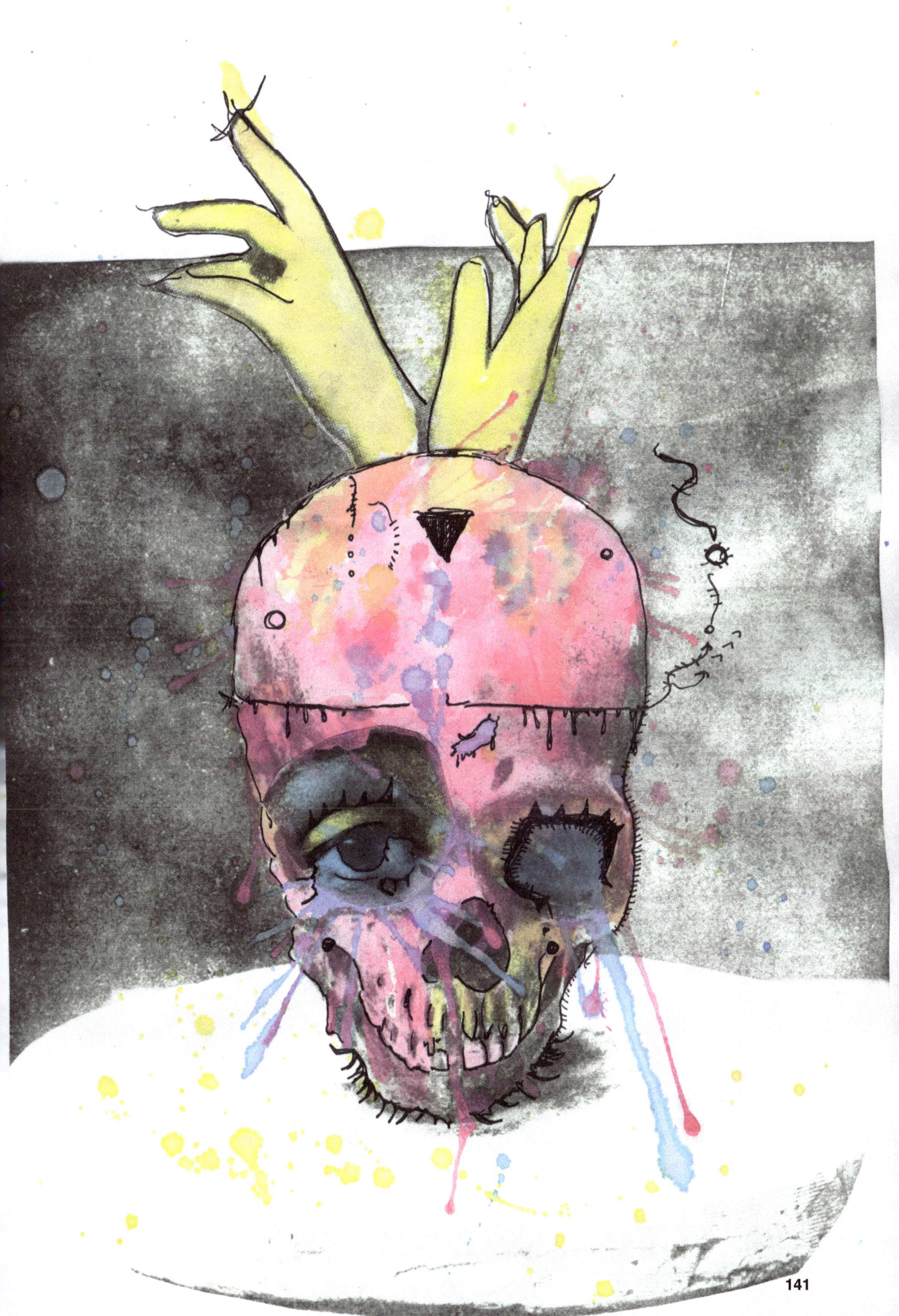

THE INTERNET
JUSTIFIES ME
THE INTERNET
THE INTERNET
JUSTIFIES ME
JUSTIFIES
INTERNET
THE INTERNET
JUSTIFIES ME
THE INTERNET
JUSTIFIES ME
JUSTIFIES
PLEASE LIKE!

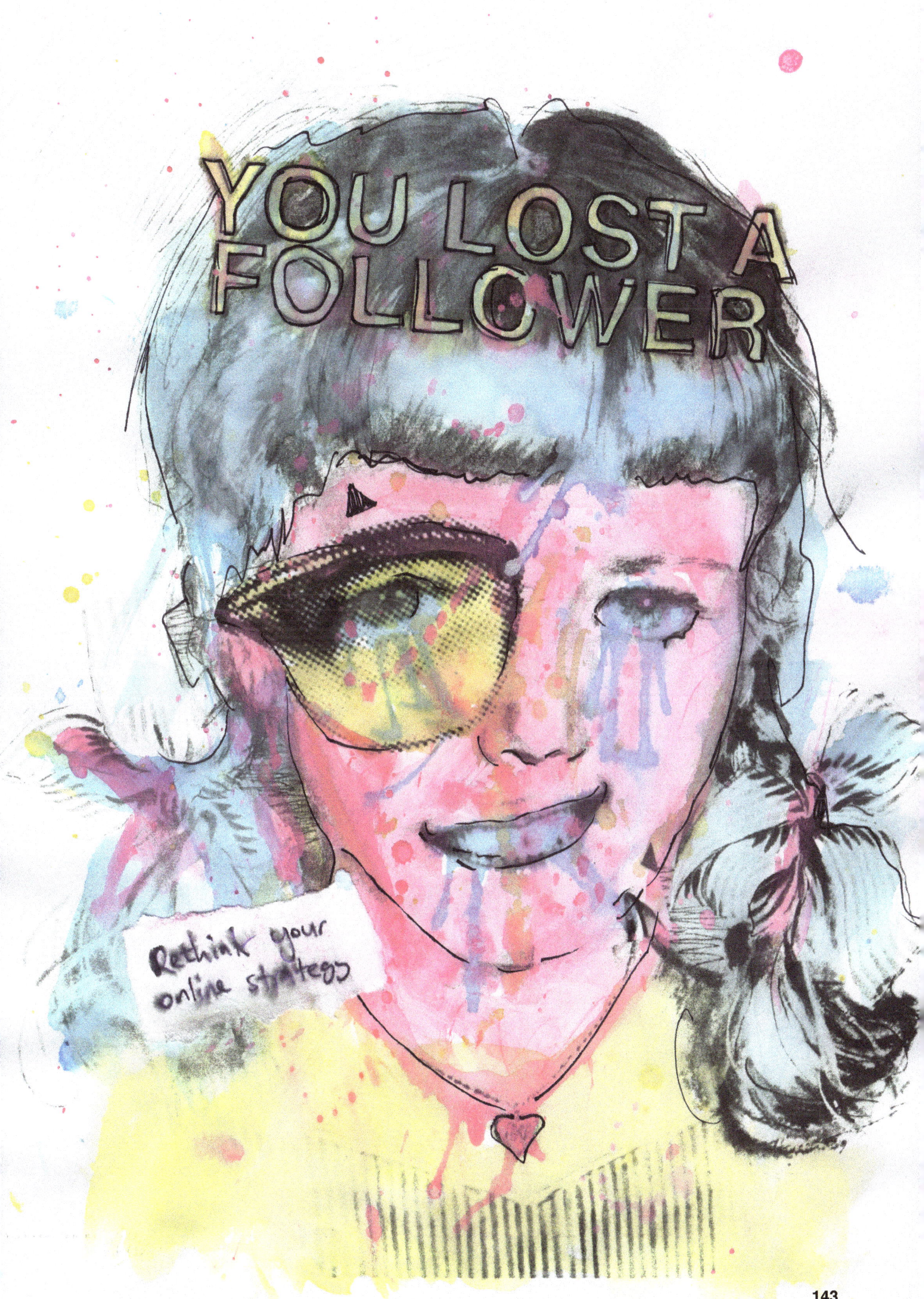

YOU LOST A FOLLOWER
Rethink your online strategy

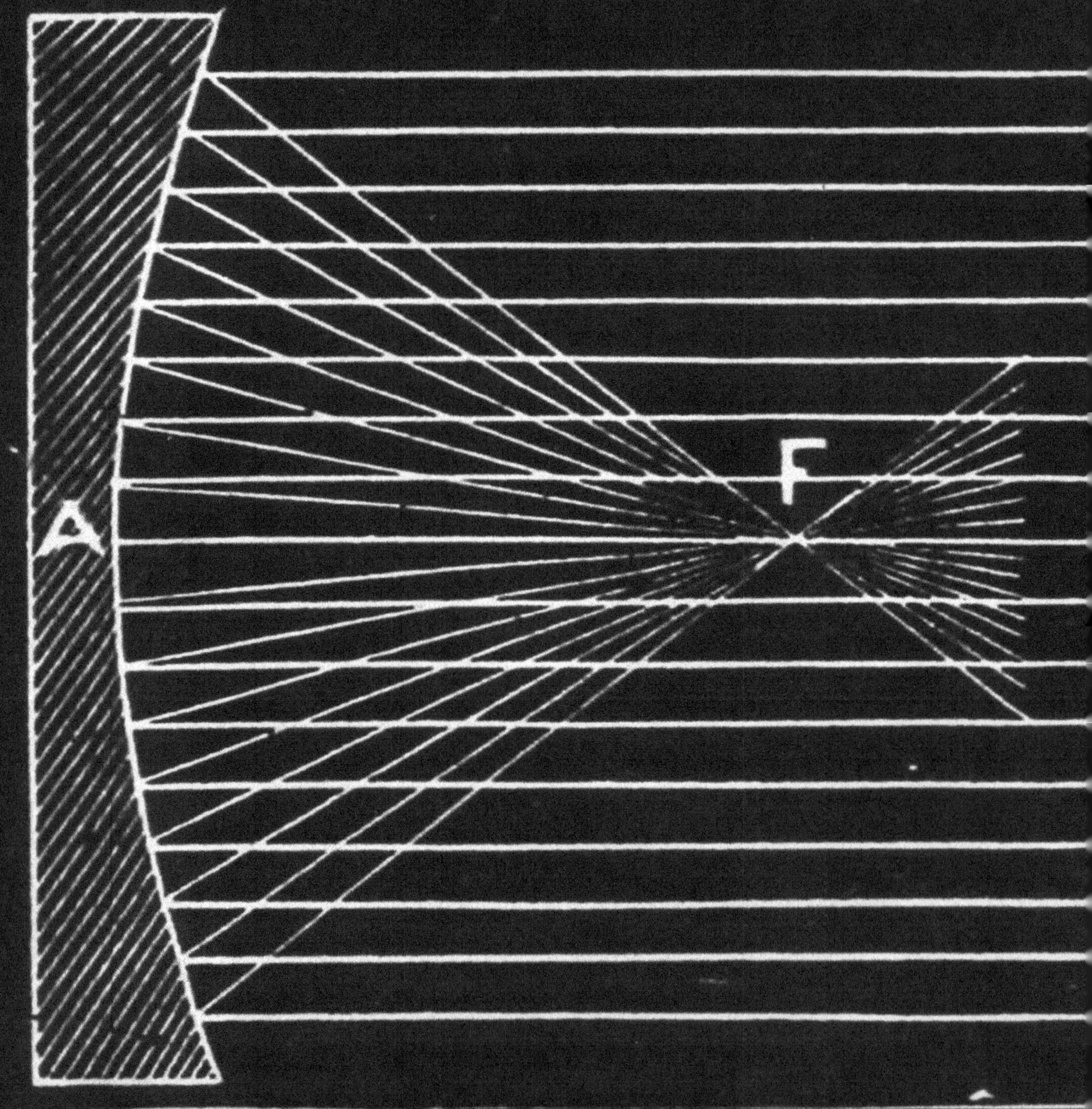

A
F

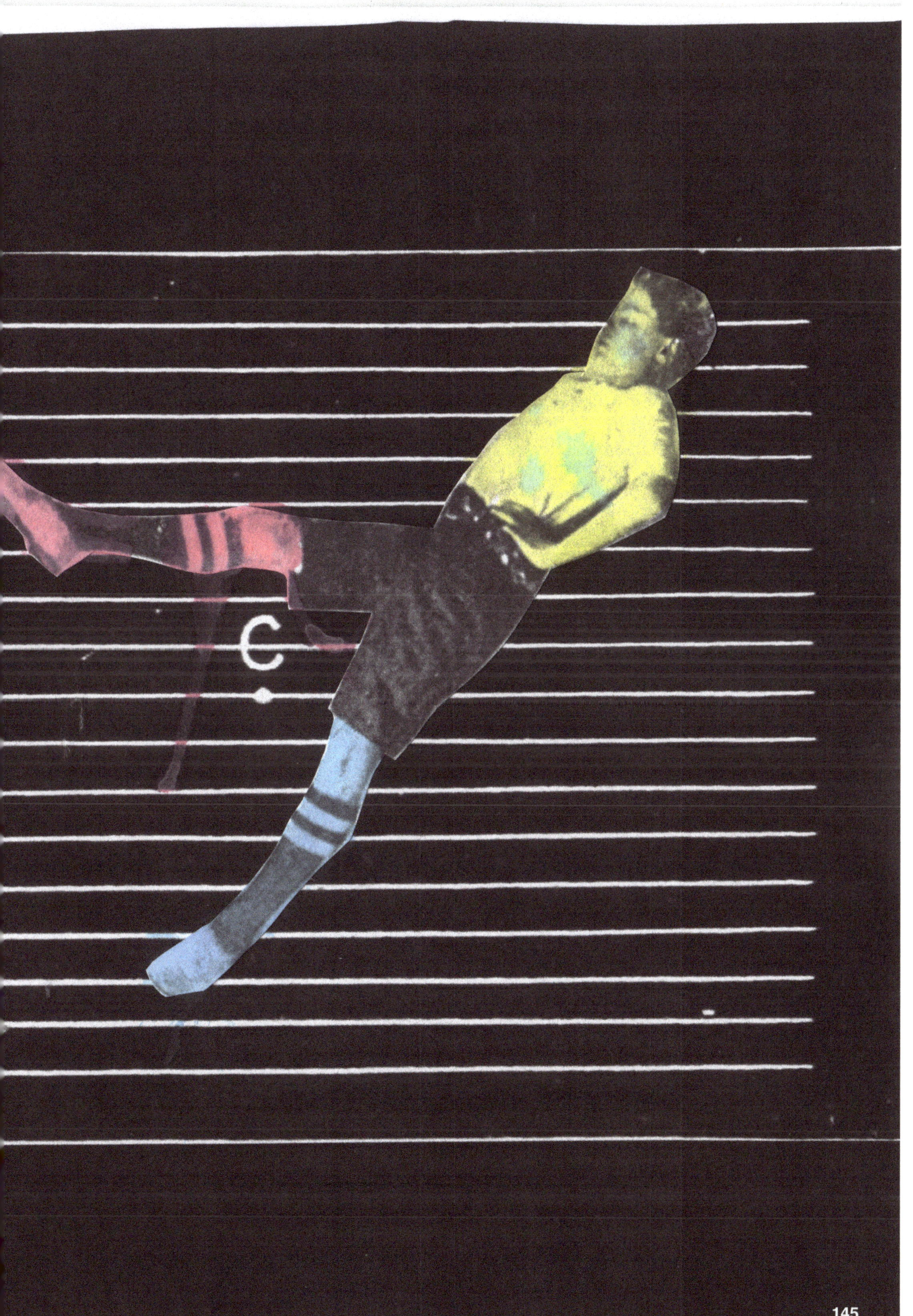

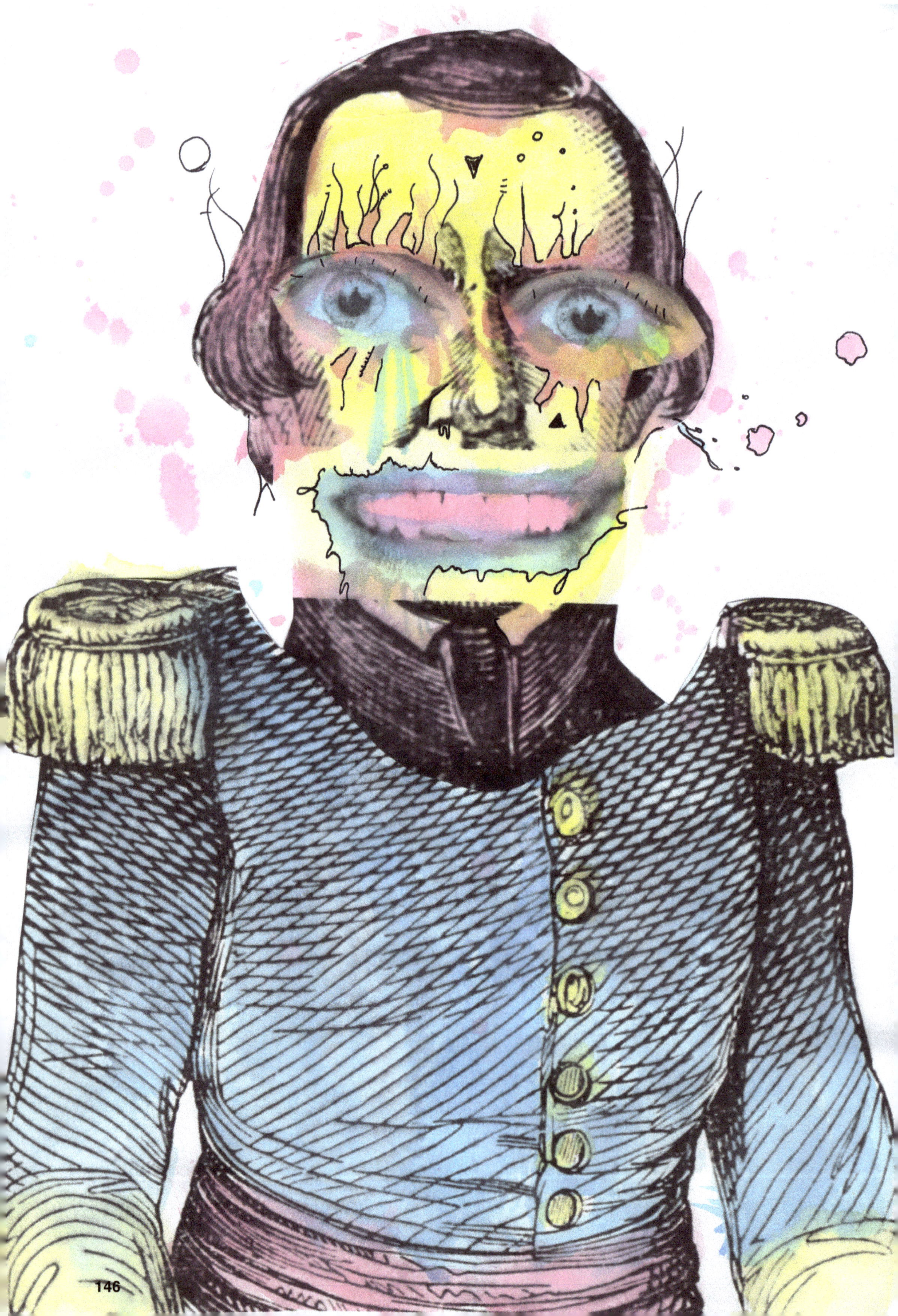

SADLY

SKIPPING

MERRILY

I wondered which of you fixed the game. To make me win my formal hen. We lived like dresses did.

The possible dinosaurs beneath my school

Young boys tend to appreciate dinosaurs. While this rule does not apply to all young boys, or just young boys, they tend to gravitate toward this interest as though fulfilling an obligation. I was, in every sense, one of those young boys and took my paleontological drive a little too seriously. It went beyond reading books, collecting toys and watching movies. In my heart, I was a fully qualified and highly regarded paleontologist and the only thing preventing the manifestation of this fantasy was reality. To me, the solution seemed simple. Whether or not I was qualified or acknowledged by others, I would simply start doing paleontology things.

My eight-year-old brain knew paleontologists often concerned themselves with the study of fossils. I was also canny enough to fully understand that most of these fossils were found underground. All I needed to do was start digging and, sooner or later, I would discover dinosaur bones. I also assumed the bones I discovered would belong to a type of dinosaur never before seen and in so making this discovery, my paleontology skills would receive the admiration it deserved. It was quite possible, I reasoned, that I would go down as the greatest dinosaur guy in history. All I needed to do was dig.

I had to consider the best way to approach an archaeological dig. Although

I lived in a country town, it was a rather large one and instinct told me that in erecting the town, any hidden dinosaur bones were already accounted for. It was for this reason I dismissed conducting the dig in the most convenient location - my garden. This is why I opted for the second most convenient location - my school grounds. While on the surface, a school ground doesn't appear to be an untapped location, the school I went to seemed different. It was replete with nooks and sprawling wastelands of dirt and, to me, these were certain to possess a menagerie of dinosaurs. Plus I had no other option.

In the 80s, school playgrounds weren't subject to the intense level of health and safety requirements found today. Our school had what was known as the 'adventure playground,' which was a large wooden structure with bridges and multi-level platforms. We injured ourselves while playing on the adventure playground frequently and were happy to do so. Giving our blood to the majesty of the playground was a rite of passage. What caught my attention were the steep inclines of compact dirt this playground sat atop. It sprawled out far beyond the wooden structure itself and presented so many exciting excavation opportunities. I singled out a particularly steep section of dirt away from the playground and, in earnest, started to dig.

I had no tools and the school was not about to provide them, so I used sticks and flat rocks to start scraping away at the top surface of dirt. This started as a solitary task and I expected it to stay this way. I knew my goal was not achievable during one lunch break - it may take three or four, but I was prepared to last the duration.

The next day I returned to the dig and surveyed the small crater of dirt I had managed to displace the previous lunchtime. I was saddened by my lack of progress. Overnight I had built my archaeological site up a rather large amount until it contradicted reality. Nevertheless, I was determined to continue. I resumed scraping away at the dirt and soon after, a couple of friends approached me to inquire about my activity. I explained my conviction that dinosaur bones existed within the dirt and once they were found, I would be famous. They asked if I needed help. I surveyed my lack of progress and agreed. My only condition was they had to obey me absolutely. They agreed. That lunchtime, the three of us made a considerable amount more progress. Our crater had become a hole and I felt good.

On the third day of our dig, things took an unexpected turn. I learned when a group of people busy themselves obsessively with a task, others become intrigued by that task and wish to be a part of it. Especially if all the people involved are children. Our three became fifteen before the lunch break was over, which ensured the dirt was being displaced at a pleasing rate. A few years ago, I was told the most important person of any new movement is not the creator of that movement - it's the first follower of that movement. The first follower teaches others it is acceptable to follow. It should be noted that I may have learned this from a TED Talk, which means you should probably ignore it.

On the fourth day, there were easily twenty children digging into the dirt and we had still not found any dinosaur bones. I noticed everyone was contributing to the creation of one large hole and while the size of the hole was impressive, it felt counterproductive. If this dig was to yield the results I expected, I needed to manage those who were participating. I split everyone up into teams and instructed each team to dig in different locations. Their obedience was astonishing to me, but I enjoyed it. Every instruction I gave was followed dutifully and my role soon became that of manager.

The dig continued for two weeks, with more and more children joining my team. In this time, under my instruction, the environment of the playground had altered significantly. The adventure playground itself rested as it always had in its dangerous wooden grandeur, but around it were mountains of displaced dirt and a worrying lack of dinosaur bones. While I found this disturbing, the other children, who continued to dig unabated, seemed unconcerned the goal had not been met. I felt somewhat alone despite the army of people following my command. What was the point if they were digging for nothing else than its own sake? My ardent belief had been rattled and I now doubted the possibility of finding evidence of unknown dinosaurs.

An emergency assembly was called the following Monday. News of the excavation had spread among the teachers and the principal of the school addressed us gravely. He expressed confusion as he spoke, unsure why so many children had decided it was appropriate to dig up the school grounds in such a profound way. So many were involved that placing blame on any one person was impossible. Rather than discipline, we received a plea to our common sense. We were implored to cease all digging and informed that the area had now become quite dangerous to traverse. We received a warning that should we continue, the playground would be cordoned off. While this might have been beneficial given how dangerous the playground was, none of us wanted such an outcome. This grave threat ensured we stopped the excavation immediately.

Even with the cessation of our dig, the playground was cordoned off for several days. Apparently we inflicted so much damage that a crew of workmen had to restore the landscape to its pre-excavation state. Watching the erasure of everything I had instigated might have caused more sadness had the task exhibited signs of success, but in my mind, these men were burying my failure. I was thankful more than anything. I never attempted to unearth prehistoric relics again.

Contents

Breakfast lecture
Each of you forgot
Andre the (actual) Giant
Life lesson
Twiggy Smith
Constable in a shoe
Bullied goblin
Fish pisser
Monsieur sloth
Your responsibilities can be avoided
Sadly skipping merrily
Post-wank shame
I will always love you
Lucy bird tears
Last kiss
Action statue
Maestro's dick
Paste Milk
Fancy dinner
The mischief
LIVER/SPLEEN
Owl bits
Ulcer junkies

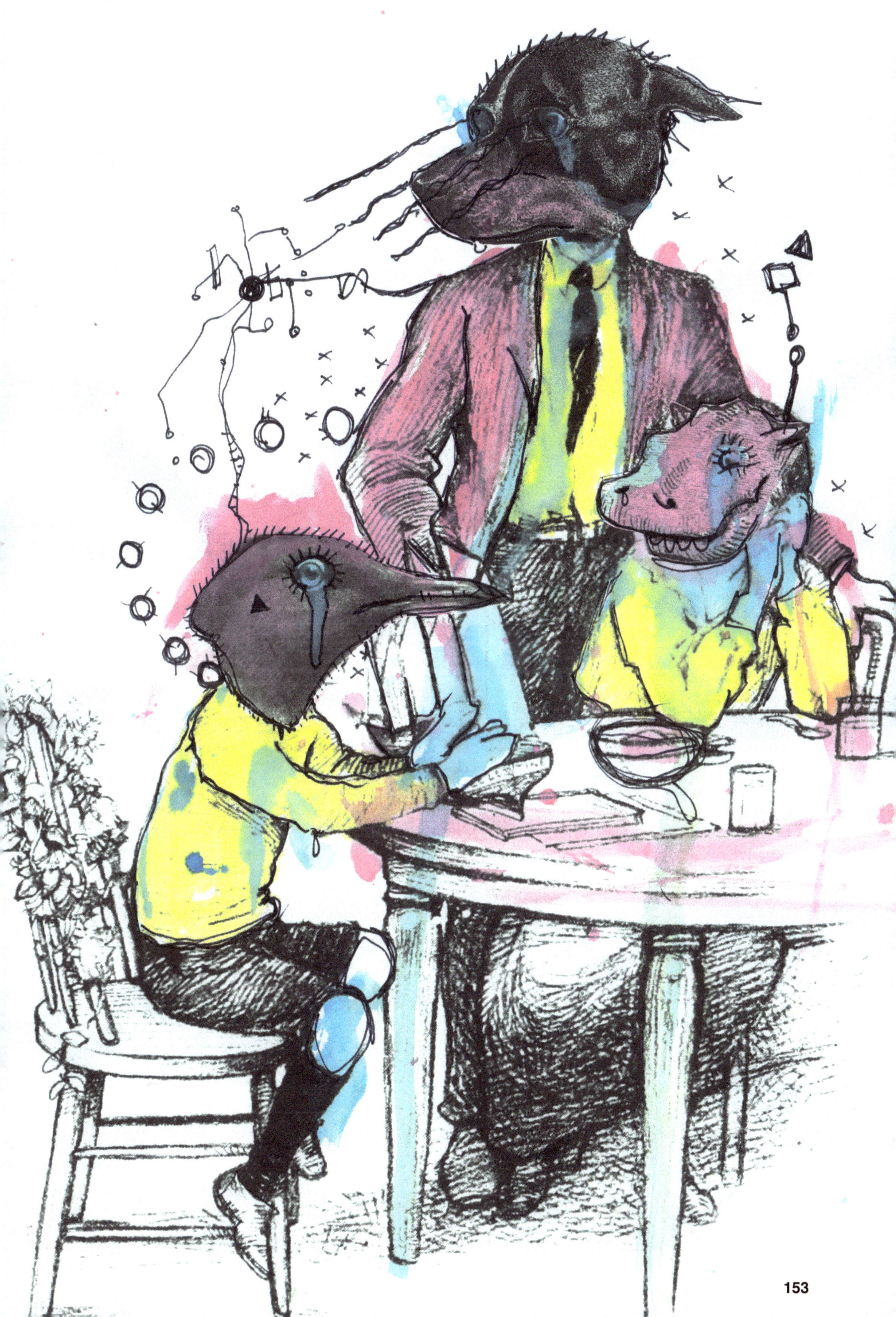

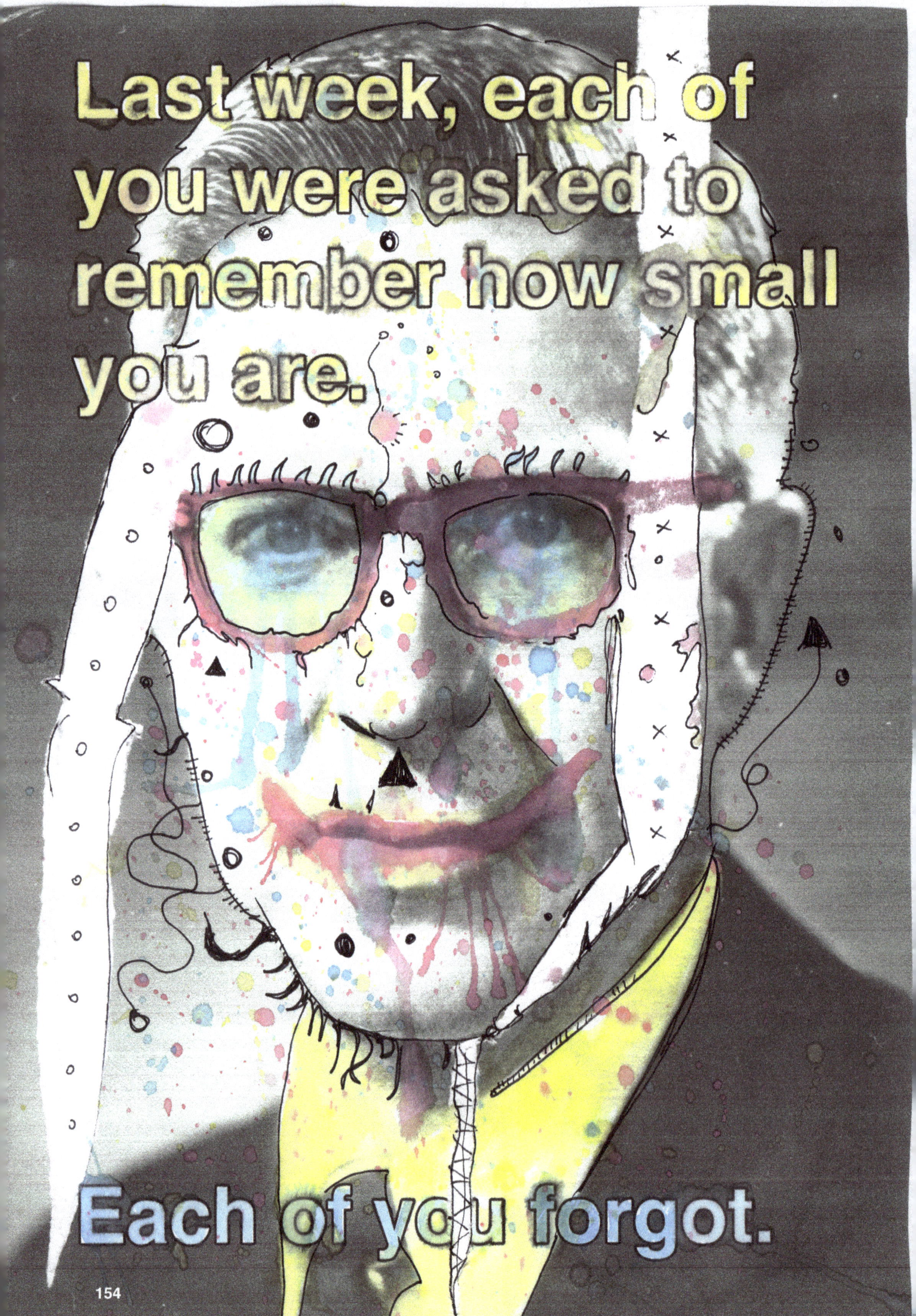

Last week, each of you were asked to remember how small you are.
Each of you forgot.

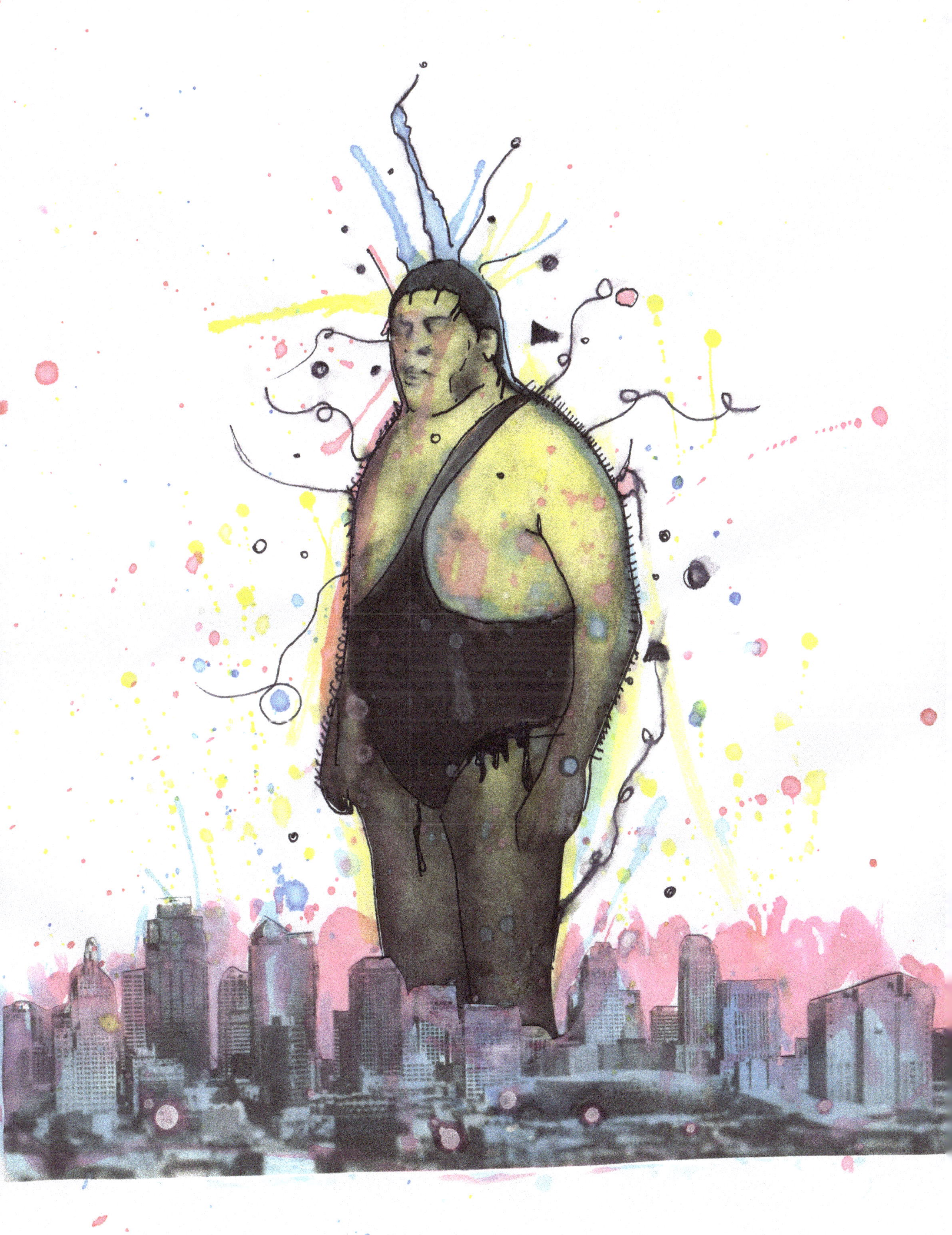

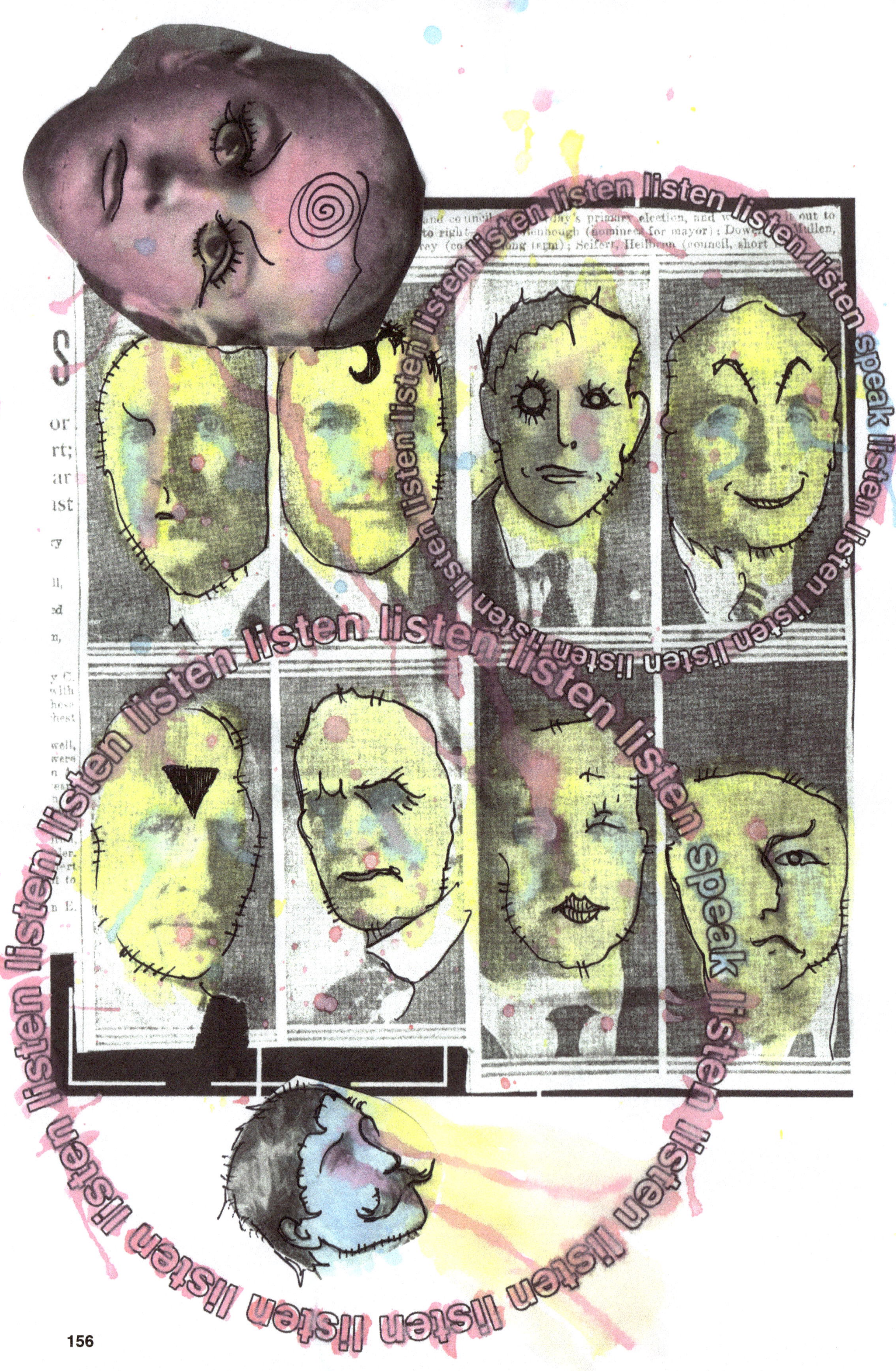

listen listen listen listen listen speak listen listen
listen listen listen listen listen listen listen
listen listen listen listen listen speak listen
listen listen listen listen listen listen

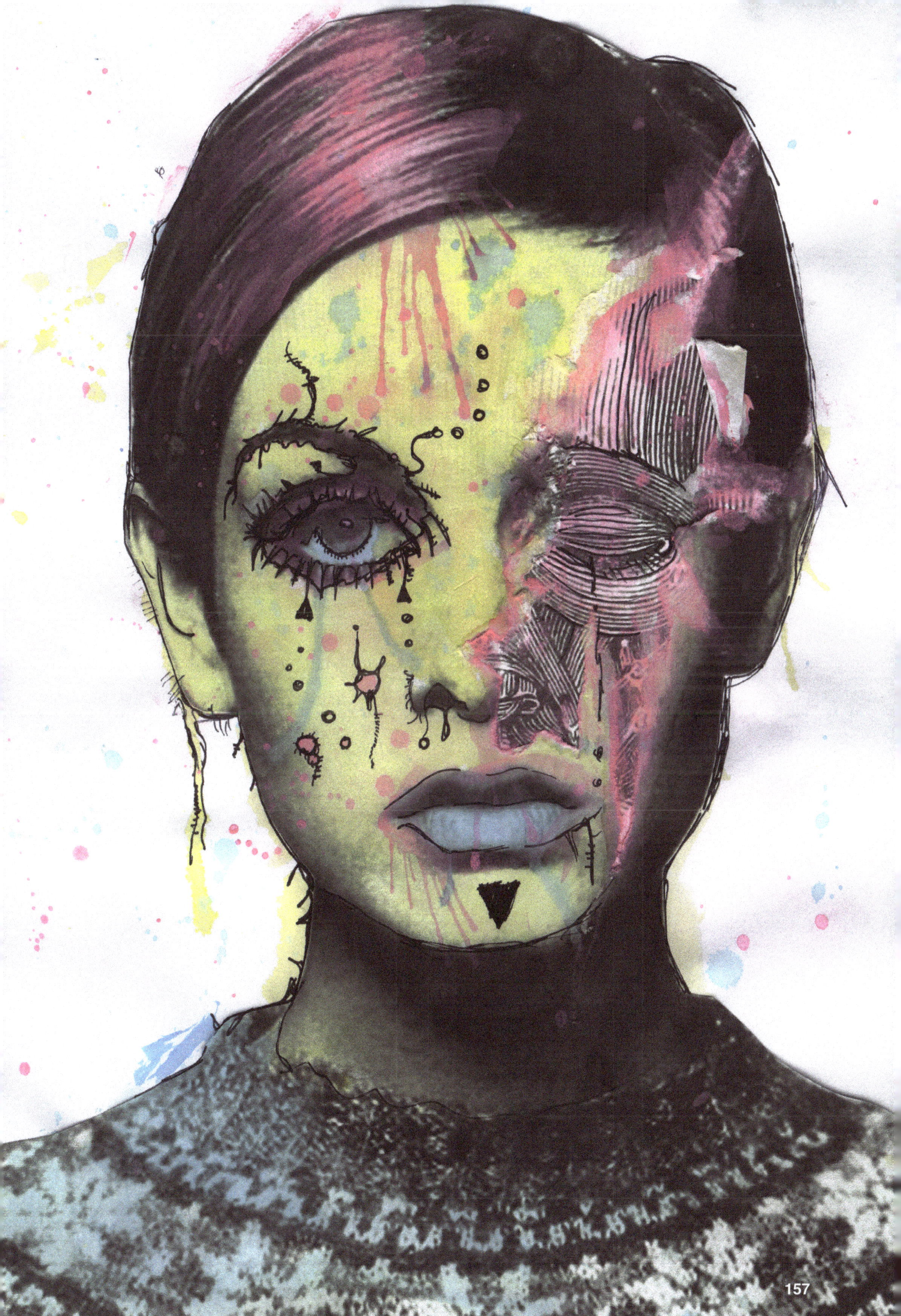

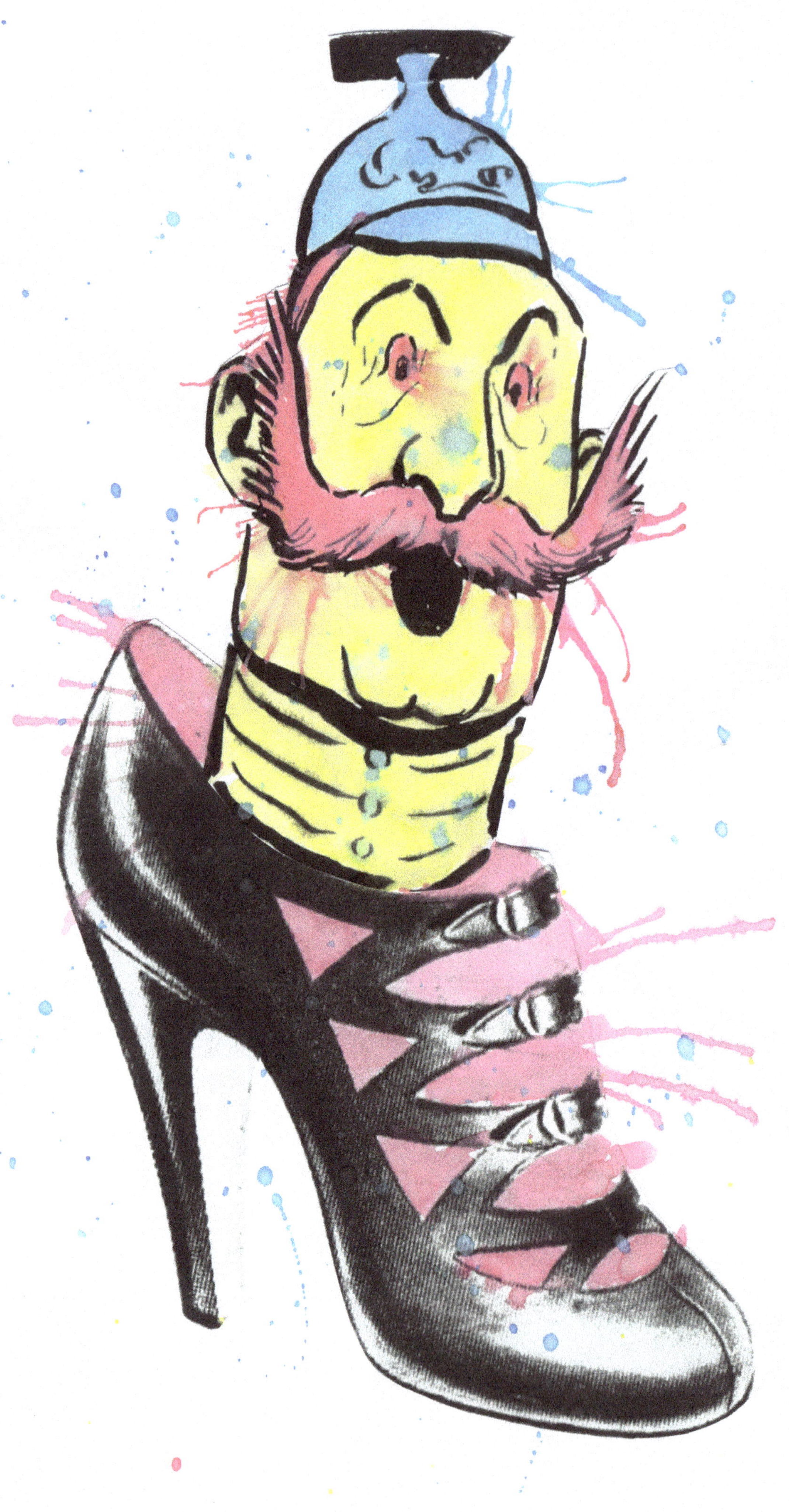

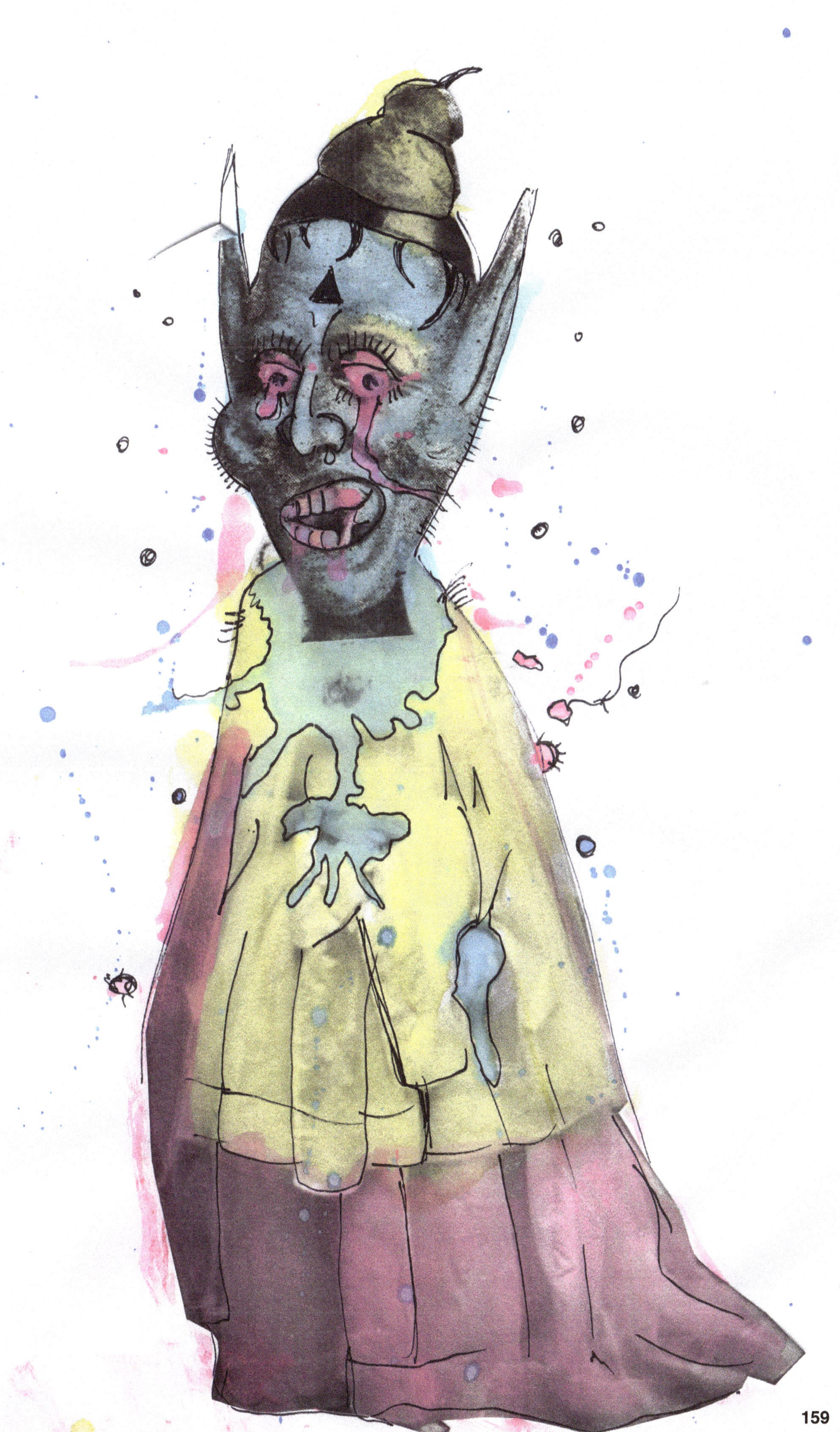

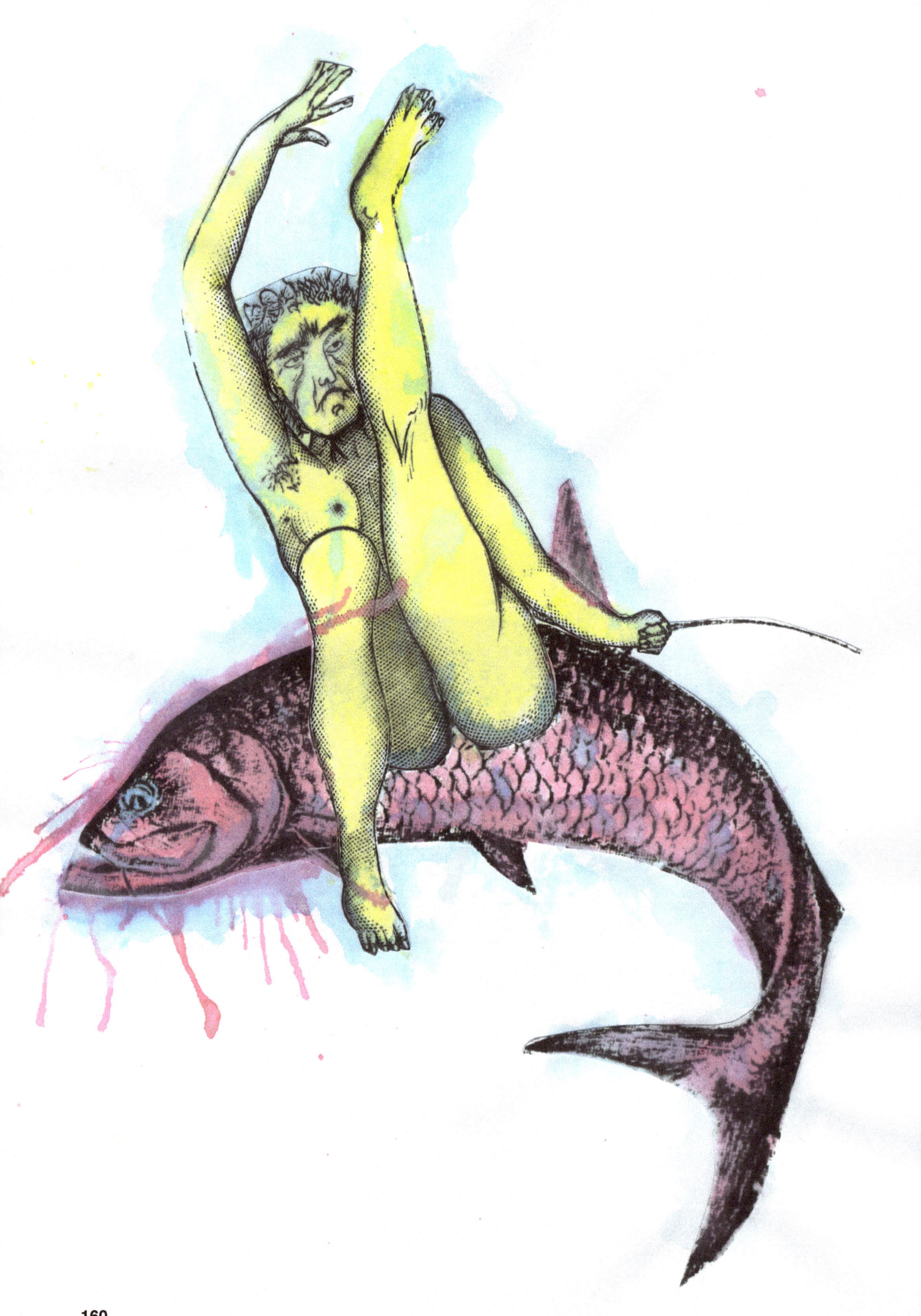

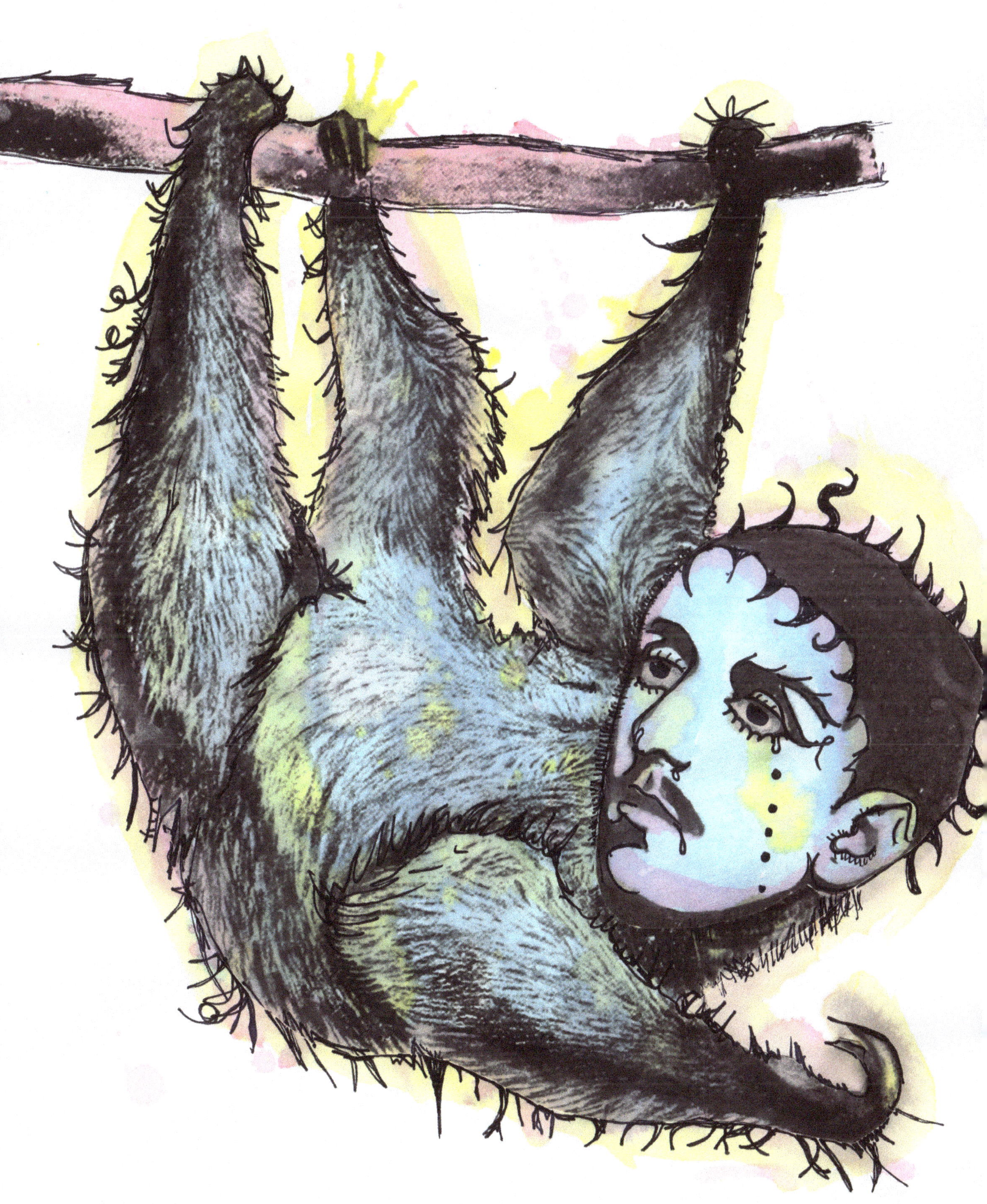

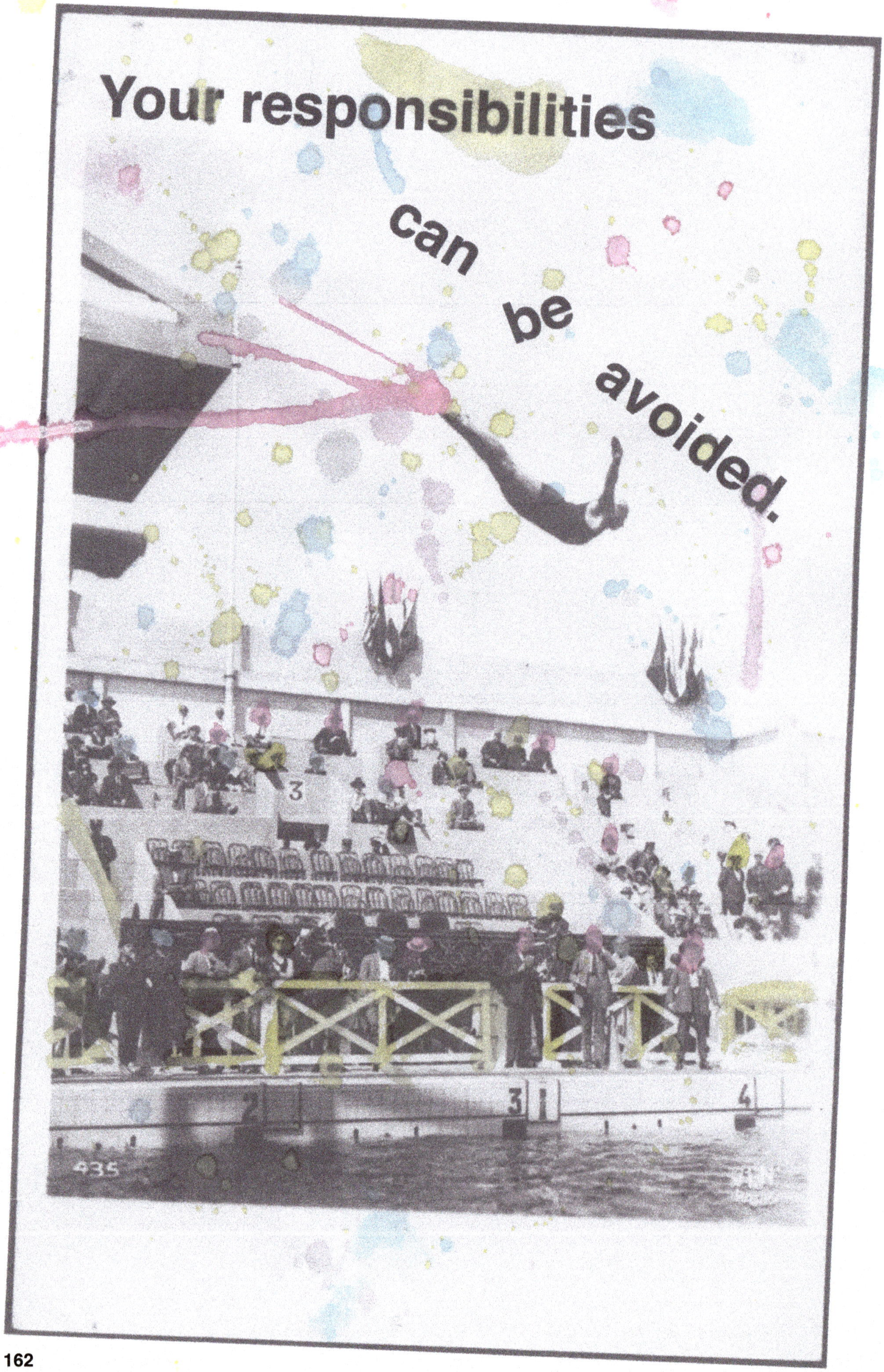

Your responsibilities
can
be
avoided.

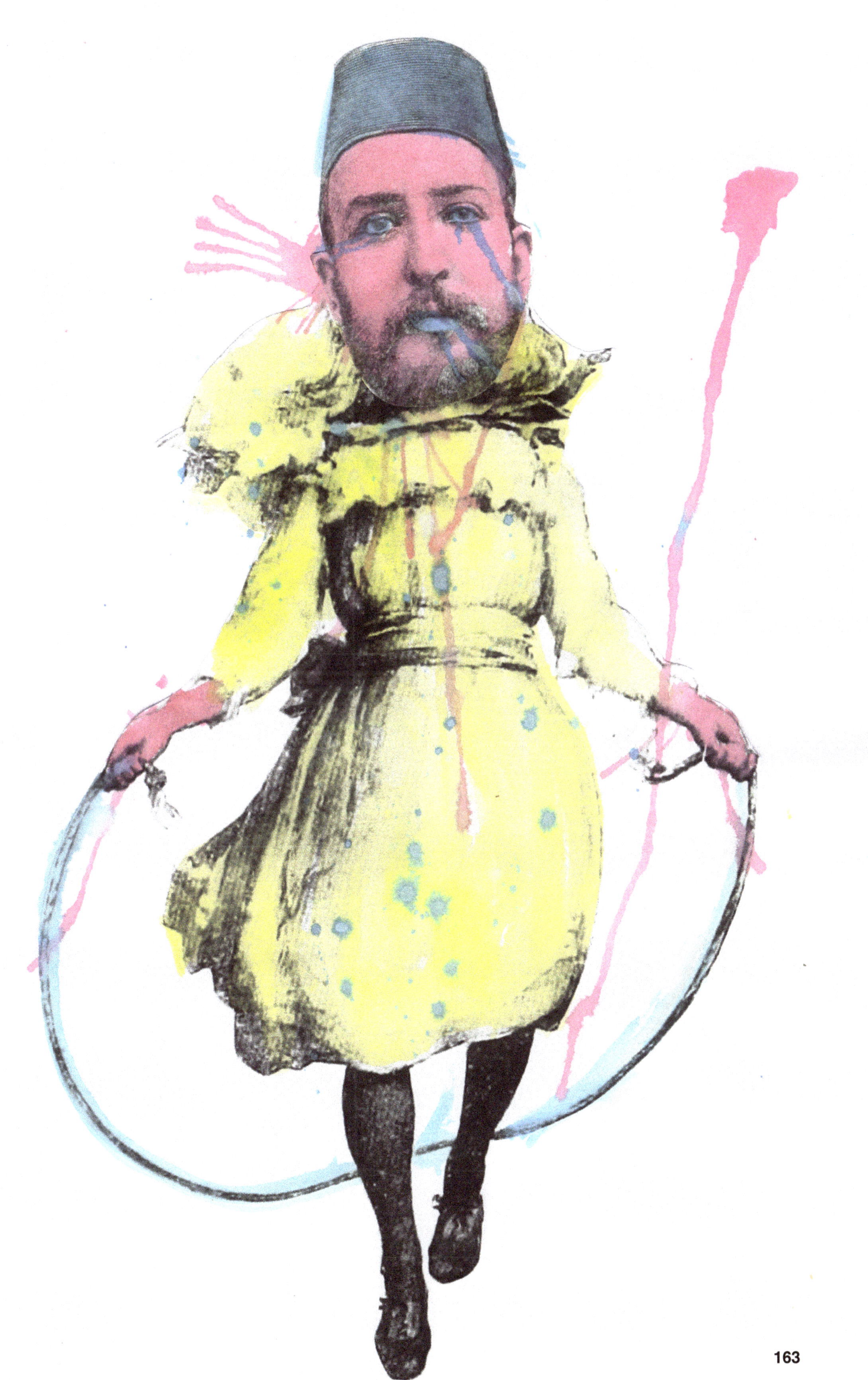

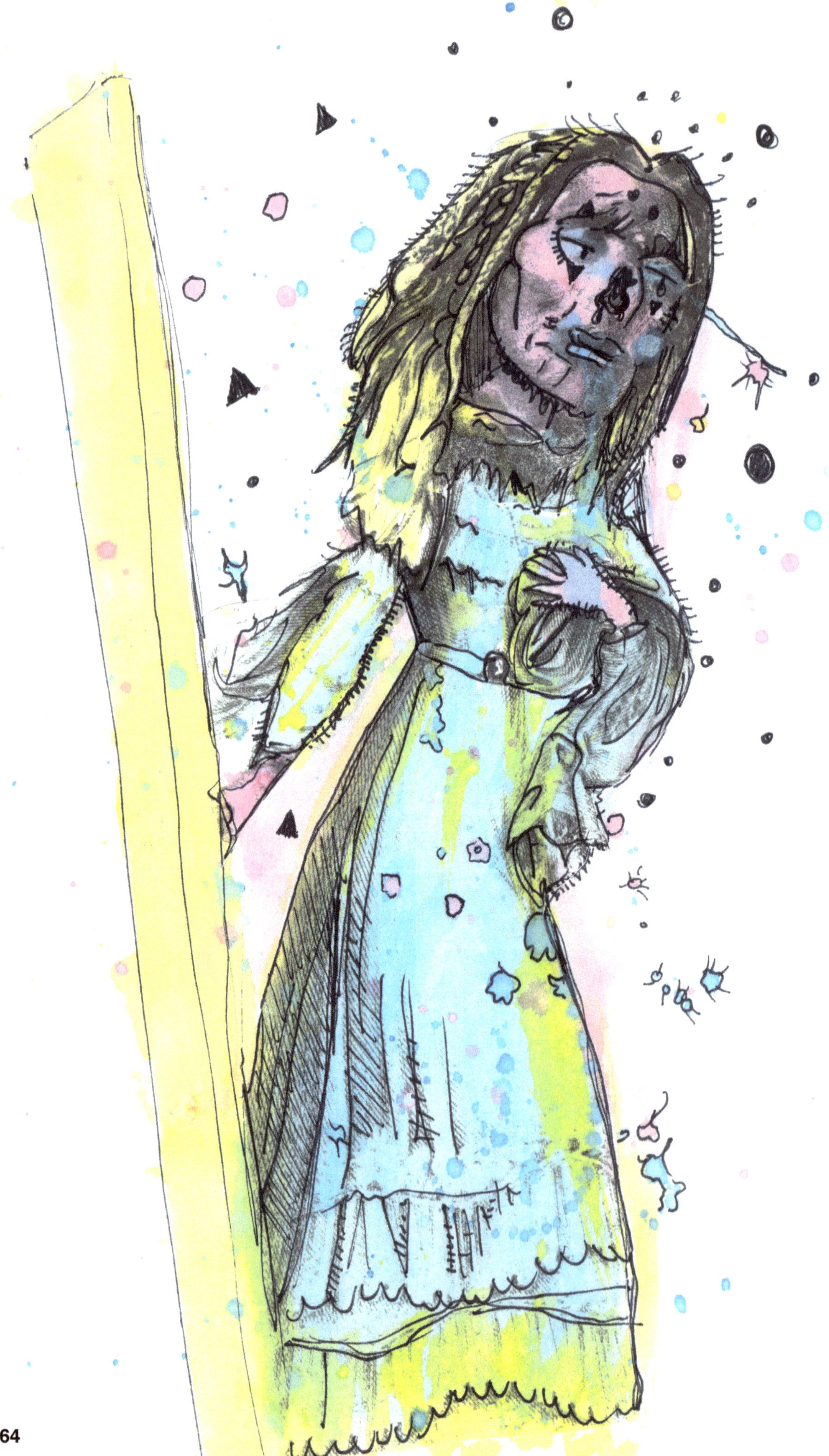

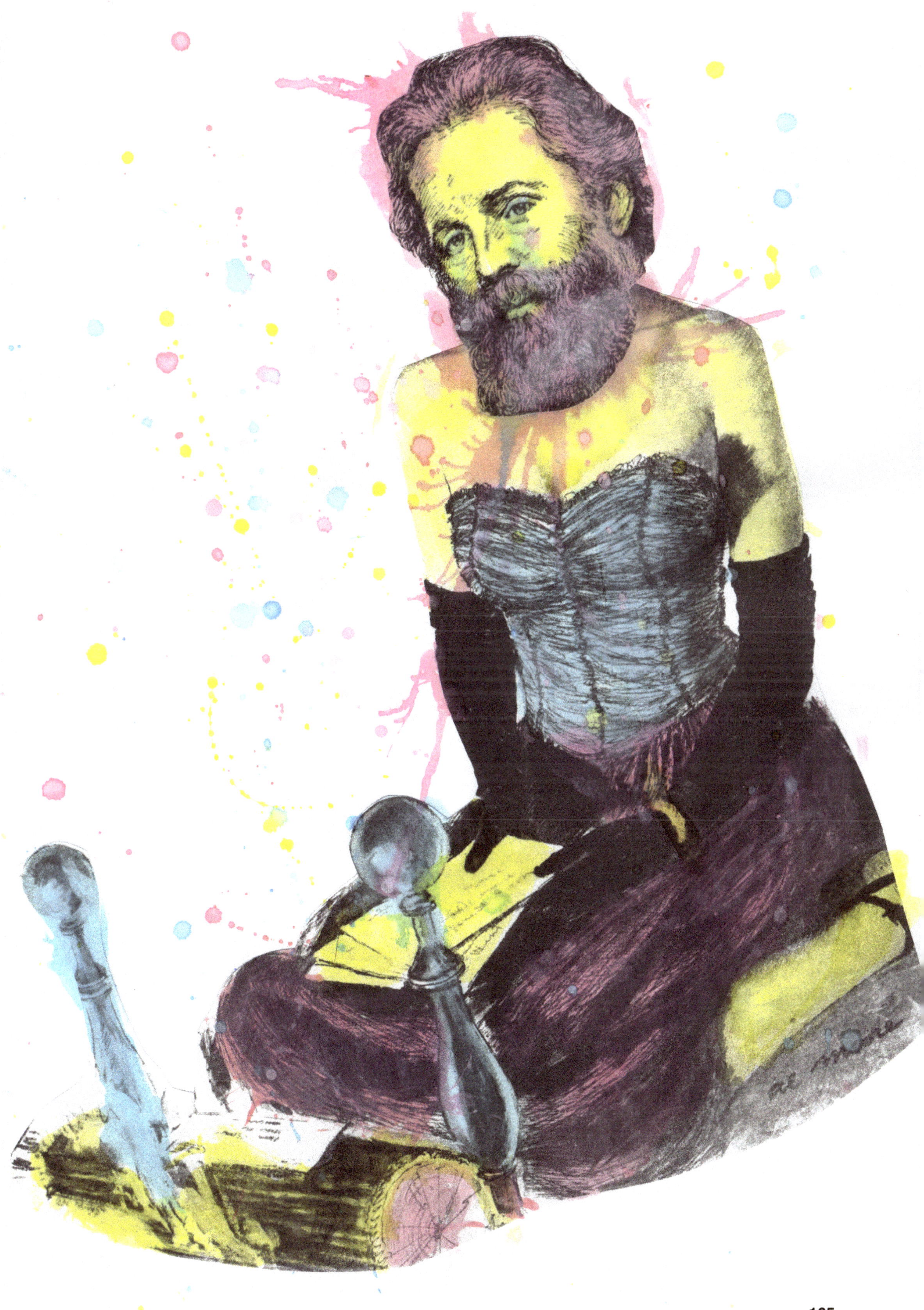

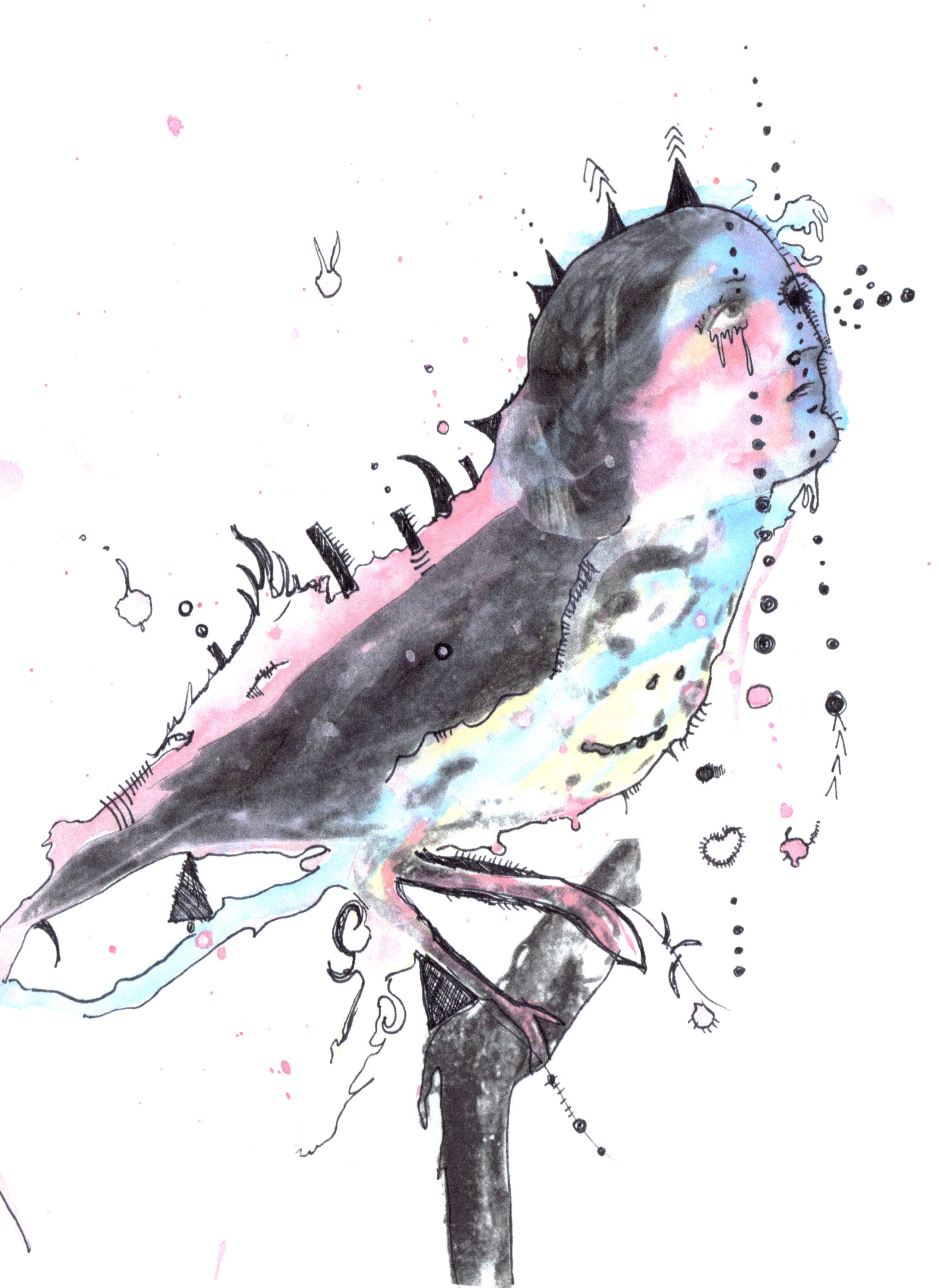

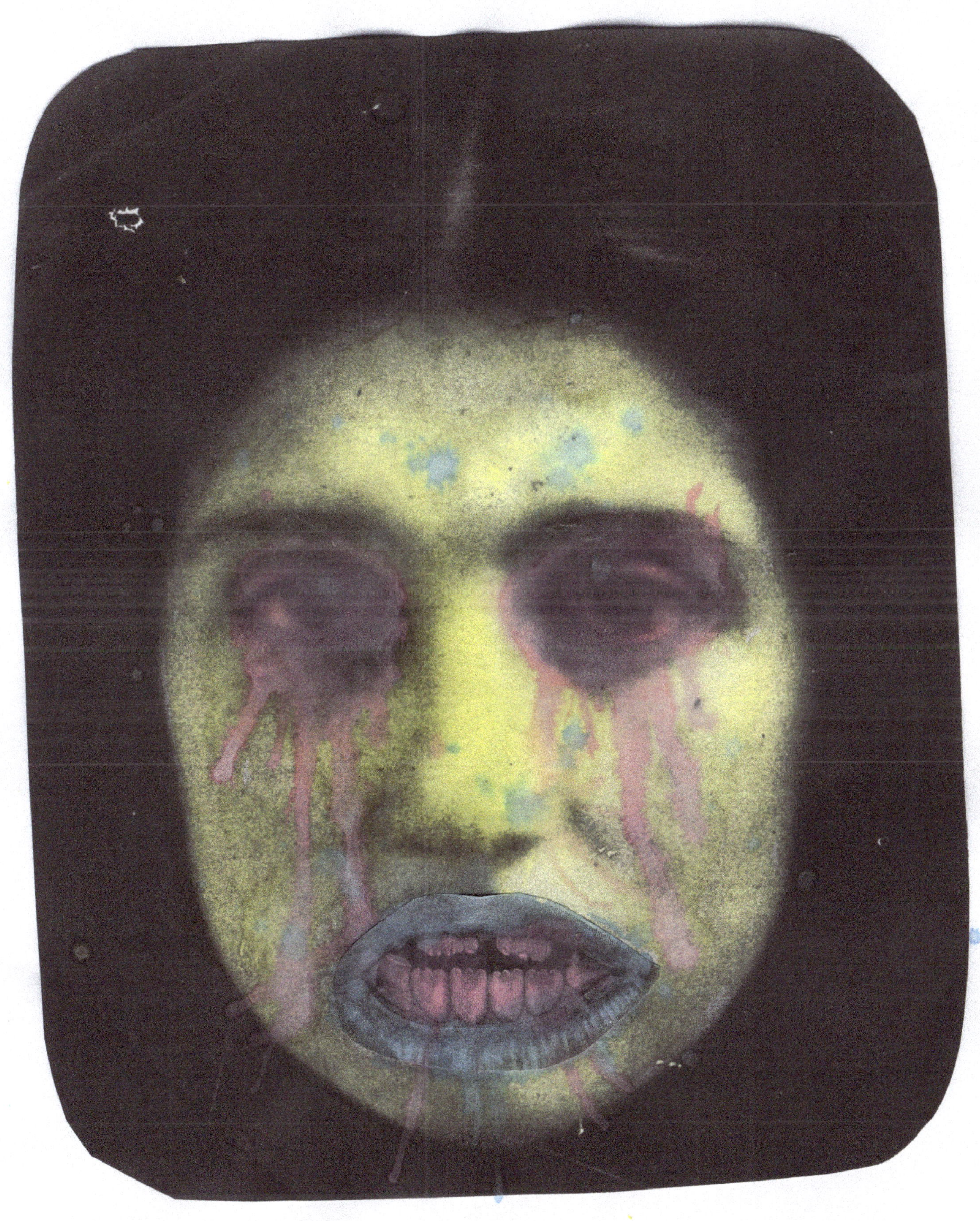

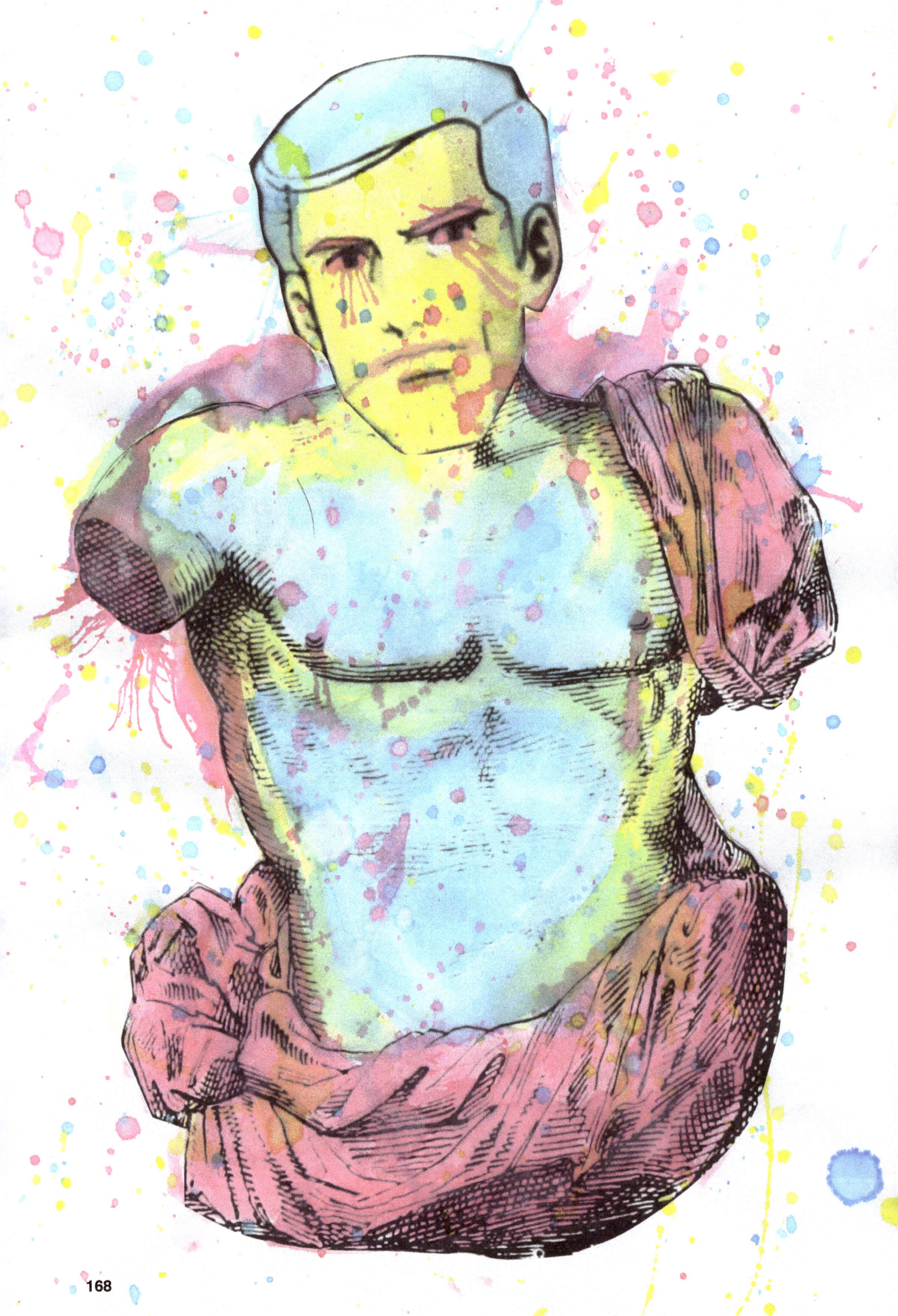

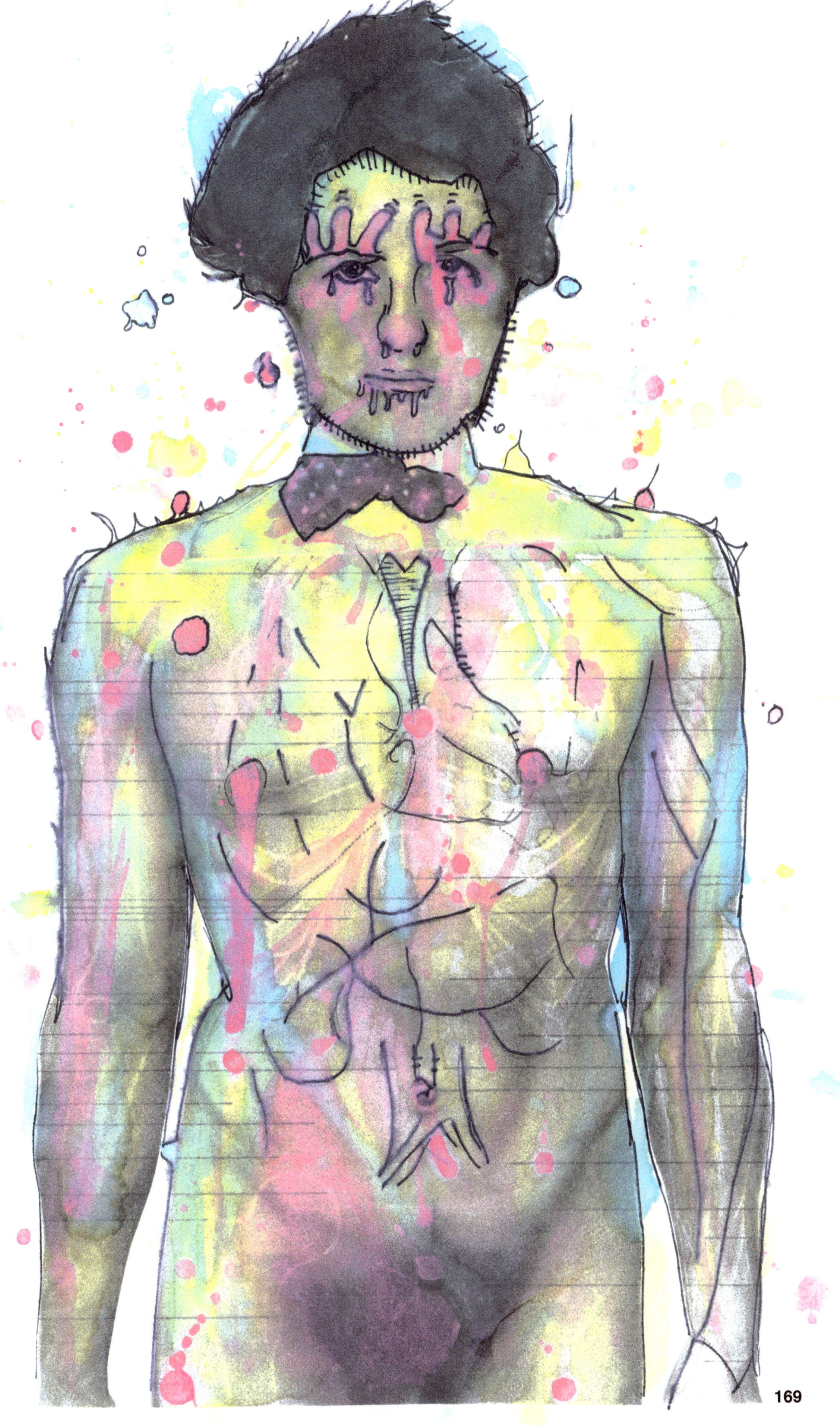

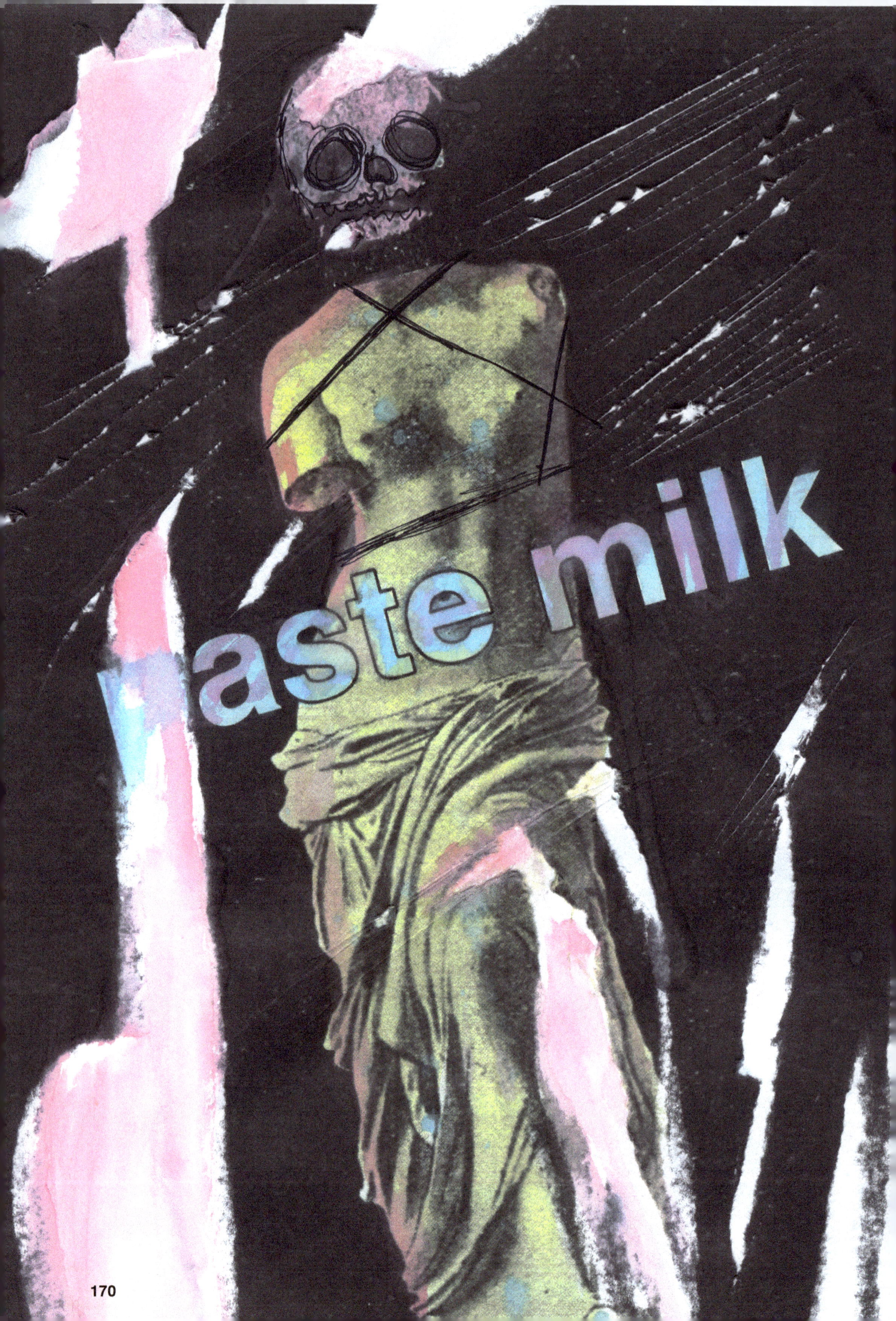

haste milk

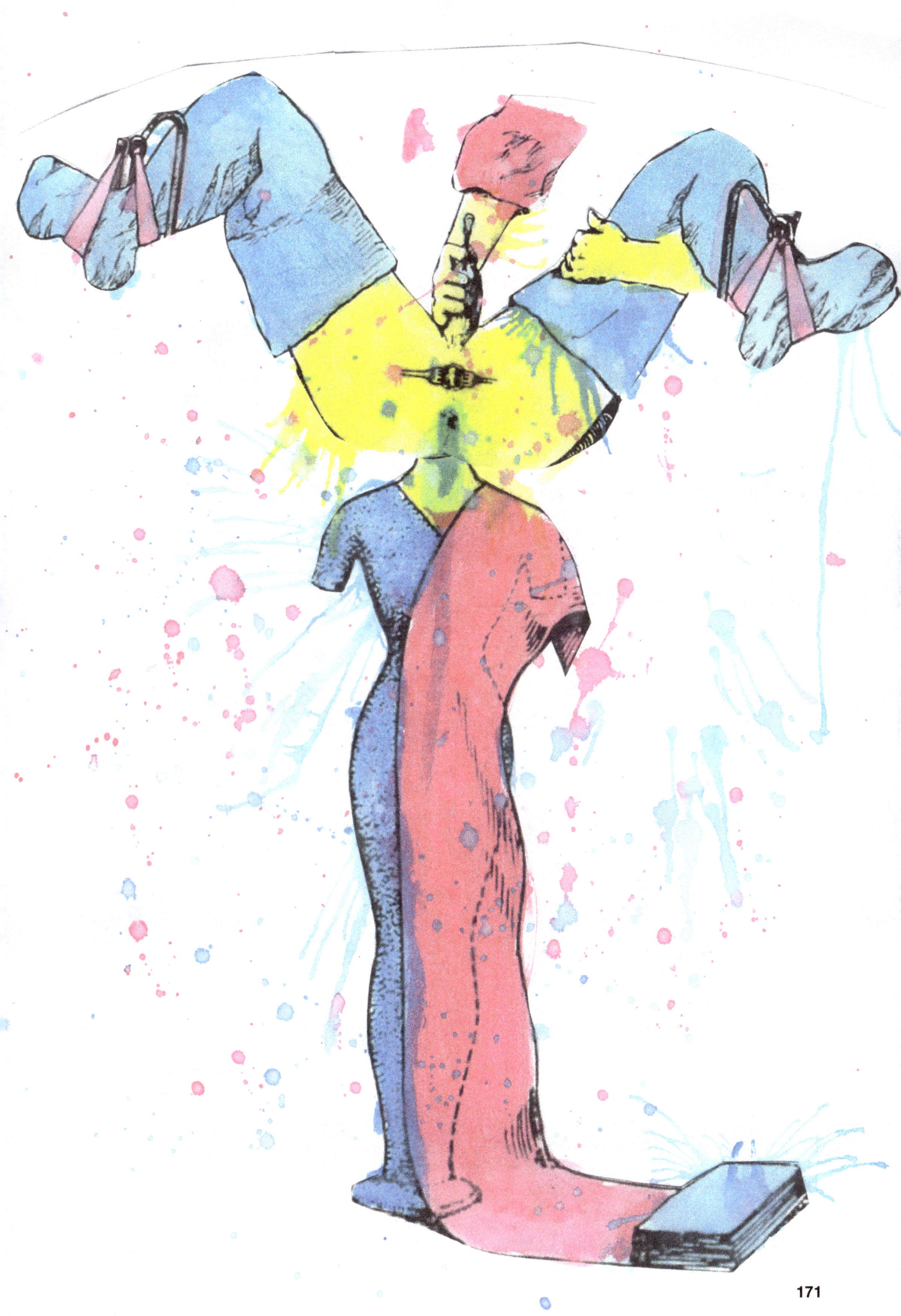

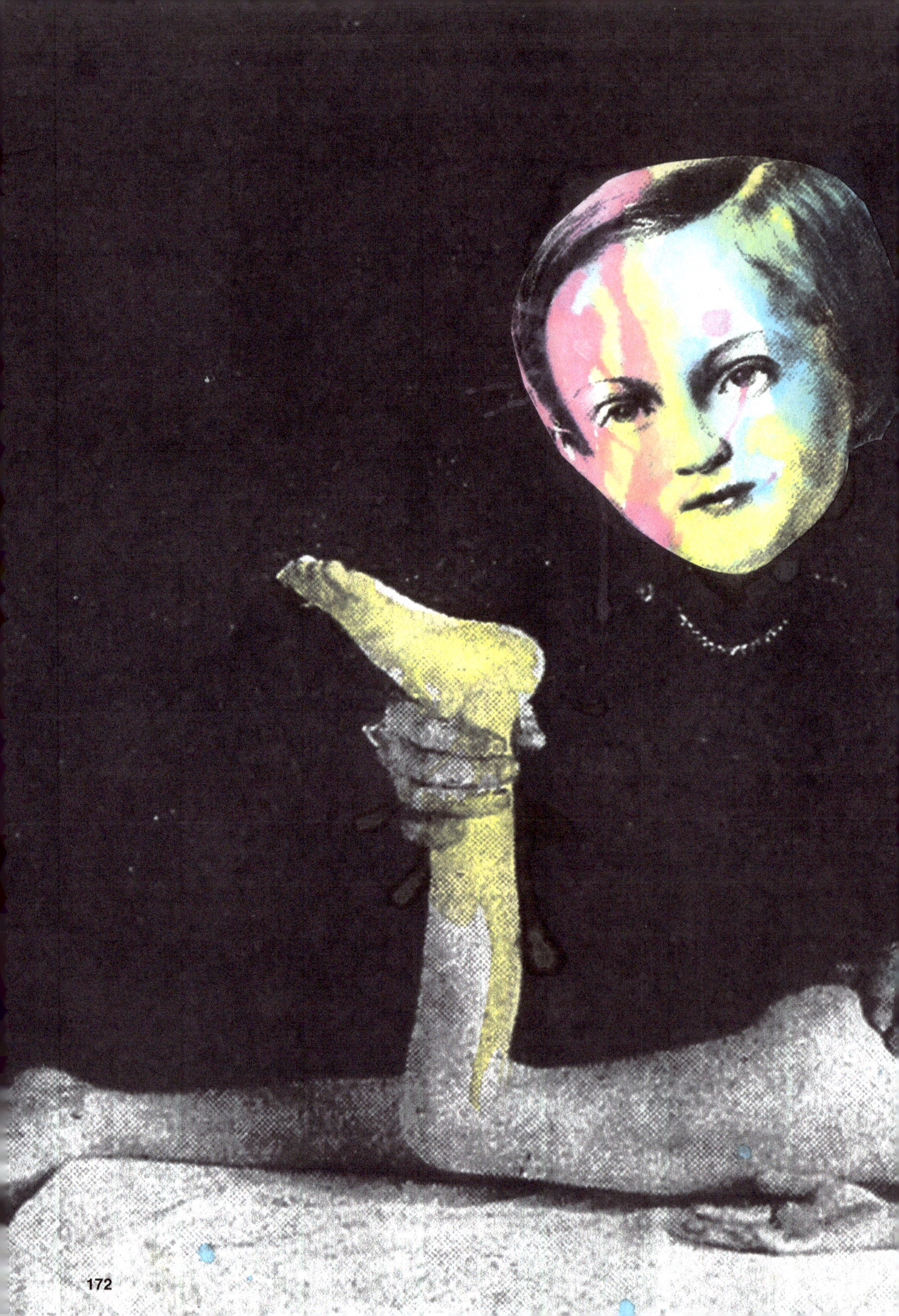

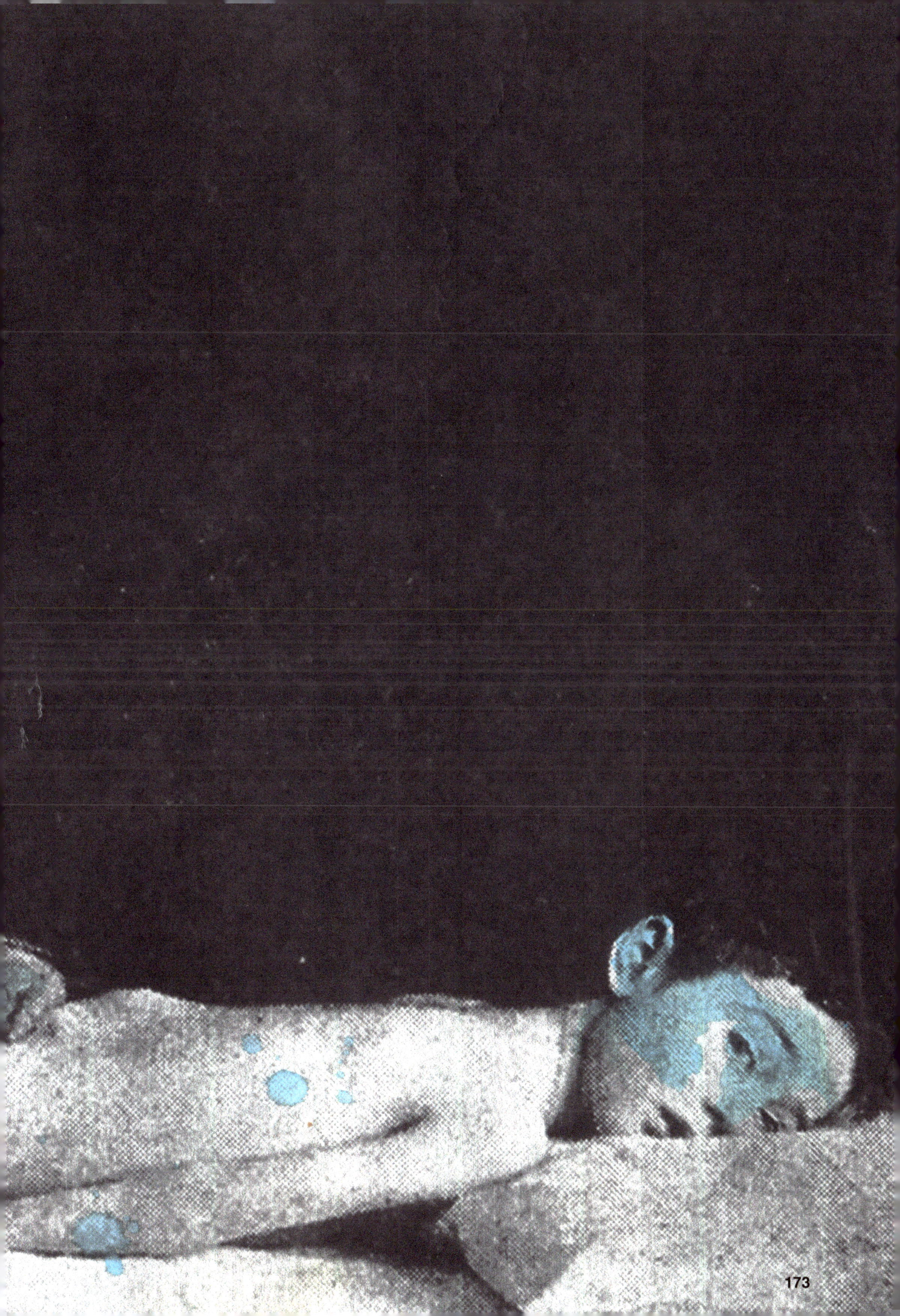

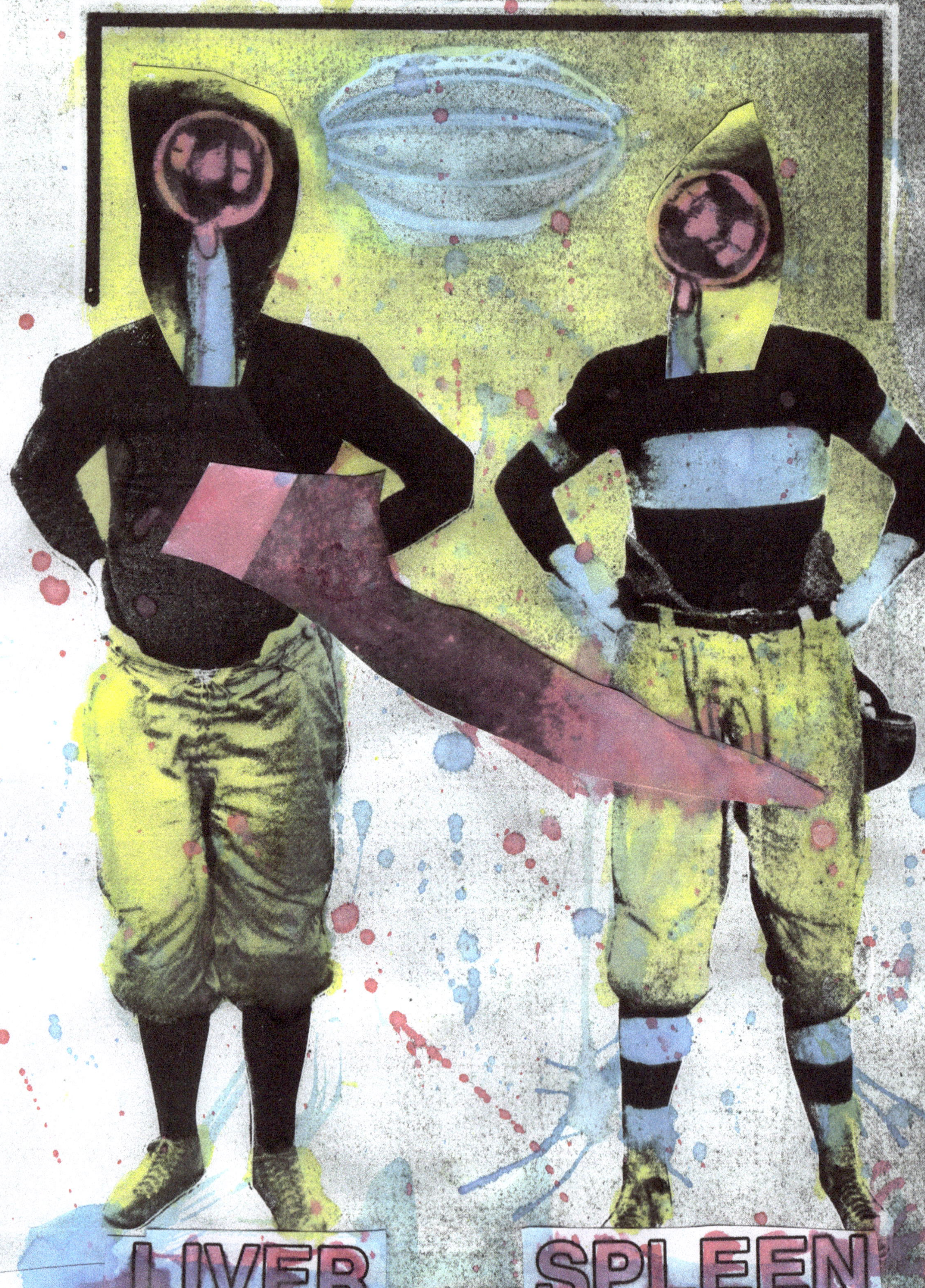

LIVER
SPLEEN

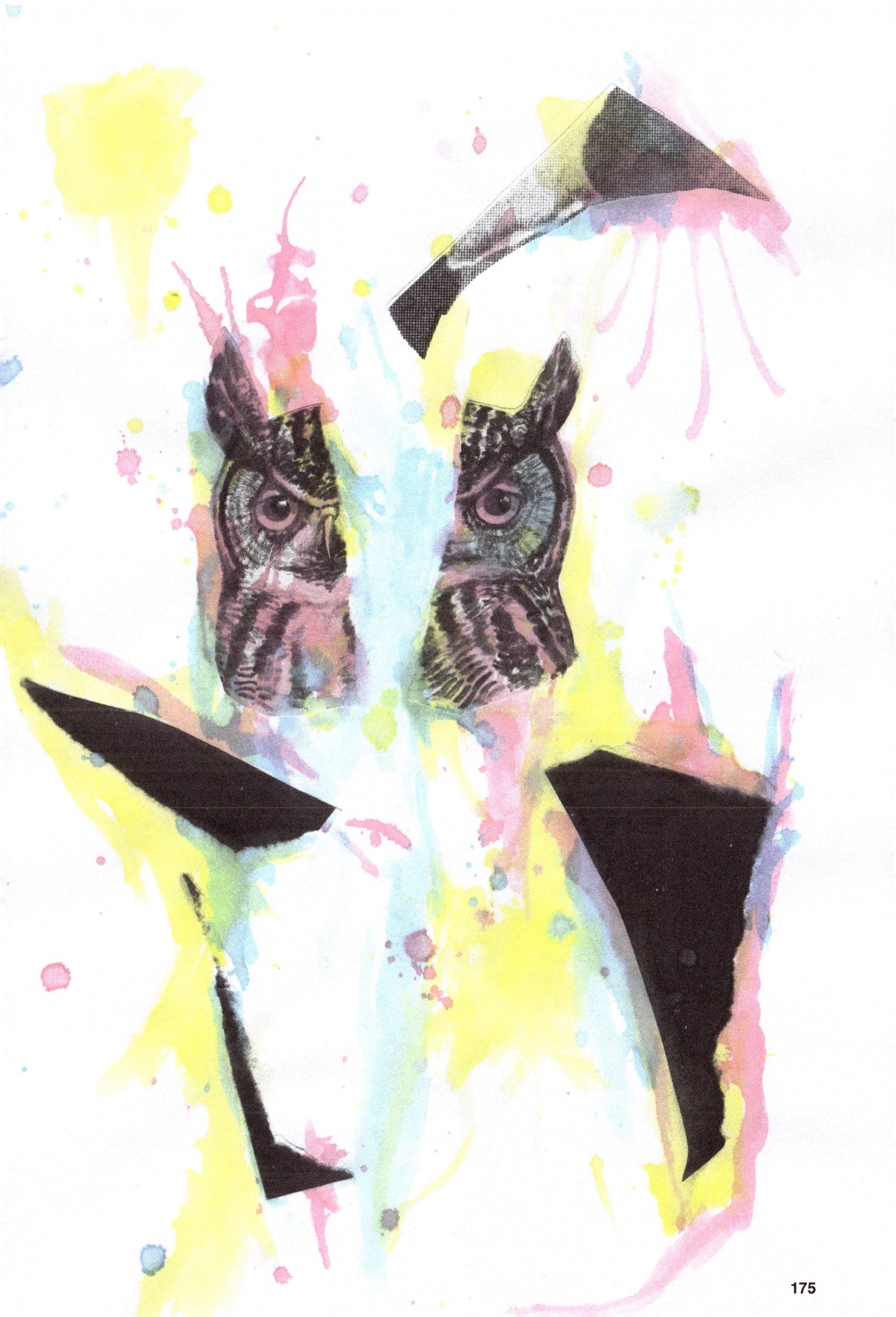

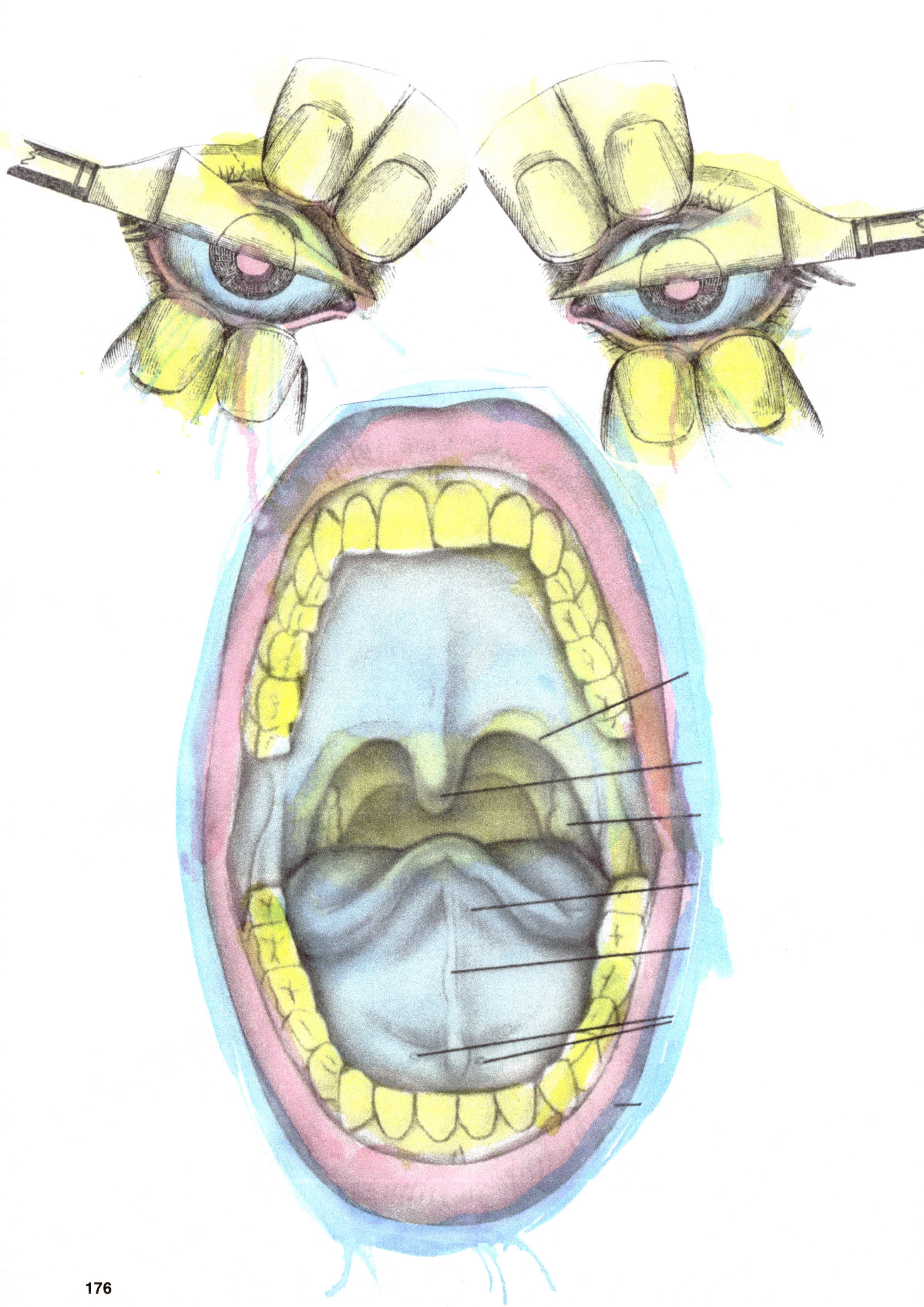

YOU
ARE
RESPONSE

Humble Walter. Flowers in hand. Ready to avoid our shadows lest he bruise them. Mending our painful hiccups with a scare.

A curious near-death on the way to camp

There is a phenomena known as 'hysterical strength' that is said to overcome people in emergency situations. Adrenaline flushes through the body, imbuing it with momentary abilities that would commonly be considered superhuman. Stories of such displays of hysterical strength are all over the Internet, but before the Internet, I just had hyperbolic stories from school acquaintances. One such story stands out above the rest and was a favorite around the schoolyard. I first heard it from a friend who is no longer a friend, but was nevertheless a friend at the time. His name was Ben. He had rosy cheeks and laughed like a cartoon. We were talking about car accidents when he mentioned an incident with a motorcyclist he had heard about. This poor anecdotal motorcyclist was obeying the road rules when a car ran a red light, which knocked him from his bike and reportedly 'broke every bone in his body.' The driver of the car responsible stared in shock from his driver's seat and witnessed a most unlikely event. This anecdotal motorcyclist with the shattered bones somehow sat up and turned to look at the guilty driver. Then, with rage in his eyes, he upped the ante by not only standing up on his broken legs, but also striding over to the car as though on a mission. Clenching his broken hand into a broken fist, the motorcyclist punched the driver, knocking him out before collapsing and dying seconds later on the road.

It is my contention the above story is an exaggeration, but it was definitely fun to think about and I wanted it to be real - I still do. No matter the veracity of Ben's anecdote, it is beyond doubt that hysterical strength exists, but the version I have experienced offers a minor upgrade at best. It could be compared to installing a new stick of ram into a computer too old for any great benefit.

I experienced my own ponderous version of hysterical strength the day my brother nearly died. Had his death eventuated, it would surely earn a place among the most pathetic deaths of all time.

It starts as most tales of near-death start - on the way to school camp. I've only ever attended one school camp as it was an expense my family had trouble affording. A part of me also enjoyed the condescending sympathy the small group of students who remained at school attracted from teachers who clearly had no plan regarding the best way to occupy the time of us non-campgoers. Perhaps because it was the first camp of my high school experience, my parents felt it important I attend.

Our family owned one sleeping bag. It was red, with a red slipcover and distinctive yellow nylon drawstring. Technically it belonged to my sister, but if a situation presented itself requiring a sleeping bag to navigate, it was the one we used.

I'm not aware of any situation requiring more than one family member needing a sleeping bag at any given time, which, as far as I'm concerned, is a hornet's nest we successfully avoided. It was this sleeping bag I took with me to school camp and, more importantly, it was this sleeping bag that nearly killed my brother.

Most students were dropped off at school with all their camp gear, but my father had to work and my mother's disability made it impossible for her to drive. As a result, I had to walk. My nine-year-old brother, who kindly offered to help, solved the conundrum of transporting so much camp gear on foot. I had a bulging backpack and a tote bag, which was more awkward than heavy. My brother's sole responsibility was the sleeping bag, the yellow nylon drawstring of which he hung around his head, like a particularly garish necklace.

We walked to school every day and this trip felt no different other than the extra baggage. I led the way with my brother a few steps behind and conversation consisted of the typical insulting comments brothers excel in. I noticed my brother was gleaning some form of enjoyment using the sleeping back around his neck as a boxing bag. The activity didn't look particularly enjoyable, but while he was helping me out, I wasn't going to judge.

What I failed to notice, as my brother boxed the sleeping bag, was the yellow nylon drawstring, which began to twist around itself. Given what followed, it is apparent my brother didn't realize either. I was first alerted to my brother's ridiculous predicament by virtue of a gurgling sound assailing my ears from behind. I turned to face the sound and witnessed my brother in a panic. As you may have guessed from my heavy-handed foreshadowing, the drawstring of the sleeping bag had twisted to such an extent it was now cutting off my brother's supply of oxygen. I didn't act immediately. The situation seemed so utterly ludicrous that it took some time to even accept it was occurring. I walked toward him, assuming my brother was not actually choking but panicking in response to the unexpected turn of events. In my mind, it was a simple case of lifting the drawstring over his head and then calling him something derogatory as a finale. Reality contradicted my assumption. The sleeping bag's drawstring had indeed cut off his oxygen - his reddening face and bulged eyes were testament to that. I began to twist the string to loosen its grip on my brother's throat, but I was not able to discern which way the twisting should occur. No matter how I approached it, the drawstring seemed to tighten. This is when my panic introduced itself.

The situation was clearly an emergency. My brother's face was turning blue and his eyes contained a level of fright I have no interest in witnessing again. In response, I felt my body surge with hysterical strength and I remembered the motorcyclist with the shattered bones. Without the time required to formulate a meaningful strategy, the only course of action I could fathom was breaking the nylon drawstring with my bare hands. It's embarrassing to admit, but I was resolute in my ability to do this. I inhaled deeply, pumping out my chest in an exaggerated fashion and screamed while pulling on the string. I poured everything I had into the act until my muscles were screaming, but the drawstring didn't care. It's as though it was unaware of hysterical strength and had little interest in the fact it was supposedly coursing through me as I tried to best it. Rather than a sensation of superhuman ability, it felt very much like my regular strength with some added desperation.

I tried my hand at breaking the drawstring several times, but with each repetition, it seemed my strength was only waning. My brother's death was the only outcome I could see as his state grew worse. His eyeballs were beginning to roll backward and I tried to predict the difficult conversation I would have with my parents and whether they'd still make me go to the school camp. I wondered if any of the remaining family members would ever want to use the sleeping bag again. Sleeping bags were expensive. As these thoughts careened throughout me, my brother stood up desperately and started to take erratic steps in every direction at the same time. He stumbled as he did, but I noticed something important. As he stood, the twisted drawstring began to dictate itself and, with the power of momentum, began to untwist. I ran to my brother and weighed him in place with a hand on either shoulder, alternating my gaze between his eyes and the untwisting drawstring. I yelled that he should stay still and he obeyed. The grip on my brother's throat lessened enough for him to gorge on the oxygen around him. We both fell to the ground with my brother's desperate breathing the only sound I could hear.

"Are you ok?"

"Yes."

"You sure?"

"Yes."

"Let's not tell mum and dad about this."

"Ok."

During school camp there was an archery competition. Post-it notes with various monetary values written on them were adhered to the targets. If any of us managed to pierce these post-it notes, we got the value written upon them. The highest value was two dollars, which, via some fluke, I managed to pierce with one of my arrows. To this day, I have never received the promised two dollars and I'm still a little salty about it.

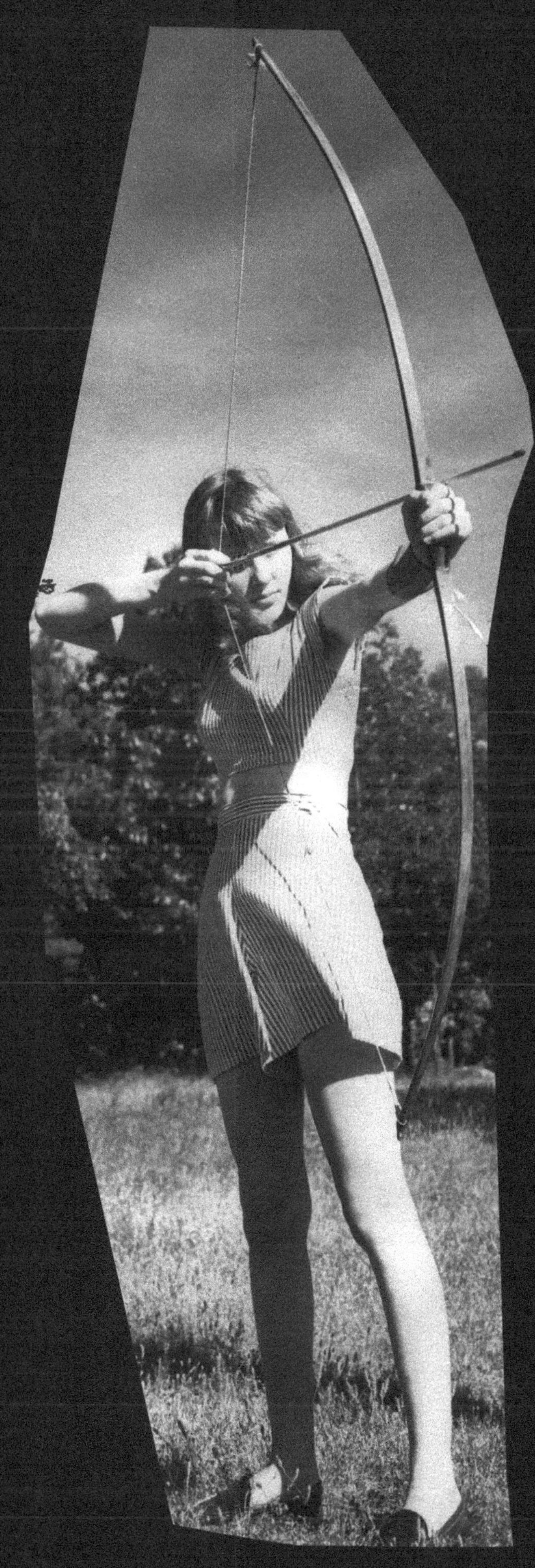

Contents

183	Illegal hat
184	Fig. 3
185	The saddest of cads
186	Officer and the gentle tan
187	The groomsman
188	Mother song
189	You are response
190	The pizza fan
191	Miss OOOOOH YEAH!
192	Lollies and coitus
193	Amusing neck
194	My skin
195	Zelda II
196	Mother elephant
197	Rad tigerman piece
198	Swan
199	Transit home
200	Time hands
201	Three cows as seating
202	Duck
204	The plate job
205	Blessed be the hag
206	Going home
207	Jack on Jill
208	Saved by the bellend
209	Memories often sting the heart
210	Today in your life
211	Never forget
212	You are love

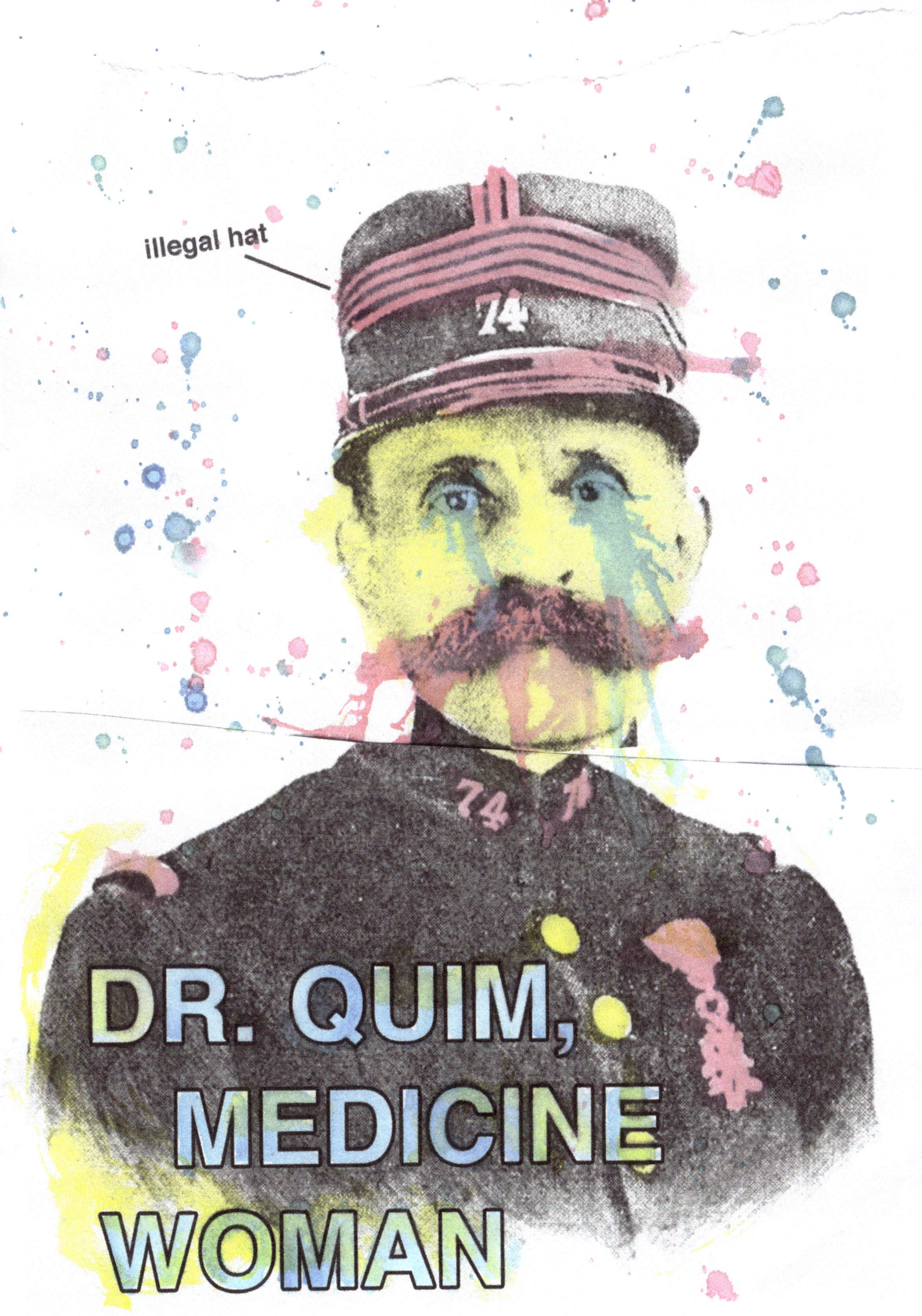

illegal hat
DR. QUIM,
MEDICINE
WOMAN

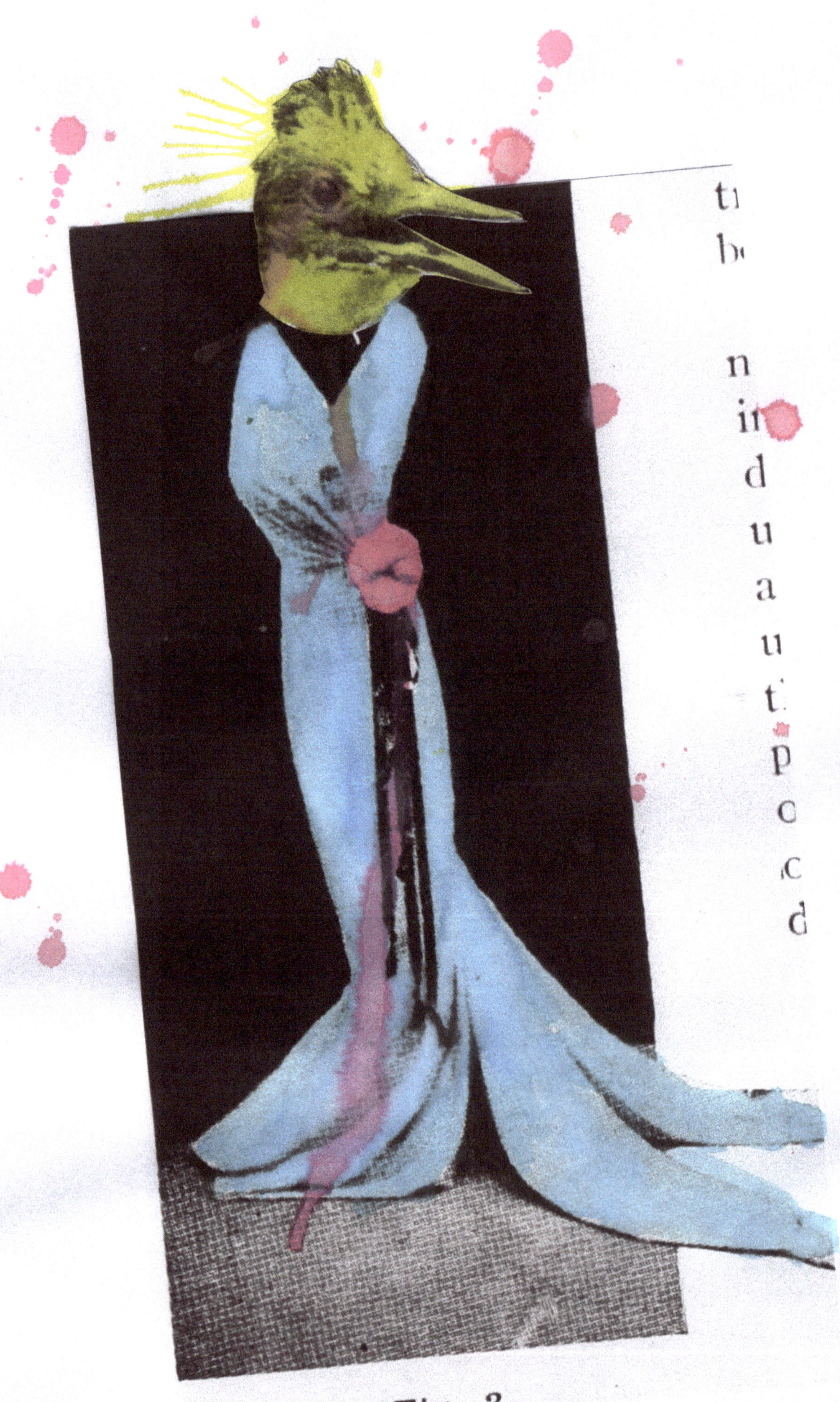

Fig. 3

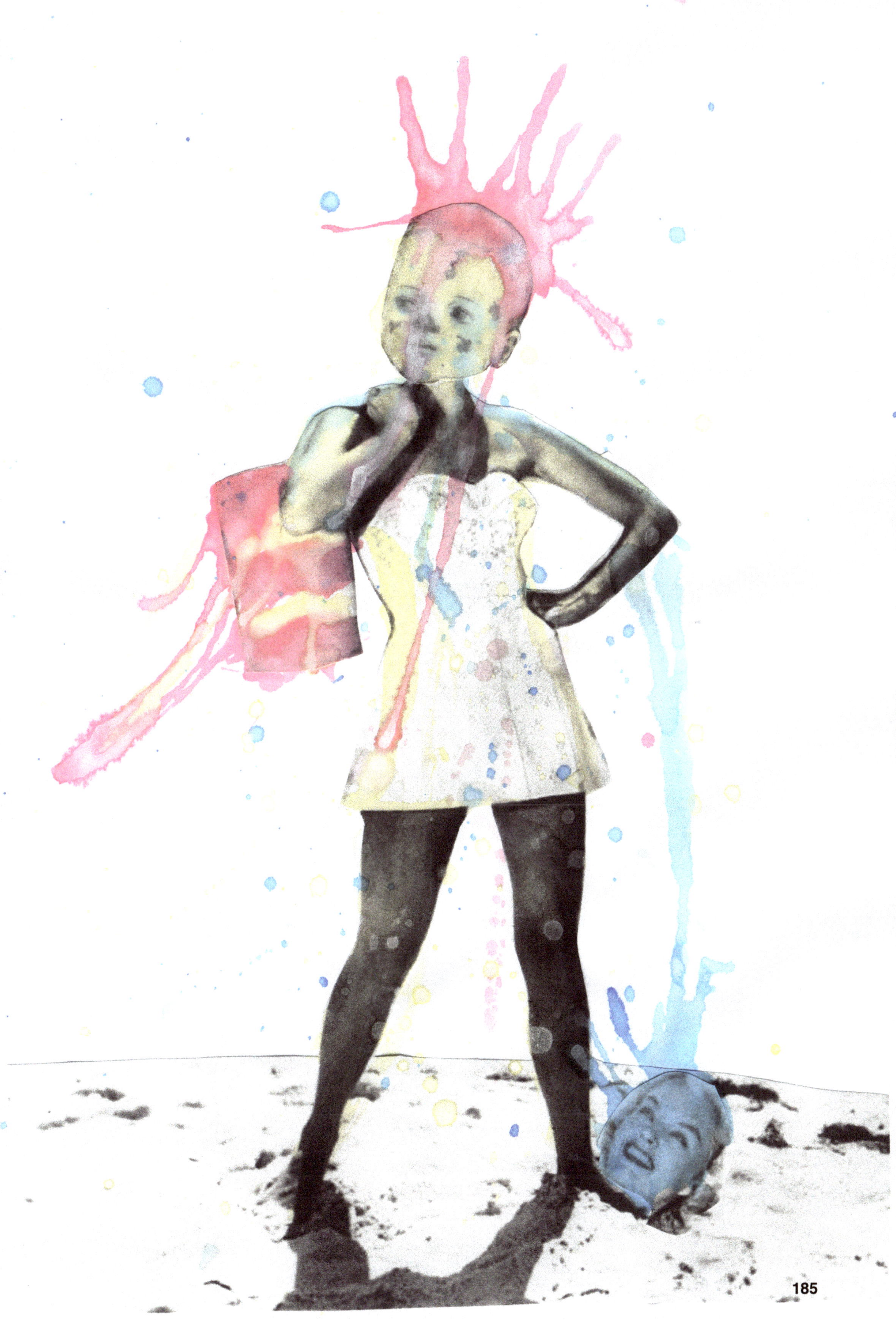

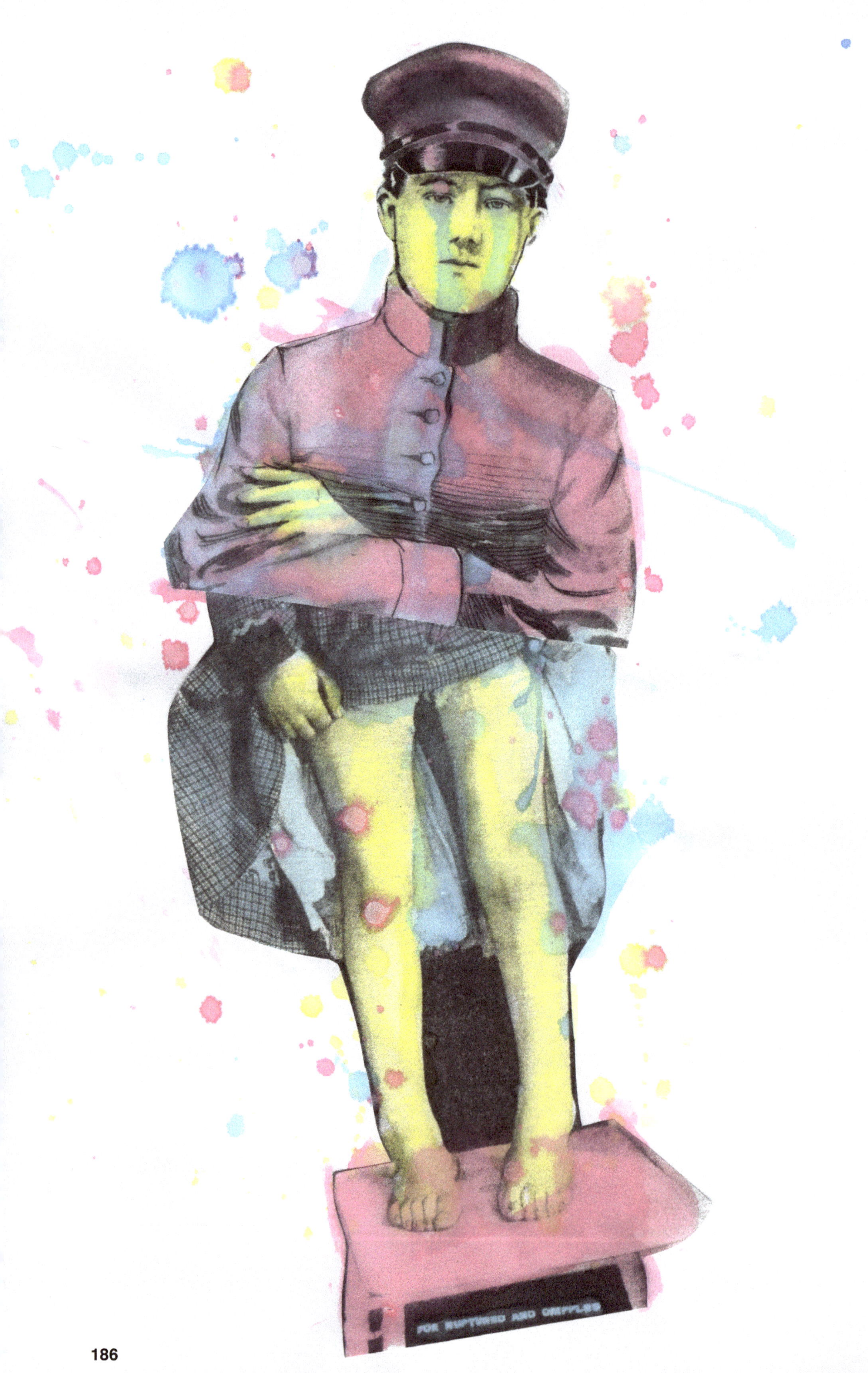
FOR RUPTURED AND CRIPPLED

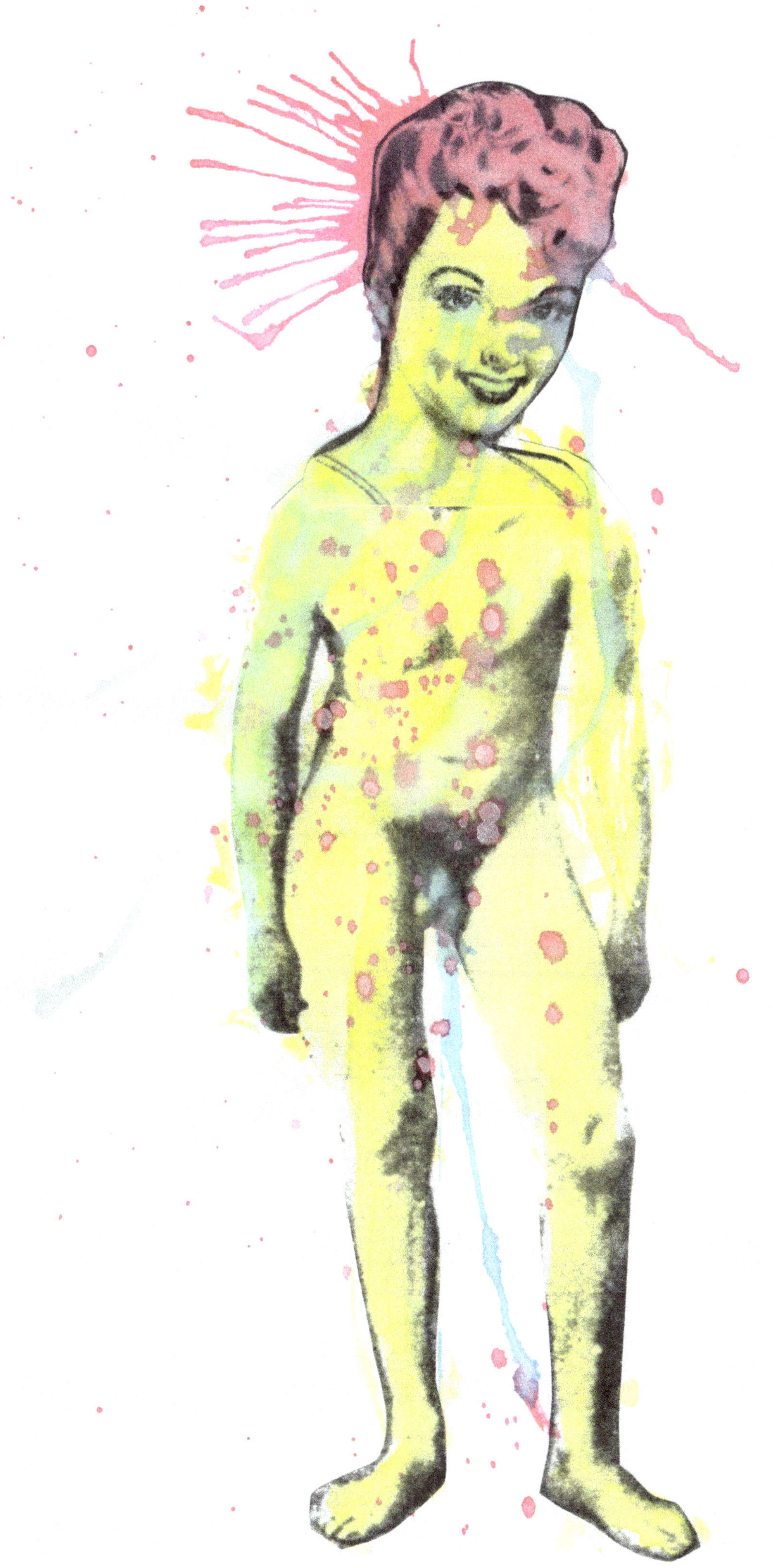

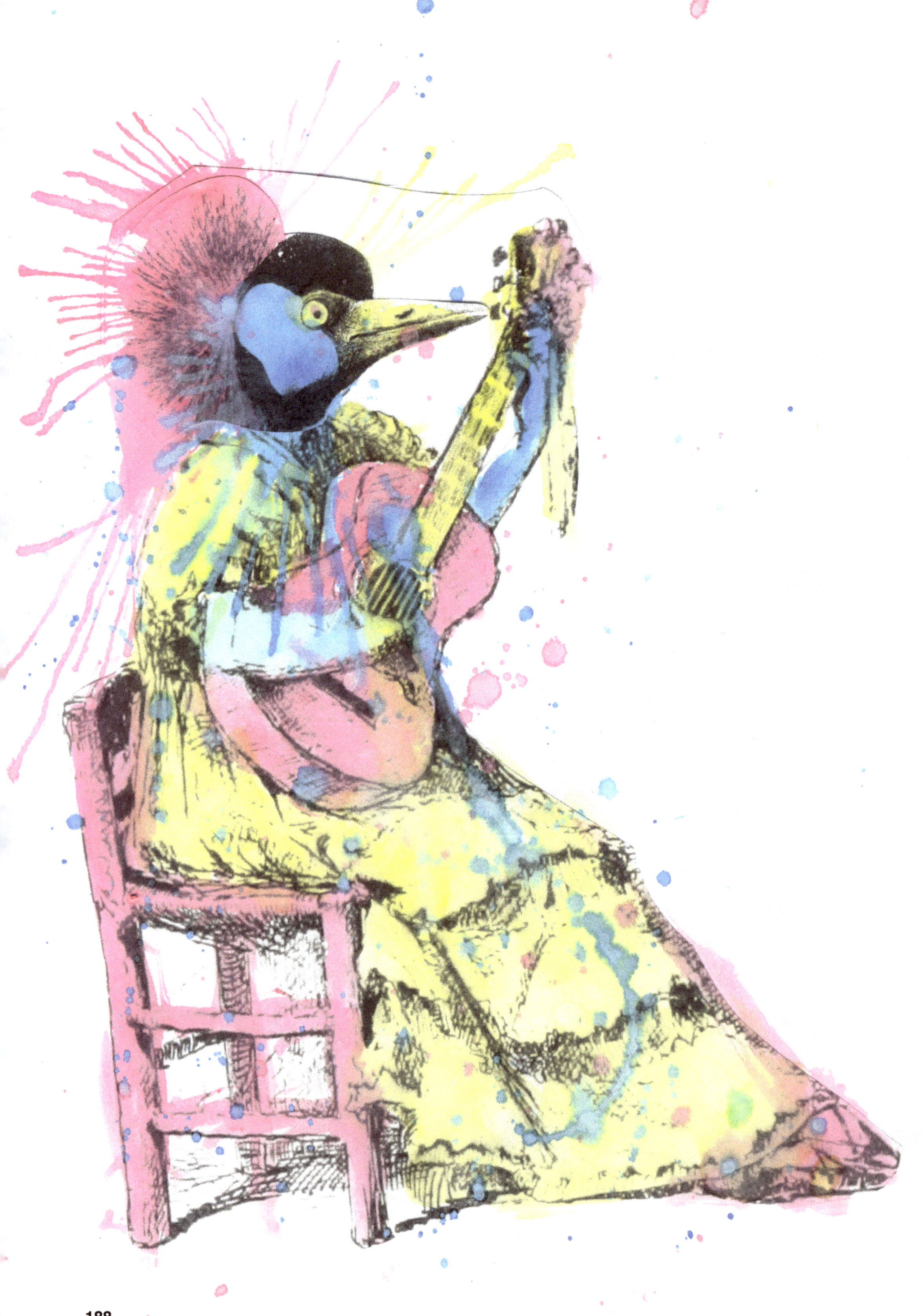

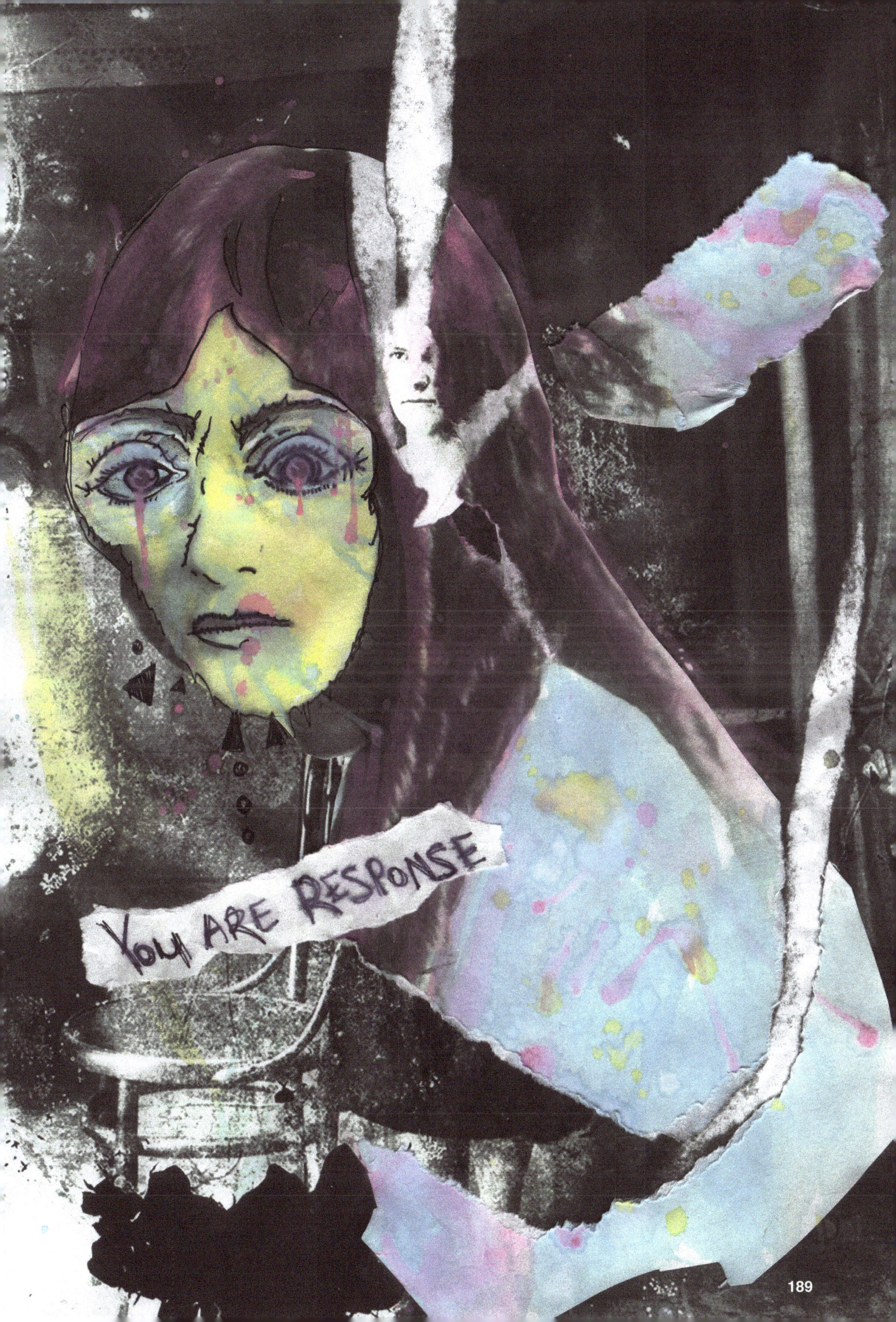

YOU ARE RESPONSE

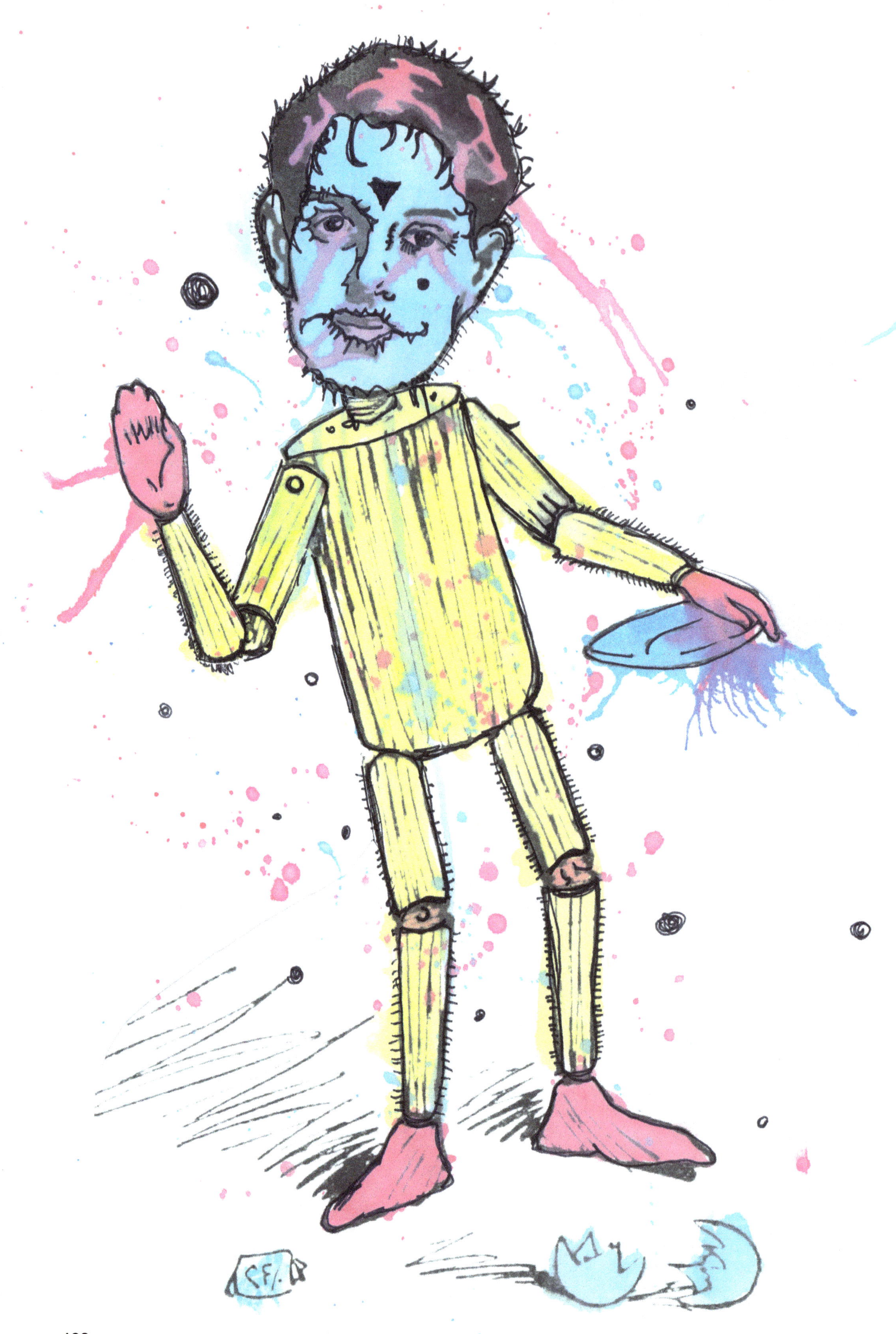

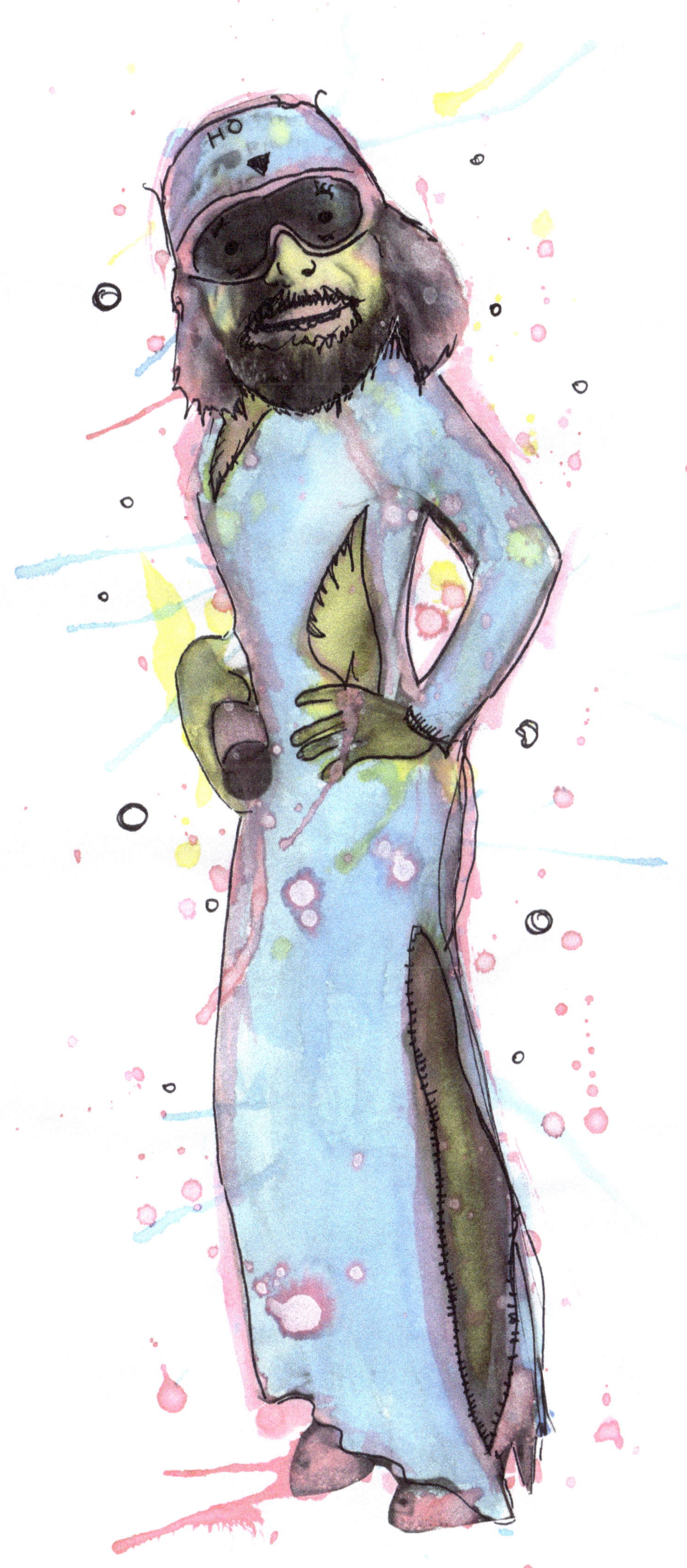

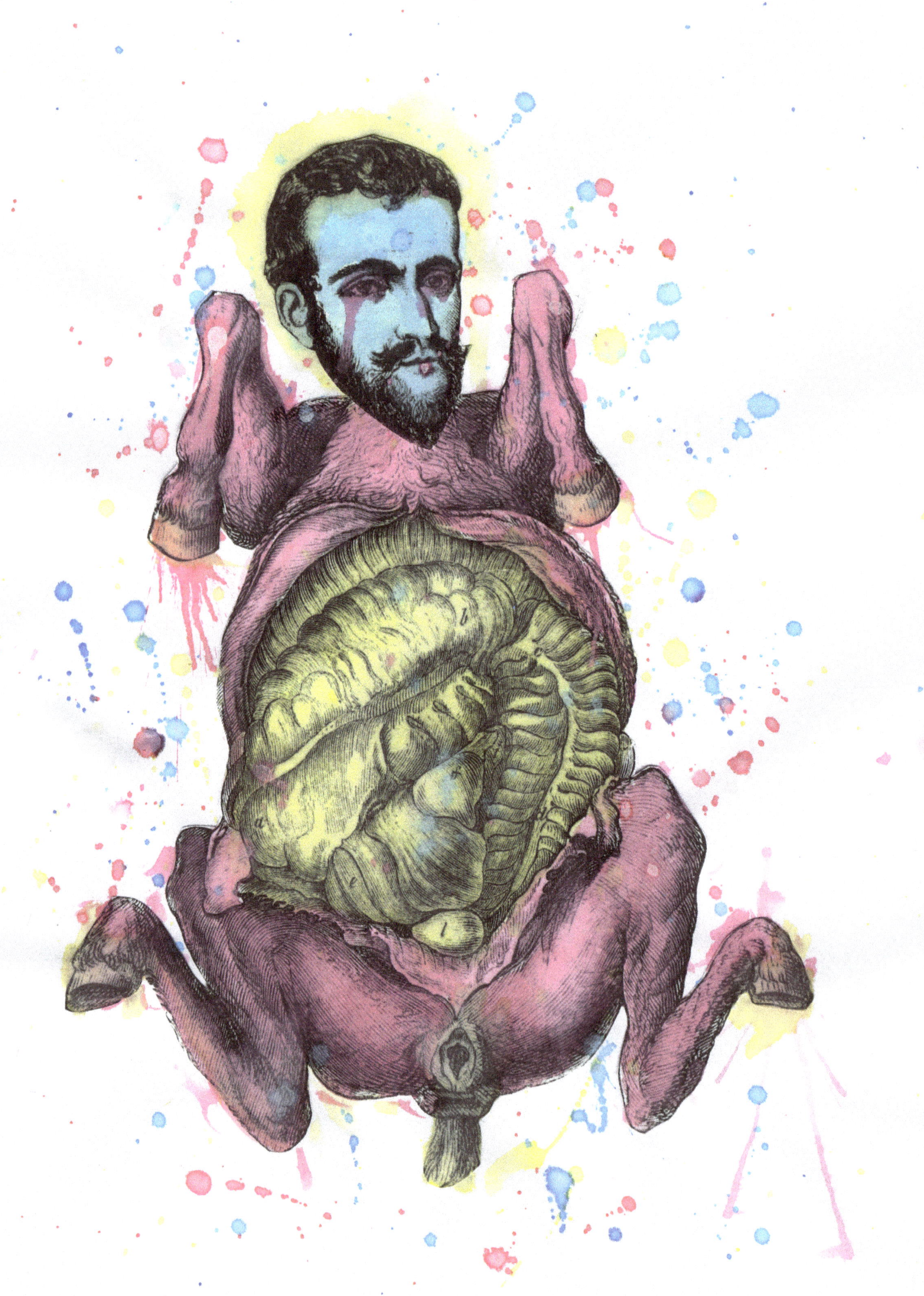

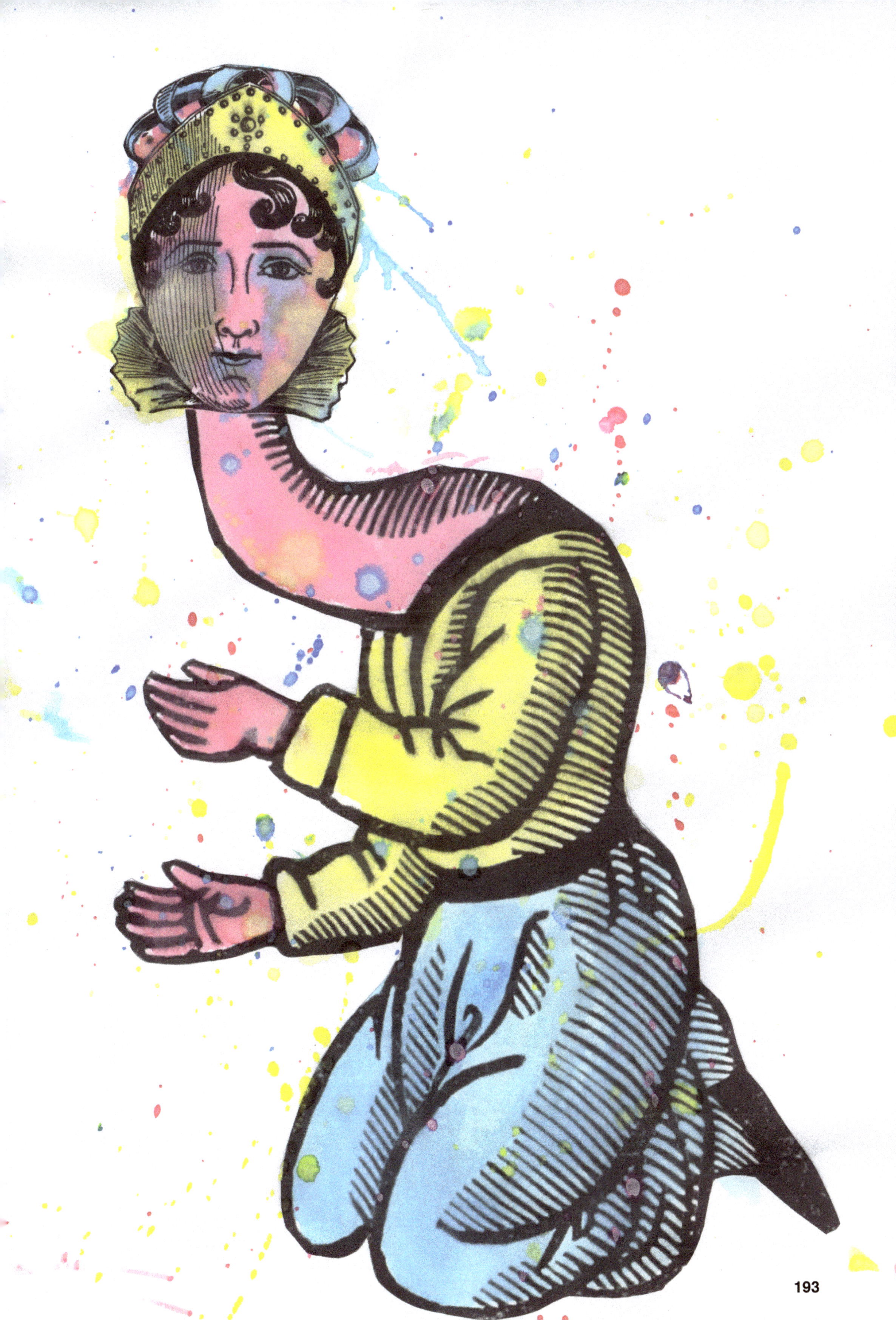

i am tired of washing my skin

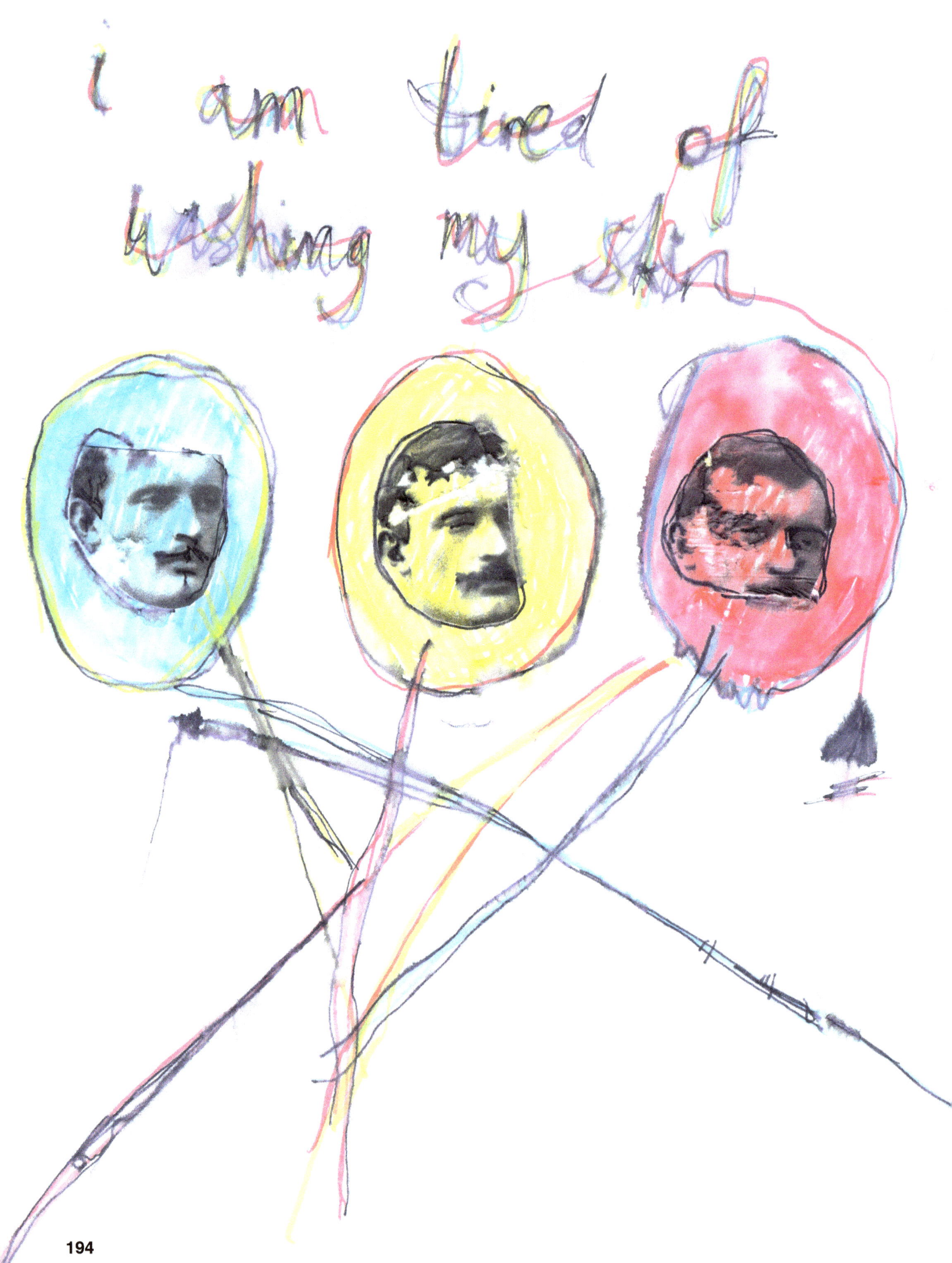

"**While different to other games in the series, 'Zelda II: The Adventures of Link' is still a very good game in its own right.**"

— George Clooney, 1952

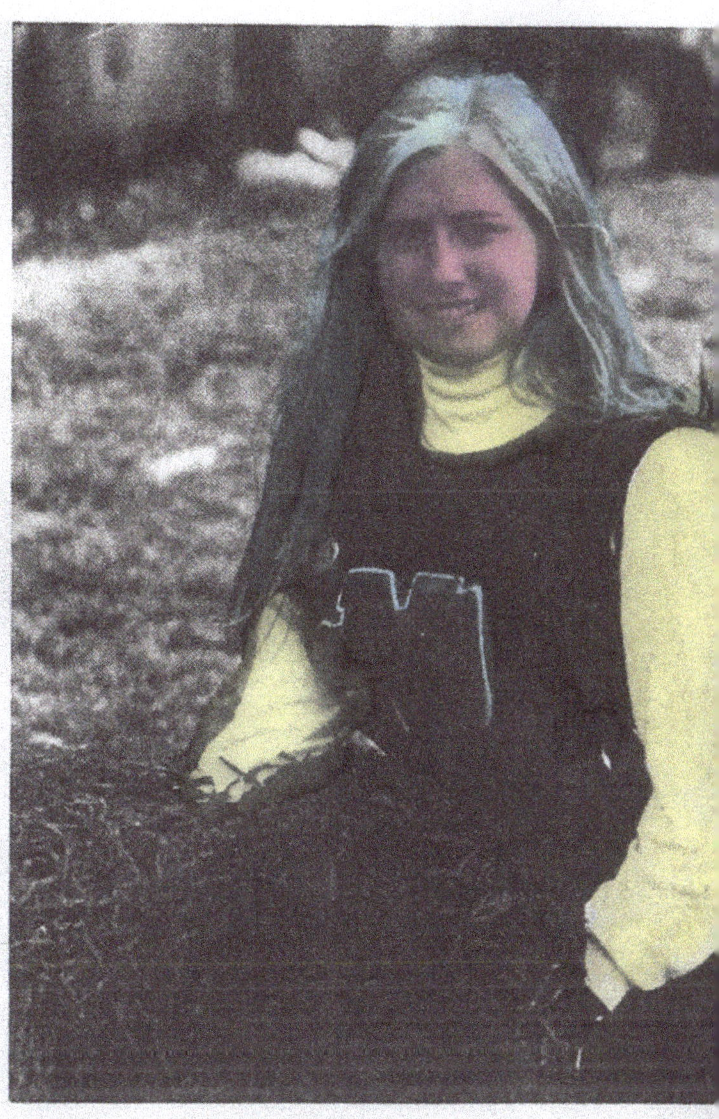

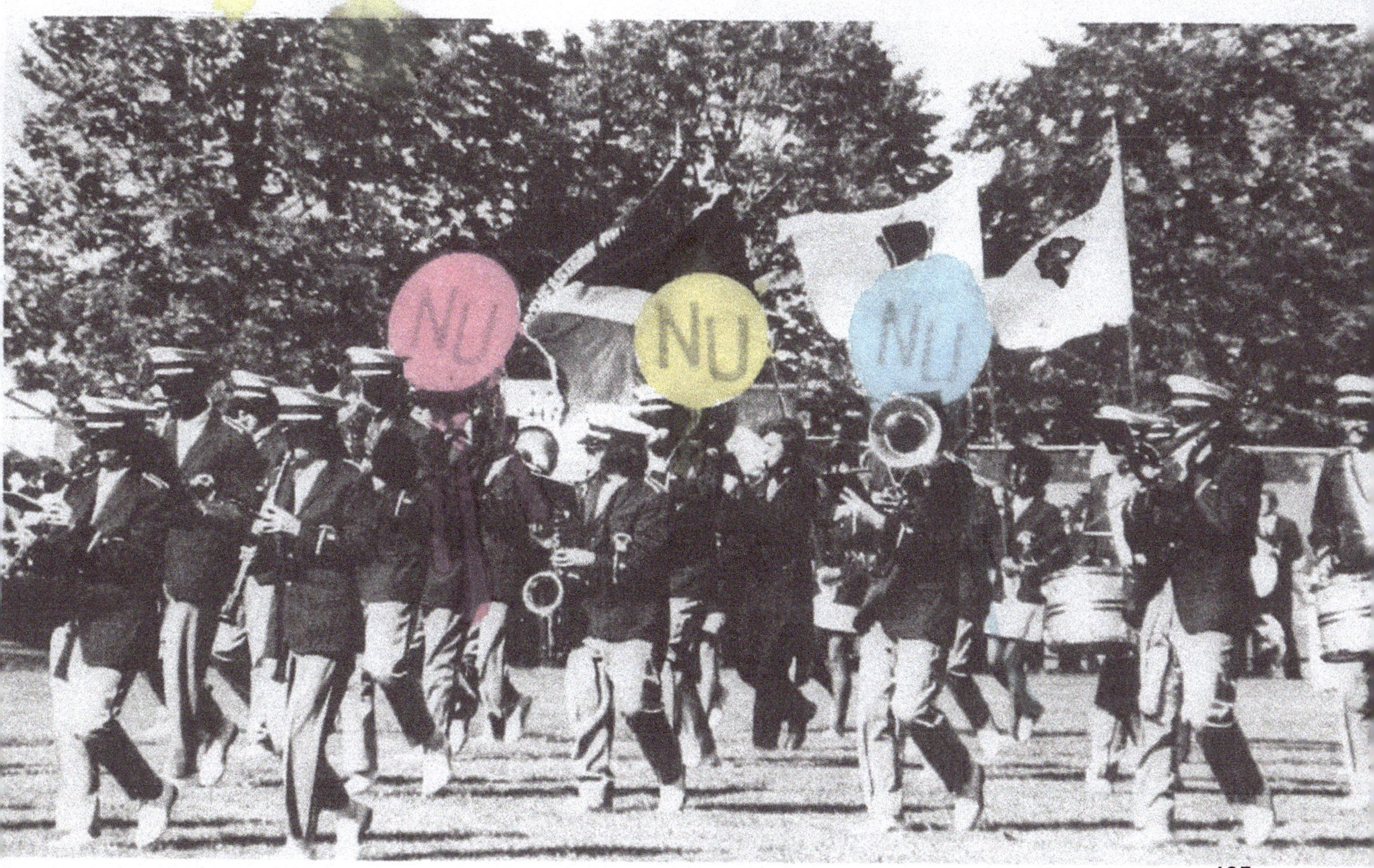

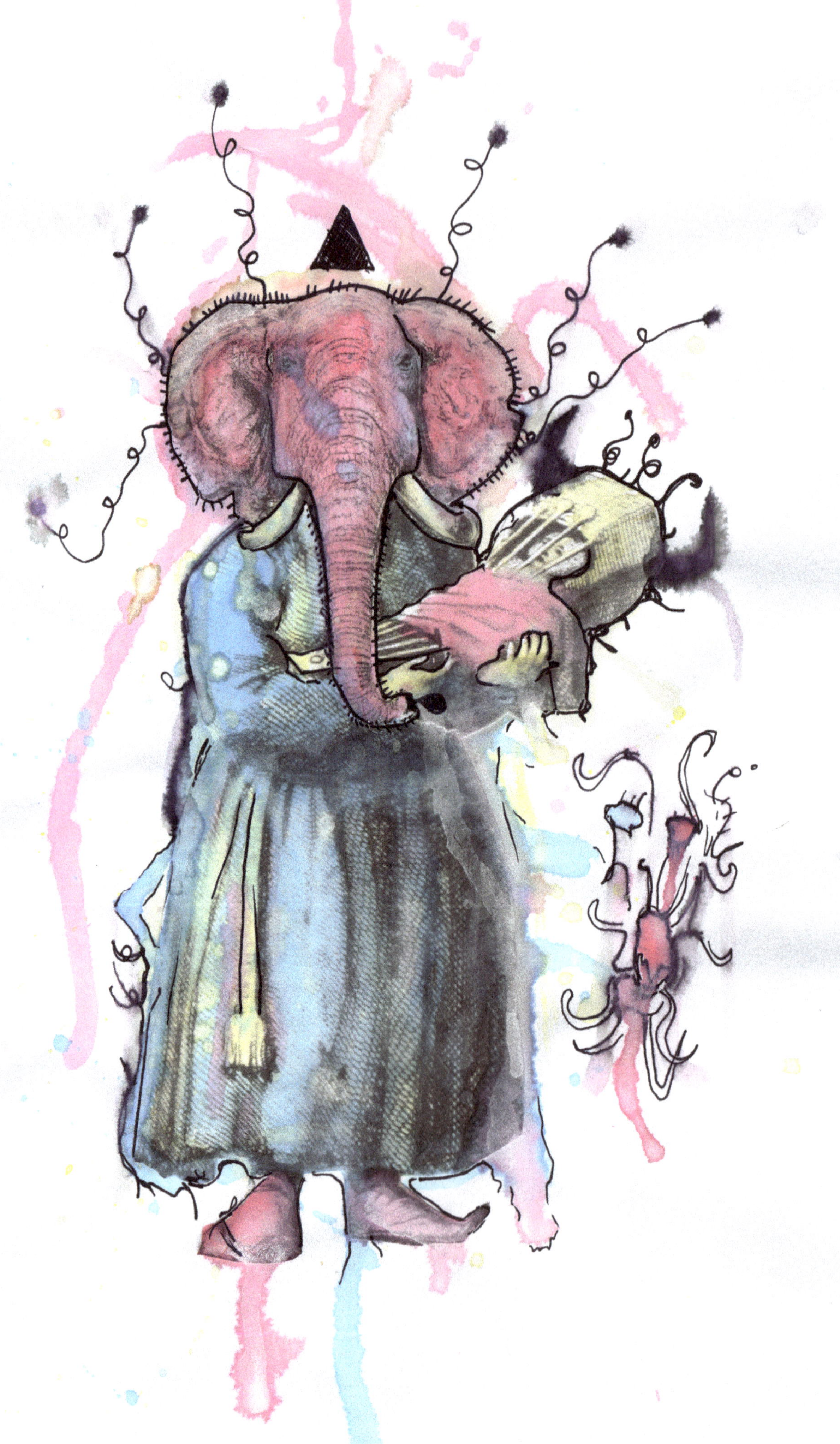

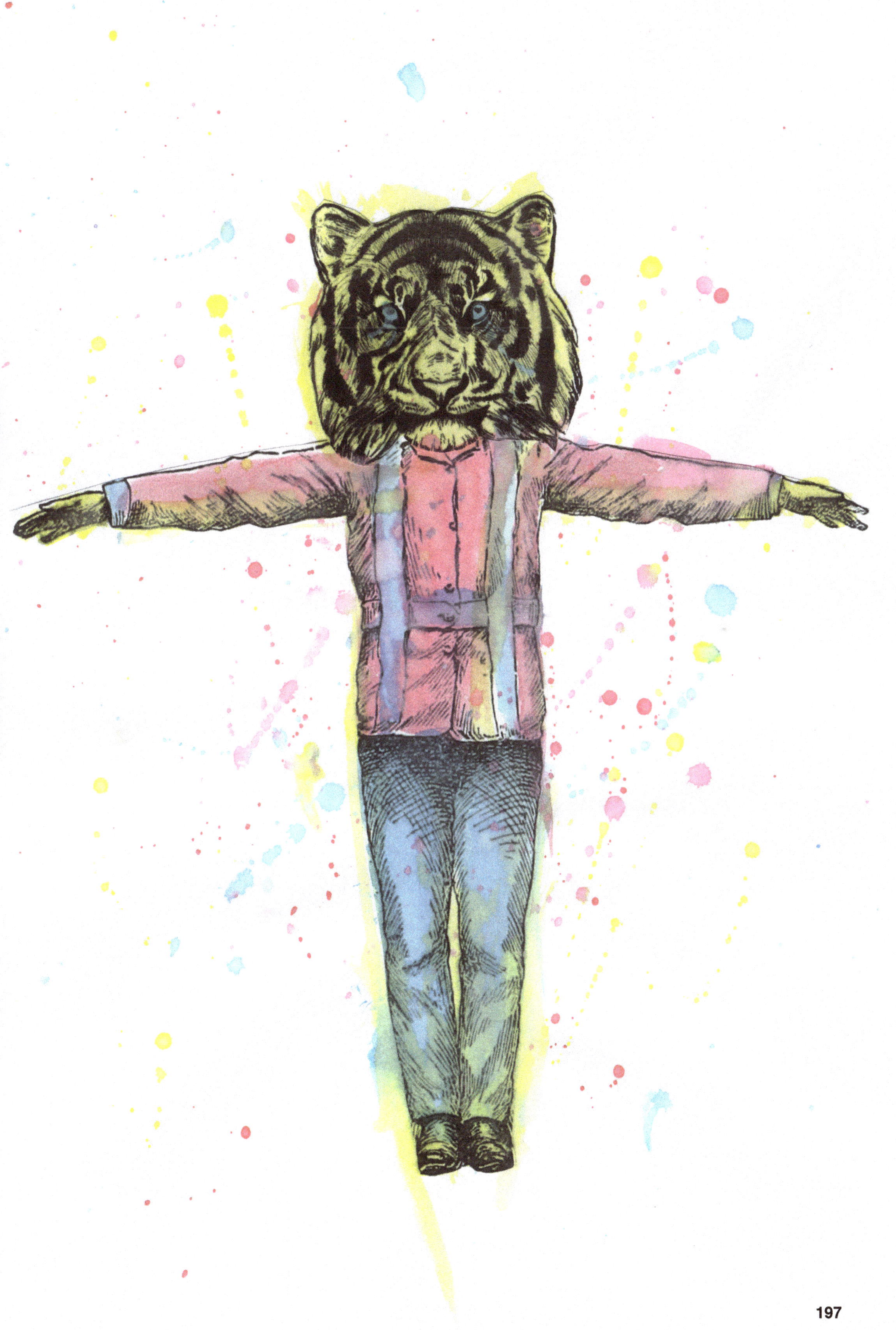

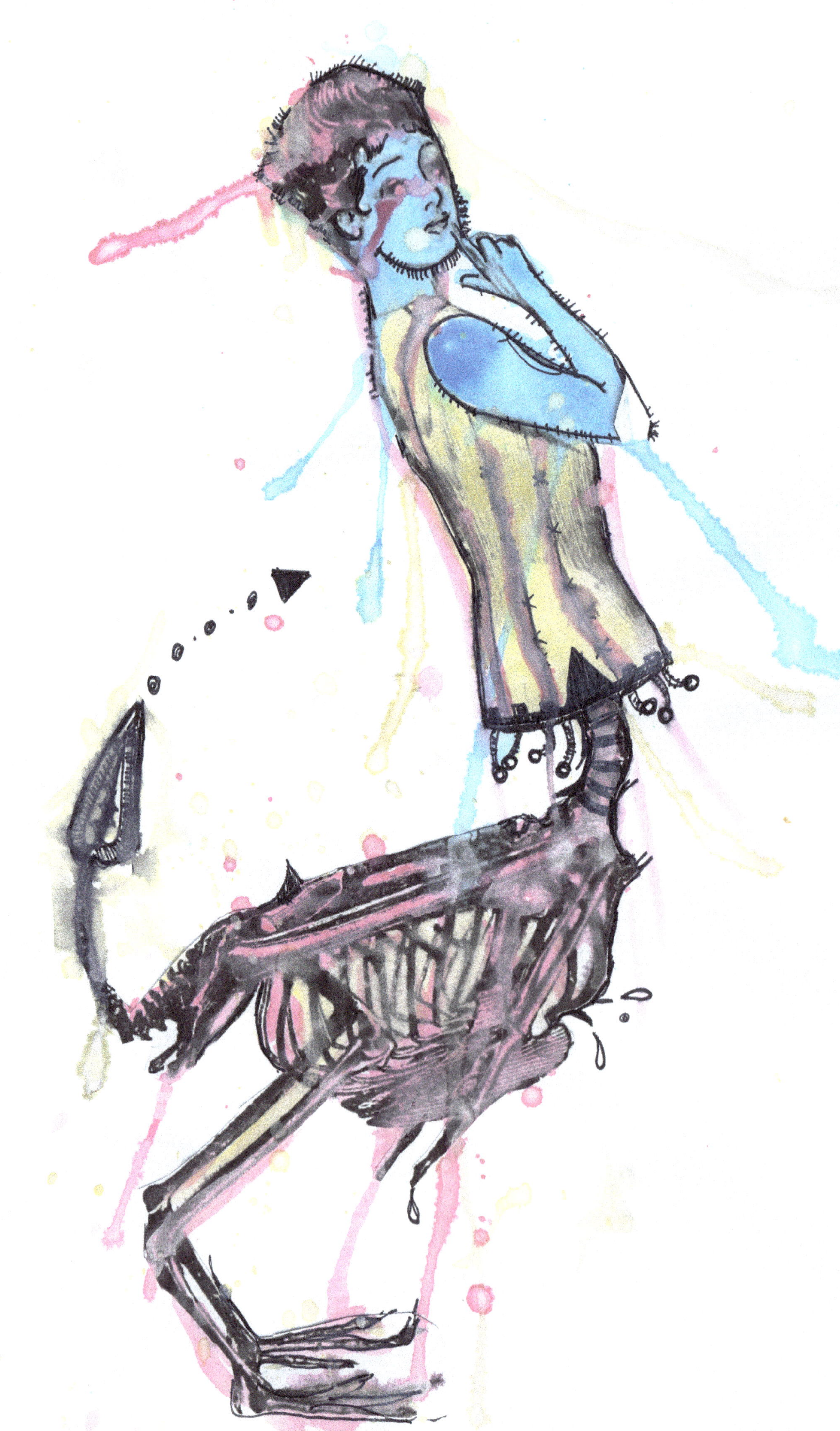

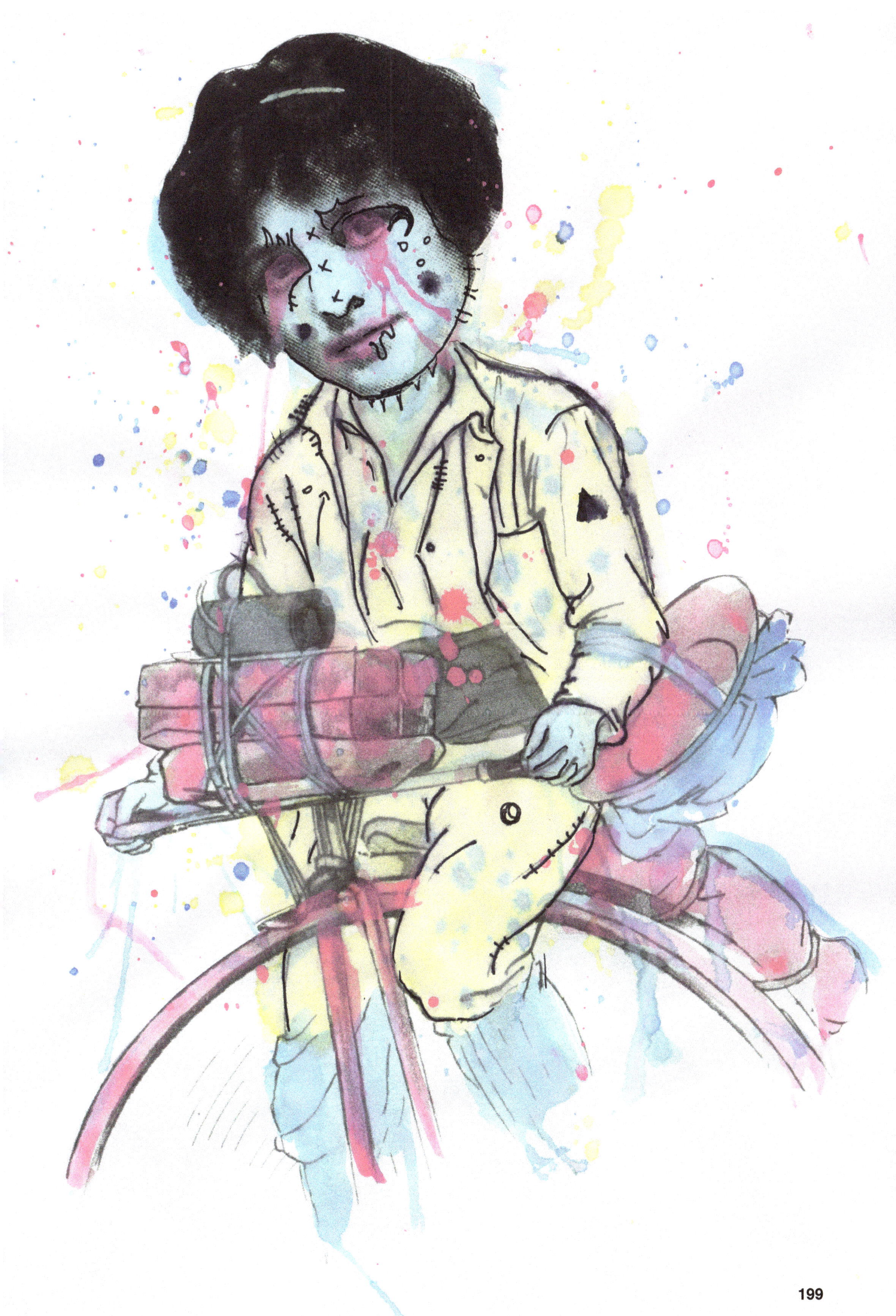

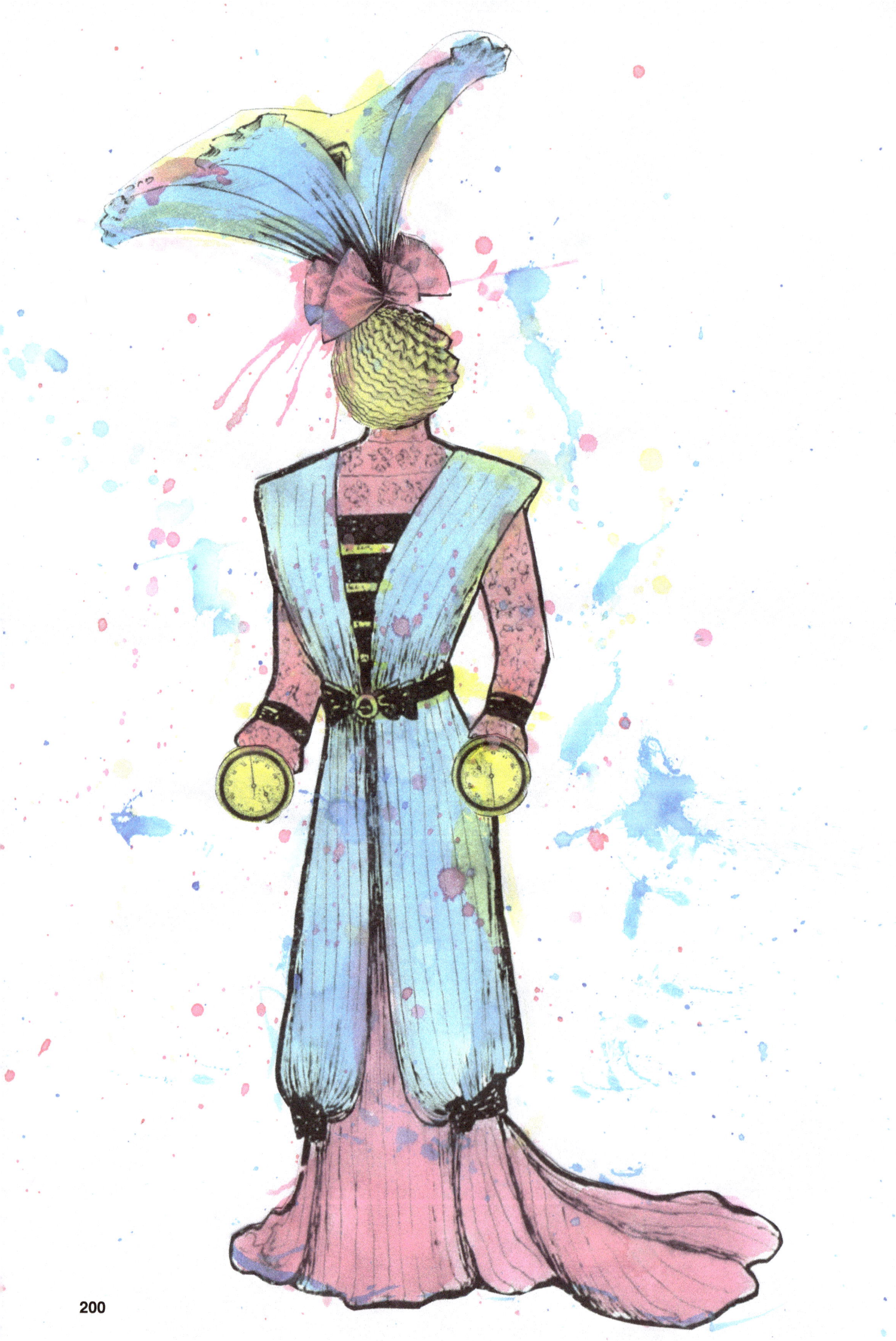

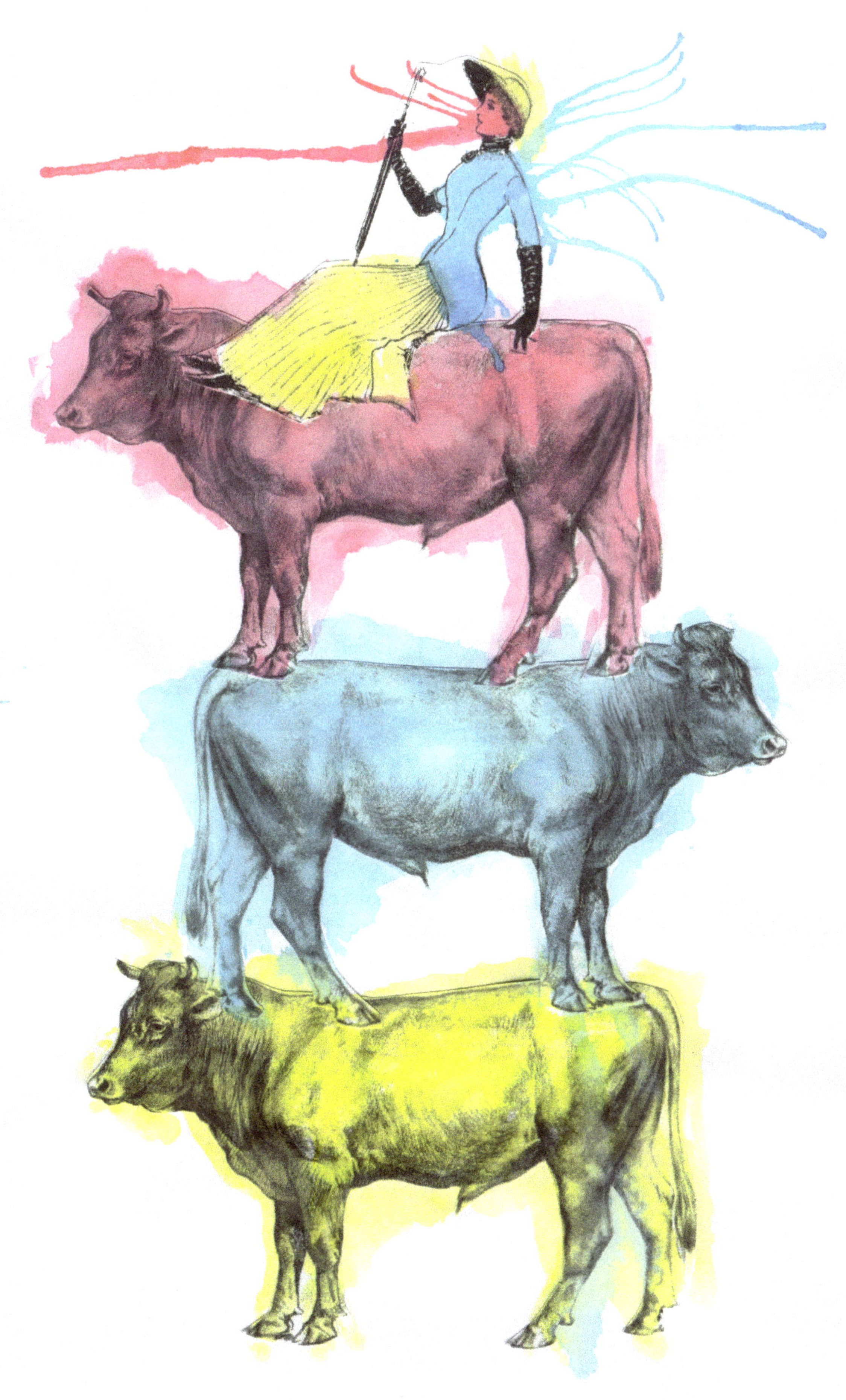

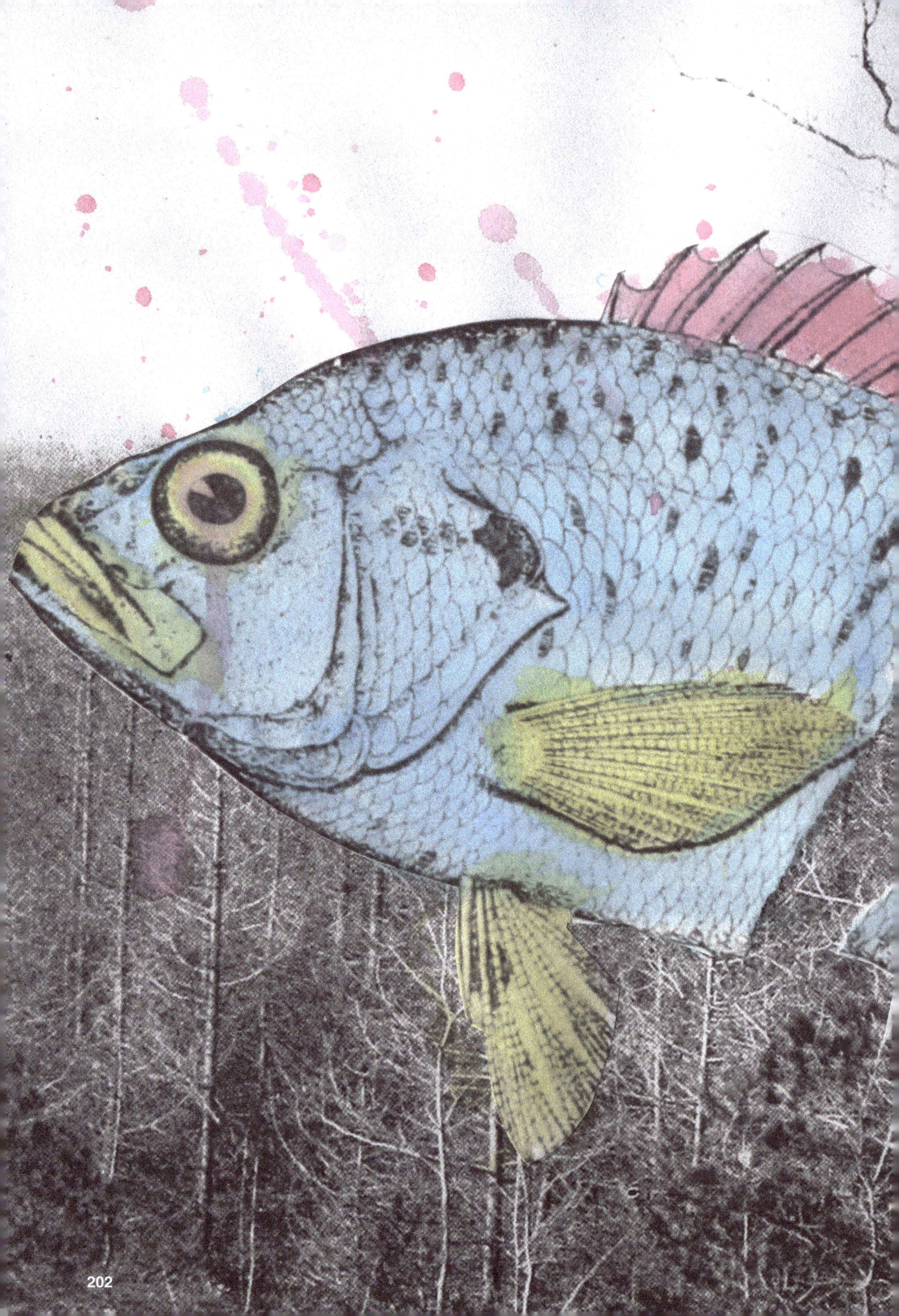

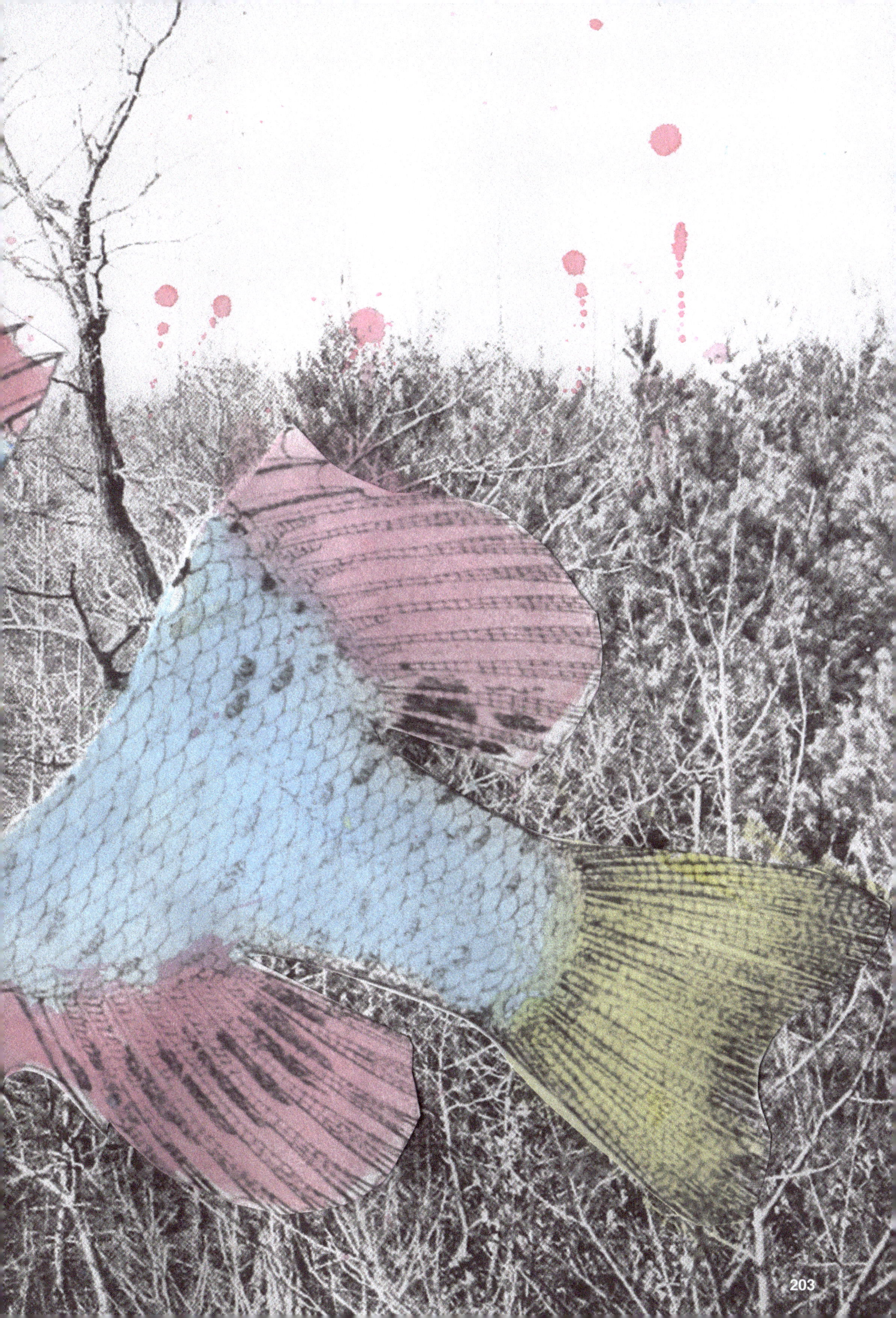

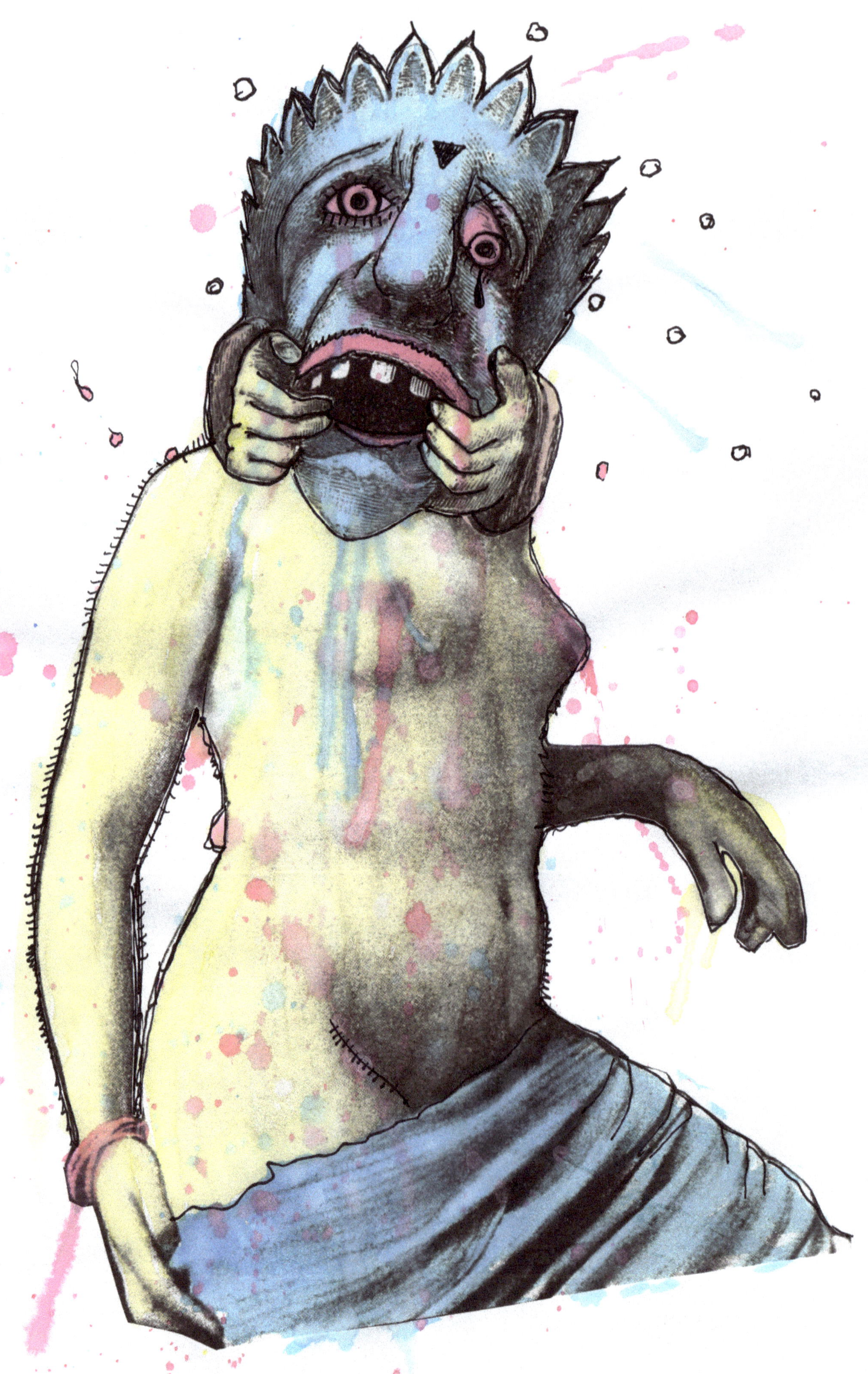

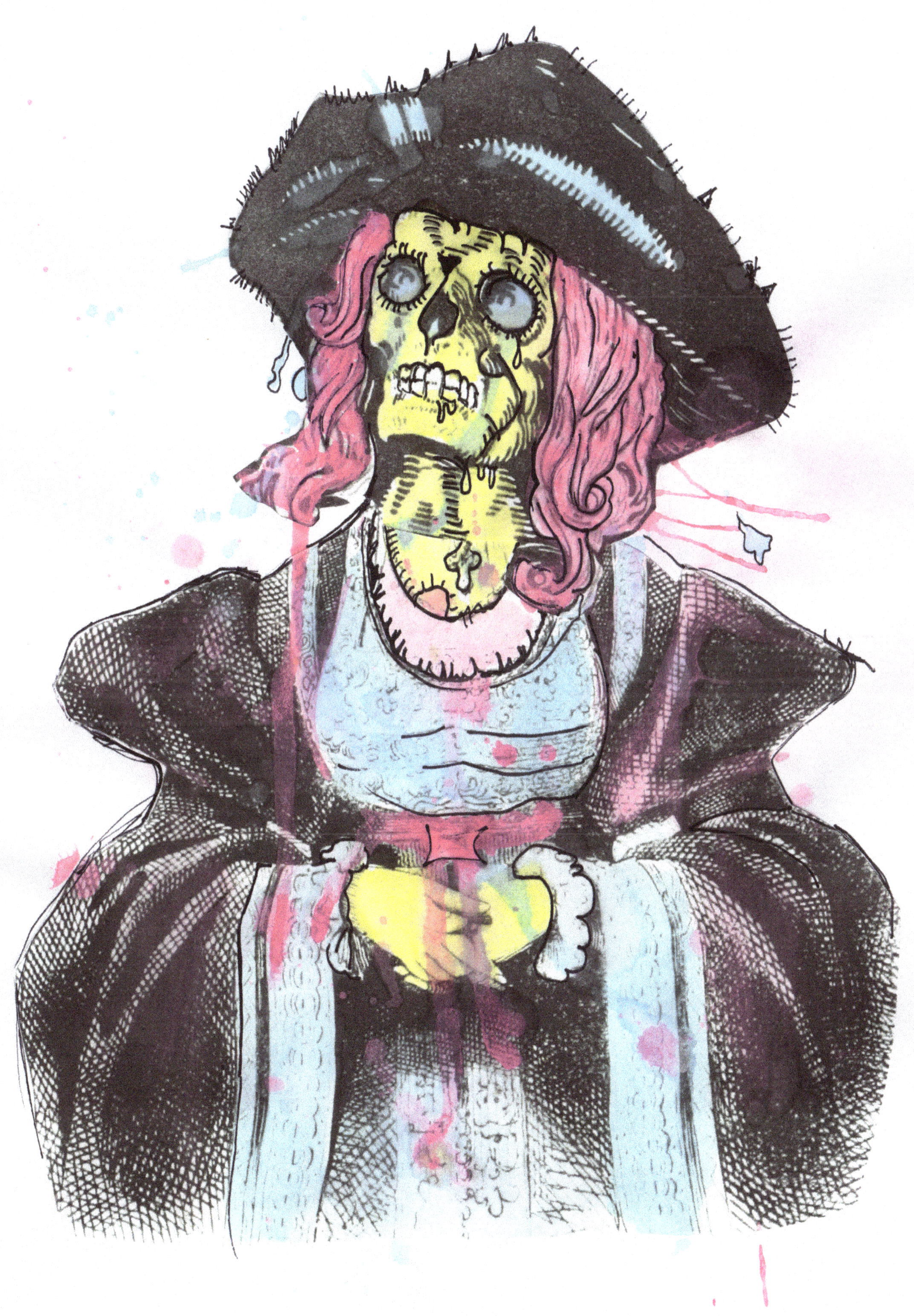

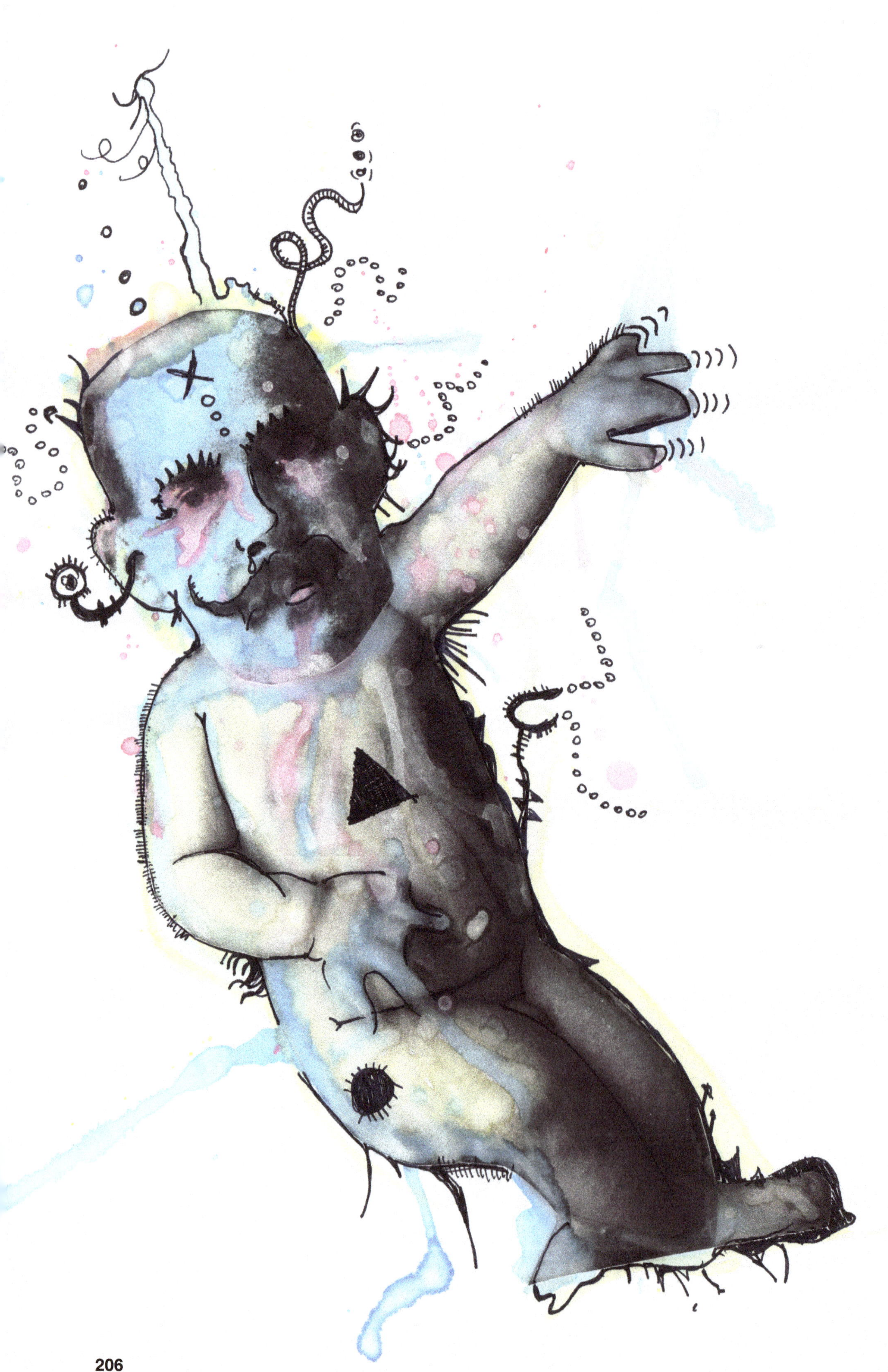

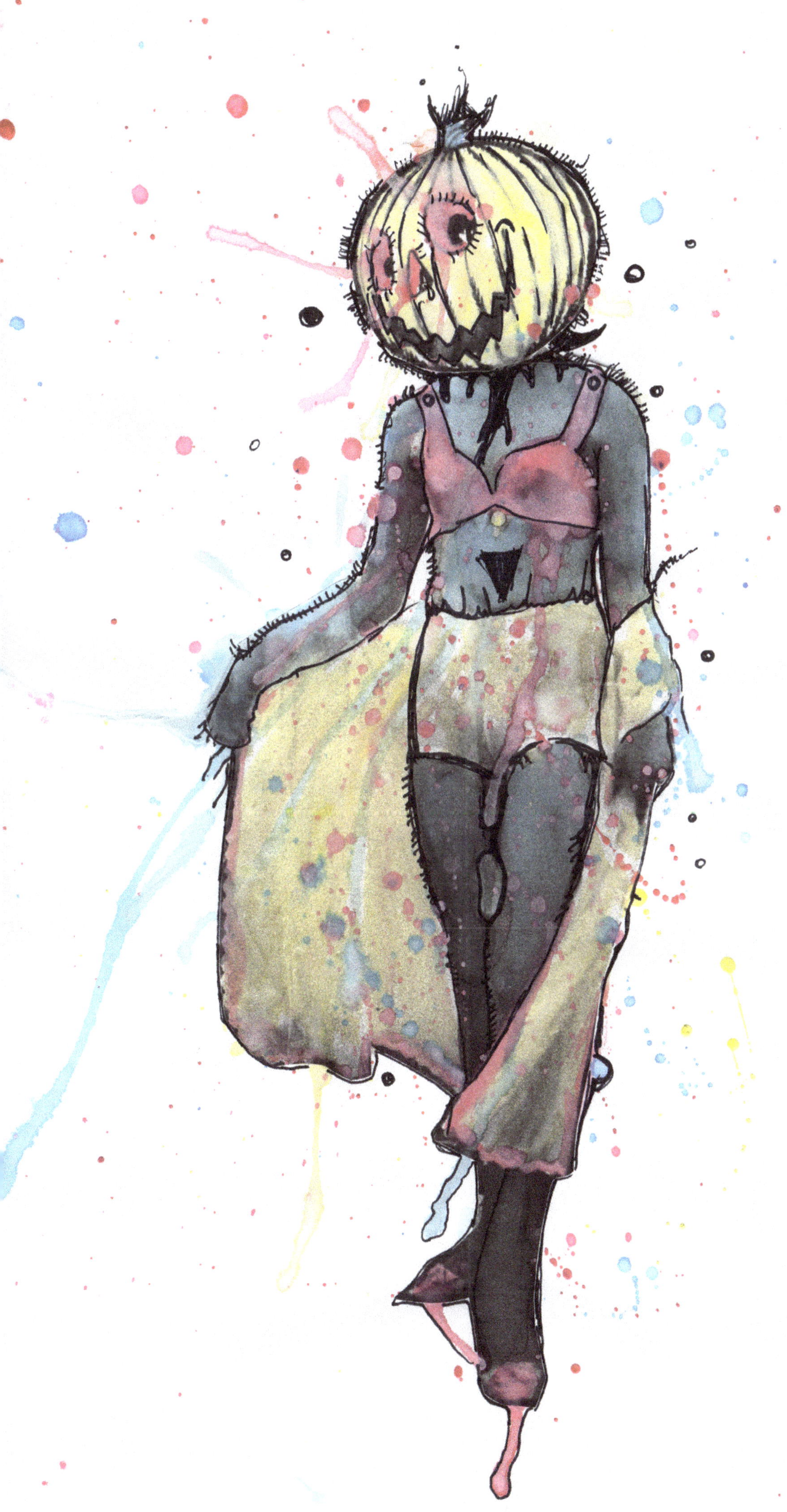

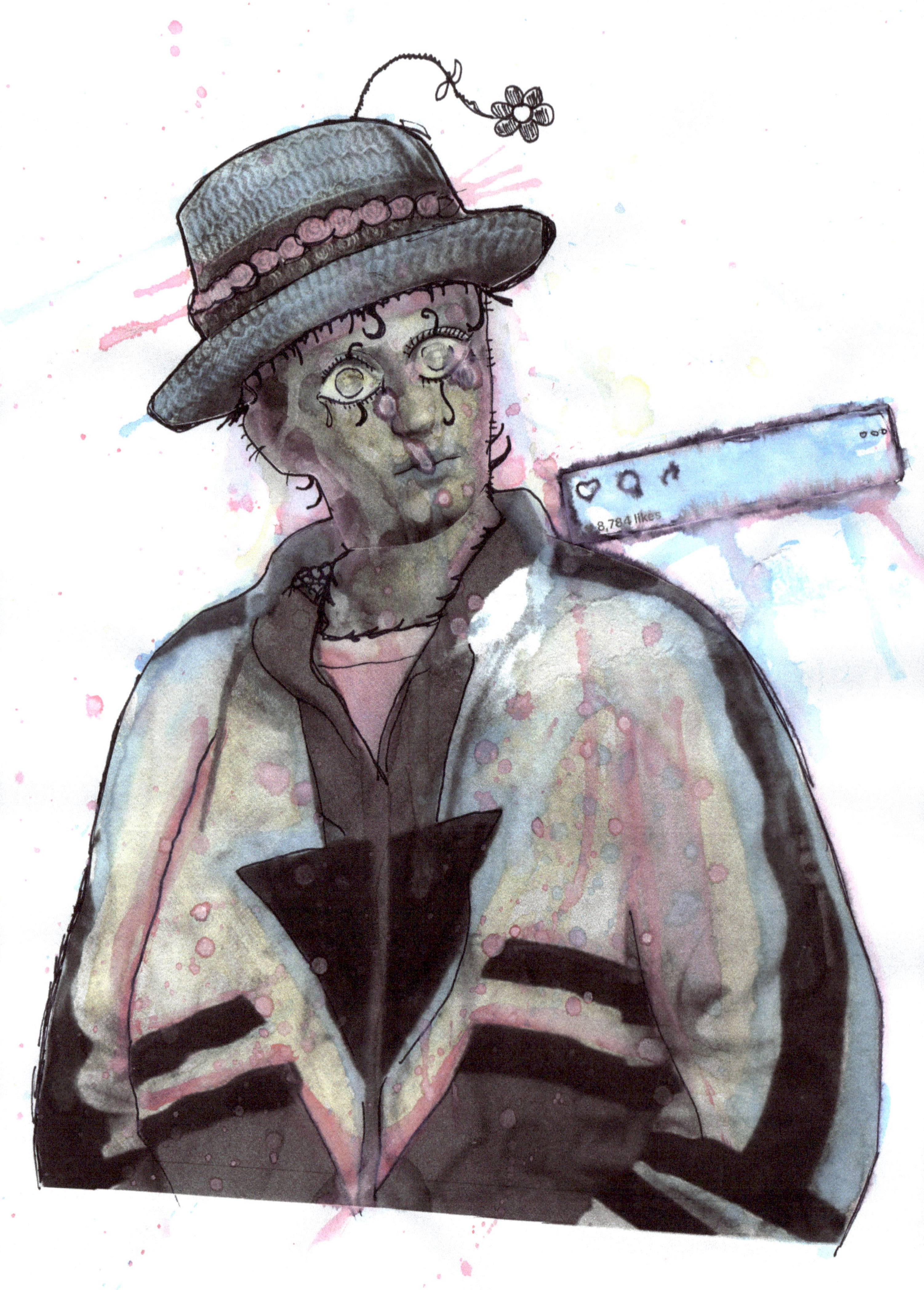

8,784 likes

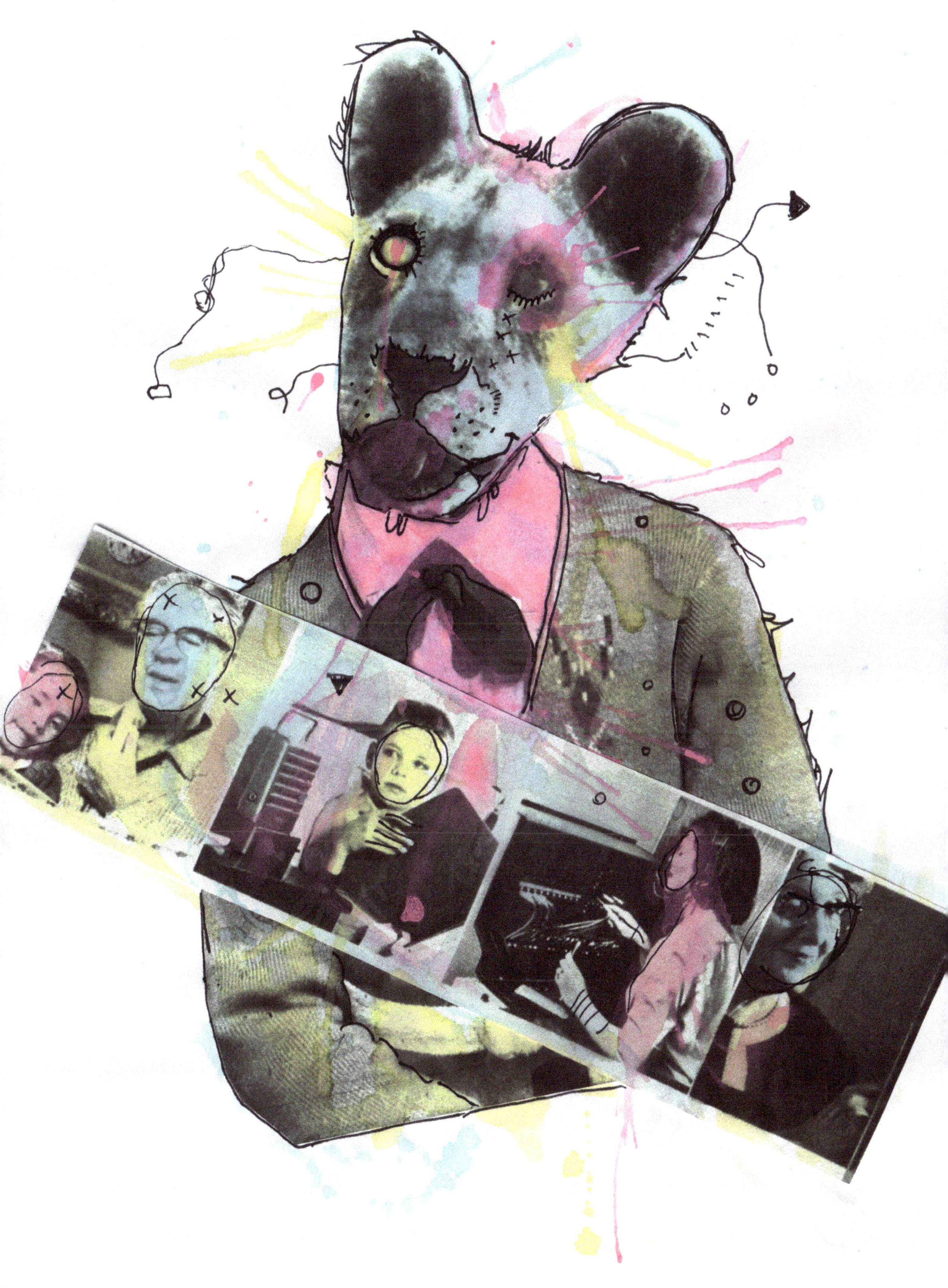

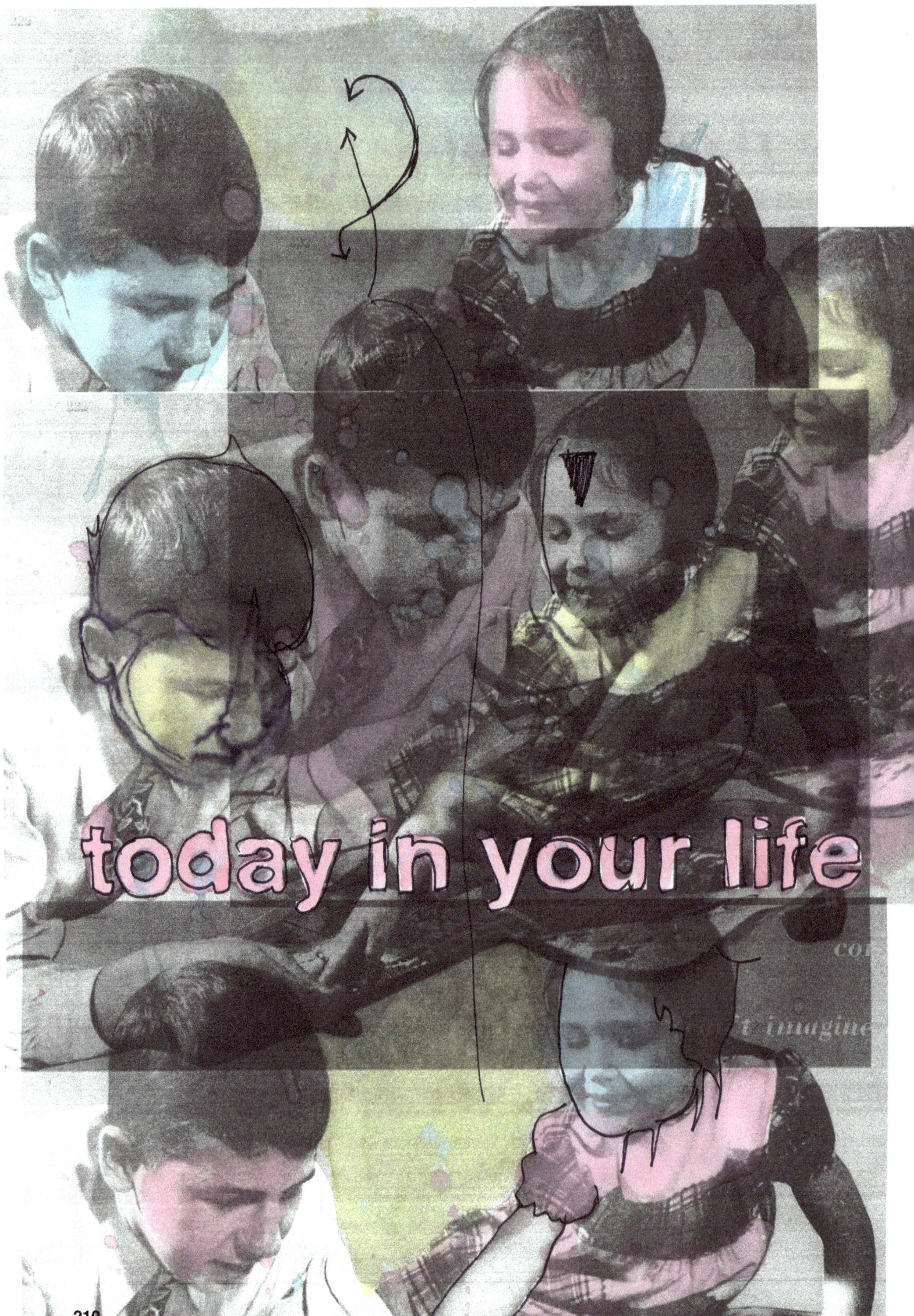

today in your life

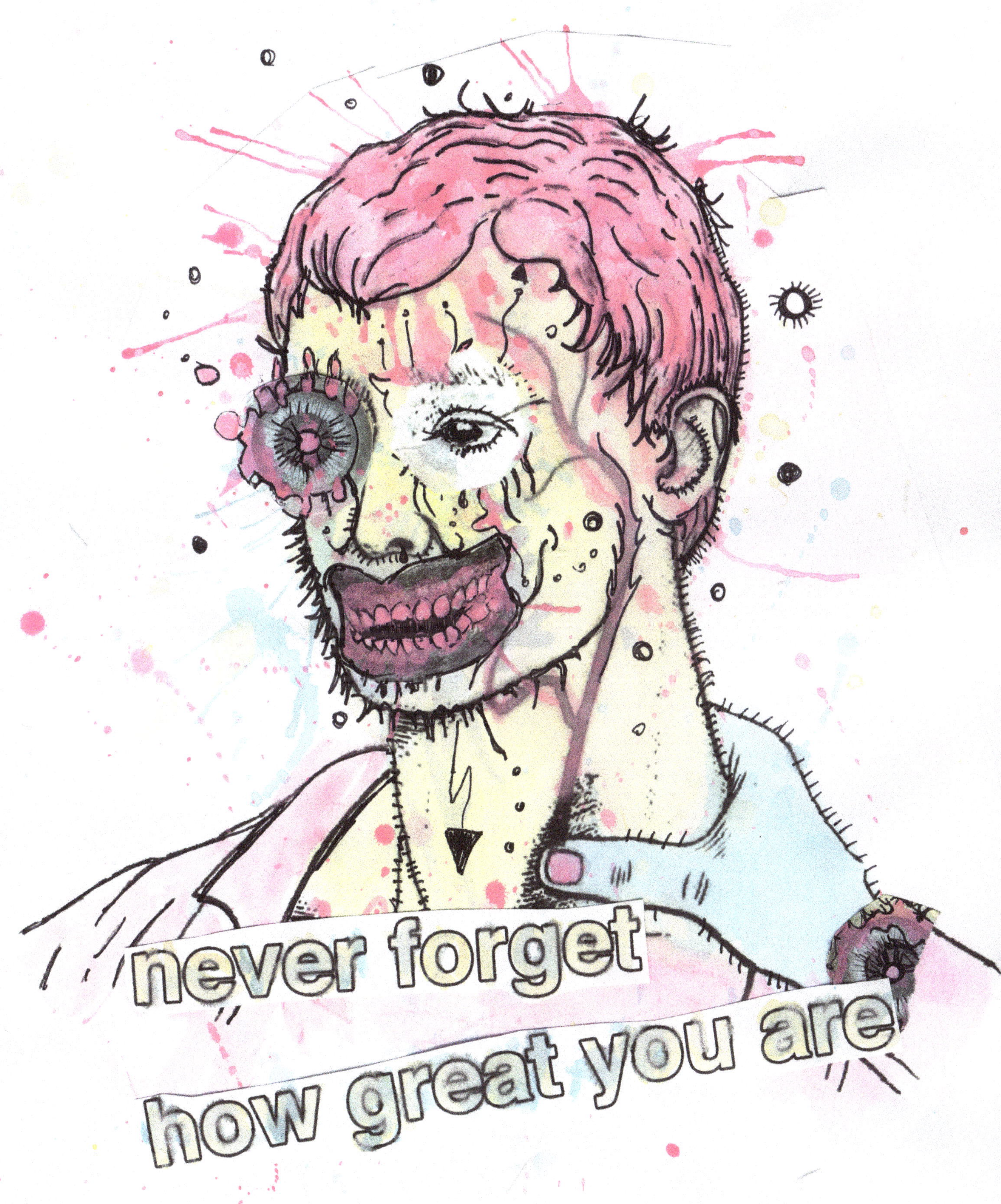
never forget
how great you are

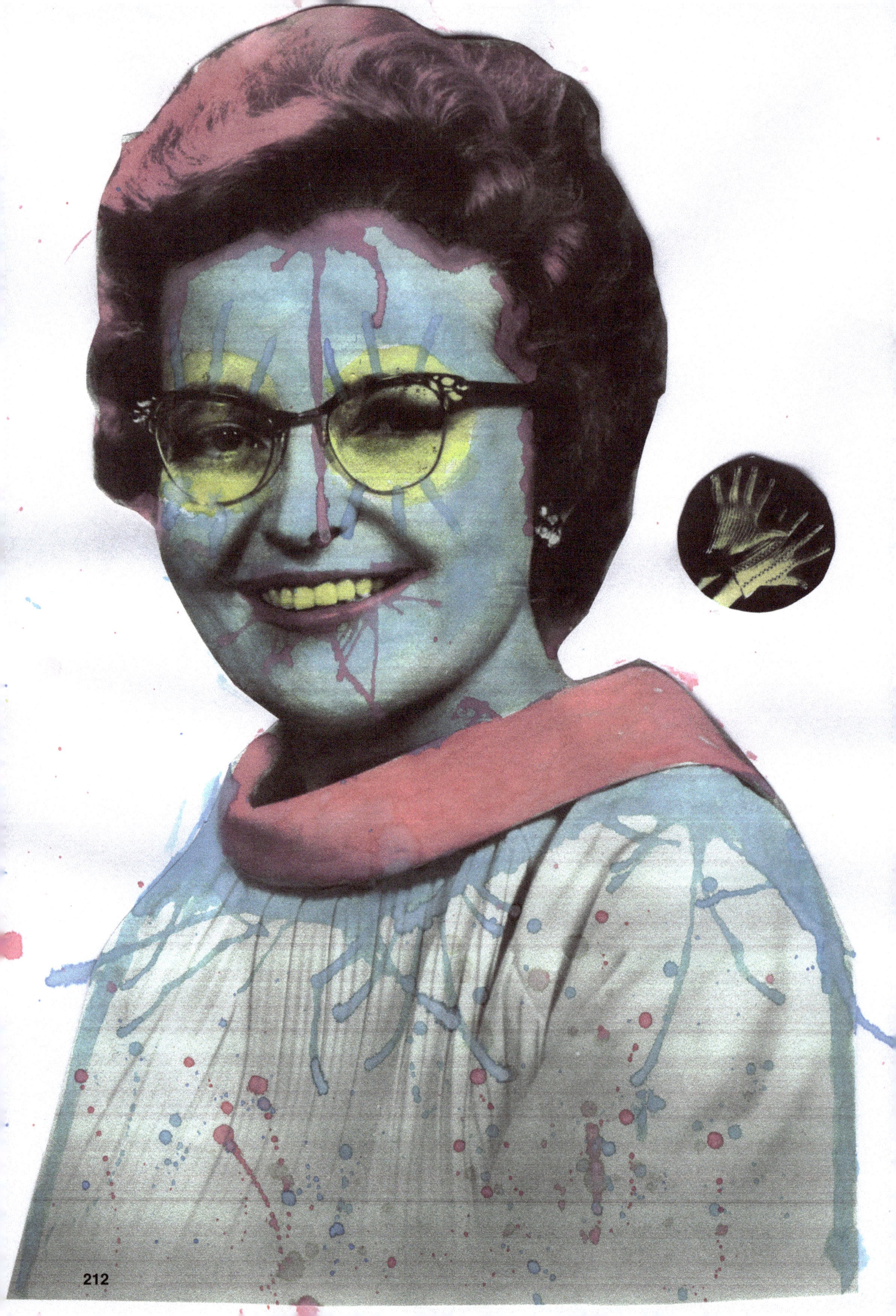

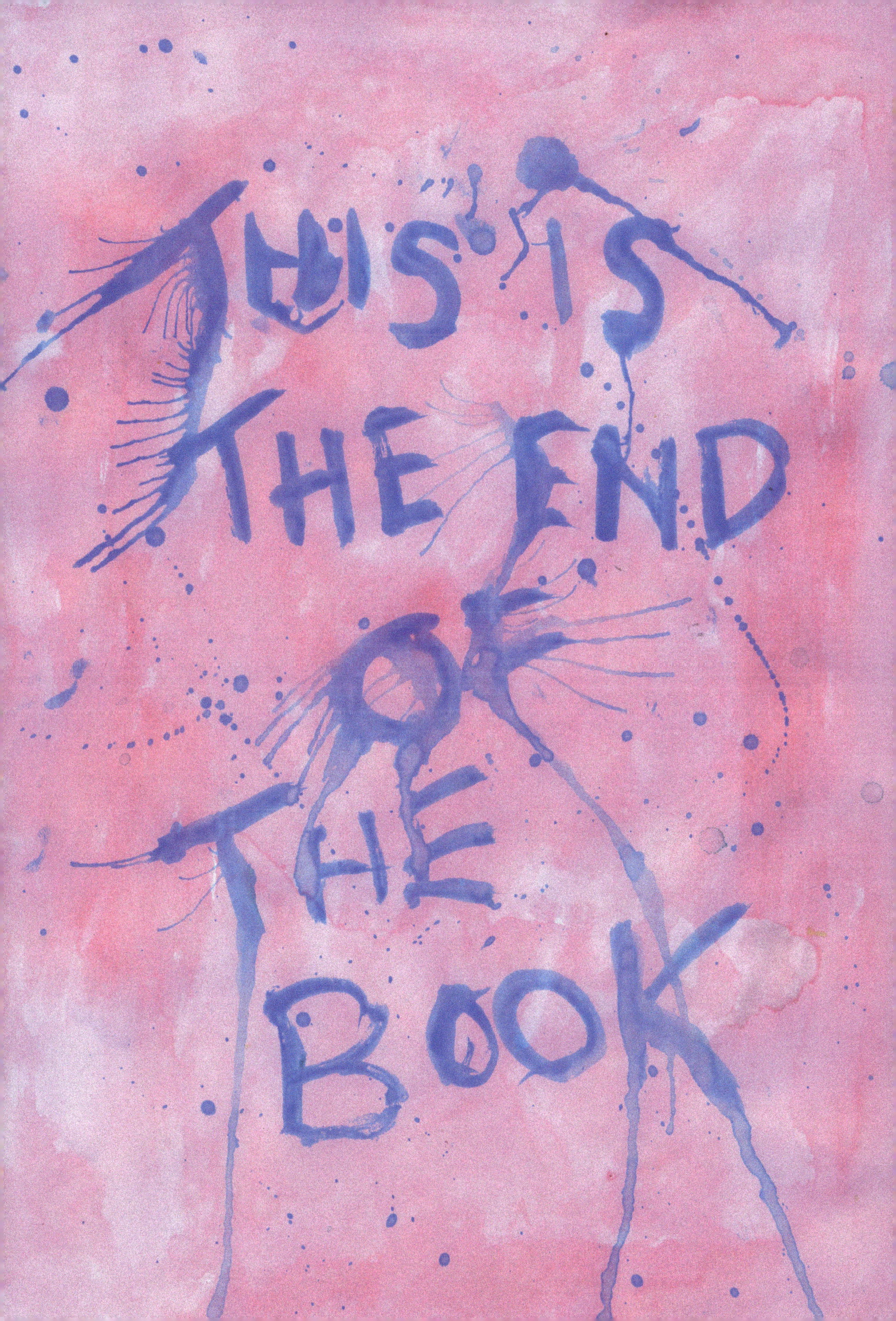

THIS IS
THE END
OF
THE
BOOK

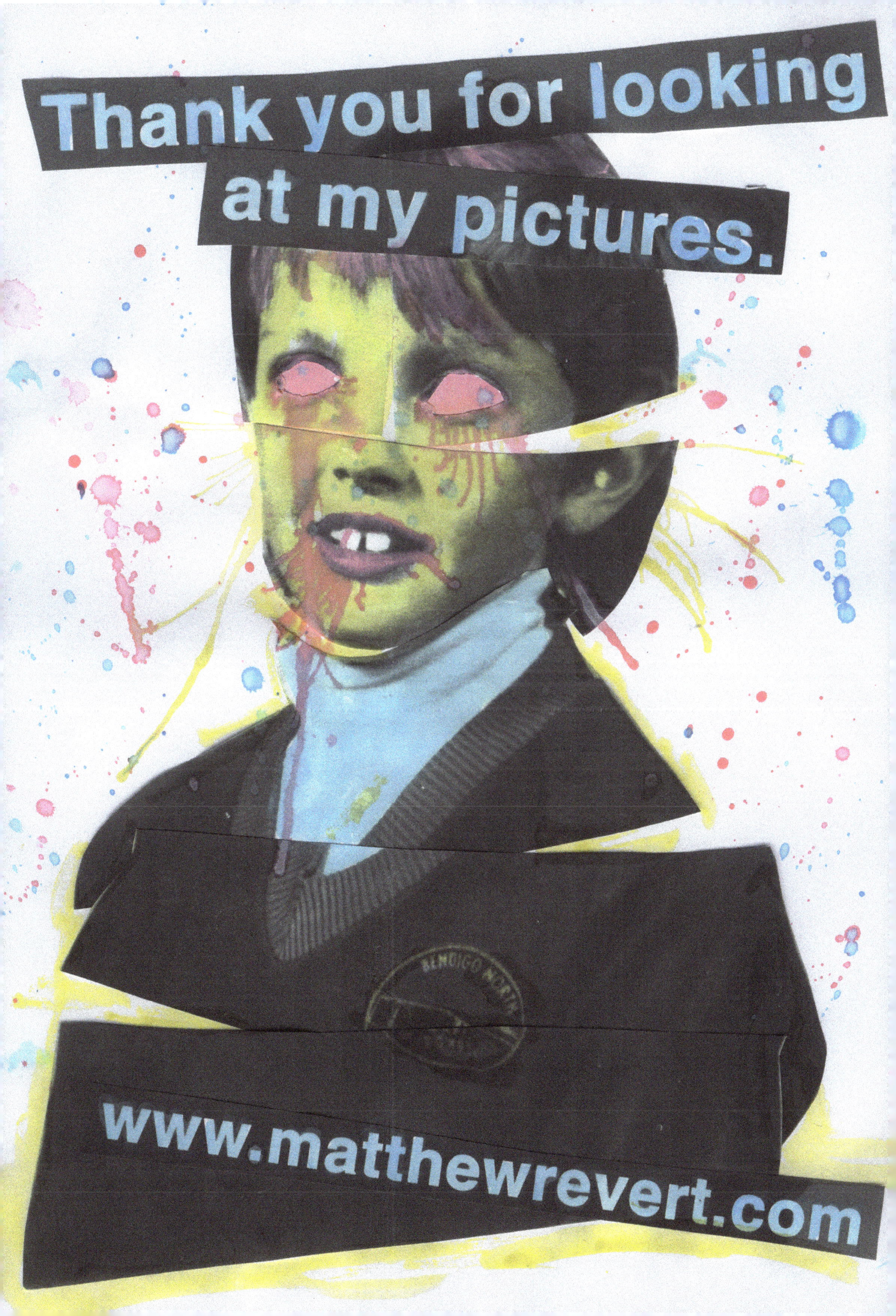

Thank you for looking
at my pictures.
www.matthewrevert.com

This

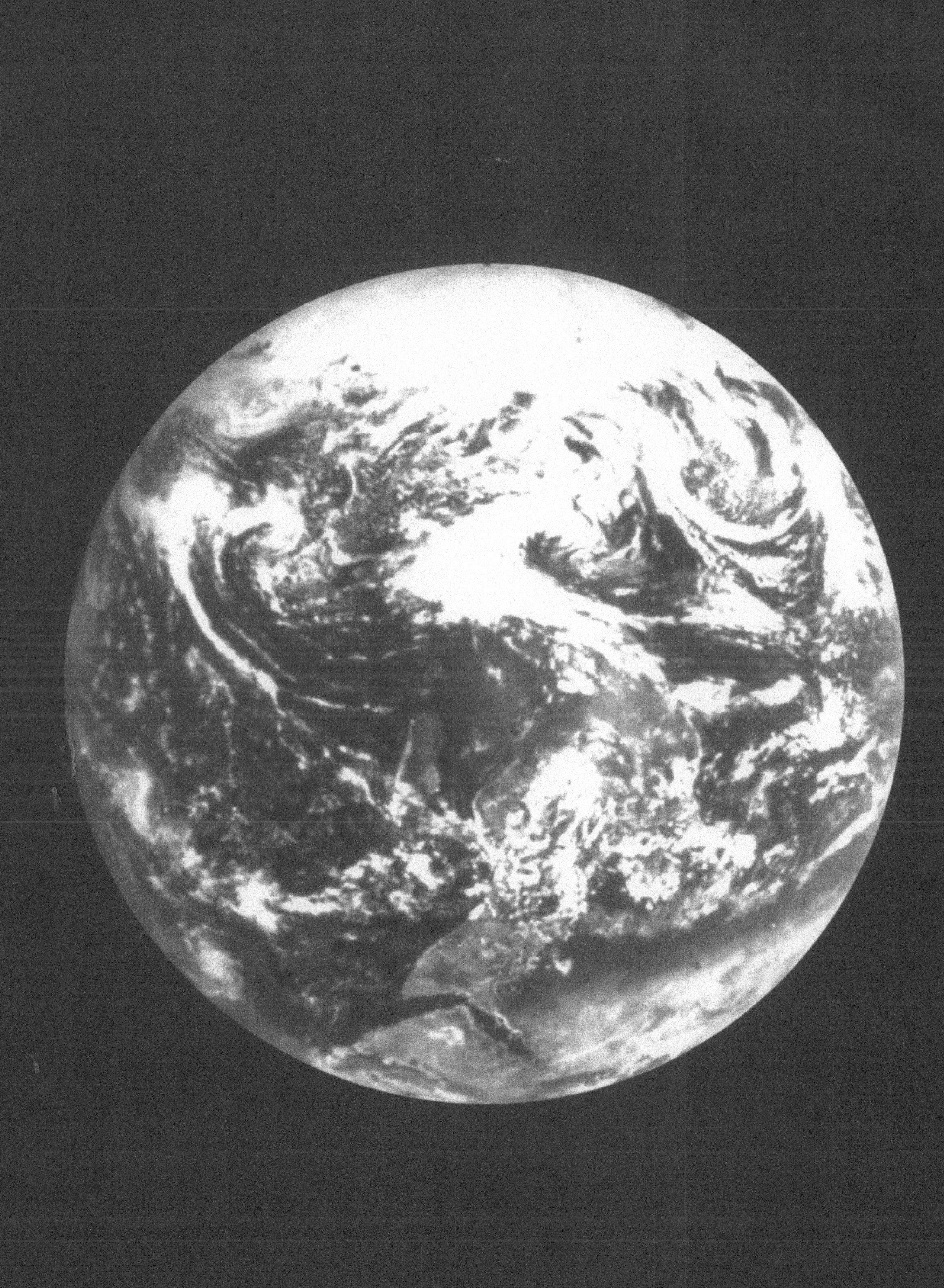

is

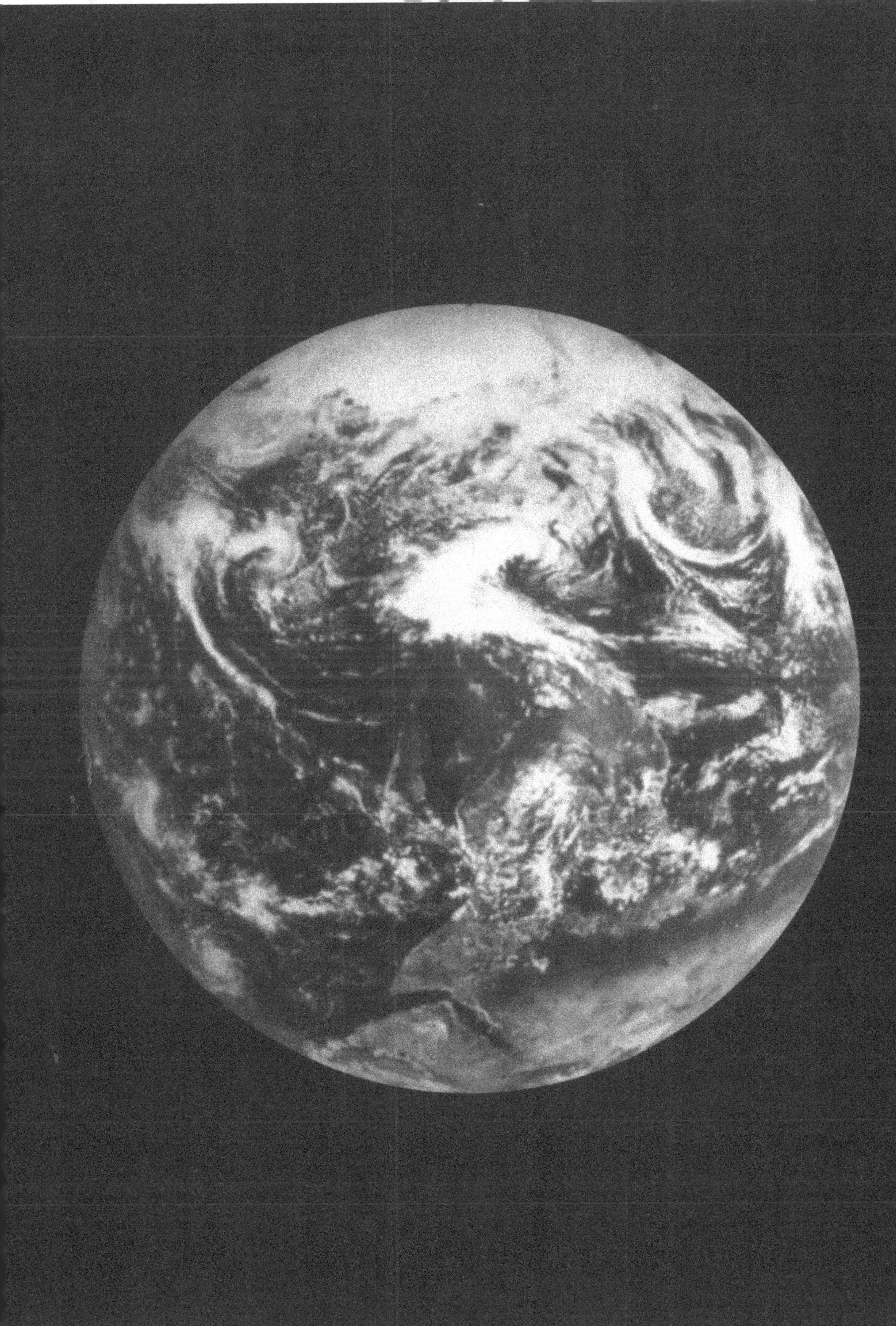

the

earth

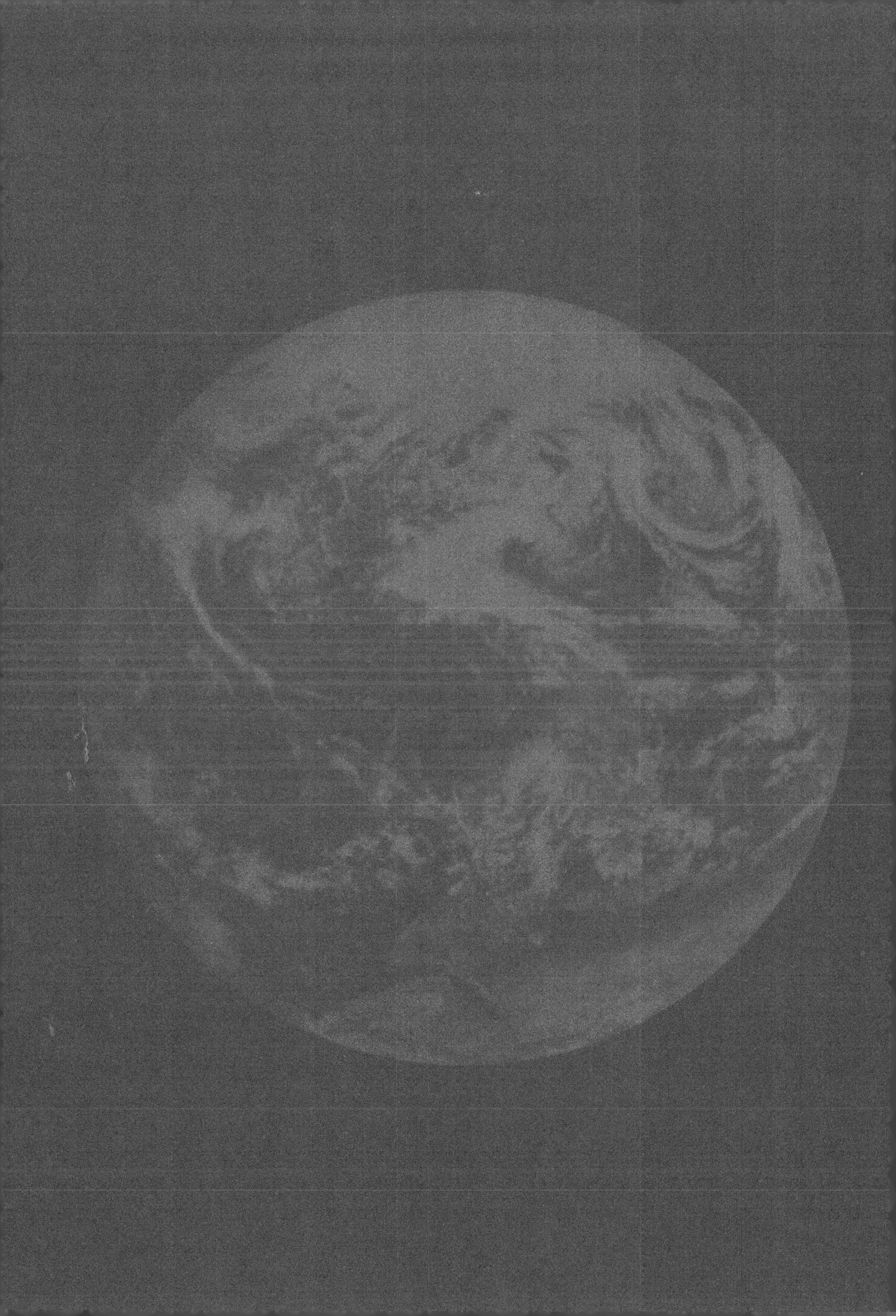

erasing
itself

ALSO BY CLASH BOOKS

TRAGEDY QUEENS: STORIES INSPIRED BY LANA DEL REY & SYLVIA PLATH
Edited by Leza Cantoral

GIRL LIKE A BOMB
Autumn Christian

CENOTE CITY
Monique Quintana

99 POEMS TO CURE WHATEVER'S WRONG WITH YOU OR CREATE THE PROBLEMS YOU NEED
Sam Pink

THIS BOOK IS BROUGHT TO YOU BY MY STUDENT LOANS
Megan J. Kaleita

PAPI DOESN'T LOVE ME NO MORE
Anna Suarez

ARSENAL/SIN DOCUMENTOS
Francesco Levato

THIS IS A HORROR BOOK
Charles Austin Muir

HEAVEN IS A PHOTOGRAPH
Christine Sloan Stoddard

FOGHORN LEGHORN
Big Bruiser Dope Boy

I'M FROM NOWHERE
Lindsay Lerman

SEQUELLAND
Jay Clayton-Joslin

JAH HILLS
Unathi Slasha

GIMME THE LOOT: STORIES INSPIRED BY NOTORIOUS B.I.G
Edited by Gabino Iglesias